SELLING SEX OVERSEAS

Selling Sex Overseas

Chinese Women and the Realities of
Prostitution and Global Sex Trafficking

Ko-lin Chin and James O. Finckenauer

NEW YORK UNIVERSITY PRESS
New York and London

NEW YORK UNIVERSITY PRESS
New York and London
www.nyupress.org

References to Internet websites (URLs) were accurate at the time of writing.
Neither the author nor New York University Press is responsible for URLs
that may have expired or changed since the manuscript was prepared.

Library of Congress Cataloging-in-Publication Data
Chin, Ko-lin.
Selling sex overseas : Chinese women and the realities of prostitution and global
sex trafficking / Ko-lin Chin and James O. Finckenauer.
p.   cm.
Includes bibliographical references and index.
ISBN 978-0-8147-7257-7 (cl : alk. paper) — ISBN 978-0-8147-7258-4 (pb : alk. paper) —
ISBN 978-0-8147-6968-3 (ebook) — ISBN 978-0-8147-6381-0 (ebook)
1. Human trafficking—China. 2. Prostitution—China. 3. Transnational crime—
China.   I. Finckenauer, James O. II. Title.
HQ281.C58 2012
306.74'20951—dc23   2012028089

New York University Press books are printed on acid-free paper,
and their binding materials are chosen for strength and durability.
We strive to use environmentally responsible suppliers and materials
to the greatest extent possible in publishing our books.

Manufactured in the United States of America

c   10 9 8 7 6 5 4 3 2 1
p   10 9 8 7 6 5 4 3 2 1

For Catherine and Midge (Margaret)

CONTENTS

ACKNOWLEDGMENTS

We would like to express our gratitude to the many people who helped us with the research that is the basis for this book. First, we thank all the Chinese sex workers (or *xiaojies* as they are called in China), who agreed to take part in our research and who willingly shared their stories with us. We owe our deepest thanks to these women, who are anonymous except for some pseudonyms here. Second, we are grateful to the various "facilitators" in the sex trade (agents, escort agency owners, mommies, brothel keepers, etc.) who not only let us talk to them, but also let us enter their world and see how they operate their businesses. Again, we can only thank them anonymously because their identities will not be revealed.

Because of Ko-lin Chin's wide range of family and friends, we were able to rely on them to help directly and indirectly on the project. We owe a debt of gratitude to Huilin (a cousin), her husband C.Y. Shaw, and their son Rui Shaw for helping us in Singapore. In Hong Kong, we were assisted by Ah Ping (a cousin). We would also like to thank our friends: Yulan Chu, Chuanqiang Zhao, and Guanxuan Cao in Macau; Tiva Jentriacharn in Bangkok; Philip Tien, Benny Phan, and Ferry Siddharta in Jakarta; Punky Pang in Kuala Lumpur; Wei Chen and Jimeng Tang in China. We thank Robert Chu and his wife Jinfeng Gao in Vancouver. In the U.S., Meilan (a sister) and her husband Frank Su offered their help when we were in Los Angeles. We would also like to take this opportunity to express our heartfelt gratitude to our considerate and caring neighbors and friends—the Gundersen family (George II, Barbara, Teresa, and George III)—for support and encouragement, and for providing an ideal environment in which to live and write. Finally, we were also helped by Diana Hadel (Midge Finckenauer's niece), who assisted with some translation from Indonesian.

Among the many individuals from the academic community who offered us their invaluable help, we are especially indebted to Yiu Kong Chu of the University of Hong Kong, Chuen-Jim Sheu of the National Taipei University, Pei-Ling Wang of Jinan University, Shu-Lung Yang of the National Chung Cheng University, Sandy Yu-Lan Yeh of the Central Police University, Narayanan Ganapathy of National Singapore University, Sheldon Zhang of San Diego State University, Mohd Kassim Noor Mohamed of Birmingham City University, and Yong Wang and Changrong Zhang of the Fuzhou Police Academy.

Many people in government and law enforcement also offered their help. We would like to thank Mark Taylor of the Office to Monitor and Combat Trafficking in Persons, U.S. Department of State; Kevin Shu-sing Lau, Paul Fuk-chuen Cheng, Sunny Kai-chor Lam, Man-chung Wan, and Philip Kincheung Choy of the Hong Kong Police Force; Eric K. K. Chan, K. K. Yip, and Cindy So-ying Yeung of the Immigration Department of Hong Kong; Mathew Tyson of the U.S. Consulate General in Hong Kong; Chih-Kun Chiang of the Coast Guard Administration of Taiwan; Ann Hurst, Gary Phillips, and Gary Kiernan of the U.S. Embassy in Bangkok; Mathew King and Trung Vu of the U.S. Embassy in Singapore; Wong Choong Mann and Jason Loke Choy Seng of the Singapore Police Force; Stanley Harsha, Thomas Daniels, and Robert Barlow of the U.S. Embassy in Jakarta; Law Hong Soon of the Royal Malaysian Police; Lee Baca of the Los Angeles County Sheriff's Department; Pamela Chen and Nancy Fabrizio of the U.S. Attorney's Office, Eastern District of New York; David Stein and Tania Hedlund of the New York City Police Department; and Barbara Stolz of the U.S. Government Accountability Office.

We would also like to express our heartfelt gratitude to those people working for various nongovernmental organizations and social service agencies who gave us their time and help. We are particularly grateful to Elise Chung of Zi Teng in Hong Kong; Kendy Yim of Action for REACH OUT in Hong Kong; Fran Gau and Sally Chou of the Women's Rescue Foundation of Taipei; Ruengrawee Pichaikul Ketphol of the Asia Foundation in Bangkok; Michael Chong of the Malaysian Chinese Association in Kuala Lumpur; Selvi of Pink Triangle in Kuala Lumpur; Lee Soo Choo of Tenaganita in Kuala Lumpur; Elizabeth Dunlap of the International Organization for Migration in Jakarta; Debbie Marulanda of Refugee Resettlement and Human Trafficking in Newark, New Jersey; Gilbert Ortiz of the Human Trafficking Information and Referral Hotline in New York City; and Wenchi Yu Perkins of Vital Voices in New York City.

Ilene Kalish, Executive Editor at NYU Press, was critically helpful in shortening and improving the manuscript. She offered us many excellent suggestions, and above all was just a most pleasant person with whom to work. We are also indebted to Despina Gimbel, Managing Editor, and Aiden Amos, Editorial Assistant, of NYU Press for helping us in the transformation of our manuscript into a book.

Thanks also to five anonymous reviewers (in addition to Sheldon Zhang and Barbara Stolz) for their helpful comments on earlier drafts of this work. Judy Mellecker edited the manuscript and we would like to thank her for doing an excellent job. Thanks to Min Liu for managing our data sets. In addition, Phyllis Shultze of the Don M. Gottfredson Library of Criminal Justice, Rutgers University, deserves a special mention here for providing us with so much information and material on prostitution and sex trafficking.

The research project was supported by Grant No. 2006-IJ-CX-0008 awarded by the National Institute of Justice, Office of Justice Programs, U.S. Department of Justice. The points of view expressed here are solely those of the authors and do not necessarily represent the official positions or policy of the U.S. Department of Justice. We thank Karen Bachar, Jennifer Hanley, and John Picarelli of the National Institute of Justice for their support.

Finally, but most importantly, we would like to thank our wives—Catherine and Midge (Margaret)—for their encouragement and patience throughout the course of this project. Without their full support, this study would not have been completed. This book is dedicated to them.

1

What Is Sex Trafficking?

Within the space of just three years, in different parts of the world, three women were brought to justice for their roles in what has become a high profile form of global crime. There are a number of common threads among these women and their cases. They exemplify in microcosm a host of issues that surround the illicit movement of people around the world. As such, they provide a kind of backdrop for the theme and focus of this book.

Perhaps the best known of the three cases is that of Cheng Chui-ping, or, as she is better known, Sister Ping. Sister Ping was an international human smuggler—in Chinese, a *shetou* or snakehead.[1] She charged tens of thousands of dollars to assist illegal Chinese emigrants to come to the United States. It was Sister Ping who was one of the masterminds behind the infamous *Golden Venture* (the name of a smuggling ship) incident in which hundreds of Chinese illegals were unloaded into the ocean off Long Island in 1993—ten of whom drowned after the ship ran aground.[2] Described as the Mother of All Snakeheads, Sister Ping is estimated to have made some $40 million in her two decades of human smuggling. On June 22, 2005 a federal jury in New York convicted Sister Ping of conspiracy to commit alien smuggling, hostage taking, money laundering, and trafficking in ransom proceeds. She was sentenced to the statutory maximum of thirty-five years in prison for her crimes.[3]

Wei Tang emigrated from China to Australia in 1998. There, she ran a brothel called Club 417, in Melbourne. In June 2006, she too was convicted of crimes, in her case possessing and using sex slaves in her brothel. The sex slaves in question were five Thai women. According to court documents in the Tang case, the five women had worked in the sex industry in Thailand, and had consented to go to Australia to continue this line of work in Melbourne. Despite this initial consent, the court found that the "debt bondage" nature of Tang's arrangement with the women constituted slavery, because they were "effectively restrained by the insidious nature of their contract." That insidious nature included having to perform sex acts for no pay while working off their debt of $45,000 each. Tang, who was sentenced to ten years in prison, was the first person in Australia to be found guilty of sex slavery.[4]

The third woman, Wei Qin Sun, was sentenced on February 22, 2008 in a U.S. federal court in the Northern Mariana Islands following her conviction for sex trafficking. A jury found her guilty of luring a young woman from China by promising the woman a job as a waitress in a karaoke club managed by Sun. Sun charged the woman $5,000 for "recruitment fees" and travel expenses. It was only after the woman began to work at the club that she was informed that she would have to work as a prostitute to repay Sun. Sun was convicted of coercion and enticement for prostitution, foreign transportation of a person in the execution of a fraudulent scheme, and criminal conspiracy. She was sentenced to three and a half years in prison.[5]

So what can one make of these cases? Actually, many things. We have three Chinese women who exploited, for money, the basic human desire of people to improve their condition. In each case, things did not turn out as the victims hoped or had been promised. There was debt bondage and deceit, but there was also consent of a kind. Sister Ping was a human smuggler, whereas Tang and Sun were convicted of human trafficking, and specifically of sex trafficking. That distinction is important for our purposes. So too is the matter of the victims' consent and of coercion. And then there is the way their crimes were organized—how did the three women arrange to carry out their crimes, and who else was involved? These issues and more will be the basis of our discussion. We begin with some background on migration and the distinction between human smuggling and trafficking.

Human Smuggling and Trafficking

A little known topic just a decade or so ago, the illicit movement of people both within and across national borders has began to draw worldwide attention since then.[6] A variety of developments account for the growth in both the size of the problem and in the attention paid to it: the collapse of the Soviet Union, the breaking up of Yugoslavia, vast socioeconomic disparities between Mexico and the United States, burgeoning economic development and social inequality in China, rapid advances in global communication and travel, increasing demands for cheap labor, a growing sex industry. The list could go on and on.

These developments taken together comprise what have come to be called the "push and pull" factors driving human migration. Push factors include both societal conditions—lack of opportunity, discrimination, persecution, civil war, and the like—and personal issues such as domestic violence and divorce that push the individuals suffering them to want to migrate. The pull factors are the opportunities—real or perceived—in developed and developing countries for jobs, freedom, safety, and so on. In most instances, the most dramatic difference between source countries and destination countries is economic opportunity. The demand for cheap labor in industrialized countries creates opportunity. With specific reference to the sex industry, countries that have lucrative commercial sex venues—brothels, massage parlors, karaoke lounges, topless bars, escort services, and so on—and/or that are tolerant toward or have legalized prostitution create a simultaneous demand and pull for commercial sex.[7]

Would-be migrants with connections, professional skills, or education can and do pursue legitimate channels to follow their dreams. For thousands of others, however, the legitimate channels are closed off. For them, the choice is to give up their ambitions, or to seek alternative means. This is where smuggling and trafficking come in. Here certain facilitating factors usually work in concert with the push/pull scenario. Those facilitators include liberal or porous border policies and corruption. Greasing the palms of officials is almost always necessary to secure documents and to avoid detection, especially when smuggling is involved.

Unable to follow the legal route of migration, one can approach a Sister Ping or one of her many counterparts. For a price that can vary from a few hundred dollars in the case of Mexican coyotes (as those particular smugglers are called) to well up into the tens of thousands, all travel and necessary documentation will be arranged. Human smugglers are in the business of illegally moving people across national borders. Their clients are willing customers. Once the fee has been paid in full and the transaction has been completed, the customer, the person smuggled, is generally free and clear of the smuggling operation, although they are illegal aliens in their destination country.[8]

Human trafficking is defined by the exploitation of victims. These victims are forced to work with little or no pay; they are beaten or raped; they and their families are threatened; they are deceived by being promised one job and then forced to work at another; they are controlled in their movements; and their documents are held.[9] The Tang and Sun cases above had one or more of these characteristics. Our focus here will be on this more insidious form of human movement and exploitation.

As mentioned earlier, a good deal of attention has been devoted to this subject during the past decade or so. Literally hundreds of articles, books, and reports have been published, especially in the past several years.[10] So why do we need yet another examination of the issue? Despite the concern and attention heaped on this problem, there is still much about it that is unknown or subject to controversy.[11] In general there is little empirical research on the issue, as was suggested by Sheldon Zhang, a sociology professor, in his review of the literature on human trafficking:

> Much of the current discourse on human trafficking has not been guided by empirical research. The increased urgency in U.S. government policy and funding priority to combat trafficking in women and children has been influenced more by a moral panic that continues to gain momentum rather than by solid and systematic assessment of the problem. Research on human trafficking remains challenging due to its secrecy and political sensitivity.[12]

Where there have been empirical research studies on sex trafficking, these have mostly been narrowly focused, for example relying on a single type of prostitute, mostly street prostitutes. As suggested by Anthony DeStefano in his book *The War on Human Trafficking*, prostitution is a multifaceted industry with a proliferation of high-priced prostitutes, and it is essential to study women in different sex markets to have a nuanced and balanced understanding of the sex trade.[13] Sociologist Ronald Weitzer likewise argued that "prostitutes vary tremendously in their reasons for entry, access to resources for protection, number and type of clients, freedom to refuse clients and specific sex acts, relationships with colleagues, dependence on and exploitation by third parties, experiences with the authorities, public visibility, and impact on the surrounding community."[14]

One of the shortcomings in the extant body of research on human trafficking, we believe, is the fact that it has included almost exclusively rescued subjects who were in the hands of law enforcement officials, advocates, or service providers.[15] In a review of more than a hundred scholarly journal articles on human trafficking, Sheldon Zhang found that "only a handful involved some forms of empirical data" and "the information was mostly obtained from law enforcement officials, representatives from advocacy groups, and a few interviews with victims in shelters or 'safe settings' as Raymond and Hughes would call them."[16] Such subjects, we believe, constitute an unrepresentative sample of the larger population of trafficking victims. Not included, for example, are any persons who may have initially been trafficking victims, but who have subsequently removed any indebtedness and have chosen to remain and to work wherever they are. Also excluded are any victims who escape on their own without contact or assistance by law enforcement or others, and any victims who fall through the cracks because agency contacts fail to recognize them as being victims. Individually complex real life circumstances can get reduced to simple labels or categories by agency workers. And since affixing the label "trafficking victim" is highly dependent upon who is doing the labeling, it can come to serve strictly administrative purposes such as establishing eligibility for temporary housing, and medical and psychological support.[17]

In contrast to this approach of relying upon subjects defined by others, we think it is critical to find subjects by casting the broadest net possible, and to interview subjects under the broadest range of possible statuses. We also believe interviews should be conducted under circumstances that will maximize the probability that subjects will be forthcoming and not constrained by other motives or agendas. By this we mean it is preferable to interview them in their own natural settings, without the presence of a third party. This helps assure subjects that the interview is confidential, and that regardless of what is said there will be no repercussions and nothing to be gained by being untruthful.

We also think it is important not only to compare women from different sex venues, but also in different destination countries. Again, the available empirical research on sex trafficking has mostly focused on only one group of women from one source country and in one destination country.[18] This approach overlooks the possibility that women from the same source country might have significantly different traveling and working experiences, handlers, clients, payment arrangements, and so on in different destination countries.

We do not promise nor assume that we will lay to rest all the controversies or definitively answer all the questions related to sex trafficking. Instead, our goals are to shed light on one group of women who go overseas to engage in prostitution—in this case women from the People's Republic of China (PRC)[19]—and to provide a more nuanced understanding of the movement of these women and its possible relation to sex trafficking. Our underlying assumption is that commercial sex, the transnational movement of women to overseas sex venues, and sex trafficking are linked. In this study, we sought to explore that linkage, and to consider whether that linkage is as characterized by the U.S. government and the United Nations in their respective codifications of human trafficking. A secondary goal was to provide information to facilitate the development of better strategies and responses to cope with these phenomena.

Sex trafficking, our focus, is not the only form of human trafficking. The demand for cheap labor and their own relative socioeconomic deprivation entice migrants into many situations having nothing to do with the sex industry. Typical examples are domestic workers, farm laborers, and construction and factory workers who will work for less than the locals are willing to take for the same jobs. They receive less than minimum pay, and no benefits or job security of any kind, and thus their status is that of being in servitude, of being little more than a slave.[20] For example, a couple in Long Island who came from India were convicted for forced labor after treating two Indonesian maids as slaves through starvation, beatings, and torture and paying them only $100 a month for working seventeen-hour days with no days off.[21]

Sex trafficking has most if not all of these same characteristics. But in addition it raises further issues that link it more closely to our overall interests in crime and criminal justice. Prostitution is a crime in many places. Picking potatoes, or sewing shirts, or digging holes is not. Nor have these forms of work, unlike prostitution, been historically linked with organized crime and vice. Because of the sex aspect, prostitution also poses dilemmas about consent and coercion that factory and farm work do not.

The Making of a Trafficking Paradigm

Some years before the United Nations and the U.S. government set out their official definitions of sex trafficking, Kathleen Barry, an influential sociology professor, offered the following definition that subsequently became a model for later depictions:

Traffickers are traders in human beings who either buy women from husbands, buy children from parents, fraudulently promise them well-paying jobs or lucrative marriages at the other end, or they abduct them. Traffickers take their acquisitions to market via overland routes or, through the more sophisticated crime gangs such as Yakuza in Japan, they transfer women and girls by air to their destination, usually a brothel where acquired women and children are sold as merchandise.[22]

Following this definition, the U.S. Trafficking Victims Protection Act (TVPA) defines "severe forms of trafficking" as:

a. sex trafficking in which a commercial sex act is induced by force, fraud, or coercion, or in which the person induced to perform such an act has not attained 18 years of age; or
b. the recruitment, harboring, transportation, provision, or obtaining of a person for labor or services, through the use of force, fraud, coercion for the purpose of subjection to involuntary servitude, peonage, debt bondage, or slavery.[23]

After the TVPA was passed in 2000, a number of high-ranking U.S. government officials began to publicly denounce the cruelty of human trafficking. When the first Trafficking in Persons or TIPs report was published in 2001, then Secretary of State Colin Powell said the following: "The overwhelming number [of trafficking victims] are women and children who have been lured, coerced or abducted by criminals who trade in human misery and treat human beings like chattel."[24] Then-FBI Director Louis Freeh was also quoted after he delivered a speech in Romania: "This is a modern-day form of slavery—women and children stripped of their freedom and dignity, subjected to forced labor and prostitution, repeatedly beaten and abused."[25]

At just about the same time, and in response to the growing problem of transnational organized crime, the United Nations adopted its *International Convention against Transnational Organized Crime* in Palermo, Italy, in November 2000. This Convention was supplemented by the *UN Protocol to Prevent, Suppress, and Punish Trafficking in Persons*.[26] According to that protocol:[27]

Trafficking in persons shall mean the recruitment, transportation, transfer, harboring or receipts of persons, by means of the threat or use of force or other forms of coercion, of abduction, of fraud, of deception, of the abuse of power, or of a position of vulnerability or of the giving or receiving of payments or benefits to achieve the consent of a person having control over another person, for the purpose of exploitation. Exploitation shall include, at a minimum, the exploitation of the prostitution of others or other forms of sexual exploitation, forced labor or services, slavery or practices similar to slavery, servitude, or the removal of the organs.[28]

Soon after, there was an explosion of discussion on the issue of human trafficking. Below are some examples that will illustrate how the nature of sex trafficking was usually depicted and understood. The first is from a report on the movement of Thai women to Japan for commercial sex, prepared by Human Rights Watch:

> The intermediaries who arrange these women's travel and job placement used deception, fraud, and coercion to place them into highly abusive conditions of employment, where they must repay outrageously high "debts" before they can earn wages or gain their freedom. While in debt, women are kept under constant surveillance and forced to satisfy all customers and all customer demands. Disobedience can lead to fines, physical violence, and even "resale" to higher levels of debt. Escape from these conditions is difficult and dangerous, and may lead to violent retaliation.[29]

This depiction includes all the main elements of human trafficking: force, deception, fraud, or coercion in recruitment, as well as debt bondage, restricted movement, forced labor, violence, and buying and selling of victims as commodities. *The Natashas*, a book by investigative journalist Victor Malarek, depicted the new global sex trade involving women from Eastern Europe—women who came to be known as "Natashas" in the European sex industry. Malarek characterized the Natasha sex trade as follows:

> Most end up in situations of incredible debt bondage, unable to earn enough to pay back the high interest on their travel and living expenses. They become victims of the worst possible forms of sexual exploitation. They are not free to leave, nor can they easily escape. They are sold to pimps or brothel owners on the open market, and soon find themselves trapped in abusive situations in which they are forced to have sex with as many as ten, twenty or thirty clients a day. They cannot refuse a customer or a demand. They are not allowed sick days. They do not get time off for their period. Some end up pregnant and having abortions. Many acquire HIV or other sexually transmitted disease, not to mention the

physiological and medical problems that come from constant abuse and gang rape. Some become alcoholics. Others become drug addicts.[30]

The stories of the plight of the trafficked victims tended to get more and more horrifying as the anti-trafficking discourse grew stronger. In an edited volume entitled *Enslaved: True Stories of the Modern Day Slavery*, Jesse Sage and Liora Kasten, directors of the American Anti-Slavery Group, described what they called modern-day slavery this way:

> Sex slavery ensnares millions of women and girls, some as young as four (young men and boys are also victims). These individuals are often kidnapped, deceived by the promise of legitimate jobs, or even enticed to work as prostitutes—only to find themselves coerced to work without pay and denied the freedom to leave or choose their clients.[31]

There have also been many individual stories of human trafficking cited in the trafficking literature.[32] The two stories presented below are fairly typical: the first is the story of a Thai woman in Japan, and the second that of a young woman in India.

> Thip came to Japan in March 1999, having been promised a job as a waitress in a restaurant where she could save money. But when she arrived she was told that she owed 4.5 million yen (approximately $38,500) for the cost of her travel and job placement, and she was put to work in a brothel, where she was kept in a small room and forced to provide sexual services to customers. Thip escaped after working fifteen to sixteen-hour days, every day, for two weeks. The customers paid 12,000 yen (approximately $100) for eight-minute sessions, but Thip's share was only 2,000 yen. From this amount, Thip was expected to pay 34,000 yen a day for rent and protection money. This meant that she had to serve eighteen clients each day before any earnings were applied toward her debt.[33]

> *Anjali from India*: My family never had enough to eat. I wanted a life different from that. I met someone who promised he would find me a job in the city, but once we arrived in Bombay he left me with one of his female cousins and said that he would return very soon. He didn't come back, and a few days later I found out that his "cousin" was actually the owner of a brothel to which I had been sold. She made me accept all the men who came to me, and when I got sick as a result, she threw me out in the street.

I am seventeen years old and have no money to pay for medicine. All I wanted was a better life, and now I am dying.[34]

These horror stories clearly present one of the slices of the truth about human trafficking. But is this the whole truth? Is it even a large part of the truth? These are questions we will address. One of the goals of our research project was to see whether the transnational movement of Chinese women for the purposes of prostitution fits the picture of sex trafficking as defined by the U.S. government and the United Nations. For the past decade, discussions of sex trafficking have been dominated by government officials, faith-based groups, feminists, and NGOs. Numerous assumptions about the phenomenon have taken hold and been taken for granted by the media, the public, academics, and policymakers. But recently, some people have begun to question some of the core assumptions and beliefs that have provided the underpinning for most of the antitrafficking policy.[35] Our research is a further effort along this path of inquiry.

It is our belief that sound public policy, irrespective of the particular problem or issue, should be firmly grounded in the best and most accurate information available. It should, in other words, be well-informed, and not be driven simply by assumptions and beliefs. In that spirit, we will ultimately be comparing and contrasting our findings with the dominant antitrafficking paradigm's depiction of sex trafficking to see how well the two fit, or do not fit, together.

Sex Trafficking and Organized Crime

Although not at the same level of intensity as some other sex trafficking controversies, such as whether or not all prostitution should be considered a form of sex trafficking or about just how big a problem human trafficking is, a fair amount of discussion and debate have also centered on whether sex trafficking is a criminal activity dominated by well-established organized crime groups.[36] The nature of this discussion revolves around a contention by some skeptics that certain special interests advocate for a big organized crime role to hype interest and gain attention.[37] If it seems that a particular crime can be associated with the "mafia," people and politicians will take it more seriously.[38] On the other side, those who argue that organized crime is very much into human trafficking cite the scale and sophistication of some of the cases.[39] They say the ways the trafficking is carried out suggest the hand of professional criminals and not "mom and pop" amateurs. The latter especially focus on the violence and corruption that is often involved—factors which are indeed hallmarks of organized crime.

What difference does it make? you may ask. The gravitas that being labeled organized crime and especially mafia brings, does get high level attention, does make something a priority, and does get resources.[40] Mafia control connotes threats, violence, and intimidation. It scares off the amateurs; it silences witnesses; and it cows potential victims. Organized crime also has the bankroll and the political reach to protect its operations via corruption. And sophisticated criminal organizations can mount more complex operations, including transnational ones.[41]

The tools that are available to combat organized crime are rather specialized.[42] They go beyond what is typically relied upon to go after more run-of-the-mill everyday crime. Ironically, a mismatch between the law enforcement methods used and the crime they are being used against, means that these specialized tools for combating organized crime are far less effective—in fact may be ineffective—when applied to nonorganized crime. What is "nonorganized" crime? Well, at least one example would be some of the loose networks of individuals who have so far been like those generally seen to be engaging in human trafficking. As we will see, they lack most of the characteristics that we tend to associate with "real" organized crime. On the flip side of the mismatch of methods to problem, using everyday crime fighting techniques has long been shown to be ineffective in dealing with organized crime. That was why the special tools were developed in the first place. Thus, it is quite important to know just who the enemy is in this case.

What would be signs of organized crime involvement? On one level, the criminal organizations involved in organized crime generally make use of corruption and violence, and they often attempt to gain monopoly control over whatever criminal enterprises they are engaged in.[43] Their corruption is not low-level, nickel and dime stuff, but instead bribes and payoffs that extend into the upper reaches of law enforcement and politics. Likewise, violence is used purposely to establish credibility and reliability, in order that the actual use of violence becomes only a limited necessity—reputation alone is enough to intimidate and strike fear into its targets.

Organized crime is the province of criminal organizations that have a degree of criminal sophistication—their crimes are planned rather than impulsive; they make use of technology; they have accounting and legal expertise available, and so on. These organizations usually have a structure that has a stable division of labor—different members have specific roles and jobs. There is self-identification with the organizations through such means as wearing colors, swearing oaths, and the like. And, as indicated, the organization has the authority of reputation. The more of these sorts of characteristics a criminal organization has, the greater its capacity to wreak harm of all kinds, including economic, physical, and societal. They are made up of professional criminals who operate continuously over time and over crimes.[44] So, what criminal organizations fit these exclusive criteria? The best-known examples would be the Sicilian[45] and Russian mafias,[46] Italian La Cosa Nostra,[47] the Hong Kong triads,[48] the Japanese Yakuza,[49] and the Colombian drug cartels.[50]

We are not suggesting that it is only these particular criminal groups or others nearly identical to them that we would have to find to conclude that human trafficking is really an organized crime problem. But we are suggesting that whoever the traffickers are, they have to have more (rather than less) of the kinds of characteristics outlined above for us to reach that conclusion. As one of the authors has suggested, "crimes that are organized" and "organized crime" are not the same.[51]

Some previous investigations hint at what is likely to be the conclusion. For example, relying upon a variety of information sources, Galma Jahic, a professor at Bilgi University in Istanbul, said that while it is frequently assumed that organized crime figures run the trafficking business, there is little evidence that trafficking is actually centrally and tightly organized.[52] The plausible counterargument is that trafficking organizations are instead loose and rather fluid networks. This will be one of the core issues we will be addressing here.

Research Approach and Rationale

Research Sites

Although prostitution exists everywhere, it is not the same everywhere. Sex for sale is a much bigger business in some places than it is in others. And it is in cities with lucrative commercial sex venues that the demand for fresh sex workers can be expected to be the greatest. The cities we chose to look at fit that bill.

We included ten research sites in our project; eight in Asia and two in the United States. The eight Asian sites are Hong Kong, Macau, Taipei (Taiwan), Bangkok (Thailand), Kuala Lumpur (Malaysia), Singapore, Jakarta (Indonesia), and Shenzhen (China), and the two U.S. sites are Los Angeles and the New York City metropolitan area.[53] We selected these sites first because of reporting in the media, government reports, and popular books that there are large numbers of Chinese prostitutes in these locations;[54] next, because we had visited some of these cities in 2003 and 2004 for a research project on transnational organized crime, and witnessed that many Chinese women were active in the sex sectors there;[55] and thirdly because we happened to have good connections in these cities and were thus confident that we would be able to recruit and interview hard-to-reach subjects at each location. We were well aware that Chinese women were also reportedly going to Australia, Burma (Myanmar), Cambodia, the Philippines, Japan, South Korea and some countries in Western Europe, the Middle East, and Africa to engage in prostitution. We excluded those sites because we did not have the same access there, and because we were limited by time and resources. We believe that there is sufficient variability among the ten sites we selected to give a relatively good representative picture of the situation.

Data Sources

PRIMARY DATA

Among the major premises upon which our research approach is based is our belief that the best sources of information about prostitution and sex trafficking are the very people who are most directly involved in it. These include women who are providing commercial sex services, the owners, operators, or managers of the venues where those services are being provided, law enforcement and other government officials who are charged with combating sex trafficking, victim services providers who work with sex trafficking victims, and certain local individuals who can be key informants because they have good "street" knowledge and connections. The latter are the kind of people found in nearly every city, such as cab drivers, bartenders, and hairdressers who "know where the action is."

Between December 2006 and August 2008, we conducted 350 face-to-face interviews with the following groups of subjects: prostitutes (or prostituted women), sex ring operators, government officials/law enforcers, and NGOs/other key informants (see Table 1.1). To conduct these interviews, we took three trips to Asia (lasting for a total of seven months), numerous trips to New York City and towns in New Jersey, and one trip to Los Angeles.

PROSTITUTES

Women who engaged in prostitution are obviously vulnerable research subjects, and commercial sex is a clandestine business. Thus, our approach to identifying and approaching possible interview subjects, and then actually interviewing them, had to be done within these parameters. In the

Table 1.1. Sample (N = 350)

Site	Sex workers	Sex ring operators	Law enforcers	NGOs and other key informants	Total
China	15	9	24	4	52
Hong Kong	15	2	9	3	29
Macau	18	9	1	3	31
Taiwan	16	14	13	5	48
Thailand	17	5	5	2	29
Malaysia	18	7	3	4	32
Singapore	15	6	7	2	30
Indonesia	18	9	7	4	38
Los Angeles	16	6	2	4	28
New York	16	9	5	3	33
Total	164	76	76	34	350

identification process, we excluded any women who were under arrest or were otherwise under the control of government authorities. Similarly, we also excluded any women who were being housed or otherwise assisted by various victims' assistance entities.

Instead, given that the ultimate goal of all sex trafficking is making money, we proceeded on the premise that sex trafficking victims must somehow be engaged in providing sexual services for money. This means they must be in settings or venues that are discernible to and accessible to potential paying clients. They cannot, in other words, be so hidden as to be completely inaccessible. We do not deny that accessibility may in some instances be so limited, such as for example in the case of child victims, that we would not learn about them. But child victims were not included in our projected population, and the extent to which adult females may have been so secreted as to make their presence unknown to our various informants is itself unknown. Keeping with our overall premise, we sought venues where our informants indicated that the word was that sex services were being bought and sold. Depending upon the legal status of prostitution in a particular jurisdiction, those venues are more or less clandestine. The venues include the most visible prostitutes, namely, the street prostitutes, as well as those who work in front businesses such as massage parlors, bars, and so on, and in KTV lounges, private apartments, and in establishments that are purely brothels.

In each site we interviewed between 15 and 18 women who engaged in paid sex, for a total of 164 subjects. All but 15 of these subjects were in overseas locations (outside China), as shown in Table 1.1. The 15 interviews in Shenzhen, China, were done more informally, meaning they were not asked every question in the questionnaire we used to interview women in overseas locations. Those particular interviews were conducted mostly for additional understanding of the context of commercial sex, and because of the possibility that some of the women might be returned prostitutes from overseas.

The following domains of information were gathered from the female subjects by asking both open-ended and closed-ended questions:

- Background characteristics: Age, marital status, number of children (if any), education, place of birth, place of residence before leaving China, work and income history (including work experience in the sex industry, if any), and parents' occupation.
- Recruitment: Under what circumstances did the subject come to know the recruiter or facilitator, characteristics of the recruiter, what terms and conditions were discussed between the subject and the recruiter, what types of arrangements were made for the trip to the destination country?
- Reasons for going to the destination country: Personal, family, and social factors surrounding the decision-making process; what was the deciding reason; did the subject know that she was going to be involved in prostitution; if not, had the subject been deceived, forced, or coerced by the recruiter?
- Social processes of moving from China to the destination country: How long did it take to leave China after an agreement was reached with the recruiter; what method was used to go to the destination country; how long did it take to travel to the destination country; what persons were involved in the process and what kinds of assistance did they provide?
- Immediately after arriving in the destination country: Who came to meet the subject in the destination country; where was the subject taken; what arrangements were made to prepare the subject to start work; how soon did the subject begin to work, what kinds of problems (if any) did she encounter during the initial period of work; was the subject being coerced?
- Prostitution: How was the subject's work organized; what was the nature of the social organization of the subject's sex ring or network; the subject's work schedule and routine; how tightly was the subject controlled and by what means; who were the customers and where did the meetings take place; what was the subject's perception of her customers; and what were the problems associated with working in the sex industry?
- Income: Amount of money owed to people for bringing the subject to the destination country; amount of time needed to repay the debt; how much did the subject charge a customer per session; how was the money shared by all the people involved; what were the fixed expenses (for the fake husband, the driver, food, lodging, etc.) for the subject; how many sessions per day on average; how much money had the subject saved so far, if any?

- Leisure and life-style: Routine activities; leisure activities; level of freedom of movement; social network (if any) in the destination country.
- Perception of involvement in the sex industry: How the subject saw it; what plans did the subject have for her future both in the destination country and in China?

SEX RING OPERATORS/FACILITATORS

We also conducted face-to-face interviews with 76 sex ring operators and others who facilitate commercial sex operations. This group of subjects includes sex establishment owners or managers, pimps or intermediaries, drivers, and telephone operators. As with the women who engaged in commercial sex, we also interviewed the vast majority of this group in their own settings, although five subjects were interviewed inside a prison in Taiwan. An interview guide was developed to help us with the interviews with all the subjects in this particular group.

The interviews with operators/facilitators focused on the following domains of information: (1) individual characteristics, (2) group characteristics, (3) what factors determine subject's involvement in the sex business, (4) types of sex rings or establishments, (5) the processes of recruiting, transporting, and managing women from China, (6) the economic aspects of the sex trade, (7) problems encountered in the sex trade and the subject's coping mechanisms, (8) subject's involvement in licit and other illicit activities, (9) possible membership in organized crime groups, and (10) subject's perceptions of his or her involvement in the sex business.

GOVERNMENT OFFICIALS AND LAW ENFORCERS

We interviewed 76 criminal justice and other related officials.[56] The majority of the subjects in this group were either police or immigration officers. A small number of judges, prosecutors, customs or coast guard officials, and American officials working for the U.S. embassies in Asia were also interviewed.

Interviews with the authorities emphasized the problems of and prospects for preventing and suppressing the movement of Chinese women for the purpose of prostitution. In regard to their own jurisdiction, they were asked about (1) the organization of sex trafficking; (2) examples of cases in which either arrests, prosecutions, and/or convictions have occurred; (3) problems in investigating, prosecuting, and punishing trafficking offenders; (4) specific examples of measures being taken and their assessments of the effectiveness of these measures; and (5) their recommendations on how to improve bilateral and multilateral strategies to combat sex trafficking and the sex industry.

NGOS AND KEY INFORMANTS

Finally, we interviewed some social service providers, NGOs, and other advocacy group members who were responsible for serving and protecting trafficking victims. The number of NGOs and service providers who had actually had experience in dealing with prostitutes specifically from China was very small. We thus additionally recruited and interviewed in an informal way many key informants who, as previously mentioned, due to their work, leisure activities, or simply residency, have special knowledge and understanding of the social organization of prostitution involving Chinese women in their locales. Taxi drivers who also work as middlemen, businessmen who frequented sex venues, and longtime residents of certain places were included in this group.

The formal interviews with NGOs and service providers focused on (1) the history, goals, and structure of their organizations, (2) their services or functions, (3) the problems they encountered in pursuit of their goals, (4) their assessments of the magnitude and nature of the movement of Chinese women for commercial sex, (5) their working relationships with local government authorities, and (6) what their needs were.

FIELDWORK

To better understand the social organization of commercial sex work, fieldwork was conducted whenever there was an opportunity to do so. For example, one of the authors simply spent time eating with various subjects, normally before or after the interviews. He also spent many hours visiting and observing various red-light districts in Asia. Most red-light districts he visited were packed with people, and because he is ethnic Chinese and speaks both Mandarin and Cantonese (a dialect most people in Hong Kong and Macau and many overseas Chinese in Southeast Asia and North America speak), he was able to blend in easily. Consequently, he was able to talk to a variety of people, including the owners, the managers, the pimps, the women, and their clients, and to ask them in detail about the local sex business. Very often, he would ask a pimp who was soliciting business in the streets to take him to where the girls were, simply to have an opportunity to observe these places. After he became acquainted with the owner of a sex venue and he let the owner know that he was conducting a research project, he also asked the owner to allow him to hang out, just watching the people who came and went and talking to the women who were working there.

In Taiwan, we were able to observe up close how an escort agency works by following the owner of an escort agency for three evenings. This owner also allowed one of the authors to ride along with a so-called jockey (a driver) and a prostitute for two nights. All parties were informed about the nature and purpose of the participant observation and consented to his involvement. The rides started around two in the afternoon and lasted until dawn. In the process, we were able to observe the interactions and power dynamics between the prostitute and her driver, and between the woman and her employer (the escort agency owner). We also spent a number of evenings in Taipei eating dinner and/or drinking coffee with a key figure in the sex trade (a woman), and with several women who were working for her.

In all these instances, we remained fully alert to the many ethical issues that might arise while doing this kind of ethnographic fieldwork.[57] We believe the unique opportunity to gain first-hand knowledge about the inner workings of the sex trade more than outweighed any potential ethical concerns that might have arisen. We are confident that our fieldwork neither facilitated the business of the sex ring operators we were studying nor put our female subjects in harm's way.

SECONDARY DATA

We collected a large amount of secondary data from government officials and law enforcement authorities at the research sites, including statistics, reports, criminal indictments, and sentencing statements. We also visited the libraries of various universities in the research sites and downloaded thousands of pages of newspaper, magazine, and scholarly articles in English or Chinese. When we visited the NGOs and social service providers in these sites, we also collected information about the history, structure, and functions of these organizations.

DATA COLLECTION

At the very beginning of the data collection stage, we placed an ad in a Chinese newspaper in New York City, indicating that two college professors were hiring research assistants/interviewers who were familiar with the sex industry. We were hoping that some current or former prostitutes or sex ring operators might call us for the job. Quite a few people, mostly women, did call; but once they learned how little we would pay our interviewers and interviewees, they simply chuckled and hung up the phone. An immigration consultant in New York who had helped many Chinese prostitutes as clients had this to say about the challenge in finding prostitutes for us to interview:

> I don't think you will find any Chinese prostitute who is willing to participate in your study, even if you are willing to pay $500 for the interview. You have to understand that these women are making $300 to $500 a day.

Your best chance of getting close to them is to open a massage parlor yourself. You open a store, hire them, and see how they work. There is no other way for you to approach them.

Of course, we were not ready to run a commercial sex venue in order to carry out a research project, so we took the advice of another caller, a Chinese woman who identified herself as a former massage parlor owner: "You really do not need anyone to help you to conduct the interviews or to refer prostitutes to you. Because you are a male, all you need to do is call the phone numbers listed in the local newspapers, ask them where they are located, walk in as a customer, and once inside a room with a woman, tell her you just want to interview her. You must tell her she need not do anything else, and you will pay her the normal charge. I assure you every prostitute you approach this way is going to talk to you!"

Eventually, we relied on three methods to locate and interview our female subjects. First, we found them on the streets. For example, in Singapore, we found most of our subjects in the streets of a red-light district where they were soliciting business, and interviewed them in a nearby hotel.[58] We also located and interviewed quite a few streetwalkers in Kuala Lumpur the same way.

Second, we located them at the indoor sex venues where they worked. After we arrived at a research site, we would first find out where the various sex venues were located by asking any colleagues, friends, and relatives who happened to live and work there. Sometimes these contacts would refer us to individuals who became key informants. In some cases, we found locations by reading advertisements in the local newspapers or by asking taxi drivers to take us to sex venues. For example, when we were in Hong Kong, we visited several so-called one-woman studios and conducted the interviews inside these premises. We found their advertisements on the internet, called them, and asked for their addresses. After arriving, we told the woman we were just doing research and would simply like to interview her. We also used the same approach to find subjects who were working out of small hotels or old residential buildings in Macau, and likewise those who ply their trade out of small apartments in New York City. Because the women working in these types of venues were most likely to be working on their own, the process of finding them, entering their premises, and asking them to participate in our study was not that difficult, because there was no third party involved.

The challenge came when we approached subjects who were working in premises that were owned and operated by someone else. For example, when we tried to interview women in the massage parlors of New Jersey, we had to deal with the fact that they were working for someone else, and we needed to get their consent as well. The same was true with the "houses" (brothels) in Los Angeles: not only did we need the consent of the women to talk to us, but also the consent of the man or woman who owned and managed the house. Certain sex venues were well-established and had more than a hundred women working there under the supervision of a dozen or so so-called "mommies" or "mammies" (women who were in charge of the girls). In these large sex venues, it was not feasible to seek the consent of the owner. Instead, for those particular sex venues, like the spas in Macau and Jakarta and the KTVs (karaoke TV lounges) in Bangkok, we sought the consent of a mommy or a manager first and then the consent of a subject.

The third way we found our subjects was through referrals. For example, we asked a relative living in Hong Kong to ask her hairdresser to introduce us to a mommy and we later asked the mommy to introduce some of her girls to us. In Hong Kong, we also were acquainted with a mommy who was soliciting business on the streets for her girls, and we asked her to bring her girls to us to be interviewed. In Shenzhen, we also relied on a street mommy to refer several girls to us. The same is true with all the escorts we interviewed in Taiwan and Malaysia. In both countries, we were able to meet a number of escort agency owners through referrals. Once these owners decided to help us with our project, we not only interviewed their girls, but also interviewed them and even observed up-close how they conducted their businesses. In no instances, however, did any owners, managers, or mommies demand or otherwise require the female subjects to speak with us or coach the female subjects what to tell us, at least not to our knowledge. In Bangkok and Jakarta, we asked those female subjects we found on our own to refer their friends and colleagues to us.

In adopting our research approach, we paid attention to what fellow researchers such as Ronald Weitzer had to say about what he thought was the best way to study the sex industry: "Absent a random sample, the best that can be hoped for is a strategy of interviewing people in various geographical locations and in different types of prostitution, in a rigorous and impartial manner. Researchers must strive to create samples that draw from multiple locations and types of workers and that are not skewed toward any particular subgroup. This procedure is known as purposive sampling."[59] We adopted the purposive sampling method in our study.

Table 1.2 shows the number of subjects we located using the three approaches (i.e., those we approached while they were soliciting business on the streets, those we found at the indoor venues where they were working, and through referrals) by research site. We recruited 17 street prostitutes (11%

Table 1.2. Methods in Locating Sex Workers, by Research Site (N = 149)

Site	Street	Sex venues	Referral	Total
Hong Kong	1	6	8	15
Macau	1	17	0	18
Taiwan	0	1	15	16
Thailand	0	4	13	17
Malaysia	6	1	11	18
Singapore	9	5	1	15
Indonesia	0	8	10	18
Los Angeles	0	6	10	16
New York	0	14	2	16
Total	17	62	70	149

of the overseas sample of 149), mostly in Singapore and Malaysia. But most Chinese prostitutes in Asia and the United States do not walk the streets, instead working in some indoor setting.

We located 62 subjects (42%) by visiting their venues as potential customers. We relied on this method heavily in Macau and New York, but less so in Jakarta, Los Angeles, and Hong Kong. The majority of the subjects we found this way were working in brothels, hotels, or massage parlors. We did not use this method to locate women working in nightclubs and KTVs because, first, it is quite costly considering cover charges and other charges; and second, it would have been seen as unusual to be visiting these sorts of places alone and also quite difficult to arrange a one-on-one meeting with a hostess.

Seventy subjects (47%) were referred to us by their employers, colleagues, or friends, and that was how we found most of our subjects in Taiwan, Thailand, Malaysia, Indonesia, Los Angeles, and Hong Kong. In Taiwan, we relied on an escort agency owner and an agent (a person who fronted the money to bring a Chinese woman to Taiwan) for referrals; likewise in Malaysia, the owner of a large escort agency made referrals. In Indonesia, we were helped by several agents[60] and middlemen, and in Los Angeles, by two "house" owners. A street mommy in Hong Kong referred to us several women for whom she was soliciting business near a park in a tourist area.

Interviews with the women we recruited on the streets were conducted at a nearby coffee shop, restaurant, or hotel; whereas interviews with women we located at their workplaces were conducted in their own settings. For those who were referred to us, we interviewed them at a coffee shop or a hotel restaurant. In sum, 31 interviews (21%) were conducted inside our hotels (most likely to be the hotel's coffee shop), 45 interviews (30%) in a public place outside our hotel, and the rest (49%) in the subjects' own setting (where they saw clients). All the interviews were conducted one-on-one, without the presence of a third party.

Most of the interviews lasted for about an hour to an hour and a half. When we were in Macau interviewing women working out of the hotel lobbies, we were asked to complete the interviews in just 30 minutes, the amount of time they would spend with a customer per session. Since it was not possible to complete an interview in 30 minutes, we decided to pay for two to three sessions per interview, thereby allowing us to have 60 to 90 minutes to conduct the interviews. For certain subjects, the interviews lasted more than two hours, especially if they were not working that day, or they were in the mood to talk, or we were willing to pay them more money. As will become clear later, we are confident that the money we paid for the interviews was kept by our subjects, and was not taken away from them by their pimps, agents, or employers.

Ethical Issues

According to a 2003 report by the World Health Organization (WHO), "interviewing a woman who has been trafficked raises a number of ethical questions and safety concerns for the woman, others close to her, and for the interviewer. Having a sound understanding of the risks, ethical considerations, and the practical realities related to trafficking can help minimize the dangers and increase the likelihood that a woman will disclose relevant and accurate information."[61] WHO recommends the following ten guiding principles for interviewing trafficked women: "(1) Do no harm; (2) Know your subject and assess the risks; (3) Prepare referral information—do not make promises that you cannot fulfill; (4) Adequately select and prepare interpreters, and co-workers; (5) Ensure anonymity and confidentiality; (6) Get informed consent; (7) Listen to and respect each woman's assessment of her situation and risks to her safety; (8) Do not re-traumatize a woman; (9) Be prepared for emergency intervention; and (10) Put information collected to good use."[62] Five years later, in 2008, the United Nations Inter-Agency Project on Human Trafficking (UNIAP) also developed a guide to ethical and human rights issues in conducting research on human trafficking and recommended seven guiding principles that were similar to the WHO guidelines.[63]

When we were in the field interviewing our subjects, we abided by all the recommendations made by WHO and UNAIP. We did nothing to harm our subjects; we went in with information about various local intervention agencies in case our subjects needed it; we did not collect any identifiable information about the subjects; we asked for their verbal informed consent and we did not pressure anyone to participate in our study; we did not ask any questions that might upset our subjects and let them decide what questions they would answer and to what extent; and, we believe we are putting the information collected to good use. We were especially mindful of the first principle—not to harm our subjects.

We also did not deceive our subjects. Once our interviewer was alone with a female subject, he immediately told her who he was and the purpose of his being there. He then told her the key points in our verbal informed consent statement, emphasizing that (1) participation was completely voluntary, (2) refusal to participate would involve no penalty or loss of benefit, (3) even if consenting to participate, the subject could refuse to answer any question she wished to, and (4) the subject could terminate the interview at any time. No interviews were conducted without the subject's full consent and understanding of the process.

If a woman said no to our request for an interview, we did not pressure her to change her mind. In that instance, we gave the woman a small amount of money and simply left. Table 1.3 shows the number of such rejections by research site, and the sex markets where those rejections occurred. Altogether, 17 women we approached refused to be interviewed, a relatively low

Table 1.3. Number of Rejections, by Research Site

Site	Number	Remarks
Hong Kong	1	A streetwalker in the Jordan area.
Macau	0	
Taiwan	1	One woman said no even after her former employer (an escort agency owner) brought us to her apartment and asked her about participating in our research project.
Thailand	2	Both were KTV/nightclub hostesses we tried to recruit in front of their nightclub.
Malaysia	2	A streetwalker in Kuala Lumpur; a hotel-based sex worker in Ipoh.
Singapore	3	At the very beginning of the field research, we were rejected by three streetwalkers when our interviewer told them on the streets about his intention to interview them. After the interviewer changed his tactic (requesting an interview only after he was inside a hotel room with the woman), there were no more rejections.
Indonesia	1	A woman soliciting business inside a restaurant.
Los Angeles	4	All four were house prostitutes in the San Gabriel Valley area.
New York	3	One woman from a massage parlor in New Jersey and two apartment-based prostitutes in Manhattan's Chinatown. All these women thought our interviewer was an undercover law enforcer.

rejection rate (about 9%). There were no refusals with respect to the other three categories of subjects (sex ring operators, law enforcers, and NGOs and other key informants) because nearly all these subjects were located through referrals, and the interviews were prearranged.

We also tried our best to protect the interviewer. WHO recommended that: "If interviewers are going to conduct an interview alone in a high-risk location, an interviewer should make certain that an outside contact person knows where she/he is going, what time she/he is conducting the interview, and what time she/he expects to complete the interview. Arrangements should be made to get in touch with the outside contact person once the interviewer is safely out of the interview location."[64] When our interviewer was interviewing a subject, a locally hired assistant, a friend, or a relative was made aware of the time and place of the interview.

Validity and Reliability

A study of this nature poses many challenges in terms of validity and reliability. Our subjects from the sex business risked being ridiculed, arrested, deported, or imprisoned if their identities and activities were revealed to the media or the authorities. Their willingness to participate and the level of their truthfulness may therefore be affected by these concerns. We used the following strategies to increase the validity and reliability of the data collection.

We were especially aware of the sensitive nature of interviewing women who engaged in prostitution, and we had explored the field logistics and reliability issues repeatedly during our prior interviews with prostitutes in various Asian cities for another project. To ensure that we would collect rich and reliable data from these subjects, we thus took a number of precautions. First, we conducted all the interviews face-to-face, one-on-one without the presence of another person. Second, we conducted the majority of the interviews in the subjects' own settings or in public places with which they were familiar. Third, we employed conversational interview techniques to gain the trust and confidence of the interviewees. Fourth, we did not collect any identifiable information. And last, we told our subjects before the interviews that if they did not want to answer a question, to just say "I don't know" or "I forget" and we would move on to the next question. And in fact, some subjects did just that.

Despite these many precautions, we cannot say with complete confidence that none of our subjects gave us misleading or incomplete information. But this is true of any interviews with any subjects on any topic. We also realize that interviewing prostitutes inside a sex venue or a public place for an hour or so has its own restrictions in trying to understand transnational sex trafficking. But by maximizing the variety of the prostitutes and the sex ring operators we interviewed, and by utilizing other sources of data (e.g., court cases, interviews with government authorities and NGOs, analyzing secondary materials, and especially fieldwork and participant observation), we hoped and believe that we have succeeded in learning much more about the pieces of the puzzle known as the international sex trade.

Limitations of This Study

As is true with any research, there are limitations; and this study has several such limitations. It is important to point these out in order to give our readers a basis for judging for themselves the weight to be given our findings and conclusions.

- We have studied only sex trafficking, meaning we have excluded other forms of human trafficking such as labor trafficking and child trafficking. Consequently, our findings are only relevant to sex trafficking and cannot be generalized to other forms of human trafficking. We agree that there is a need to pay more attention to other forms of human trafficking.[65]
- We studied only Chinese prostitutes and the people and processes involved in the transnational movement of these Chinese women. As a result, our findings are pertinent to that population, but may not be generalizable to the experiences of women from other source countries such as Nepal, Thailand, Nigeria, or Moldova. We cannot emphasize enough that whatever our findings are, they may be applicable to one group of women only—women from the People's Republic of China.
- Our samples of prostitutes, sex ring operators, law enforcers, and NGOs are all small because of time and resource constraints, and are also not fully representative samples. Even though we recruited women with diverse backgrounds in terms of age, marital status, and place of origin; included women from a variety of sex markets (street, massage parlors, brothels, nightclubs, etc.); and interviewed women in eight Asian and two American cities, the sample could be skewed in terms of age, marital status, earnings, and the like. Women who are younger, single, and capable of making substantially more than the average prostitute are probably underrepresented in our sample, simply because we were constrained by our budget to reach them. The sex ring operator sample is not equally distributed by research site, and the majority of the subjects in this subsample are the mommies. Certain other actors such as chickenheads (male pimps), fake husbands, and big business owners are

not included because we did not have the opportunity to approach persons in these roles for a formal interview. This too limits generalizabililty.

- All the interviews with Chinese prostitutes were conducted by a male interviewer. Not having a female interviewer could be construed as a weakness because female subjects might not be as candid with a male interviewer, or be willing to tell a male interviewer about physical aspects of their engagement in commercial sex. The original plan was to hire professional female interviewers to conduct the interviews with female subjects, but after encountering many difficulties in the process (i.e., it not being easy to find a professional interviewer who speaks Mandarin, candidates wanting more money than we could pay, candidates not being flexible with the work schedule, and/ or being unable or unwilling to go into sex venues to interview subjects, etc.), we abandoned that plan.

- Some of the interviews were conducted in the subjects' own settings and readers may consider it to be a weakness because they assume that most subjects may be afraid to tell us the truth while they were under their controllers' watchful eyes. However, we want to point out that, even though we interviewed them in their own settings, many were independent prostitutes and so the question of being watched by one or more controllers was not an issue. Moreover, because the interviews were conducted one-on-one in private and without the presence of a third party, subjects' fear was also in this respect minimized. Since the interviews were conducted face-to-face, we were also able to observe whether our subjects appeared to be fearful while being interviewed; and we did not encounter anyone who was afraid to talk to us because she thought her boss or mommy might get upset. In fact, subjects were more concerned about us (the interviewer) than their employer or manager, if they had one.

- Some subjects were referred to us by their employers, agents, or mommies and some readers might be concerned that these subjects could have been instructed by their sex ring operators to tell us falsely that the subjects were willingly engaged in prostitution and that they were not being victimized or exploited by their handlers. Again, we do not think this is a major concern because, as we think you will see in reading the stories of the women in the following pages, their stories ring true; and in fact most were not shy in complaining about their dealings with their handlers if they were not satisfied.

- The last issue may or may not be a limitation, but it clearly is a finding. It is the issue that will perhaps (probably) be likely to garner the most attention and controversy. This is the fact that, even though we set out to study the transnational movement of women for commercial sex and its possible links to sex trafficking, and given our best efforts using the approaches described, we

were not able to find many *transnational* trafficked victims who either explicitly told us they were, or who otherwise gave the appearance of, or described
experiences of being deceived, forced, or coerced into their current situations.
One of the exceptions was an underage subject, a 17-year-old streetwalker in
Singapore, who was by legal definition a trafficking victim simply because of
her age. Another woman in Bangkok said she felt like she was deceived by
her "auntie" who brought her there because the auntie did not tell her that
as a hostess, she would have to sleep with men. This is not to say that some
other subjects, more than a few as will be seen, had not been victimized or
otherwise exploited at some point during their involvement in commercial
sex. We did encounter a number of subjects who can be considered to have
been *domestic* trafficking victims, because they were coerced or tricked into
prostitution in China.

We have already detailed our research approach and rationale, as well as
why we rejected the notion of depending upon defined groups of trafficking
victims such as other studies have done. Nevertheless, we were made starkly
aware of the potential risks we were running in using that strategy very early
on in the study. A college-educated, 33-year-old prostitute from Harbin City
(Heilongjiang Province, in northeastern China) working in New York City
criticized our proposed approach after she was told that we were looking to
interview women who were trafficked:

> If you are looking for trafficked victims like this, you are never, ever going
> to find them. If you can find a girl through a newspaper advertisement,
> that means the girl is not being deceived or controlled, because the girl can
> tell her customers about this. Those who are tricked here are most likely to
> be locked up, and the brothel owner is unlikely to advertise his business.
> He is going to do business with only regular customers, and the girls are
> going to be locked up in a small hotel or an apartment. (116)[66]

Interestingly and importantly, we believe, she then added: "Of course, I
know this happens in China, but I don't know whether it also exists in the
United States." Similarly, most of our subjects, while denying that they had
been forced, deceived, or coerced into doing what they were currently doing,
also indicated that they knew of no such cases involving other women, although sometimes some had witnessed or heard of this happening.

We will have much more to say about this later, but simply want to add
here that no matter how reasonable the criticisms from the above woman
about our ways of locating our subjects, we also believe that it would be very

difficult (albeit not impossible) for sex ring operators to do a lucrative business the way she described: locking up women and accepting new customers only with referrals from regulars. Guri Tyldum and Anette Brunovskis from the Fafo Institute for Applied International Studies in Oslo made the same point when they wrote: "Even women in situations of serious exploitation and abuse can never be totally invisible in the prostitution arena, as their organizers need to sell the women to clients."[67] Sheldon Zhang also argued: "Despite sensational claims by the news media and advocacy groups, prostitutes are typically not locked up in cages and let out only to have sex with customers and then sent back to their cages again. As long as these women and children come in contact with the outside world, there will be venues to study them."[68] Even Victor Malarek, some of whose conclusions are in contrast to ours, echoed this point in his book *The Natashas*: "To make money, brothel owners and pimps have to make their victims readily available to clients, night in and night out. It is virtually impossible, therefore, to run an underground sex trafficking enterprise. Johns have to know where to find these women whenever the urge strikes. Their quest has to be simple."[69] Again, we will revisit this issue at some length.

Discussion Roadmap

In the next chapter, we will examine the main reasons for Chinese women to go overseas. We will also explore whether these women have been to other countries before they arrived in the country where we interviewed them. We will also take a look at who the recruiters were, if any, and under what circumstances the women met their recruiters. Finally, we compare the background characteristics of the subjects in various research sites.

In chapter 3 we will introduce the women we interviewed. We will provide some basic demographic information about them, such as age, education, family background, marital status, and employment history. And because a substantial number of these women were engaged in prostitution before they went overseas, we will explore how and why that came about. This includes a discussion of what has been called "bounded rationality," as well as gender inequality and the objectification of women in China, and how these macrofactors seem to combine with microfactors to steer some Chinese women into prostitution. We conclude chapter 3 with a discussion of life in the commercial sex business. We examine how our subjects viewed paid sex in general and their engagement in prostitution in particular. We then discuss how our subjects were coping in a foreign country, and how people in the destination countries reacted to the arrival of Chinese prostitutes.

In chapter 4, we will discuss the unique character of the commercial sex business in each of our destination countries, and examine how Chinese women penetrated or were embedded into the local sex trade. We will also take a look at the sex trade in Shenzhen, China. At the end of the chapter, we will take a comparative look at the background characteristics of the subjects in each destination country.

We will explore the social organization of prostitution in chapter 5 by focusing on the modus operandi of various sex venues in the ten research sites. We will categorize the sex markets into three main categories: independent, partnership, and employed. Within each main category, we will further examine the various settings where our subjects were engaged in commercial sex. At the end of chapter 5, we will explore the curious phenomenon wherein certain of these women maintained a stable relationship with a customer by becoming a mistress, and the pros and cons in their view of having a "husband."

In chapter 6, we will take a look at the people who facilitate the movement of Chinese women from one country to another and engage them in prostitution. We will examine all the participants in the sex trade: chicken-heads, agents, mommies, escort agency owners, brothel keepers, jockeys or drivers, fake husbands, and others. We will conclude the chapter with an examination of whether or not transnational commercial sex seems to be controlled by Chinese organized crime groups such as the triads in Hong Kong, organized gangs in Taiwan, and Chinese tongs and street gangs in the United States.

We will examine the economics of transnational prostitution in chapter 7. Specifically, we will explore how much, if anything, Chinese women must pay to go overseas, how long it takes them to clear their transportation fees, how much they make from prostitution, and how they manage their money. Here we will argue that transnational commercial sex is a business, and that the sex business is, like any other business, organized and functional in such a way that the benefits to all the participants are maximized, without certain participants having to be sacrificed or exploited. We will then focus on the customers, the sex buyers. We will examine the socioeconomic and ethnic backgrounds of the men who bought sex from our subjects. We will also explore the issue of abuses by clients. Lastly, at the end of the chapter we will discuss the nature of buying sex.

We will examine the role of the police and other governmental and non-governmental agents in chapter 8. We will begin the chapter with a discussion of how government and police agencies in various research sites are responding to the increase in foreign prostitutes in their jurisdictions. We will then describe our female subjects' experiences with the police. We also will explore the problem of police corruption in combating human trafficking.

In chapter 9, in order to assess whether our subjects can be truly considered to be trafficked victims, we will compare our subjects' experiences and situations with those set out in the description of the nature and characteristics of sex trafficking as promulgated by both the United Nations and the U.S. government. Finally, in the concluding chapter we will probe the politics of prostitution and sex trafficking, the issue of defining and estimating the volume of sex trafficking, and then end with a discussion of what we see as the need to reexamine the predominant trafficking paradigm.

Clarification of Terms

Thus far, we have been using the word "prostitutes" or "women who engage in commercial sex" to refer to our female subjects mainly to avoid using the terms "sex workers" or "prostituted women," as we fully understand the ideological construction and controversy surrounding the use of these terms.[70] We want to make it clear, however, that our position is that whether commercial sex is "sex work" or "violence against women" is an empirical question to be settled by facts, data, and evidence, and not by ideological posturing on either or any side of the issue. Our study is actually about the social organization of the transnational movement of Chinese women for commercial sex, and thus we hope will have relevance for sex trafficking as well as for prostitution. Therefore, at the very outset, we would like to clarify what we mean by the terms that follow.

PROSTITUTE OR *XIAOJIE*

A prostitute is a woman who willingly engages in sexual intercourse for money. Of course, agreeing on what is "willingly" can be a problem, but we will return to this question later in the book. For our purposes, we will use the Chinese word *xiaojie* interchangeably with the word "prostitute" because *xiaojie* was the term used by the vast majority of our female subjects in the sex business to refer to themselves. The term *xiaojie* is composed of two characters: *xiao* which means "little," "small," or "young," and *jie* which means "older sister." *Xiaojie* can be translated as "miss," and people in Taiwan and Hong Kong often use the word *xiaojie* to refer to any young woman, regardless of whether the woman is a stranger, a waitress, a celebrity, and so on. As a matter of fact, not all prostitutes in China are referred to as *xiaojie*, nor are all *xiaojie* prostitutes. Because prostitution is illegal in China, most of the women who are engaged in prostitution in China are necessarily categorized as *xiaojie, jishi* (technician), or *falangmei* (hair salon lady).[71] Strictly speaking, a *xiaojie* is someone who works in a nightclub, a KTV, or a dance hall as a hostess. She can claim that she is not a prostitute because she only entertains customers by sitting at their tables (*zuotai* or on stage) and does not go out with them (*chutai* or off stage). However, in reality, it is rare that a *xiaojie* is able to resist going out with a customer, at least not for long. A streetwalker is also normally referred to as a *xiaojie*. A *jishi*, or technician, is a formal name for someone who works in a spa or a sauna as a masseuse, and most *jishi* also engage in providing sexual services. A *falangmei* is someone who works in a "hair salon" as a prostitute. The meaning of these terms will become clearer when we discuss the operations of various sex venues in chapters 4 and 5. To keep it simple, we will use the word *xiaojie* to denote all the Chinese women who are (1) hostesses (*zuotai xiaojie* or *sanpei xiaojie*) in nightclubs, KTVs, and dancing halls; (2) technicians (*jishi*) in spas and saunas; (3) hair salon ladies (*falangmei*) in hair salon-style brothels; and (4) streetwalkers.

We also want to clarify that, although we use the word prostitute to refer to our female subjects, some of these subjects did not regularly (i.e., on a daily basis) engage in sexual intercourse with their clients, or they engaged in sexual intercourse only with certain customers, or even with just one particular customer whom they referred to as their "husband." Some of them regularly provided hand jobs and blow jobs rather than sexual intercourse. However, it is safe to say that all our subjects can be considered to be prostitutes because they did in fact provide sexual services for money, regardless of the nature of those services and how frequently they were provided.

TRAFFICKED VICTIM

A sex trafficking victim is a person who unwillingly engages in commercial sex as a result of force, fraud, or deception. If the processes of force, fraud, and/or deception occur within the borders of one country (namely, China in this case), we will refer to the victim as a *domestic* trafficked victim; and if it occurs overseas, we will consider the subject a *transnational* trafficked victim. Of course, if the subject is a minor, then we will consider her to be a trafficked victim regardless of how she was recruited into the sex business. As will be discussed later, the U.S. TVPA (Trafficking Victims Protection Act) created a two-tier definition: "severe forms of trafficking in persons," in which a commercial sex act is induced by force, fraud, or coercion, and "sex trafficking," defined simply as the recruitment, harboring, transportation, or obtaining of a person for the purpose of a commercial sex act. Here, when we use the term "sex trafficking," we are referring, unless otherwise specified, to "severe forms of sex trafficking" that involve force, fraud, or coercion.

Among our female subjects, there were domestic trafficking victims (who were tricked into prostitution in China). These subjects should not, however, be considered to be transnational trafficking victims, because no force, fraud, or deception was involved in their *transnational* movement. This is an important distinction that bears repeating. We will categorize certain subjects as having been domestic trafficking victims, but we will not continue to view them as victims when we discuss their engagement in prostitution overseas, if they were not deceived or forced to go overseas. The matter of determining whether a subject was a transnational trafficked victim or not will be discussed in chapter 10, when we apply various other criteria besides the presence of force, fraud, or deception (i.e., whether there was a recruiter or a facilitator in the process of the women going overseas, whether payment was involved in the transnational movement, whether there was debt bondage, whether a subject's travel documents were withheld) to get a better picture of the reality of sex trafficking. While this book deals mainly with the overseas experiences of Chinese women, we will not ignore their experiences back home in China.

Since we interviewed women who had not already been identified as victims, and since the interviews were conducted either in these women's natural settings or in public places, some readers might want to argue that what we are studying is actually prostitution, and not sex trafficking. If our purpose is to study the latter group, these readers might suggest, we should interview identified trafficked victims and trafficked victims exclusively. However, were we to do that, we would simply be repeating what the majority of other studies have done over the past ten or so years.[72] Instead, our plan was to examine the broader issue of the transnational movement of Chinese women for commercial sex, and in the process, determine what constitutes prostitution and sex trafficking, respectively. How are the two related? We think we can show that the prevailing human trafficking discourse fails to capture the many nuances of prostitution and sex trafficking, and that the definition of sex trafficking needs to be reevaluated to reflect the reality in the field.

TRAFFICKER OR CONTROLLER

A trafficker or a controller is anyone who plays a role in the transnational movement of a woman for the purpose of commercial sex. Many different roles have been identified in the literature on trafficking, and these include recruiter, transporter, trafficker, brothel owner, and pimp. As will be clear later in chapter 6, within the Chinese context at least, many more roles are involved in the transnational movement of Chinese women. We will use the terms used by our female subjects and sex ring operator subjects when we refer to these people (i.e., chickenhead, agent, mommy, escort agency owner, fake husband, jockey, etc.). We will often use the term sex ring operator as a generic term to refer to all the people who facilitate the transnational movement of Chinese women.

ORGANIZED CRIME

In this book, only certain groups will be referred to as organized crime groups. This means that we are going to use a more restrictive definition than that put forth by, for example, the United Nations. According to the United Nations Office on Drugs and Crime, an organized criminal group is "a structured group of three or more persons existing for a period of time and acting in concert with the aim of committing one or more serious crimes or offenses . . . in order to obtain, directly, or indirectly, a financial or other material benefit."[73] If we were to use the U.N. definition, certainly many of the groups that are engaged in the transnational movement of Chinese women could be considered to be organized crime groups. However, based on our many years of extensive research on organized crime in Asia and the United States, we have come to the conclusion that, at least within the Chinese or Asian context, only the following groups should be considered to be true organized criminal groups: (1) U.S.-based tongs (e.g., On Leong, Hip Sing, Tung On, etc.) and street gangs (e.g., Ghost Shadows, Flying Dragons, Fuk Ching, Green Dragons, etc.); (2) Hong Kong-based triads (e.g., Sun Yee On, 14K, Wo Shing Wo, etc.); (3) Macau-based triads (e.g., the 14K, the Water Room, etc.); (3) Taiwan-based organized gangs (e.g., United Bamboo, Four Seas, Celestial Alliance, etc.) and *jiaotou* groups (e.g., Fang Ming Kuan, Nyo Pu, etc.); (4) China-based mafia-style gangs (e.g., the Liu Yong group in Shenyang, the Li Qiang group in Chongqing, etc.); (5) Thailand-based *jao pho*; (6) Singapore-based *tangpai*; (7) Malaysia-based Chinese gangs (e.g., 390, 18K, Dragonhead, etc.); and, finally, (8) Japan-based yakuza groups (e.g., the Yamaguchi-kumi, the Inagawa-kai, the Sumiyoshi-kai).[74] We believe that the vast majority of government officials and law enforcers in Asia and the United States agree with us on this characterization.

2

Going Down to the Sea

In the late 1970s, not long after the Cultural Revolution (1966–1976) was over, China reestablished ties with the West and adopted its Open Door policy.[1] China also began to move from a centrally planned economy to a market-oriented economy. Government-owned enterprises crumbled quickly in the face of the rising private ventures. Foreign investors were lured to China to open up factories in the many newly established special economic zones in the coastal areas.[2]

Chinese leaders, especially the then paramount leader Deng Xiaoping, encouraged Chinese people to work hard and get rich with slogans such as "Let Some People Get Rich First" and "To Get Rich Is Glorious." Deng also came up with his famous motto of "whether a cat is black or white makes no difference—as long as it catches mice, it is a good cat!" In other words, he was urging the Chinese people to brush aside ideology and focus on practicality. All of a sudden, China began to embark on a reform movement that helped usher it into the new millennium with impressive economic achievements.[3]

As China began to open up and its people began to improve their living conditions, there were also a large number of Chinese citizens longing to go overseas.[4] Such persons who actually live and work abroad and then return to China are known as "overseas Chinese." People living in the two provinces with the largest numbers of overseas Chinese—Guangdong and Fujian—were especially eager to go abroad because they were impressed by the wealth of overseas Chinese who returned to China for the first time after having been away for many decades. As a result, in the early 1980s many people from Guangdong looked to be smuggled into Hong Kong, and people from Fujian, into Taiwan.

After the Chinese authorities' violent crackdown on the student democracy movement in Tiananmen Square in June 1989, the U.S. government responded by allowing many Chinese citizens in the United States to become permanent residents by granting them political asylum, regardless of whether they were students, visitors, or illegal immigrants.[5] Coincidently, it was also a time when tens of thousands of people from certain rural areas around Fuzhou City (Fujian Province) began to clandestinely arrive in the United States with the help of professional human smugglers known as snakeheads.[6] In June 1993, a human cargo ship by the name of *Golden Venture* arrived near New York City and unloaded more than 260 passengers. Ten Chinese citizens drowned while attempting to swim ashore.[7] When the United States stepped up its efforts to stop Chinese citizens from entering the United States illegally, many potential migrants from China shifted their efforts toward Western Europe and other parts of the developed world.

The early outward migration of Chinese citizens was dominated by male migrants. In the late 1990s, however, there was a dramatic increase in the number of Chinese women going overseas. The latter included both legal as well as illegal, and temporary as well as permanent migrants. For example, when Chinese citizens were smuggled into Taiwan in the late 1980s and early 1990s, most were men who were brought to Taiwan to work in the manufacturing, construction, and fishing industries.[8] But by the late 1990s male workers from China had begun to disappear from the Taiwan job market. They were replaced in part by Chinese women who were smuggled into Taiwan for work in the local sex sector.[9] This feminization of the illegal immigration of mainland Chinese into Taiwan was dramatic and pervasive.

In 1997 the British returned Hong Kong to China, and two years later the Portuguese handed Macau back to the Chinese. After the conversion of these former colonies into special administrative regions (SARs) with their own political and judicial systems, the Chinese authorities worked hard to improve their economies in order to win over the local populations. As a result, Hong Kong was promoted as the shopping center, and Macau the gambling mecca, for China's 1.3 billion people. In order to encourage mainland Chinese to go to Hong Kong and Macau to buy and gamble, the Beijing authorities loosened the restrictions on mainlanders' visits to these two regions.[10]

The economic miracle in China (especially in the coastal provinces) can be attributed to the large "floating" (or transient) population whose members have fled their villages in order to improve their lives. Using this same logic, even those with connections and financial wherewithal have sought options to go overseas to look for opportunities. The search for better paying jobs has been voracious, fanned largely by a freshly opened society having a weak safety net and few social resources. The prevailing belief in China is that the only security anyone can achieve is to make as much money as possible in one's lifetime. Coupled with the longstanding cultural practice of showing off one's success in the form of material possessions, Chinese people—young and old, men and women—have for the past two decades spawned a massive tidal wave of job hunters. Under intense competition to survive in a new economic system, even morality has come to be measured by material success. In China there has long been a saying: people will laugh at poverty but not at prostitution (*xiaopingbuxiaochang*). To be poor is to be looked down upon.

As China's economy continued its vigorous growth in the 1980s and 1990s, many government officials and entrepreneurs began to travel overseas. Soon they were followed by increasing numbers of students going overseas to study. In the twenty-first century, as a new middle class began to develop in China, the world community, especially countries in Asia and Western Europe, began to relax their visa restrictions for Chinese citizens in hopes of bolstering their own tourism industries. Quickly, Chinese tourists became the predominant group of visitors in many countries that rely on tourism as a major source of income. Of course, the increased ease of traveling to neighboring countries in Asia, and even to Western Europe, enabled both men and women to go overseas. This was true whether they were tourists or were actually seeking opportunities to make money abroad.

The marketing of the sexual services of Chinese women in Asia and in the United States was made possible because the women who went abroad to make money in commercial sex largely catered to the Chinese men working or living in those countries. In fact, Hong Kong, Macau, Taiwan, and Singapore are all Chinese societies, and there is as well a large Chinese presence in Thailand, Malaysia, Indonesia, and the United States.

Reasons for Going Abroad

Of the 149 Chinese women interviewed outside China, 106 or 71 percent, said they knew they were going overseas to engage in the sex business even before

Table 2.1. When Subjects Knew They Would Engage in Prostitution Overseas (N = 149)

Site	In China (%)	Right after arriving overseas (%)	Not long after arriving overseas (%)	Long after arriving overseas (%)	N
Hong Kong	80	0	7	13	15
Macau	94	0	6	0	18
Taiwan	88	6	0	6	16
Thailand	82	0	18	0	17
Malaysia	94	6	0	0	18
Singapore	93	0	7	0	15
Indonesia	94	0	6	0	18
Los Angeles	0	13	50	37	16
New York	6	0	44	50	16
Total	71	3	15	11	149

they left China (see Table 2.1). Four subjects (or 3%) said they realized they would work as prostitutes right after they arrived in the destination country, twenty-two not long after they had arrived, and seventeen long after they had settled down abroad. The last two categories of subjects—those who entered the sex sector either not long after or long after they had gone abroad—were predominantly women we interviewed in Los Angeles and New York. These women in the United States were quite different from the other women in Asia in terms of age (older), marital status (more likely to be married or divorced), education (better educated), region of origin (came from the northeast rather than from the south), and commercial sex experience (most were not prostitutes in China). Even though these women said they did not go to America with a plan to sell sex, we do not know how many of them knew back in China that, if they struggled in the United States, there was always a chance for them to enter prostitution as a last resort. If we exclude women in Los Angeles and New York from the calculation, then 105 out of the remaining 117 (90%) said they went overseas with the knowledge that they would be engaging in providing sexual services.

This same point has been made by Johan Lindquist (a professor at Stockholm University) and Nicola Piper (a professor at the University of Wales) in their review of the research on prostitution in Southeast Asia: "What has become clear in existing studies in Asia and elsewhere is that migrant women rarely fit the ideal-type image of the victim of trafficking. Many migrants understand prior to migration what their working destination consists of, and even if their choice is constrained by economic and social circumstances, they cannot be understood as innocent victims on a general level."[11] The same is true with Thai women working in the sex business in Germany, as observed by social worker Prapairat Ratanaloan Mix, who said that "more than 80 percent of these women were sex workers in Thailand before going to Germany. Many of them were aware of what was waiting for them in Germany."[12]

For our subjects, the reasons for engaging in prostitution overseas include two main ones: making money for oneself (54%) and making money to help their families (31%). As will be discussed in chapter 3, these two factors were also often cited by our subjects when asked why they got into prostitution *in China*. The other 15 percent offered a variety of other reasons for becoming involved in commercial sex overseas, including (1) it was not so easy to make money as prostitutes in China anymore, especially given the frequent crackdowns by the authorities; (2) they had run into a chickenhead who urged them to go overseas; and/or (3) to get away from certain people, mainly husbands or boyfriends.

Money for Self

More than half the women in our sample said the main reason for them wanting to go overseas was simply to make money for themselves. Their most frequent answer was: "I was looking for an opportunity to make money, and then I met a returned *xiaojie* who told me how easy it was to earn money overseas. I said I want to give it a try, too." Let us take a look at how the women who were already engaged in commercial sex compare with the others with respect to their motives for going abroad.

Ah Dong,[13] a 30-year-old married woman who was a streetwalker in a red-light district in Singapore,[14] said: "I came here mainly to make money. I was making only $48 to $60 a day as a *xiaojie* in China; here I make $260 to $330 a day. As far as making money is concerned, there is no comparison whatsoever between these two places" (2). Angie, a 37-year-old woman from Yiyang (Hunan Province) who was selling sex in Shantou (Guangdong Province) before she went to Hong Kong, explained why she went overseas:

> I wanted to make lots of money quickly. At that time, I just broke up with my boyfriend in Shantou. I did not work for the two years we were together. In the beginning, he gave me some money, but later, he was spending my money. Therefore, I did not have any money when we broke up. Besides, I adopted a daughter, and I was desperate for money. So I came to Hong Kong to make money. (80)

Another subject, Xiao Tao, said she came to Macau because a returned *xiaojie* told her she could make more money abroad:

> The girlfriend of my boyfriend's friend came back from Macau and told me that it was easy to make money in Macau. At any rate, while I was working [as a prostitute] in Zhanjiang and Shenzhen, I met many girls who came back from Hong Kong, Macau, and Singapore, and it seemed like they came back with lots of money. So I have always wanted to come out and give it a try, or I would regret it one day. (85)

In brief, some of the subjects who were already engaged in prostitution in China were willing to go overseas because they learned that they could make more money abroad than in China, and they met someone who could help them to go abroad.

The overseas sex industry attracts not only women who are already prostitutes in China but also Chinese women who had never been involved in commercial sex. Among these women are some who had worked for many years in the legitimate labor market and were frustrated by how little money they were making. According to Xiao Song, a 24-year-old single woman who was looking for clients in the lobby of a small hotel in Macau:

> I quit school after the first year of high school and worked in Shashi [Hubei Province] for a few months. Then a cousin brought me to Dongguan [Guangdong Province] and I worked in a shoe factory. I made only about $50 a month and I often worked until midnight. Later, another cousin [who is a shoe designer] brought me to Zhuhai [Guangdong Province] and I worked for a small shoe factory. I made a little more than $120 a month in Zhuhai, but I still felt short of money. How can I get by with that kind of money? At that point, I met a *xiaojie* who just got back from Macau. She said: "Why don't you take advantage of your youth to make money, otherwise you will not have the opportunity to make a 'youthful meal' (*chinchunfang*) any more." She told me that I could make more than $2,400 a month in Macau, so I came. (98)

Bing Bing, 25 years old, single, from Changchun (the capital of Jilin Province), explained why she went to Taiwan and became an escort even though she had never been involved in commercial sex in China:

> After dropping out of school during my last year in high school, I worked as a salesgirl in a boutique. Later, I started my own clothing business. At

the beginning, I was doing fine, but not long after, my business went down-hill. At that point, I was also splitting with my boyfriend. I was in a bad mood, and when my friend said she wanted me to go to Taiwan with her, I thought for a moment and said yes. Both of us knew a woman who just came back from Taiwan who bought a house and a new car. That woman did not tell me and my friend how much she actually made in Taiwan, but we could sense that she was rich, and we were really envious. (144)

Ah Lian, a 35-year-old divorced woman from Xinhui (Guangdong), was working on the streets of a red-light district in Singapore when we inter-viewed her. Her reason for going to Singapore and working as a prostitute was very simple: "I came to make money. The amount of money you make a month in Singapore is about the same as what you make in ten years in China. I made $70 a month in China. After deducting $7 a month for lodg-ing at the factory, I took home $63 a month and $750 a year—$7,500 in ten years. I can make $7,500 a month in Singapore"[15] (14).

Money for Family

Some of our subjects entered prostitution not because they needed money for themselves, but rather for their family. The reasons why these subjects' families were in dire financial situations can be categorized into (1) there was a crisis in the family, (2) the head of the household was not supporting the family, (3) the husband was not supporting his wife, and (4) a divorced woman needed to support her family.

CRISIS IN THE FAMILY

Some of our subjects went overseas because there was a crisis in the fam-ily and they needed to earn a substantial amount of money in a hurry. Miao Miao, a 24-year-old single woman from Liuzhou (Guangxi), who was not a *xiaojie* in China, explained why she went to Macau and took up commer-cial sex: "I needed to make a large amount of money in a very short time. My brother was arrested for assault. My family spent plenty of money on his case. In the end, he was sentenced to prison and my parents owed a huge debt. After witnessing how devastated my parents were with my brother's imprisonment and our financial predicament, I decided to come to Macau to engage in prostitution to help them repay the debt" (90).

Common people in China, as opposed to those of higher status, are un-likely to obtain a loan from a bank, and poor people are also unlikely to find relatives or friends who are willing to lend them money. When there is a crisis and money is needed to deal with the crisis, many ordinary families must thus rely on sometimes drastic measures to find the money. Becoming a prostitute may be one such drastic measure.

IRRESPONSIBLE FATHER

Some subjects we interviewed went overseas and became prostitutes because they were unhappy with their fathers' lack of support for their families, and thought that they, as daughters, should sacrifice themselves to help their mothers and siblings. Wang Min, a 24-year-old single woman from Nanning (Guangxi), who was working for an escort agency in Kuala Lumpur, explained why she became a *xiaojie* in Malaysia:

> My father was originally a farmer, and he became a car driver later. He is a womanizer and he also loves gambling. I have an elder sister and a younger brother and we all feel sorry for our mother. The main reason that I am in this line of work is that my father does not take care of us. He spends a lot of money. I have to shoulder the burden of this family. I do not care for myself. I used to have three jobs because my family needed money. I have a friend who is a *xiaojie* in Malaysia. Learning that I was doing three jobs, she urged me to work as a prostitute in Malaysia. I thought about it for two months and decided to come. (23)

Our subjects were more likely to blame their fathers than their mothers for their predicaments. Some subjects repeatedly made fun of how their fathers call them only when they want money.

BAD HUSBAND

Some married women who think their husbands are not making enough, or are indulging in drinking, gambling, or paid sex, consider prostitution in a foreign country as an option to both improve their families' financial situations and to be away from their husbands. This is especially so if they also happen to know someone who can help them go overseas. Xiao Wei, a 43-year-old married woman from Zhoushan (Zhejiang Province) with an 18-year-old son, explained how she ended up being a *xiaojie* in Bangkok:

> I knew a fellow villager who worked as a *xiaojie* in Bangkok. She told me that men in Thailand are very nice. If you eat and chat with them, they will give you tips. At that point I was in a dire financial situation because my husband was earning only $40 a month as a fisherman. Worse, he likes gambling and he often lost all his earnings. What can I do in China? There

is no job opportunity for me in Zhoushan. My husband never took money home, he is a gambler, and our relationship is bad. So I came here. (56)

DIVORCE

Women are also vulnerable when they are divorced and have children to raise, because they do not get adequate support in a divorce and do not have any other safety net to rely on. For divorced women with little education, no connections, and who have been out of work for many years, finding a job in China is an almost insurmountable challenge. Because of their age, their possibilities for entering the commercial sex business in China are also restricted. As a result, if they know someone who can help them to go abroad for prostitution, they might seriously consider that option. Cui Cui, a 34-year-old divorced woman with a 12-year-old son, was soliciting business in front of an old residential building in Macau. She told us:

> I came out to work after dropping out of middle school. I started as a salesgirl for a clothing store and later I did it on my own. Then I worked at a garment factory for almost ten years. During that time, I got married, gave birth to my son, and then divorced. My husband and I quarreled frequently due to a shortage of money. Then he met a rich woman, we divorced, and he married her. I can't make much money in China and my fellow villagers told me that I could do this in Macau and make lots of money. I am divorced and have a son to support; how can I get by with so little income in China? (97)

Recruited by a Chickenhead or a Middleman

Thirteen subjects went abroad to work in commercial sex simply because they were recruited by chickenheads—men who assist women to work as prostitutes for a fee or a cut of the women's earnings. Both prostitutes and non-prostitutes in China can be recruited by chickenheads to go overseas. Yan Yan, a 20-year-old single woman who was a *xiaojie* in China told us how, after she went back to her hometown to try to live a normal life, she was brought to Macau by a man she loved:

> I had been a prostitute in Shenzhen for two years. Then I decided to go back to my hometown to have a normal life because I was sick of being a prostitute. However, I met a man in Changde [Hunan] who is a chickenhead and I liked him. He told me one day after we had been together for half a year that he lost money in his business and needed money to pay the debt. He wanted me to help him and suggested I go to Zhuhai [near

Macau] and work as a prostitute. So I went to Zhuhai and worked in a nightclub. Not long after I went to Zhuhai, he sent me to Macau. (87)

C C, a 31-year-old woman from Fushun (Liaoning) who had no commercial sex experience, explained how she became a prostitute in Macau after she met a chickenhead in Zhuhai:

A friend and I traveled to Zhuhai from Fushun to look for work. After arriving in Zhuhai, we met a man in a restaurant. He told us that working in Zhuhai was not as good as in Macau; we can make more quick money in Macau by drinking and chatting with customers. To be honest, I knew at that time that it was not that simple. We knew definitely that we must sleep with customers. But we could not be concerned so much at that time because we did not have any money left. This man applied for travel passes in Zhuhai for us. He took us to Macau and tried to find us jobs at a nightclub. (101)

Besides chickenheads, there are also middlemen in China acting as recruiters for overseas sex establishments. These middlemen charge a fee to help women obtain the necessary travel documents to go abroad. Middlemen, unlike chickenheads, are highly unlikely to have any sexual relationships with the women they help, nor do they play any role in the women's activities overseas. These facilitators have a critical role in the migration process because they are often the key to a woman's deciding to go abroad and being able to do so.

Some of the subjects who were prostitutes in China also mentioned a variety of other reasons to go overseas. For example, they thought they would save more money if they worked overseas simply because they had no friends abroad, were not familiar with the new place, and as a result, had less opportunity to spend money. Also, because they were so far away from home, family members were less likely to approach them for money. Others went abroad because they wanted to avoid the Chinese authorities.[16] According to Liu Li, a 34-year-old divorcee who was working at a spa in Jakarta:

In 2004, I was working as a hostess in Beijing and I also went out with clients. Because of the frequent police crackdowns, being a *xiaojie* in China was really nerve-racking: you were worried all the time about being arrested. On one occasion, I was with a famous movie star in a hotel room in a remote place outside of Beijing. It was very cold and it was snowing heavily that day, and yet the police came to check our room. I had to crawl out of a window to escape. After that I wanted to leave Beijing.

Coincidently, I met my classmate who had just returned from Indonesia and she brought me here. (48)

As mentioned, other subjects went overseas mainly because they wanted to get away from their husbands or boyfriends. A small number of subjects said they were interested in going abroad because they thought the commercial sex business overseas was less competitive than in China, and that they would get more business and make more money. Dan Dan, a 31-year-old woman who had been to Singapore and Malaysia, explained why she began to go overseas after being a *xiaojie* for about ten years in China:

> When I was in China, I met a *xiaojie* who came back from Indonesia. She said she was willing to be my agent. She told me that I could make more than $2,500 a month there. At that time, the price for "an hour" [one session] in China had decreased to $40 from $125. Not only had the price decreased, but it became more competitive because not only were there more girls entering this line of work, but they were also younger. That's why I wanted to go overseas.[17] (50)

In addition to their desire to make money or having been recruited by a chickenhead, some of our subjects went overseas just to travel and to see the world. Even if they returned home without much money, they thought it would be fun and exciting to be abroad for a short time and to see what it was like to live in a different culture and a different climate. Sociologist Laura Maria Agustin, in her research on foreign women selling sex in Europe, also made the point that many women have a "desire to travel, see the world, make money and accept whatever jobs are available along the way," and they "do not fall into neat categories: 'victims of trafficking,' 'migrant sex worker,' 'forced migrants,' 'prostituted women.' Their lives are far more complex—and interesting—than such labels imply."[18] Unpacking these categories and the often blurred distinctions among them does create a much more complicated picture—a picture that does not lend itself to simple policy and practice prescriptions. On the other hand, that much more realistic picture would certainly be more accurate and could lead to better targeted and more cost-effective solutions.

Other Overseas Experiences

Of our 149 subjects, 89 (60%) had only been to the country where we interviewed them. Among the 60 (40%) who had been to other countries as well, 32 (53%) said they went to those countries also to engage in prostitution.

Table 2.2. Subjects' Other Overseas Experiences,
by Research Site (N = 149)

Site	Been to other countries? Yes (%)	For prostitution? Yes (%)	N
Hong Kong	53	27	15
Macau	78	44	18
Taiwan	25	13	16
Thailand	12	6	17
Malaysia	28	17	18
Singapore	47	40	15
Indonesia	50	39	18
Los Angeles	25	0	16
New York	44	6	16
Total	40	21	149

Women we interviewed in Singapore and Indonesia, and who had been to other countries, were more likely to have engaged in commercial sex in multiple countries. On the other hand, subjects in the United States who had visited other countries were the least likely to have engaged in prostitution in those countries. This was largely because they had gone to these other places for a purpose other than prostitution (see Table 2.2). This will be explained in chapter 4.

Meng Fei, a 32-year-old single woman from Hefei (Anhui) who was working as a street prostitute in a tourist area of Hong Kong, described her overseas experiences as follows:

Before I came to Hong Kong for the first time in 2004, I went to Singapore and worked at a nightclub for more than a month. The year before last year [2005], I went to Indonesia and worked at a nightclub in Jakarta for two months. I like Singapore, but I was unable to obtain a Singapore visa again. I do not like Indonesia but you get more money going out with men in Indonesia, about two or three *tiao* [between $200 and $300]. In Singapore, it is $143 to $200; in Hong Kong, about $200. Customers are the best in Singapore, followed by Hong Kong.[19] (74)

Miao Miao, a 24-year-old woman whom we interviewed in Macau in a brothel located inside an apartment building, told us she had previously worked in the sex sectors of Singapore and Malaysia:

I have been to Singapore and Malaysia. In Singapore, I worked as a street-walker for more than 20 days. I charged $40 or $50 per session and I made a little more than $6,300 that trip, but I also paid more than $2,500 to those who helped me to get there. Later, I returned to Singapore for the second time and still worked as a streetwalker. I did not ask anybody to help me the second time, but my charge also decreased to $30 or $40. Even so, I earned more than $5,000 the second trip. (90)

The Intermediaries

Of the women we interviewed, only ten (less than 7%) said they went abroad on their own without any help from anyone. The majority of the subjects (79 out of 145, or 54%), were assisted by a returned *xiaojie* only, or a returned prostitute *and* a company (a labor broker in China), or a returned *xiaojie* *and* an agent (an investor in Taiwan or a representative in Indonesia). In the first scenario, a returned *xiaojie* helps a subject to apply for a visa, brings the subject along when she goes overseas again, or simply introduces her to a mommy or a sex venue owner in the destination country. In this process, no third party is involved. In the second and third scenarios, the returned prostitute needs someone else, either a company or an agent, to help the subject obtain the necessary travel documents or to make employment arrangements with a sex venue in the destination country. Women we interviewed in Taiwan, Thailand, and Malaysia were most often helped by a returned *xiaojie*, who assisted them in going abroad, with or without the assistance of a company or an agent (see Table 2.3).

Returned *xiaojies* were interested in helping other women to go overseas for one or more of the following three reasons. First, they make money. The woman who is being helped, or the agent for whom the returned prostitute is

Table 2.3. Intermediairy, by Research Site (N = 149)

Site	None (%)	A returned xiaojie (%)	A company (%)	A chickenhead (%)	Husband or boyfriend (%)	Others (%)	N
Hong Kong	40	47	0	13	0	0	15
Macau	6	50	0	33	11	0	18
Taiwan	0	87	0	0	13	0	15
Thailand	0	88	0	12	0	0	16
Malaysia	5	83	6	6	0	0	18
Singapore	0	66	27	7	0	0	15
Indonesia	6	55	33	6	0	0	18
Los Angeles	7	7	36	0	29	21	14
New York	0	0	75	0	12	13	16
Total	7	54	19	9	7	3	145*

* 4 missing observations

recruiting, or the sex venue owner for whom the recruit is going to work, pay the returned *xiaojie* recruiter a certain amount of money for her help. This payment is generally made without being requested, and money is usually not the strongest factor for these particular recruiters, as this comment by Wen Wen from Wuhan, a 22-year-old woman working as an escort in Taipei, illustrated: "I introduced two women to my agent. If the women I introduced come here as tourists, I will get a $700 referral fee per person; if they get here through fake marriages, I will get $1,400 per person. Regardless of how a woman gets here and how much the referral fee for me is, the road fee is always $6,700. When we refer someone in China to our agent in Taiwan, we are not doing it just for that small amount of money" (146). Wen Wen was already making about $8,750 a month (excluding tips and gifts) in Taipei, and it was our impression that she was referring other women to her agent more as a favor and not because of the referral fee.[20]

Second, by bringing someone along on their next overseas trip, returned *xiaojies* can establish a small and close network among the group so that they can look after one another in the destination country. For many Chinese women working in overseas commercial sex, having someone they can trust, rely on, or at the very least talk to after work, is as important as making a commission. Third, for many women in Thailand, bringing a younger and prettier friend, relative, or neighbor with them on their next trip to Thailand is also a way for them to maintain a niche in the sex market. Ah Chan, a 38-year-old divorced woman, with a 19-year-old son who was attending college in Wuhan, explained why Chinese women in Bangkok were bringing other women to Thailand:

> When you hear an older woman here saying this or that younger woman is her cousin or niece, she is lying. This is one way for the older woman to get some money from a man who is interested in the younger woman. It's like, well, if you like my younger cousin, you've got to do something to please the elder cousin (me) who brought her here, right? Besides, many women here are willing to go home and bring other women here because they can make some *haochufei* [benefit fee], which is about $250. (62)

Twenty-eight of our subjects (19%) were helped by a company to go overseas. These subjects, most of them in Los Angeles or New York, were helped by "broker companies" that specialize in assisting Chinese citizens to go abroad. In this scenario, no returned prostitutes are involved; the subjects take the initiative, contact a broker company, and ask the company to help them leave China. After these women arrive in the United States, their relationship with the broker company ends, and they later enter the sex business on their own. Their migration experiences are actually quite similar to the Fujianese who are smuggled into the United States by human smugglers for a fee, except that these women paid significantly less than the Fujianese and almost always flew into the United States as opposed to the Fujianese use of sea or land routes.[21]

As mentioned previously, thirteen subjects (9%) were assisted by chickenheads—men who help Chinese women to enter the profession and then take a cut of the women's earnings, or in some cases actually take all the earnings. Women we met in Macau were significantly more likely to be engaged with chickenheads than subjects in any other sites.

Another ten subjects (7%) were helped by their husband or boyfriend to go overseas. Of the ten, six were women we interviewed in Los Angeles and New York, and they arrived in the United States after they had married American citizens.

There is also evidence that the various intermediaries in different sites tended to recruit in particular areas. Consequently, we observed a noticeably large number of women from Sichuan in Hong Kong, from Hunan in Macau, and from Beijing in Los Angeles. This could be attributed to the effect of the network development described earlier.

The issue of intermediaries is very much related to the definition of sex trafficking. Some scholars and practitioners have argued that if a woman is helped to go overseas to engage in commercial sex, then she is a trafficking victim, regardless of who the helper is or how the help is provided. If this is the case, then more than 90 percent of our female subjects could be considered to be trafficking victims. We, however, believe such a view to be an overly broad and simplistic perception of how the process actually works, and will pick up the issue again when we discuss the definition and prevalence of sex trafficking in chapter 10.

A Comparison of Subjects in Various Sites

Table 2.4 shows the individual characteristics of the *xiaojie* subjects by research site. As far as age is concerned, subjects in Macau were the youngest, with a mean age of 25, followed by subjects in Taiwan (mean age of 26). Subjects in New York were the oldest (39 years), followed by Los Angeles (38 years). The average age for the entire sample of women we interviewed outside China was 31. This clearly indicates that the vast majority of women who go overseas to sell sex are not teenagers, but rather are women who are

Table 2.4. Subject Characteristics, by Research Site (N = 149)

Site	Mean age	Mean years of education	Single (%)	Sell sex in China (%)	Helped by a returned xiaojie (%)	Most common mode of entry
Hong Kong	31	9	60	85	78	Tourist
Macau	25	9	78	56	53	In Transit
Taiwan	26	10	94	50	87	Fake Marriage
Thailand	33	8	24	13	88	Tourist
Malaysia	30	8	50	56	88	Tourist
Singapore	27	11	47	33	67	Tourist
Indonesia	27	10	72	50	59	Business
Los Angeles	38	14	19	6	8	Business
New York	39	12	6	6	0	Business
Total	31	10	50	39	59	Tourist

at least in their mid- to late twenties or early thirties. They do not fit the stereotype of being young, naïve, and particularly vulnerable girls.

Women in New York and Los Angeles were comparatively better educated than those we interviewed in Asia. Many subjects in Los Angeles had attended or completed college, whereas subjects in Thailand and Malaysia were the least educated, with an average of only eight years of education (meaning most of them had not completed middle school). The average period of education for the entire overseas sample was 10 years—most of them did not finish high school.

Table 2.4 also shows subjects' marital status by research sites. Subjects we interviewed in Taiwan are most likely to be single (94%), followed by Macau (78%), and Indonesia (72%). Subjects in New York were the least likely to be single (6%), followed by Los Angeles (19%), and Thailand (24%). For the entire sample, 50 percent said they were single. Again, it shows that one in every two Chinese women who are selling sex overseas were or had been married, and in addition many of them were mothers.

Table 2.4 also shows the percentage of subjects who said they had been *xiaojies* in China by site. This commercial sex experience was significantly different by site; few if any of the women in New York and Los Angeles had engaged in prostitution before they arrived in the United States, whereas the vast majority of the women in Hong Kong (85%), and slight majorities in Macau (56%), and Malaysia (56%) said they had been selling sex in China. Some four out of ten women in our sample told us they had engaged in paid sex in China before going overseas. And most of these women had been involved in commercial sex in China for quite a few years before they went overseas to continue the practice.

When we compare the backgrounds of the persons who helped our subjects go overseas by research site, it is clear that the great majority (59%) of the sample was assisted by a returned prostitute, with or without the help of another party such as an "agent" or a "company." Subjects in Hong Kong, Taiwan, Thailand, and Malaysia were most likely to be assisted by a returned *xiaojie*, whereas subjects in Macau were more likely to be helped by a chickenhead, and subjects in Los Angeles and New York City were aided by a broker company. None of the women in New York arrived with the help of a returned prostitute.

The mode of entry into the country also differed by site. Whereas most subjects went to Hong Kong, Thailand, Malaysia, and Singapore as tourists, subjects entered Macau as tourists in transit who were heading for a country in Southeast Asia. By contrast, subjects in Indonesia, Los Angeles, and New York were most likely to arrive with a business visa. Because Chinese women are highly unlikely to enter Taiwan with a tourist or a business visa, the majority of them entered Taiwan as the "wives" of Taiwanese men through fake marriages.

Examining the information in Table 2.4, it is obvious that the transnational movement of Chinese women for the purpose of commercial sex is country-specific. We cannot therefore equate the situation, for example, in Taiwan with the situation in New York, and vice versa, because we are talking about two very different groups of women with very different motives, different travel arrangements, and different commercial sex experiences both in China and in the destination countries. This echoes our observation that the reality is a fairly nuanced one, and that one size does not fit all. However, we again caution our readers that our *xiaojie* sample is not a random sample, and as a result the characteristics of our female subjects may not be a good representation of the population of Chinese women who are engaged in transnational commercial sex. And we certainly do not claim that they are representative of sex workers from other ethnic backgrounds.

3

The Women

Little is actually known about the women who sell sex overseas. The general assumption is that they are most likely young, have little education, and come from poor families, usually in rural areas.[1] Indeed, the image of the typical sex trafficking victim presented by the media, as well as by many government agencies and nongovernmental organizations, is that of a young, innocent, vulnerable female.[2] The common belief is that the women involved have been tricked, forced, or otherwise coerced into commercial sex after having been trafficked to some other country. We are sure that this occurs —in fact we know it does—but is it the whole story?

Rarely, if at all, is the possibility entertained that some of these women may have been engaged in prostitution before they went overseas. Likewise, not much consideration has been given to the possibility that some women may actually elect to travel abroad to become involved in commercial sex as the best option that appears to be available to them. Or, that once having gone overseas, whatever their original motivations, commercial sex comes to be seen by some to be their most viable option. Are there, in other words, lumped in with the population defined as sex trafficking victims, distinct subgroups? Of course, our study pertains only to Chinese women working in commercial sex outside China, and whatever our findings about these Chinese women, they may not apply them to other ethnic groups such as the Nepalese, the Thais, the Nigerians, or the Ukrainians who are likewise engaged in commercial sex abroad.

Actually, we are not even claiming that our findings are absolutely applicable to the larger population of Chinese women engaging in commercial sex outside China, because as already described, ours is not a random sample. Irrespective of these limitations, we firmly believe that what we have learned about the characteristics and experiences of our particular subjects tells us a lot about the women who are engaged in transnational commercial sex.

The *Xiaojie* Sample

Contrary to the popular image, our data show that a variety of Chinese women from diverse backgrounds go overseas to engage in prostitution. This suggests that there may be more diversity among the parties involved in transnational prostitution than is commonly supposed. Of the 149 women we interviewed outside China, many were young, single women, but a large proportion of them were also married women in their thirties or forties (see Table 3.1). Most of them were indeed from rural areas. Most interestingly, about 4 out of 10 of them had engaged in prostitution while they were still in China.

Age

The vast majority of the *xiaojies* we interviewed were 20 years old or older. The average age of our subjects (N = 149) was 30.79; only one subject in our sample was a juvenile—a 17-year-old girl we met in Singapore. Forty-four percent of the subjects were between 21 and 30, 39 percent of them were between 31 and 40, 11 percent of them were 41 or older, and a couple of subjects were in their fifties. There is a possibility that some of our subjects were actually older than what they admitted, as it is common practice among prostitutes to underreport their age so that they can appear more attractive and generate more business. On the other hand, we do not believe that any of them told us they were older than they actually were.

Education

Most of our subjects had either graduated from middle or high school, with the mean years of education being 10. Twelve percent of them had only an

Table 3.1. Demographic Characteristics of the Xiaojie Subjects (N = 149)

	N	%
Age		
20 and younger	8	5
21 to 30	66	45
31 to 40	58	39
41 and older	16	11
Education		
Elementary	17	11
Middle school	56	38
High school	50	34
College	25	17
Marital status		
Single	75	50
Married	35	24
Divorced	39	26
Occupation		
Prostitution	59	41
Ordinary worker	24	17
Professional	19	13
Unemployed	16	11
Private business	13	9
Entertainment	9	6
Government job	4	3

elementary school education, 37 percent middle school, 34 percent high school, and 17 percent college (undergraduate). Taken together with age, these women are both older and better educated than has been commonly portrayed. And we think that both these factors are related to vulnerability to exploitation. Many subjects said they did not like school when they were young, so they stopped attending after graduating from elementary or middle school and stayed home to do house chores. Authorities in China normally do not make much of an effort to keep girls in school. When our subjects reached a certain age, they left school and some went out to work. Others spent a lot of time just hanging out with friends—singing, dancing, and having fun—until eventually they met someone who recruited them (not necessarily using force, fraud, or deception) into prostitution, or who simply sold them on the idea.

Some dropped out of school because there was a crisis in the family and they had to work to support their families. Others said they actually liked school and hoped to receive a good education, but that their parents were not very supportive simply because they were girls. Since some of our subjects were from poor families in rural areas, their status as females put them in a precarious position, because poor families in rural areas have traditionally preferred to have sons rather than daughters. Xiao Zheng, a 23-year-old from Liuzhou (Guangxi Province, located in southwest China bordering Vietnam) told us why she was forced to quit school:

> I dropped out of school two months before graduation from middle school because my father was diagnosed with cancer. I am the youngest of six siblings. Actually, I really wanted to continue school. My father was always against my desire to attend school—he said that girls should not attend school. It was my mother who insisted that I go to school. Because of this, my father put a knife to my mother's neck and demanded that she stop me from attending school. (83)

Some of these women, with relatively little education and/or connections to people of influence and power, ended up working in the manufacturing or service sectors. There, because of low pay and unrewarding work experiences, many changed jobs frequently, until they ultimately ended up in prostitution.

Family

Even though our female subjects came from all over China (a total of 59 towns or cities), many of them were from areas around Chongqing and Changde (Hunan Province) in central China, from Harbin (Heilongjiang Province), Changchun (Jilin Province), and Shenyang (Liaoning Province) in the far northeast, and from the capital Beijing. Subjects from Hunan Province made up 14 percent of the sample, Chongqing City and Sichuan Province made up 13 percent, and Liaoning Province 12 percent. The three major source areas for *xiaojies* in China are believed to be Sichuan Province, Hunan Province, and the three provinces in the northeast (Heilongjiang, Jilin, and Liaoning). It is important to point out that very few of our subjects were actually born in the major cities mentioned above. Most were born in the rural hinterland around those big cities, and it was not unusual for them to travel for many hours by bus or train from where they lived to a big city nearby. Moreover, many of them were already living away from home, usually in coastal areas, for several years before they left China. According to Tiantian Zheng, of the two hundred hostesses she studied in Dalian (Liaoning Province), only four were from cities.[3]

As already mentioned, most of our subjects came from poor families.

Thirty-six percent of our subjects said their fathers were farmers, 30 percent laborers, and 8 percent of fathers were retired or unemployed. Thirty-six percent of the subjects said their mothers were farmers, 22 percent laborers, and 21 percent were retired or unemployed. Only a very small percentage of our subjects' parents had professional jobs. There is no doubt that the majority of our subjects belonged to very ordinary families with very little power or privilege.

Marital Status

Half of our subjects were either married (24%) or divorced (26%), and 40 percent of them had at least one child. All the married or divorced women became prostitutes only after their marriages. There is a possibility that a very small number of subjects might have deceived us about their marital status, telling us they were divorced when in fact their marriages were intact, or saying they were single when they were actually married. Juan Juan, a 42-year-old married woman from Yingkou (Liaoning Province) who was working as a hostess in Bangkok, explained why they might do this: "I am married and I have a good relationship with my husband, but I tell my customers here that I am divorced. Otherwise, why would they give me money? If I say I am married, they will think that I will give all the money they give me to my husband" (59).

Work Experience

Given their typical circumstances, it is not difficult to imagine that these women did not have especially good, high paying jobs in China. But that does not mean they were necessarily only ordinary workers or unemployed. Instead nearly a third of them reported doing what is considered professional work, or they worked for the government or in a private business, or were involved in the entertainment business. The latter is of particular interest because the entertainment sector has been considered a target for the recruitment of young women with aspirations for glamorous jobs as dancers, singers, actresses, and so on. As previously indicated, the largest portion (41 percent) told us they were already engaged in prostitution before they went abroad. We want to stress that this does not preclude the possibility that they may have been victimized earlier. Likewise, it also does not mean that these subjects could not have been subsequently victimized through physical abuse or various forms of deception or coercion when they went overseas.

Reasons for Becoming a Prostitute

Of the 59 subjects who said they had started in prostitution in China, 44 (75%) of them said they went into the commercial sex business voluntarily. Most single women became prostitutes so that they could make money. Most of them began their commercial sex careers as hostesses at nightclubs or karaoke establishments. In China, to be a hostess in these two types of venues means only that a woman is entertaining her customers through singing, dancing, drinking, and chatting—even though most people also know that very few hostesses can refuse to go out with customers who want them to engage in sexual activities.[4]

The reasons offered by our subjects for taking up commercial sex can be grouped into five categories: (1) they wanted to live a good life but did not want to work that hard; (2) they tried to make money through conventional work but found that it was a bitter life and the money was not enough; (3) there was a financial crisis in the family and they needed to do something quickly to help their families; (4) they were divorced and were desperate to earn and save some money while they were still young; or (5) they were deceived or coerced into prostitution by their boyfriends, or by pimps or chickenheads.

Easy Money

Some of our subjects told us they became prostitutes simply because they realized that they could make a lot more in the commercial sex business than they could make in the legitimate labor market. Meng Fei, a 32-year-old single woman from Hefei (Anhui Province) and a streetwalker in Hong Kong, described how she originally entered sex work in China:

> I worked with my sister as a tailor after I graduated from middle school. Then I went to Wenzhou [Zhejiang Province] and worked in a garment factory. Later, I worked in a hair salon in Shanghai, where I met a Taiwanese man. He invited me to dinner and then to a nightclub. There, I saw hostesses making $24 to $36 just by drinking and chatting with customers. At that time, I was making about $85 a month in the hair salon. It was very easy for those hostesses to make money. As a result, I went back to the nightclub the next day and told the boss that I wanted to be a hostess. He hired me. . . . I made about $1,000 a month just sitting at tables. After working there for two to three months, I began to go out with customers and my monthly income increased to more than $1,500. (74)

Xiao Dai, a 24-year-old woman from Leshan (Sichuan Province) whom we interviewed in a spa in Jakarta, told us why it was easy for her to make up her mind to become a *xiaojie*:

> After I finished middle school, I had a variety of jobs, but nothing lasted long. I was very lazy, so I tended to look for work that was easy. Finally, I worked as a DJ at a nightclub and began to have contact with *xiaojies*. Working as a DJ was relatively easy and my monthly income was more than $375. However, I also thought that being a *xiaojie* might be even easier, and I would make more money. Therefore, I eventually entered this line of work. How else can girls like me make $1,250 to $2,500 a month? (51)

Qian Qian, a 34-year-old divorced woman working in a massage parlor in Singapore, was quite straightforward when asked why she became a prostitute: "I needed money. What can I do when I don't have much of an education? If I had an ordinary, regular job, I would make less than $100 a month. How can I survive in a place like Shenzhen with less than $100 a month? Besides, I like name-brand handbags and perfume, so I decided to work in a KTV" (10).

Desperate for Money

Some of our subjects sacrificed themselves to help their parents or siblings overcome financial crises or to provide their family members a better life. According to Chun Chun, a 24-year-old street prostitute from Chongqing in Hong Kong:

> My mother worked part-time in a variety of manual jobs. My father used to be an auto mechanic. Later, he borrowed money to lease a bus and start a small transportation business. But the business failed and he lost a lot of money. Debtors came to our home and asked us to repay them. I am the only child and life was hard when I was young. I did not want to study anymore after my father's business collapsed, even though I liked school. At first, I worked as a waitress at a restaurant and made a little more than $25 a month. That was not enough to help my family. So I went to Yunnan with a friend and we both decided to enter the sex industry. (78)

Some of our subjects were married women, and they turned to prostitution because their husbands were not supporting them and their children. Chen Hung, a 39-year-old from Jinzhou (Hubei Province) became a prostitute because her husband was arrested. At the time of the interview, she was divorced and was soliciting clients at a food court in Kuala Lumpur; her daughter was a college student in Wuhan:

> I married when I was 20. My husband was a gangster. We had a baby girl one year after the marriage. My husband not only gambled, he also frequented sex venues. One day, my husband demanded that a friend repay his debt, and under pressure the friend killed a taxi driver and took his car. He gave the car to my husband and asked my husband to sell it or consider it as repayment. Later, my husband was arrested and sentenced to three-and-a-half years. At that time, I was really desperate; I had a daughter to raise, and we owed lawyers and others a lot of money. I had no choice but to go to another city to be a KTV hostess. (26)

Deceived into Prostitution

Some girls and women (about 10 percent) were lured into prostitution in China, either by their boyfriends or by the so-called chickenheads. Thus, they fit the definition of being domestic trafficked victims. For example, Xiao Ya, a 20-year-old single woman from Chongqing whom we interviewed at a one-woman apartment in Hong Kong, said:

> I worked as a waitress in a restaurant after I dropped out of middle school. I quit a few days later because it was hard work. Then I became an apprentice at a hair salon. I was there for more than one year, and I was not paid at all. Thereafter, I went back to work at a restaurant, met a boyfriend, and had sex with him. My mother slapped me when she found out about this. I took it hard and fled to another city with a female friend. We checked into a small hotel. I bought ten sleeping pills and swallowed all of them, but I woke up the next morning. At that time, all we had left was $3. We took a bus to where my boyfriend lived and he took both of us to a place to sell sex. (75)

Xiao Zheng, a 23-year-old woman from Liuzhou (Guangxi), described how she was coerced into prostitution by a man:

> A friend introduced me to a man who was about 30. He treated me very well and he was aggressively after me. Later, we lived together. I was working and financially independent at that time. He asked me not to go to work and often made me late for work so that I would lose my job.
>
> In order to show that he intended to marry me, he took me to meet his

parents. He was also from the Liuzhou area, but came from a different village than mine. His parents were honest people; they did not know what their son was up to.

Not long after, I stopped working because my boss was unhappy that I often did not show up for work. Even without a regular income, we went out every day and we spent all our money. That's their [the pimps'] tactics. First, they make you lose your job. Second, they make you broke. Third, they ask you to go to another city to make money, insinuating that after we make enough money together, we will go home to marry, build a house, and buy a car.

He brought me to Foshan [Guangdong].[5] There were plenty of chickenheads there and they had girls they brought from all over China working for them. I did not know until I arrived in Foshan that he wanted me to be a prostitute. I, of course, said no, and a few days later he yelled at me: "Now that you are here, why the hell are you not making money right away? If you don't act quickly, I am going to tell your family that you are a prostitute here in Foshan." I was very scared. I came from a very conservative village located in the hills. I can stop going home, but what about my family? He also said something like: "I am also going to tell your family that while you were working as a prostitute, a customer stabbed you to death, and the police could not find your body."

After resisting it for a few more days, I gave up. He also asked other chickenheads to talk to me, emphasizing that I can make good money and the job is easy. Once I agreed to work, he asked a *xiaojie* to take me to a small hotel. I had to pay the hotel $50 a day to work there, and he gave me that money. The hotel kept all the girls in a big room, where there were more than a dozen girls working at any given time. When a guest in the hotel needed a girl, we all went to his room for him to select. The charge was $12 per session, and all the money went to the girls.

My boyfriend treated me very well after I returned home from work. He massaged my feet, cooked dinner for me, and washed my clothes. He treated me very tenderly, and he often made love to me. (83)

Li Na, a 30-year-old from Guilin (Guangxi Province) who was working as a freelance prostitute in Kuala Lumpur when we interviewed her, was also forced into prostitution by a group of men she and two female friends met at a train station in China:

When I was 16, I went to Harbin [the capital of Heilongjiang Province] with two other girls. We slept at a bus station for two nights because we

had no money. We met three men who found a hotel for us and later introduced us to hostessing at a KTV. They told us we will make $4 an hour
sitting tables. After working for a week, we thought that we had earned
about $125 and we could go home. But these men told us that we owed
them another $125 because they provided us with meals, lodging, clothes,
cosmetics, and transportation. So we had to continue to work. (31)

Yang Fei is a 21-year-old call girl whom we interviewed in Kuala Lumpur.
She was originally from Changde (Hunan), and she described how she was
forced by her boyfriend to become a *xiaojie* in China:

> I did nothing but have fun for two years after quitting middle school. Later,
> I went to work in a factory in Changpin [Guangdong Province]. There, I
> met my boyfriend. Later, we moved to Haikou and he forced me to work at
> a bar lounge. A lot of girls sat in the lounge for customers to choose from,
> and after being chosen, went into a room to have sex. I gave all the money
> I made to my boyfriend. (25)

According to our data, domestic trafficked victims in our sample were
more likely to be found in Hong Kong, Macau, Malaysia, and Indonesia.
These women were also more likely to have engaged in organized commercial sex abroad (i.e., an escort service or spa/sauna) and owed money to a sex
ring operator to go overseas. None of the fifteen domestic trafficking victims
went to the United States. The majority of these victims came from Chongqing City, Guangxi Province, and Hunan Province, and they were generally
less well-educated than the others.

Our estimate of 10 percent as the prevalence rate of domestic sex trafficking in China is probably an underestimate because, of the other 90 percent
who said they were not forced, deceived, or lured into prostitution and thus
are not counted as domestic trafficking victims, some of them could have
entered prostitution as minors and thus would also be defined as trafficked
victims. But because we do not have the data for all our subjects on the age
at which they entered prostitution, we are not able to definitively answer
this question.

Trajectories and Paths to Prostitution

Most of the subjects who had engaged in the commercial sex business in
China went through various stages before finally becoming a *xiaojie*. Typi-

cally, after quitting school at a tender age, they stayed home for a short period of time before they ventured out to look for work. Because most of them were from rural areas in interior China, they traveled to a nearby city to find work. Some of them even traveled to a distant coastal city for employment. Very often, they began by working in the manufacturing industry, making about $50 a month and working long hours.[6] Yan Yan, a 20-year-old *xiaojie* in Macau worked in several factories before she made up her mind to engage in providing sexual services:

> After dropping out of middle school, I worked in a relative's factory in Changde [Hunan Province]. I was only 13 then. Later, I went to work in another factory. I also went to Jiansu Province to work, also in a factory. After returning to Changde, I stayed home for a while and eventually decided to go to Shenzhen. Before I left for Shenzhen, I had already made up my mind to be a *xiaojie*. It was a decision I made on my own. (87)

Some subjects became *xiaojies* after they began to work in one of the precursor venues: a hair salon, an acupressure massage parlor, or a nightclub/ KTV lounge, even though they did not intend to sell sex when they initially applied for the job in these venues. For example, there are large numbers of so-called *falang* (hair salons) in China and some hair salons are actually legitimate businesses that provide haircuts and shampoos, facial care and facial massages, and sometimes body massages. However, there are also many hair salons that are essentially brothels, and some that provide both licit and illicit services. Many girls and young women in China are employed in the hair salon business because there are plenty of job opportunities that do not require much education, and the conditions of work are more appealing and trendy than working in a factory. However, many young women working in this business also end up as prostitutes simply because the business is poorly regulated, and many places function as a venue for male customers and female employees to engage in paid sex. Xiao Qian, 22, an independent, hotel-based prostitute in Macau, explained how she entered the life:

> I dropped out of middle school after attending for only one year. I then went to work in a factory in Zhuhai. A year later, I found a job at a hair salon because the pay at the factory was very poor. Not long after, I met my boyfriend and I began to do bad things. With my boyfriend's tacit approval, I began to enter this line of work. I became a prostitute at the same hair salon where I was already working. (88)

Massage parlors are another venue where many young women who start as legitimate masseuses may gradually move into commercial sex. In China, there are large and small massage parlors everywhere, and these venues provide ample employment opportunities for young women who want to make good money but do not have the educational qualifications or professional skills to find other well-paying jobs. Many females employed in massage parlors also are lured into providing sexual services by their employers, or they shift their role after they find out that they can make substantially more if they are willing to be accommodating. Xiao Tan, 20, single, was an independent, hotel-based prostitute in Macau at the time of the interview. She described how easy it was for her to move into sex massage from pure massage:

> After struggling to make money in the legitimate sector away from home, I came back to my hometown and worked in a massage parlor [pure massage] and earned almost $250 a month, but I still felt the income was not enough. At that time, even though I was doing pure massage, it wasn't difficult for me to get acquainted with women who were doing sex massage. Once you have connections with these people and know that they make plenty of money, it is not hard to enter this line of work. So I went to Shenzhen to do sex massage. I was 21 then. (84)

The third route to prostitution is through hostessing. In China, there is a huge demand for hostesses because there are many nightclubs and karaoke TV (KTV) clubs where young women entertain male clients by singing, drinking, and chatting with them in private rooms.[7] For many businessmen and government officials with money and power, these places are ideal to entertain their friends, business partners, clients, and superiors. When men go to these places for fun, buying sex is not necessarily the outcome; many men simply go there and have a good time with a bunch of hostesses and then go home. But there is also always the possibility that a hostess may catch a man's eye, and he will then try to get her to go out for sex. There is no rule that a hostess must go out with a client, and some hostesses never venture out of their workplaces with customers. According to our interviews, however, it is rather difficult for a hostess to refuse a customer's request for extra service, simply because a customer can come back again and again until he gets his wish; and other hostesses, the mommy, the manager, or the employer may put pressure on her to sleep with the customer. Certain men will double or triple the payment offered for taking out a hostess until she gives in.

Choices and Bounded Rationality

In all the instances described to us, we saw that economic factors were a driving force behind the choices the women made. Many had already been the victims of circumstances. Whether they would have behaved differently or made different choices if they had had other options is, of course, unknown. Nevertheless, greater economic opportunity for women in China—and elsewhere as well—would certainly reduce the pressure of economics as a major push factor in prostitution.

One way to view the process through which these women moved is in terms of what some scholars call "bounded rationality."[8] Originally theorized to explain organizational behavior and various forms of economic and management decision making, bounded rationality has since been taken up by various social scientists, including some criminologists.[9] Criminal justice professor Jody Miller's analysis is particularly a propos here because she describes the role of gender inequality as a factor limiting the rational choices of women. She points out that the structural inequalities in society certainly shape the choices girls and women have available to them, but that they do nevertheless exercise choice, and are not "simply passive victims of male oppression."[10]

These and a number of other works addressing bounded rationality attempt to explain decision making in a variety of contexts. In essence, the theory of bounded rationality posits that when individuals make decisions, they do not do so under optimum conditions that allow them to be completely rational and able to fully weigh all the possible risks and rewards surrounding their decision and choice. There may, for example, be time constraints; there may be a lack of information or misinformation about certain options; there may be peer pressure; certain alternatives may simply not be accessible, and so on. Because they lack information and/or are unable to fully comprehend the information they do have, people are said to "satisfice." That is, they make what may appear to them to be the best decision or choice given their circumstances at the time. Consequently, their decision making is bounded —constrained or restricted—by their social, physical, and situational contexts, and their perceptions of those contexts. The individual assessments of the costs, risks, and benefits involved are subjective, which is why in this case different women in the same circumstances might make different choices; and why the same women may make different choices at different times.

In her study of prostitution in China, Min Liu, a criminologist, looked specifically at this issue of bounded rational choice among the prostitutes she interviewed.[11] She concluded that there are a number of factors in contemporary China that affect both the range of options available and the perception of those options by Chinese women. Liu notes that attitudes toward sex have become more liberal, with both premarital and extramarital sex being more acceptable. At the same time, traditional Chinese views of women as being subordinate to men have reemerged, putting women in a less advantaged position than before. In addition, the expanding and omnipresent entertainment venues and countless customers mean the opportunities to work as prostitutes are numerous. And finally, attitudes toward money and wealth have changed dramatically, giving way to much more materialistic perspectives. "The extent to which a woman accepts these liberalized attitudes toward sex, how she views her body, and her attitudes about money are," says Liu, "the decisive forces determining whether she will enter prostitution, given certain financial circumstances."[12] This last point suggests that personal economic circumstances are usually the critical spark for considering sex work as a viable option.

There is another consideration that might enter into the choice to become a prostitute as well, and that is the moral qualms that may have to be addressed. Liu found, for example, that one of the greatest concerns of her subjects was the fear that their friends or families would find out what they were doing. This suggests that they are ashamed of what they are doing. Therefore, their choice process would seemingly also be bounded by the force of any moral qualms, and in instances where women choose to act against their deeply held values, they are probably going to have to rationalize and adopt what sociologists Gresham Sykes and David Matza originally termed "techniques of neutralization" in order to justify their deviant behavior.[13]

The data presented in chapter 2 on the women's reasons for going overseas, and in the first half of this chapter on their reasons for entering prostitution, suggest that bounded rationality is probably the most salient theoretical framework in which to think about the Chinese sex business and the transnational movement of women for commercial sex. Most of our female subjects entered prostitution in China or went overseas to engage in prostitution to make money. They also traveled afar (either to a coastal city in China or outside of China) to engage in prostitution because it offered them anonymity. It decreased the likelihood of being discovered by their family as being involved in sex for pay. Many of our subjects also mentioned selling sex overseas instead of China because it offered them further benefits such as a better class of clientele, the ability to save more, the fun and excitement of traveling to a foreign country, and the chance to perhaps marry a foreigner and settle down abroad. Becoming a prostitute in China or going overseas to engage in commercial sex certainly had its costs and disadvantages, but under the circumstances in which our subjects generally found themselves, the benefits, at least within their bounded rationality, outweighed the costs. When the choice to enter prostitution and to go overseas was presented, by whoever and however it was presented, they opted for it.

Gender Inequality and the Objectification of Women

While the concept of bounded rationality is important to understanding what individual decision-making processes and microlevel forces may be at play, we also need to take into consideration how larger sociocultural forces can also bound or limit the rational choice of Chinese women to engage in prostitution.

Chinese women have clearly been treated unfairly by both the legal system and the society at large throughout Chinese history.[14] Chinese norms and values put considerable pressure on women through the cultural expectation that a daughter must obey her father, a wife must obey her husband, and a widow must obey her eldest son.[15] Under many rigid gender norms and values, the exploitation of women has been a serious problem in China for many centuries.[16] Even in modern China, Hong Kong, and Taiwan, women face many forms of victimization: infanticide, slavery, child prostitution, forced marriage, rape, and wife abuse.[17] Traditionally, boys have always been considered more precious than girls among the Chinese people for both economic and cultural reasons. Compounded with the one-child policy adopted in contemporary China to control population growth, this has resulted in the pervasive practice of Chinese couples abandoning newborn girls in hopes of having a son instead. If the baby girls are not discarded, they often become the sacrificial lambs when there is a crisis in the family (sickness, legal problems, failed business, divorce) and money is needed to deal with the crisis.

As described by our female subjects, most felt that their parents (especially their father) had not treated them as being as equally valuable as boys. Most parents, particularly those from rural areas, were not supportive of their daughters' wishes to receive a good education because the parents wanted to retain their limited resources for the use of their sons, and/or they thought their daughters would belong to their husbands' families and thus become "outsiders" after they were married. As a result, as illustrated in Table 3.1, most subjects received very little education; and the parents' indifference was a key factor in prompting them to terminate schooling while they were still very young.

Women with limited educations are naturally not in a position to enter the already small white-collar job market in China. For women from poor families in rural areas, their families' lack of connections to people in power also denies them the opportunity to land good jobs in government, for example. Thus, for the majority of these poorly educated women from rural areas the only jobs available to them are low-paying jobs in the manufacturing, food, and retail industries that do not offer much of a career path. Inevitably then, some women enter certain service industries that serve as pathways to their ultimate entrance into commercial sex.

Financial pressure aside, the labor market is also structured in such a way that it can propel some women toward prostitution. For example, women are not physically fit for certain jobs in construction or other heavy lifting jobs. There are only so many electronic and clothing businesses, and these tend to be limited to the coastal provinces in China. As already mentioned, other available jobs are in the service or entertainment industry, and these often involve much more physical contact with men. Massage parlors, hair salons, tea houses, and karaoke bars—these are places (with jobs) frequented by men with money who may be looking for sexual adventure. These jobs put women at a clear disadvantage and often trap them. Lured by the money and pressured by their bosses, women may begin selling sex. But this is not to downplay the attractiveness of the earnings potential in these businesses. Without the tempting financial possibilities, we suspect fewer women would choose to go this route. But once they realize how much money they can make and the lifestyle they can attain, it becomes difficult for them to go back to their old ways.

The strong demand for sexual services in China is also a major factor in causing so many Chinese women to enter the sex business. Young women who migrate to urban centers for work are bombarded with the hiring announcements posted in newspapers, on street poles, in restaurants, in public phone booths, and at the entrances of entertainment centers and hotels; and it is simply impossible to ignore them or not notice them.[18] Selling sex is also glorified or romanticized by the existence of a large number of so-called *xiaomi* (little honey) or *ernai* (second wife)—the mistresses of high-ranking government officials and rich businessmen who can be seen living in luxurious apartments in so-called "mistress villages" in coastal cities. The reality for young women from rural areas who have migrated to the big cities along the coast and are struggling to survive is this: find a relatively easy job as a salesclerk in a retail store and make $50 to $100 a month; work in a factory for long hours and with limited freedom for $150 to $200 a month; work as a masseuse or a hostess and make about $1,000 a month; or sell sex and earn more than $1,500 a month. Of course, there are also women who do not want to go into commercial sex regardless of how much money they can make, but they may be compelled to sell sex when they are desperate for money to deal with a family crisis. They soon find out that the only way to earn a large amount of money in a short time is to sell sex. As explained by some of the subjects quoted above, there was a crisis in their family—one of their parents was sick, one of their siblings got into trouble with the law, their father's business failed, or their husband left them—and they became the sacrificial lamb who had to sell herself to overcome the crisis in the family. According to our subjects, their parents were ready to sacrifice them, as they would not do with their brothers, because sons were more precious to parents. Cola, a 25-year-old single woman working for a *falang* (hair salon-style brothel) in Shenzhen, had this to say about how daughters and sons are treated so differently in China:

> In China, sons are not required to take care of their families. All they have to do is grow up, marry, and have children to continue the family lineage. They also need not travel far to make money because parents want them to be nearby. As a result, only girls are asked to support their families. Since parents do not care whether their daughters are around or not, girls can also travel far away to find jobs. It's all taken for granted. (153)

The other factor in the push and pull of prostitution in China is the existence of male pimps who are called chickenheads. In many source villages in the provinces of Sichuan, Hunan, and Liaoning, networks of chickenheads work aggressively to recruit young women to move to the coastal areas to engage in prostitution. There are also substantial numbers of women pimps called *chipor* (chicken lady) who are orchestrating the movement of girls and women from villages in the inland provinces to coastal cities like Shenzhen to engage in street prostitution. As mentioned by a spa manager in Shenzhen, many women he met in the sex business were being "brought" to Shenzhen by someone. This is because it is not easy for a village woman to come to Shenzhen on her own and to enter prostitution without an intermediary (see Figure 3.1 for a pathway to entering prostitution in China).

As Figure 3.1 demonstrates, socioeconomic circumstances clearly put many Chinese women into a vulnerable category. Faced with these circumstances, some of these women end up in prostitution. Some of them may then subsequently choose to go abroad to practice their profession in what they see as more lucrative environments. It may be that once the crucial threshold of opting to make a living by selling sex is crossed, the further decision to seek to go abroad for that purpose is quite simply an economic one. For other women in our sample, although they had not become prostitutes

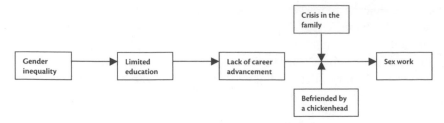

Figure 3.1. Pathways to prostitution in China

initially, they later had the opportunity and chose to go abroad, and once relocated, they ended up in prostitution. And then there are, of course, the faceless majority of similarly situated Chinese women—faceless because they were not included in our study—who struggle on, not becoming prostitutes either at home or abroad.

In sum, economic reform and marketization in China since the 1980s has yet to ameliorate the problem of gender inequality there. In fact, according to Sally Engle Merry, "the shift to a more capitalist economy and the closing of many state-owned enterprises has hurt women's economic status, as they are often the first fired and last hired and are forced to retire at younger ages than their husbands."[19] Sociology professors Xialing Shu and Yanjie Bian conducted a study on the impact of the growth in market economies on gender inequality in China and concluded that:

> Our analysis shows that by 1995 Chinese men and women in the cities differ in level of human and political capitals, labor market placements, and work earnings. Compared with a man of the same individual characteristics living in the same city, a woman has fewer years of education and is less likely to have a college education, be a Communist party member, be in the state sector, be a cadre or manager in a state enterprise, and be in manufacturing, mining, construction, and transportation. . . . These findings support the assertion that within the realm of gender relationship there are relatively separate and autonomous components from the economic domain not readily penetrable by economic forces.[20]

Limited opportunities in the professional and governmental labor markets, coupled with abundant opportunities in the entertainment or sexual service markets, might have channeled Chinese women into the sex industry, especially when there was enormous pressure for both men and women to get rich by any means possible.

Western films and literature have often portrayed Chinese women as submissive, docile, obedient, and sexy. Even though racial/ethnic or cultural stereotypes of Chinese femininity or sexuality are strong in many parts of the world, we do not think that these stereotypes play a role in the objectification or commodification of Chinese women. The buyers of Chinese female sexual services are mostly Chinese men, even when these services are being purchased outside of China. Because of their personal experience, these men are less likely to be influenced by the stereotypes. As will be discussed later in chapter 7, most of the women in our study told us that the majority of their clients were Chinese men; only a few of them serviced any non-Chinese clients. As a result, it is fair to say that the demand for Chinese female sexual labor is not related to the cultural stereotypes of Chinese female sexuality. According to the many people from diverse backgrounds we talked to while we were in the research sites, Chinese women were in demand overseas because they were: (1) younger, (2) prettier, (3) cheaper, and (4) *ganwan* (dared to "play"). Cultural stereotypes were neither mentioned nor alluded to by any of our contacts.

The Life

Let us turn now to how the women we interviewed actually feel about their involvement in commercial sex, and about the nature of prostitution itself. How do they relate to other *xiaojies*? What do they see as society's reactions to women like themselves who sell sex? If they had it to do over again, would they take the same path? And finally, what do they think about their futures?

Feelings about Selling Sex

A few of the women were not particularly disturbed with being a prostitute, and in fact, three women were rather content with what they were doing. One subject said: "I want to be a woman again in my next life. That's because if I am desperate for money, at least I have a body to sell!" And another, Helen, a 34-year-old single woman in Los Angeles who said she enjoyed having sex with her clients, said this about selling sex: "This is a great job; I really like it!" (126).

But for the vast majority of the women we interviewed, they did not like what they were doing and were saddened by their experience in *xiahai* (going down to the sea). Chu Chu, a 26-year-old divorced woman from Harbin (Heilongjiang Province), was a KTV hostess in Singapore at the time of the interview:

I was a teacher when I was in China and I had never worked as a prostitute back home. That's why after I went out with a customer for the first time in Singapore, I returned to the KTV tightly holding that $200 the customer gave me and cried like hell. My colleagues all came over to comfort me, saying something like it will be OK when I get used to it. (3)

For most subjects, prostitution was not something that they got used to, regardless of how long they had been working at it. Wang Fei, a 27-year-old single woman from Zhengzhou (Henan Province) who was a KTV hostess in Jakarta, said: "We are like commodities waiting to be picked when we are standing in front of the customers. It makes you feel sick to your stomach" (39). Another subject, Chen Cui, a 22-year-old single woman from Changde (Hunan Province) who was seeing clients in a small hotel in Macau, said: "One thing that strikes me as a *xiaojie* is that, whenever men look at us, they always examine us from head to toe, and it will take them a long time to make a decision. It's like they are buying some items, not human beings" (96).

We did not find that selling sex was enjoyable for our subjects or that most women were doing it happily. Instead, most of the women we talked to were selling sex because they believed that they had no other options, especially if they did not want to live frugally or if there was some need for them to make a large amount of money in a hurry. Some subjects said the one thing that made them happy was to count their hard-earned money: "Whenever I am not working, I will take my money out and count it. This is how I find happiness" (Candy, 27, married, from Harbin, Heilongjiang Province, a masseuse in a Jakarta spa) (40). Our data lend support to the argument that prostitution is not something that women enjoy doing and that most of them would like to quit if they could.

Some women tried to establish a stable relationship (meaning usually an emotional attachment) with a man. The man might be a former customer who was willing to provide financial support to the woman in exchange for her agreement to see him on a regular basis. Or it might be a man to whom the woman was willing to provide financial support, to be her "loverboy."

Another diversion for some women was gambling. A number of subjects, especially those who were working in Macau or Malaysia where legal casinos operate, were heavily involved in gambling. As a result, these subjects had not been able to save much money despite, in some cases, many years in the commercial sex business:

I have been to Macau several times over the past years. Business was very good during my first trip, but I lost all my money to gambling. One time, my friend took me to a casino. I won more than $260 and I was very happy. Later, however, I began to lose money. I lost $6,700 during my first trip and during my last trip [two months ago] I lost $4,000. I won't work for several days if I go gambling. I have lost a total of $40,000 to $53,000 over the past few years. Gambling means when you are winning, you want to win more; when you are losing, you want to win it back. (Zhang Li, 24, single, from Huangmei, Hubei Province, a hotel-based prostitute in Macau) (99)

University of Birmingham professor Louise Brown, among others, has suggested that "drug use and dependency is a way that many women overcome their fears and unhappiness over what they do to earn a living."[21] But we did not find evidence for the idea that many xiaojies are addicted to drugs either as a coping mechanism or because their handlers were using drugs to control them. Some of our subjects who worked in a KTV or a nightclub did tell us that they were often asked by their clients to use drugs, but most said they did not enjoy using drugs—and those who used said they did so simply to get more money from their clients.

For most Chinese women selling sex overseas, there seem to be two primary things that sustain them: the amount of money they are making; and the number of days they have left before they can return to China. As most subjects told us, making money was their main motive for leaving China, and as long as they were indeed making money overseas, they could somehow swallow whatever pain and sorrow they felt about being a prostitute. They also comforted themselves by counting the number of days left before returning to China, where their plan was not to work but instead to pamper themselves with all the money they had brought back from abroad. The temporary nature of the work overseas appears to be one of the main reasons why these women can relatively easily move back and forth between China and overseas. Going back to China—back home—enables them to sort of recoup and rejuvenate themselves before they run out of money and have to look for yet another opportunity to go abroad.

Interestingly, when asked directly whether they regretted that they had traveled overseas to be prostitutes, the majority of our subjects (80%) said no. A woman in Macau explained why:

I do not regret coming to Macau; I only regret that I did not come sooner. For two years, I did not save any money while engaging in commercial sex in China, but I am saving money here in Macau. (Xiao Tao, 20, single, from Changde, Hunan Province, a hotel-based xiaojie) (85)

Xiao Li, a 25-year-old single woman from Shenyang (Liaoning Province) was also very sure that she had made the right choice about working as an escort in Taiwan: "I came here to make money. If I stay in China, how much can a woman like me with little education and no skills make? I do not have any feelings for anything anymore; for me, everything is about making money" (135).

On the other hand, the 20 percent who thought they had made a mistake by going overseas said that the sacrifice they made was not outweighed by the money they earned. Many women we interviewed in the United States especially, said they were disappointed with their living conditions and work in the United States, and that if they could do it all over again, they would not come to America. Na Na, a 28-year-old single woman from Dalian (Liaoning Province) with a college degree and working as an independent prostitute out of her own place, said: "I regret coming here. When I was in China, I did not know I would end up like this in America. Here, I am very lonely because I have no friends or relatives. I hope I can leave this line of work soon" (118).

Coping

Given their mixed feelings, moral dilemmas, and need to rationalize what they were doing, what other coping strategies did our subjects use? C C, a 31-year-old woman from Wushun (Liaoning) who was a hotel-based sex worker in Macau, not only indulged in gambling but in shopping as well, even though she was making only $27 per session:

> I shop like crazy. I may spend $400 to $530 a day shopping. I shop like I hate money. I buy clothes and shoes that do not fit me, like I will wear them after I lose weight. Besides, I like going to the casino. Altogether, I have lost as much as $40,000 in the casinos. Sometimes I gamble for more than twenty hours nonstop. I gamble even when I cannot open my eyes. One time, I lost $6,600 on one visit. (101)

Curiously, a small number of subjects told us that they occasionally visited sex venues that catered to female customers. This is called "eating duck," mainly because men who sell sex are called *yazi* (ducks) and their places are called "duck house" in Hong Kong and China. Yang Yan, a dancing hall hostess in Hong Kong, said:

> Occasionally, I will visit a *yadian* [duck house] so that I could vent my feeling. When I go, I also drink. We [several sisters] will go to the duck houses

at Kowloon City [of Hong Kong], Bangkok, or Shenzhen [China]. When we go there, more than twenty ducks will stand in line for us to select. If we are in a good mood and we like the ducks, we will take them out. Otherwise, we just sing and drink there. (69)

Anthropologist Yeeshan Yang, the author of *Whispers and Moans*, suggested that duck houses in Hong Kong predominantly catered to female customers who were mistresses and *xiaojies*. Yang explained why there was an increase in "eating duck" by women who sell sex:

Why did nightclub hostesses suddenly develop a taste for gigolos? The attraction is certainly not the price. Hostesses may charge HK$1,500 [about $200] for each sex deal, while a gigolo's price might be HK$4,000 [about $530]. The answer appears to be that within just a few short years, nightclub hostesses have evolved from social butterflies into sex slaves, who have to accept the five and seven flavor sex package deals [very elaborate and demanding sex acts] every day. The change in market conditions means they had to accept this, but without any outlet to release their stress and frustrations. Their boyfriends did not present an appropriate target for pent-up stress and self-loathing. The solution that worked best was to offload onto gigolos.[22]

Besides Hong Kong, there are also many duck houses in Shenzhen, China, a city with probably the largest sex industry in China. Wa Wa, a 24-year-old single woman from Changchun (Jilin) who was working as an escort in Taipei at the time of the interview, described an occasion involving her visit to a duck house in Shenzhen: "Me and my friends once went to a nightclub that catered to female clients. We sang and drank. The male hosts were very good at pleasing us. A male host told me he would like to go to bed with me for free, but I declined. One of my friends did take a male host out, and after sex, he did not ask for money. However, my friend gave him $250 anyway" (147).

While we were dining with a document vendor, an agent, and a money sender in a restaurant in Jakarta, we witnessed a *xiaojie* walking in with a young man dressed in a white shirt and white pants. The man who was acting as our contact in Jakarta told us that the young man was a *xiaobailian* (little white face). The contact said: "There's a saying among Hakka people in Indonesia—a ghost eats money, but the head of the ghost eats both the ghost and the money." His point was that a *xiaojie* takes away her customer's money, but a gigolo takes away both the *xiaojie* and her money. Even though the restaurant was packed with customers at that time, the woman was constantly hugging and fondling the young man as if there was no one around.

Societal Reactions

In general, Chinese *xiaojies* tend to be demeaned and degraded by the government officials in whatever country they are working in. This reaction tends to be true of the media and the public at large as well. Prostitutes from China are called *beigu* (girls from the north) in Hong Kong, *dalumei* (girls from the Mainland) in Taiwan, and *xiaolongnu* (little dragon lady) or *uya* (crow) in Malaysia and Singapore. After these terms first appeared in the media, the general public quickly picked them up as ways to depict Chinese *xiaojies*. These labels define their status, and many secondary traits—being rude, ignorant, opportunistic, manipulative, greedy, cold, lazy, deceitful, and promiscuous—go along with them. Many of the people we talked to in Asia and the United States who were not involved with the sex business, often rolled their eyes when they were asked how they felt about *xiaojies* from China. When we approached our friends or relatives in various places for help with the research and they found out we wanted to talk to *xiaojies* from China, most of them did not want to have anything to do with it. In fact, they acted as though they were trying to avoid a plague.

In Singapore, there are many young students from China whose parents had been allowed by the government to stay with them. After the media began to report that many so-called *peidumama* (mothers who accompanied their children to study) were actually selling sex to make money on the side, all mainland women who happened to be in Singapore, regardless of their marital status and age, were viewed as potential hookers. The fact that so many women from China (almost none of them were *peidumama*) were dominating the sex trade in Singapore—convinced the city state's populace that a young woman from China could be there for only one reason—to sell sex. Owners of some of the apartments in Singapore were so disturbed by the large numbers of Chinese women soliciting business in front of their buildings that they placed a big sign in both English and Chinese at the entrance to make it clear that no Chinese prostitutes lived there: THIS RESIDENTIAL APARTMENT DISAPPROVES HOOKERS FROM STAYING HERE.

The Future

In general, the women we interviewed were more concerned about their present circumstances (how much money they were making, how to avoid arrest, which was a better place to make money, and so on) than with what they might do in the future. But when we asked them about their future plans, it was clear that at least some of them had thought about this. There is a clear differentiation between married (or divorced) women with children, and single women in this respect. Most married or divorced women were determined to work hard and save as much money as possible so that they could send their children to good schools. They wanted to see their children receive a college, or better yet, a graduate school education.

Qian Qian, a 34-year-old woman who had been divorced twice, had a 5-year-old son. She had the following to say when we interviewed her inside a massage parlor in Singapore: "I am going to go all out to make and save money and then go back to China to open a business store. I will also let my son go to the West to attend college, maybe even graduate school" (10).

Some of the divorced women, especially those who were still young, hoped that they would marry again in the future. Xiao Jing, a 29-year-old divorcee with a 9-year-old son, who almost committed suicide after her divorce, was working as a hostess in Bangkok. She said: "Being a prostitute does not mean I am evil or that something is wrong with me. Any woman can become a prostitute. I still hope that I will marry someone who does not know anything about my past and I will start a new life" (68).

For most young, single subjects, a typical answer to the question of what they would do in the future was this, provided by Wa Wa, a 24-year-old escort in Taiwan: "After I make enough money, I will go home, buy a house, start a small business, and marry someone" (147).

Other single women were not so eager to marry because, after seeing so many men, they were convinced that almost all men cheat: "I want to make money to buy a house for my parents and I want to start a small business. I do not care whether I will marry or not. I have no faith in men since I entered this line of work" (Li Min, 29, single, from Mulang, Heilongjiang Province, an escort in Kuala Lumpur) (29). For all of them, the seeming futility of some of the dreams of marriage can be summed up in this comment: "I don't expect to marry a good man. No good man would marry a woman like me. Besides, I could not marry a man I meet in the sex venues" (Jin Yan, 28, single, from Changsha, Hunan Province) (77).

4

The Destinations

According to some of the people we talked to, the outmigration of Chinese women is so massive nowadays that they believe Chinese prostitutes can be found in almost every corner of the world. Not only can they be spotted in wealthy, developed countries such as the United States and Japan, but also in poor, underdeveloped countries such as Burma (Myanmar) and Cambodia. They are active not only in countries or special administrative regions where there are many Chinese (e.g., Singapore, Macau), but also in countries where there are few Chinese (e.g., United Arab Emirates, Afghanistan). They travel to places where access is relatively easy (e.g., Hong Kong, Thailand), but also to places that are difficult to reach (e.g., Taiwan, the United States).

This chapter explores the social organization of the Chinese sex business in the ten research sites we studied: Hong Kong, Macau, Taipei (Taiwan), Bangkok (Thailand), Kuala Lumpur (Malaysia), Singapore, Jakarta (Indonesia), New York (United States), Los Angeles (United States), and Shenzhen (China). What is the particular character of these overseas sites that seems to have made them magnets for women from China? What can we learn from looking closely at one prominent site (Shenzhen) in China? What is the nature of the culture of tolerance for commercial sex in each of these cities? Most importantly, is there anything about the sites' character and nature that help us to better understand how transnational human smuggling and trafficking work?

Hong Kong

Hong Kong, located on China's south coast on the Pearl River Delta, and bordering Guangdong Province, became a British colony after the First Opium War (1839–1842) between Britain and China. The territory, with a population of a little over 7 million, consists primarily of Hong Kong Island, the Kowloon Peninsula, Lantau Island, and the New Territories. After it was returned to China in 1997, Hong Kong became a special administrative region (SAR), with a degree of autonomy and self-governance under the "one country, two systems" policy of China.

Hong Kong had developed rapidly under British rule, and it became a major manufacturing center after World War II. In the 1990s, it was known as one of the Four Asian Tigers, and it is today one of the largest financial and trading centers in the world, with many corporate headquarters located there. After China adopted its open door policy in the late 1970s, and the Chinese government selected Shenzhen, a small town adjacent to Hong Kong, as the first special economic zone in China, Hong Kong became a point of entry for businesspeople who were interested in doing business in China.[1]

As a relatively free, market economy society with a large number of immigrants, expatriates, and tourists, Hong Kong has developed not only a large commercial sex business, but also one that is highly internationalized.[2] The 1960s movie *Suzie Wong* captured the public imagination of how a Chinese bar girl in Hong Kong made a living by drinking, dancing, and providing sexual services to foreigners.[3] In the 1970s and 1980s, many Filipina and Thai women began to enter the sex business in Hong Kong. According to Karen Joe Laidler and her colleagues at the University of Hong Kong: "sex work itself is not illegal in Hong Kong, but the criminal law prohibits almost everything related to sex work, including soliciting for an immoral purpose and loitering for the purpose of soliciting; putting up signs advertising prostitution; and running a vice establishment. The latter offense is interpreted strictly and includes the use of premises by two or more persons for prostitution. Thus, sex work is only legal if conducted in a one-woman brothel and if the sex worker does not solicit or advertise in public."[4] Needless to say, women, including those from mainland China, routinely violate these conditions.

Chinese women, known as *beigu* or "girls from the north," started to show up in Hong Kong in the late 1980s.[5] When the Hong Kong authorities began to crack down on prostitutes from Southeast Asia in 1993, the women from China became very prominent in the Hong Kong sex business.[6] A former police officer who is an expert on triads, told us that the financial crisis of Asia in the late 1990s was the main reason behind the changing face of the Hong Kong sex business. After the crisis, Hongkongers could no longer afford the more expensive local and exotic foreign women, and instead looked as an alternative to the cheaper mainland Chinese women. This provided these women a golden opportunity to move into Hong Kong's sex trade.

In Hong Kong, we interviewed 15 *xiaojies*, 2 sex ring operators, 9 law enforcement officers, and 3 NGO and other key informants for a total of 29 interviews. Individual information on the 15 *xiaojies* is presented in Table 4.1. The majority of our subjects in Hong Kong were in their twenties or thirties, mostly single, and came from all over China.

According to a high-ranking officer of the Immigration Department of Hong Kong, Chinese women can travel to Hong Kong in a variety of ways. First, they can arrive with a business visa. This was a major problem in the past, but after Hong Kong authorities began to scrutinize the process and the applicants, the number of business visa abuses has declined. Second, Chinese women can go to Hong Kong with a travel permit. There are more than forty-nine cities in China that can issue these permits to PRC nationals for a visit to Hong Kong; this allows the permit holders to stay for either seven or fourteen days. Third, Chinese women can be smuggled into Hong Kong, either overland or by sea. Fourth, Chinese women can use Hong Kong as a transit point. PRC nationals who are on their way to some countries in Southeast Asia can stay in Hong Kong for seven days on their way to that country, and then stay another seven days on their way back. Fifth, PRC nationals can move to Hong Kong through fake marriages. If they marry a Hong Kong resident, they can come and stay for three months and then go back and return for another three months, and so on. This can go on for several years, after which they then can become Hong Kong residents.

About half of the women we interviewed in Hong Kong (7 out of 15) came to Hong Kong with a travel permit (*tongxingzheng*) which allowed them to stay for either seven or fourteen days, and they did not pay an intermediary to obtain the permit. For example, a 37-year-old married woman from Chongqing, Mei Fang, said: "I applied for the permit on my own. In Chongqing, it was very easy to apply for a permit to go to Hong Kong. The seven-day visa costs $3, and the fourteen-day visa costs $6. After you have used the visa, you can mail the permit to Chongqing and apply for a new visa. You

Table 4.1. Xiaojies in Hong Kong (N = 15)

Case no.	Name	Age	Marital status	Visa	Travel fee ($)	Began to sell sex in	Current venue	Monthly income ($)
69	Yang Yan	35	Single	Missing	N/A	Hong Kong	Dancing hall	2,000
70	Wang Lan	45	Divorced	Marriage	N/A	Hong Kong	Dancing hall	2,000
71	Ah Feng	26	Married	Travel permit	N/A	Hong Kong	Brothel	Missing
72	Lin Xin	37	Divorced	Travel permit	N/A	Shenzhen	Brothel	1,500
73	Mei Fang	37	Married	Travel permit	N/A	Shenzhen	Brothel	2,100
74	Meng Fei	32	Single	Transit	N/A	Shanghai	Street—independent	4,400
75	Xiao Ya[a, b]	20	Single	Travel permit	N/A	Chongqing	One-woman apartment	6,160
76	Su Ting	23	Single	Transit	460	Xian	Street—with mommy	2,100
77	Jin Yan[a, c]	28	Single	Business	1,250	Changsa	Street—with mommy	1,760
78	Chun Chun	24	Single	Travel permit	N/A	Yiliang, Yunnan	Street—with mommy	3,200
79	Lin Nuan	24	Single	Travel permit	N/A	Chengdu	One-woman apartment	1,400
80	Angie	37	Divorced	Business	1,000	Shantou	Street—with mommy	6,600
81	Meng Xiang	40	Married	Travel permit	N/A	Hong Kong	One-woman apartment	1,166
82	Liu Yan[d]	36	Single	Business	N/A	Beijing	Street—with mommy	3,300
83	Xiao Zheng[a, c]	23	Single	Transit	N/A	Foshan	Street—with mommy	2,300

[a] Domestic trafficked victim
[b] Currently associated with a boyfriend pimp
[c] Currently affiliated with a chickenhead
[d] Currently protected by a sugar daddy

must apply for a permit in person in Chongqing after you are granted a permit twice" (73). People from China with a travel permit simply walk across the various checkpoints located between Shenzhen and Hong Kong, generally at the Luohu Checkpoint.

Three subjects said they were able to enter Hong Kong because they could show that they were on their way to another country, and they were using Hong Kong as a transit point solely for the purpose of working there for a short period of time. Of these three subjects, only one said she paid someone ($460) for assistance. Three other subjects said they were in Hong Kong with a business visa. For subjects with a business visa, one said she was required to pay someone $1,250 for helping her to obtain her visa, and another said it cost her $1,000. Our data suggest that only three out of the fifteen subjects (20%) interviewed in Hong Kong needed to pay someone for the trip to Hong Kong, and even these three subjects were not in debt when they arrived in Hong Kong, because they said they had paid those who helped them with their own money.

About 70 percent of the subjects (11 out of 15) said they were engaged in commercial sex in China before they traveled to Hong Kong, and that they were in Hong Kong for the sole purpose of prostitution. Only two women, one who arrived through marriage and another for an unstated reason, said they did not go to Hong Kong to get involved in commercial sex. These two, however, entered the sex business not long after they found out that selling sex was their best chance to make good money, considering that they lacked education and professional skills.

The fifteen women we interviewed worked in dance halls, brothels, one-woman apartments, or solicited business on the streets with the help of mommies. The dance hall where two subjects worked is located in Mongkok, a popular destination for shopping and dining and also for adult entertainment. This area has the highest concentration of sauna clubs, brothels, nightclubs, hostess bars, and karaoke lounges in the whole of Hong Kong. According to Wang Lan, a 45-year-old, twice-divorced woman from Beijing:

> There are about 30 *xiaojies* in our dancing hall; half are *beigu* [Northern girls, meaning from China], half are local women. Everyday, it opens at 10 a.m. and closes at 3 a.m. If there are no customers, we will play mahjong in a big room. We talk and laugh, and are very happy. Whenever someone walks in, he must buy one hour for $24, and the woman who hosted him will get $8. *Daban* [or mommy] will ask the man what kind of woman he likes, and she will help the customer pick a hostess. After that, the client and a hostess will go to a booth. We do not sell liquor, so if a patron needs

liquor, his hostess will go out and buy it for him. Client and hostess can do anything in the booth, from touching to having sex. The tips could range from $3 to $70. (70)

Indoor straight sex venues in Hong Kong are categorized as one-woman apartments (*yilouyifeng*, or one-room-one-phoenix) and villas (*malan* or horse barn). A one-woman apartment, by law, is legal in Hong Kong, as long as there is only one woman and one man inside the room and no third party is involved in the transaction or benefits from it. These places are advertised in the newspapers or on the internet, and the price can range from $30 to $120. Despite the restriction, some one-woman apartments actually involve more than one woman and are operated by a local woman who may also work as a backup *xiaojie*. Xiao Ya, the young woman who was lured into prostitution in China by her boyfriend and thus was categorized by us as having been a domestic trafficked victim, explained her experience in Hong Kong:

This is a one-woman apartment. A friend introduced me to the female boss. She treats me very well. She buys me food if I am hungry but too busy to go get it myself because I am with a customer. Of course, she is nice to me because I am making money for her.

For DUP+HJ [DUP is the Cantonese word for massage and HJ means hand job], the price is $40; ML [make love or vaginal sex] is $50; Full service [massage, vaginal sex, and oral sex] is $66. For full service, I get $37, the boss takes $29.

Every day, I begin to work after 9 or around 10. I stop working around 9 p.m. At night, I sleep in this same room. Once in a while, the female boss and I will go out for a walk. When I was here for the first time, I served 18 customers a day when business was good. Yesterday, I had 10 clients. At any rate, I usually have about 10 customers a day. (75)

According to Yang Yan, a woman who had working experience in all kinds of sex venues in Hong Kong, there are essentially three types of one-woman apartments: working for a boss; working for oneself; or being a substitute for those who have their menstrual periods and cannot provide services.

A villa or a horse barn is a type of brothel with more than one woman. According to Yang Yan, who was able to convert to resident status after spending some time in Hong Kong: "For the villa (or brothel), there should be two or three women like me who have an ID in order to show the police when they come for inspection. Those who have no ID will be in hiding. In the villa, those who have no ID are controlled and divide their income with

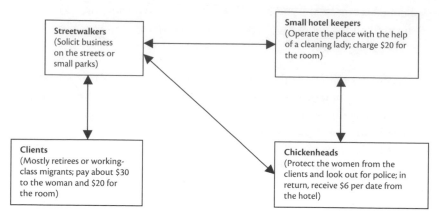

Figure 4.1. Social organization of street prostitution in the residential areas of Hong Kong

the people who control them. They make less money than those who have IDs" (69).

Besides dance halls, one-woman apartments, and villas, Chinese women also work the streets of Hong Kong. Streetwalkers in Hong Kong can be categorized into those who are working on their own in predominantly residential areas and catering to local residents, and those who are working with others in mostly tourist areas. Even though the first type of street prostitutes are working on their own, they nevertheless need to maintain an informal working relationship with small hotel keepers and chickenheads (pimps) around the area where they solicit business. Figure 4.1 illustrates how this business works in certain residential areas of Hong Kong.

The second type of streetwalker mainly works the tourist areas. Several middle-aged women solicit business in a park or a plaza by approaching male passersby, and if a potential customer shows some interest, the female pimp (also called a mommy) signals young women hanging around the plaza to come over to let the man take a look. If the man does not like any of the three or four women, then the mommy will get another group of women to come by until the man finally selects one. While the man is looking over the women, he and the mommy will also be discussing the price and the types of service provided. If the man and the mommy strike a deal, the man will tell the mommy the name of his hotel and his room number, and then will leave. A few minutes later, the selected girl will show up at the man's hotel room.

Most women from China are not able to find work in the licensed and well-established adult entertainment venues because the owners are unwilling to risk losing their businesses if undocumented workers were to be discovered. As a result, some women will, with the tacit approval of the business owners, show up as customers at a nightclub and try to solicit business. There, the women can sit at tables as hostesses, or if a male patron and a woman strike a deal, the two will leave the premises and go to a nearby hotel for a sexual transaction. According to several women we interviewed, they pay $13 for the entrance fee and charge customers $66 per table. This means they make $53 per table. If a customer wants to take a girl out, it costs the customer $200—the nightclub takes $28 and the girl gets the rest.

The subjects in Hong Kong made somewhere between $1,166 to $6,600 a month.[7] Xiao Ya, the 20-year-old woman from Chongqing who was working in a one-woman apartment, and Angie, the 37-year-old woman from Yiyang (Hunan), were the only two who were making more than $6,000 a month. The rest of them made about two to three thousand dollars, an enormous sum for women from rural China whose employment options and level of income are very limited in their home country.

Macau

Like Hong Kong, Macau is also a special administrative region of China and is located on the western side of the Pearl River Delta. Bordering Guangdong Province in the north, it is 60 kilometers (37 miles) southwest of Hong Kong. With an estimated population of 550,000, it was a former Portuguese colony before it was returned to China in 1999. Under the "one country, two systems" policy, Macau maintains its own legal system, police force, monetary system, and customs policy, and has its own delegates to international organizations. The impression of Macau is that it is a tourist mecca, dominated by gambling casinos, prostitution, and drugs. Because the Macau administration relies heavily on taxes from gambling, and prostitution is considered to be an important component to gambling, Macau authorities are reluctant to crack down on prostitution. As a result, women from China began to arrive in Macau in droves and soon dominated the sex industry there. Currently, Macau has three American casinos operating (the Sands, Wynn, and MGM Mirage). According to one source, these American casinos invested about $5.2 billion in Macau, and even though the Americans were operating only 5 of the 33 casinos in 2008, their market share was a hefty 50 percent.[8] Macau is now the world's number one gambling center, having surpassed Las Vegas in 2007.

According to the manager of a small hotel that was once a major attraction for local men looking for hotel-based paid sex, Thai women dominated the commercial sex business in Macau in the 1970s. The manager described the evolution of the business as follows: "Thai women were not streetwalkers; they worked in the sauna stores. They were expensive; at that time it cost more than $140 per visit. Northern girls from China began to show up in 1981, but just a few. A large number of northern girls appeared in 1995; the peak period was between 1997 and 2003."

In Macau, we interviewed 18 *xiaojies*, 9 sex ring operators, 1 government official, and 3 NGO and other key informants. Table 4.2 shows the background characteristics of our female subjects.

Female subjects in Macau were on average younger than those in Hong Kong, and were also more likely to be single rather than married. In the Macau sample, there was a disproportionate number of women from two Chinese provinces: Hunan and Hubei. Unlike Hong Kong, only three subjects arrived in Macau with travel permits. The majority of them (13 out of 18) were in Macau as tourists in transit. These women were on their way to a destination country in Asia and they were allowed to stay in Macau for a short period of time (normally fourteen days). After they traveled to the destination country and returned to China, they were again permitted to stay in Macau for another fourteen days. Xiao Tan, 24, who was selling sex in a small hotel, explained how she managed to enter and exit Macau:

> I entered Macau with a tourist visa issued by the Thai government. In transit, I can stay in Macau for 14 days. Then I can go back to China and return to Macau and stay another 7 days. After that, I must go to Thailand, stay there overnight, and fly back to Macau and then stay for 14 days. So I can stay in Macau 35 days altogether. The tourist visa is valid for 3 months and that means I can repeat the above process one more time. In short, I can stay in Macau for 70 days with a 3-month tourist visa to Thailand.[9] (84)

Like the subjects in Hong Kong, the majority of the women in Macau (13 out of 18, or 72%) did not pay anyone to leave China. However, there were three subjects who were required to pay a large sum of money (about U.S. $12,500) to be in Macau; one arrived with a business visa and two who were transiting Macau on their way to a country in Southeast Asia as tourists. Yin Yin, a 24-year-old single woman from Changde (Hunan Province) who solicited business in the lobby of a small hotel, explained how she had arrived in Macau:

> A friend of mine who is a *xiaojie* introduced me to a chickenhead. There is a network of chickenheads active in my hometown. He showered me with affection and he courted me, and then after we were together, he urged

Table 4.2. *Xiaojies in Macau* (N = 18)

Case no.	Name	Age	Marital status	Visa	Travel fee ($)	Began to sell sex in	Current venue	Monthly income ($)
84	Xiao Tan	24	Single	Transit	N/A	Shenzhen	Hotel	3,000
85	Xiao Tao[b]	20	Single	Transit	N/A	Zhanjiang, Guangdong	Hotel—with chickenhead	3,000
86	Yin Yin[c]	24	Single	Transit	12,500	Macau	Hotel—with chickenhead	3,000
87	Yan Yan[c]	20	Single	Business	12,500	Shenzhen	Hotel—with chickenhead	3,400
88	Xiao Qian[b]	22	Single	Transit	N/A	Zhuhai	Hotel—with chickenhead	3,000
89	Ah Min	38	Married	Tourist	N/A	Macau	Home	410
90	Miao Miao	24	Single	Transit	N/A	Macau	Brothel	2,640
91	Ah Qin[c]	29	Divorced	Travel permit	N/A	Macau	Street—with chickenhead	5,800
92	Shan Shan[c]	24	Single	Transit	Missing	Macau	Hotel—with chickenhead	12,000
93	Xiao Rou[a]	21	Single	Transit	N/A	Guangzhou	Sauna	2,200
94	Xiao Ju	23	Single	Travel permit	N/A	Jinzhou	Hotel	2,000
95	Zhou Xuan[a]	20	Single	Travel permit	N/A	Chongqing	Hotel	1,430
96	Chen Cui	22	Single	Transit	N/A	Zhuhai	Hotel	1,700
97	Cui Cui	34	Divorced	Transit	N/A	Macau	Home	2,640
98	Xiao Song	24	Single	Transit	N/A	Macau	Brothel	3,000
99	Zhang Li[a]	24	Single	Transit	1,275	Zhuhai	Hotel	2,200
100	Zhao Yan[b]	24	Single	Transit	N/A	Changsha	Hotel—with chickenhead	2,200
101	C C[c]	31	Married	Transit	12,500	Macau	Hotel—with chickenhead	3,000

[a] Domestic trafficked victim
[b] Currently associated with a boyfriend pimp
[c] Currently affiliated with a chickenhead

me to go to Macau to make money. He said he will take care of all the travel documents and will ask a woman who had been to Macau to take me there. Even though I had never been a *xiaojie* in China, I agreed to go to Macau to be a *xiaojie*. He did not tell me how much I should pay him for his help, but he made it clear that I will be working as a prostitute in Macau. He said he will find me a place to work. (86)

Ten of the eighteen subjects in Macau (56%) had been engaged in commercial sex in China. Two of these ten described being tricked into prostitution, and a third was victimized in pretty much the same way.

At the time of the interviews, most subjects (12 out of 18, or 67%) were engaged in commercial sex in a number of small hotels located in an old section of Macau. The typical routine was that a woman from China would show up at one of these hotels, rent a room, and then simply come downstairs to solicit business in the lobby. According to Xiao Tao, a 20-year-old from Changde of Hunan Province:

This is a small hotel. We rented all the rooms on the second and third floors and we provide sex services in our rooms. The 4th and 5th floors are reserved for regular customers, but there are very few regular customers here. There are two small beds in my room. One is for me to sleep in at night, the other for doing business. We charge $14 each session, and the time limit is 30 minutes, but clients usually leave once the sex transaction is completed. (85)

The hotel charges about $42 per night, so the women must start working once they arrive and if they have their period, they try to find a roommate who is also having her period to share a room and thus reduce the rent to half. Another subject told us how she was able to find the hotel where she worked:

While I was working in the sex industry in Shenzhen, I met some *xiaojies* who had returned from Macau. They told me that you can make more money in Macau than in China. They did not help me much, just provided me the names of the hotels in Macau where I can go to work. The person who helped me to obtain a visa to Thailand is not related to the hotel in Macau at all. I went to Zhuhai from Shenzhen and then entered Macau. I took a taxi after I crossed the immigration checkpoint and came directly to this hotel. I started to work after renting a room in this hotel. (84)

Chinese women are also found in the basement of a five-star casino hotel that is one of the landmarks of Macau. In the hotel basement where many expensive boutique stores and restaurants are located, more than twenty women walk the corridors at any given time, aggressively soliciting business by asking passersby whether they want to "go" or not. Unlike the women in the small hotels who charge $14 or $28 per session, these women charge $106 per date, mainly because they tend to be taller and more attractive. And the hotel costs $130 per night and only one woman per room is allowed.

There are also women working out of apartments located in old, residential areas, catering to local Macau residents or laborers from China. Most of these women are in their thirties or forties, either married or divorced, and they provide their sexual services in old and dirty apartments. Ah Min, a 38-year-old married woman with two teenage children from Shaoyang (Hunan Province) said:

> I provide sex services in my room. I solicit business downstairs at the entrance to the building and take my clients to my room. It is straight sex service and clients leave immediately after. I tell my client in advance that I do not *chuixiao* ["play flute" or provide oral sex] or I will not take him to my room. Besides, they must use a condom. Every day, I work from 10 a.m. and stop at 11 p.m., because it is possible to be arrested after 11 p.m. (89)

In Macau, there are also many sauna establishments, both large and small. The bigger and more expensive saunas are generally located in the four- or five-star hotels; the smaller and cheaper ones are located in commercial buildings and are not affiliated with other enterprises such as the hotel. Xiao Rou, a 21-year-old single woman from Chongqing working in a mid-size sauna, described her experience as follows:

> I have been working in this circle in China, so it is normal that I know some people from this line of work. A woman got back from Macau and she told me that I can make more in Macau. Besides, I won't be arrested in Macau for prostitution. Right after I arrived in Macau, I was planning to work in a nightclub where a friend was working. I went there for an interview, but the manager did not hire me because he thought I was a little overweight. So I came to this sauna place. They hired me quickly. People in the sauna establishment taught me massage. For those services including "ice and fire" [oral sex with cold and warm water], they gave me a video tape. I learned by watching the tape. (93)

There are also many Chinese women who walk the street, especially along a street not far from the Hotel Lisboa, probably the best known hotel and casino in Macau. Street women, like women working the lobby of the five-star hotel and casino, are not working on their own, but with the help of chickenheads. For example, Ah Qin, a 29-year-old divorcee from Dalian (Liaoning Province) told us this story:

> I must pay my chickenhead $8,000 for him to allow me to work on this street. Other girls need to pay more than me, like $10,000. Maybe that's because these girls were brought over to Macau by their chickenheads; I came to Macau without their help. I was recruited by my chickenhead here in Macau.
>
> On average, I have 3 or 4 customers a day. I try my best to clear my debt of $8,000 with my chickenhead. Now I only owe him a little more than $1,350. After paying off the $8,000, I must pay him $1,400 a month so that I can keep on working on this street. Some chickenheads may demand their girls split their income with them after paying off the debt. That is really ridiculous. These chickenheads are really garbage, and they are animals. After they take our money, they go gamble and lose all the money. How can they win when they gamble with the kind of money they are making? (91)

On average, subjects in Macau were making more than subjects in Hong Kong. Shan Shan, who was soliciting business at the five-star hotel, said she made about $12,000 a month, and Ah Qin, a streetwalker, made about $5,800 a month. Those soliciting business in the lobbies of the various small hotels made about $3,000 a month—none of these incomes are small, if we consider women in China normally do not make more than $240 a month.

Taiwan

With a population of almost 23 million, Taiwan, or the Republic of China (ROC) is an island located off the coast of China's Fujian Province, separated by the Taiwanese Straits. After the Communists defeated the Kuomintang in 1949, the KMT leader Chiang Kai-shek and his followers fled to Taiwan and ultimately developed the island into one of the Four Tigers of Asia. A thriving economy and a maturing democracy have enabled the people of Taiwan to enjoy prosperity and freedom unprecedented in the long history of the Chinese people.[10]

In the late 1990s, women from China began to arrive in Taiwan to work in the booming sex business there. At that time, most Chinese women, called *dalumei* (girls from the Mainland), were smuggled into Taiwan by boats across the Taiwanese Straits.[11] In August 2003, two boat captains and their crew members threw twenty-six Chinese women into the sea near Maoli County in order to escape pursuing Taiwanese coast guards, leaving six of them to drown. Under pressure, Taiwanese authorities responded by cracking down on the boat smuggling. But the traffickers in Taiwan responded by simply increasing the use of fraudulent marriages with Taiwanese citizens in order to bring Chinese women to Taiwan. When the authorities then tightened their control of these cross-straits marriages, the traffickers again reacted by flying Chinese women to Taiwan with passports issued by various countries in Southeast Asia.

In Taiwan, we interviewed 16 *xiaojies*, 14 sex ring operators, 13 law enforcers, and 5 NGO and other key informants. Table 4.3 shows the backgrounds of the sixteen Chinese women we interviewed in Taiwan. The vast majority of these women were in their twenties and single. About half of them had been engaged in prostitution in China. Eleven out of fifteen (73%) arrived in Taiwan through fake marriages with Taiwanese citizens.

Fang Fang, a 31-year-old single woman from Guilin (in China's Guangxi Province bordering Vietnam) described why and how she arrived in Taiwan:

A friend who returned from Taiwan gave me the phone number of her boss in Taiwan and told me to give him a call. She did not help me in any other way. She [and a few other women who used to work in Taiwan] told me a lot about commercial sex in Taiwan. Three to four months after the call, he [the boss] came to China to take care of some businesses and he dropped by Guilin to see me. We just met once, but he told me he was satisfied with me. He said after he went back to Taiwan, he will find a man willing to act as a fake husband and come marry me. After he left, we continued to talk by phone. Several months later, a man who had been doing business in China for many years married me. After the marriage, I applied to go to Taiwan and it went very well. (137)

Some Chinese women arrived in Taiwan as tourists from another country in Asia. For example, Wen Wen, a 22-year-old woman from Wuhan explained how she got to Taiwan:

I came here with a Malaysian passport. First, I traveled to Malaysia with my Chinese passport, then flew to Taiwan with a Malaysian passport and a tourist visa. The visa was valid for only one month, so now it is expired and

Table 4.3. *Xiaojies in Taiwan* (N = 16)

Case no.	Name	Age	Marital status	Visa	Travel fee ($)	Began to sell sex in	Current venue	Monthly income ($)
134	Xiao Ling	23	Single	Marriage	6,250	Dongguan	Outcall	Missing
135	Xiao Li	25	Single	Marriage	6,250	Taichung, Taiwan	Outcall	9,372
136	Co Co	28	Single	Marriage	6,250	Dongguan	Outcall	Missing
137	Fang Fang	31	Single	Marriage	6,250	Taoyuan, Taiwan	Outcall	6,160
138	Yu Fang	38	Married	Marriage[a]	N/A	Chiayi, Taiwan	Massage parlor	9,400
139	Zhao Shuang	26	Single	Marriage	6,250	Nanchang, Jiangxi	Outcall	8,360
140	Xiao Cai	22	Single	Marriage	6,250	Taichung	Outcall	5,000
141	Nancy	29	Single	Marriage	6,250	Changchun	Outcall	Missing
142	Michelle	25	Single	Marriage	7,180	Changchun	Outcall	7,800
143	Rainbow	26	Single	Tourist	Missing	Taipei	Brothel	Missing
144	Bing Bing	25	Single	Marriage[b]	6,250	Taipei	Outcall	8,600
145	Betty	22	Single	Marriage	5,625	Chengdu	Outcall	7,000
146	Wen Wen	22	Single	Tourist	7,180	Shanghai	Outcall	8,750
147	Wa Wa	24	Single	Tourist	7,180	Taipei	Outcall	7,800
148	Mao Mao	23	Single	Tourist	6,250	Quanzhou, Fujian	Outcall	1,875
149	Xiao Xiao	32	Single	Smuggled by boat	6,250	Xian	Outcall	6,500

[a] Genuine marriage
[b] Using another returned sex worker's identity; the subject did not go through the processes of fake marriage

I am out of status. I needed to pay $7,180 for this trip to Taiwan, and I was able to clear it within a month working here. Because I came as a tourist, I did not have to pay the *laogongfei* [husband fee]. (146)

Unlike their travel to Hong Kong, Chinese women must pay a relatively high price for the trip to Taiwan. Those who arrived through a fake marriage or by boat paid about $6,250, and those who came using a passport from a country in Southeast Asia paid about $7,180. In all cases, the agent ("owner") of a woman had paid for all the expenses to bring in the woman, and the woman then had to repay the agent from the money she made in Taiwan. Normally it took them less than a month to clear the debt.

As in Hong Kong, Taiwanese authorities are very strict in prohibiting Chinese women from working in nightclubs, karaoke lounges, and massage parlors. Not only are owners heavily punished for hiring Chinese women, but the women also find it very difficult to pretend that they are Taiwanese because of their accents. As a result, most Chinese women in Taiwan are forced to work only in an escort service. These escort or so-called outcall service operations in Taiwan are highly mobile and elusive. Customers must go through intermediaries or pimps (called *neijiang*) to hook up with escort agencies, because the agencies normally do not advertise their services. The process can either be very simple or rather complicated. A customer checks into a hotel or a motel and asks a hotel employee to find a Chinese woman. The hotel employee, through his or her contacts with various escort agencies, will call an agency. The agency is actually only a person answering phone calls using a cell phone. After receiving a call from a referrer, the agency operator will call a jockey and ask him to drive a girl to the customer's motel. After the transaction is completed, the customer pays the girl, the girl turns in all the money to the jockey once she returns to the car, and the jockey meets the operator at the end of the day to go over how much business there was that evening. The operator keeps a record of how much a girl makes and how much he owes to the various pimps who are working with him. Xiao Li, a 25-year-old single woman from Shenyang (Liaoning) described how she spent every working day: "I get up at noon and begin to work around 2 p.m. If there is business, my jockey will drive me from my apartment to where the customer is. Once we start working, we may be out in our car all day long, sometimes we may find a coffee shop to rest. I stop working at midnight and go home. I ask the [escort] company not to arrange work for me after midnight"[12] (135).

The fifteen Chinese women interviewed in Taiwan made an average of $7,218 a month, significantly more than those interviewed in Hong Kong and

Macau. As explained to us, normally the money from the customers is distributed among all parties involved as follows:

Customer pays	$94
Pimp receives	$31 (33%)
Escort agency owner	$14 (15%)
Agent	$14 (15%)
Woman	$35 (37%)

The woman is also responsible for paying her fake husband $937 a month, and her jockey $78 every working day, regardless of how much she makes on a given working day. The driver is responsible for providing a car, works from 2 in the afternoon until early dawn, and pays for the gas. In one case, a subject said she received only $23 per session, but her agent paid her rent, gave her living expenses, and took care of the monthly fee for her fake husband and daily charge for her jockey. Sometimes, on a case by case and day by day basis, an agent receives around $2,500 a month from a woman but does not take any cut.

Thailand

Thailand, population 65 million, is situated in Southeast Asia. A Buddhist country, Thailand has a very well-established commercial sex industry.[13] In fact, Bangkok is known as the world's brothel or the "world's most open city."[14] It is as well a source, transit, and destination country for trafficked women.[15] Because the sex trade is vital to the country's enormous tourist industry, Thai policemen are believed to be heavily bribed by sex establishment owners.[16] There are also a substantial number of Chinese prostitutes in Bangkok, working in the music halls, tea parlors, karaoke lounges, and nightclubs that cater to retired Thai-Chinese or businessmen from Taiwan. Like prostitutes in the Caribbean,[17] many Chinese prostitutes in Bangkok seek to establish long-term relationships with retired Thai-Chinese men that can lead to marriage, migration, and a comfortable life.

We interviewed 17 *xiaojies*, 5 sex ring operators, 5 government officials, and 2 NGO and other key informants in Bangkok. Table 4.4 illustrates the backgrounds of the *xiaojies*. Compared to Hong Kong, Macau, and Taiwan, subjects in Thailand were older, more likely to be married or divorced, and less likely to have been involved in commercial sex in China. In fact, only two women said they had been engaged in prostitution before they headed for Thailand, and only four were single at the time of the interview.

Table 4.4. *Xiaojies in Thailand (N = 17)*

Case no.	Name	Age	Marital status	Visa	Travel fee ($)	Began to sell sex in	Current venue	Monthly income ($)
52	Ah Ping	36	Married	Tourist	875	Guangzhou	Restaurant	500
53	Dong Dong[b]	26	Married	Tourist	500	Bangkok	Restaurant	600
54	Ah Hua	32	Married	Business	N/A	Bangkok	Restaurant	1,500
55	Xiao Lan	45	Widowed	Tourist	1,800	Bangkok	Restaurant	Missing
56	Xiao Wei	43	Married	Tourist	1,250	Bangkok	Restaurant	530
57	Ah Yu	40	Divorced	Business	1,560	Bangkok	Restaurant	750
58	Xiao Yao	37	Divorced	Business	N/A	Bangkok	Nightclub	1,600
59	Juan Juan	42	Married	Tourist	750	Bangkok	Restaurant	500
60	Xiao Wen	25	Single	Business	2,500	Bangkok	Flower Hall	2,200
61	Xiao Xing	28	Single	Business	N/A	Bangkok	Restaurant	625
62	Ah Chan[a]	38	Divorced	Tourist	N/A	Jorzhou, Hebei	KTV	1,300
63	Huan Huan	41	Divorced	Tourist	N/A	Bangkok	Restaurant	2,600
64	Zhao Tong	24	Divorced	Tourist	1,500	Bangkok	Flower Hall	1,250
65	Wang Chun	34	Divorced	Business	1,500	Bangkok	Flower Hall	1,000
66	Chun Xiang	23	Single	Tourist	N/A	Bangkok	Brothel	625
67	Li Qun	26	Single	Smuggled by boat	350	Bangkok	Brothel	1,300
68	Xiao Jing	29	Divorced	Business	1,875	Bangkok	Flower Hall	880

[a] Domestic trafficked victim
[b] Deceived; transnational trafficked victim

A large number of these women were brought to Thailand by their relatives. For example, a 26-year-old married woman explained why and how she came to Bangkok and how she was brought into this profession:

> I had never been a *xiaojie* in China. My sister-in-law [a returned *xiaojie*] did not tell me about going out with men before I left China. I assumed that I would accompany patrons to drink and sing. The first night I arrived in Bangkok, the man who met my aunt [also a *xiaojie*] and me at the airport drove us to where my aunt lived. Then my aunt gave me her cell phone and told me to go downstairs and stay there until she called me. About half an hour later, she called me upstairs. By then, that man was wearing only underwear and he was walking in the room. I knew right then what they did a moment ago. After the man left, my aunt told me not to make a big deal out of it and that I will come to understand it better in a few days. At that point, I did not know what she was talking about. Two days later, my aunt told a man that I just got here and asked if he wanted me to keep him company. My aunt and he agreed that he would pay me about $1,000 if I stayed with him for two weeks. I refused, but my aunt said: "Why are you here in Thailand if you don't want to do this? If you do this, you will earn back all your expenses and you won't have to worry about going back to China with a loss." So I packed and went with the man to his place. (53)

More than half of the subjects arrived in Thailand as tourists (9 out of 17), followed by those who entered with a business visa (6 out of 17). Our subjects were able to travel to Thailand with a Chinese passport with relative ease, and were also allowed to stay in Thailand for a few months per visit. According to Ah Ping, a 36-year-old married woman from Jinzhou (Hubei Province): "When I came here for the first time in March 2003, I came as a tourist. I stayed for three months, and then applied for an extension. I stayed for a total of six months during my first visit. I went back to China after that and stayed for 45 days. When I came for a second time, I could apply for a business visa, which I did. I have gone back and forth between China and Thailand quite a few times over the past four years" (52).

Those who arrived in Thailand with a one-year-valid business visa were able to stay for three months; some of them crossed over to Cambodia after three months to have their visa extended for another three months and then returned to Thailand right away, paying a total fee of about $500.

Unlike Hong Kong, Macau, and Taiwan, Thailand is not a Chinese society, even though there are many ethnic Chinese living there. Bangkok's Chinatown is one of the largest Chinatowns in the world. Chinese women working in Thailand do not penetrate into the well-established mainstream sex industry dominated by native Thai women; instead, they work in the flower halls (more or less like a KTV) and nightclubs located around Bangkok's Chinatown that are frequented by predominantly local Chinese (most originating from China's Chaozhou area) or businesspeople from the mainland or Taiwan.[18] A tour guide in Bangkok explained why this was the case: "Chinese women are not in a position to compete with Thai girls in the mainstream sex industry because women from China are older and they do not speak English or Thai. How can they win the hearts of customers from Thai mainstream society? Therefore, Chinese women can only make money from those old Thai-Chinese in Chinatown."

Of the ten research sites, only Bangkok had entertainment venues called flower halls where the majority of our subjects worked during the day, and then worked in a nightclub at night. In the flower halls, the girls eat, sing, and chat with customers, and they make money by, with the permission of their customers, going up to a podium and singing. When they do that, their customers ask a waiter or waitress to go up to the podium and put a flower ring around the girl's neck. A customer usually tells the waiter or waitress how much "flower money" he is willing to pay the girl who is singing. In Bangkok, besides the low-end flower halls visited by elderly local Chinese, there are also relatively fancier flower halls operating during the evenings, that cater to younger, wealthier customers.

Besides working in flower halls or nightclubs, many women in Bangkok also try to get ahead by establishing regular relationships with a man so that he will pay the rent, buy food, offer a monthly allowance, and be responsible for other expenses such as buying roundtrip tickets for them if they want to return to China for a break.[19] Ah Ping, the subject quoted above, explained how and why she continuously maintained a relationship with a man:

> Soon after I arrived in Bangkok for the first time, I met a man from China. He agreed to *bao* [cover] me, so he paid my rent and gave me a monthly stipend. He came to see me frequently, and he wouldn't let me go out with customers. But he was often not in Bangkok, so I went out with customers when he was not around. I did not have any emotional attachment to him. Five months later, he bought me a plane ticket and I went back to China. He probably spent about $5,000 on me during the five months we were together. But when I got back from China after 45 days, he had found another recently arrived Chinese woman. So we separated. During the four years here, I have always had a man to provide me with financial support. As a result, I do not need to work very hard. (52)

Some of the subjects we interviewed were able to maintain a relationship with more than one "husband" and work at the same time. Huan Huan, a 41-year-old divorced woman from Yinkou (Liaoning) described how she juggled jobs working at a flower hall during the daytime and entertaining two "husbands" at night: "I go to work at XXX [a flower hall, name omitted] around 1 or 2 in the afternoon; one of my Chaozhou husbands picks me up at the flower hall around 8:30 p.m. Sometimes he comes upstairs and we have sex; sometimes he just leaves after bringing me home. Another Chaozhou husband will come to my place later and he likes to drink until 1 or 2 in the morning" (63).

Compared to Hong Kong, Macau, and Taiwan, Chinese women in Thailand make significantly less. Two of our subjects were making as little as $500 a month, and the most successful subject in our Thai sample was making about $2,600. For some of the married or divorced women in China, they were willing to go to Bangkok to toil for a living because it was relatively easy and inexpensive for them to go there. In addition, when they are in Thailand, they are surrounded by friends and relatives from their hometown, not chickenheads, agents, fake husbands, or jockeys. Moreover, they don't have to sleep with men as often as do women in Hong Kong, Macau, and Taiwan. Some divorced women actually cherished the opportunity to maintain regular relationships with men who were more mature in years, given that they were generous and nice to them.

Malaysia

Malaysia borders Thailand, Singapore, Indonesia, and Brunei, and has a population of over 25 million. It is a Muslim country with a large number of ethnic Chinese who account for about a quarter of the population. The economies of most of the cities and towns in Malaysia are dominated by ethnic Chinese. According to one source, almost every Malaysian town has a red-light district, and the illicit sex culture is widespread. Sex workers from China are most likely to work in Kuala Lumpur, Ipoh, Penang, and Johor Baharu, where a large number of ethnic Chinese congregate, or in resort areas such as Kota Kinabalu and Genting.

According to the Malay authorities, 2,824 Chinese women were arrested in Malaysia for prostitution in 2005—many more than women from Indonesia (1,606), Thailand (910), the Philippines (742), and Vietnam (204).[20] Chinese xiaojies are called "little dragon ladies" or "China dolls" in Malaysia, and their presence there is more controversial and thus more likely to be reported in the Malay media than that of prostitutes from other countries.[21]

We interviewed 18 Chinese women, 7 sex ring operators, 3 law enforcers, and 4 NGO and other key informants in Malaysia. Table 4.5 shows some of the basic information about the female subjects.

The average age of the subjects in Malaysia was 30, and half of them were either married or divorced. They came from all over China, all of them arrived in Malaysia with a Chinese passport and Malaysian tourist visa, and they were required to pay someone a fee to make this possible. For example, Ah Hung, a 36-year-old married woman from Nanping (in China's coastal Fujian Province) explained how she came to Malaysia:

> I applied for a Chinese passport on my own. My fellow villagers [who were returned *xiaojies*] introduced me to a snakehead who applied for the Malay tourist visa for me. I spent about $400 altogether. We came here by helping one another. The one who is the middleman [who introduced the snakehead to us] may earn $125 in the process, but this is in the open and we all knew that. I myself acted as a middleman before, but I did not charge any money. It is not a company or an organization that is helping us. We are all sister workers, but then there are individual snakeheads who are responsible for the visa applications. (16)

Xiao Xuan, a 20-year-old single woman from Dandong (Liaoning) described why she came to Malaysia after working as a *xiaojie* in Zhuhai:

> It was not easy to make money [as a *xiaojie*] in Zhuhai any more and there were frequent police raids. Therefore I applied for documents to come to Malaysia. Here in Kuala Lumpur, I share a room with another girl. The rent is $15 a day. Our company had a working contract with XXX Spa [name omitted]. The spa will arrange work for us. We normally would provide sex service only at XXX Spa or XXX Hotel [name omitted]. We rarely go to other places. This way it is safer. We just stay home and wait for phone calls. (30)

In Kuala Lumpur, we interviewed several women who were working for one of the largest escort agencies in Malaysia. The agency's mode of operation is very similar to the escort agencies in Taiwan: after a customer asks an intermediary to get in touch with the agency, the agency dispatches a car with two or three women to the customer's place, most likely a hotel where the customer is staying. After the customer picks one of the women, he pays the driver the charge on the spot. About 45 minutes later, the driver returns to the hotel to pick up the woman. Yang Fei, a 21-year-old single woman

Table 4.5. *Xiaojies in Malaysia* (N = 18)

Case no.	Name	Age	Marital status	Visa	Travel fee ($)	Began to sell sex in	Current venue	Monthly income ($)
16	Ah Hung	36	Married	Tourist	487	Jinjiang, Fuzhou	Restaurant	1,150
17	Ah Xue	37	Divorced	Tourist	425	Kuala Lumpur	Street	1,000
18	Yi Ning	34	Divorced	Tourist	437	Jiangmen, Guangdong	KTV	2,860
19	Xiao Mei	27	Married	Tourist	913[b]	Faoshan, Guangdong	KTV	3,500
20	Xiao Chuan	32	Single	Tourist	425	Ipoh, Malaysia	KTV	4,300
21	Ah Juan	28	Married	Tourist	1,338[b]	Chaozhou, Guangdong	Street	4,180
22	Xiao Feng	33	Married	Tourist	350	Kuala Lumpur	Restaurant	924
23	Wang Min	24	Single	Tourist	4,285	Kuala Lumpur	Escort	5,100
24	Ah Shuang	42	Divorced	Tourist	525	Kuala Lumpur	Street	1,400
25	Yang Fei[a]	21	Single	Tourist	1,250	Haikou, Hainan	Escort	4,285
26	Chen Hung	39	Divorced	Tourist	500	Taizhou, Jiangsu	Street	2,800
27	Li Yin[a]	24	Single	Tourist	625	Kuala Lumpur	Escort	2,000
28	Lu Lu	35	Married	Tourist	562	Wenzhou	Restaurant	1,700
29	Li Min	26	Single	Tourist	2,500	Tianjin	Escort	1,700
30	Xiao Xuan	20	Single	Tourist	Missing	Zhuhai	Sauna	2,860
31	Li Na[a]	30	Single	Missing	Missing	Harbin	Hotel	1,700
32	Zhang Yin	28	Single	Tourist	562	Kuala Lumpur	Nightclub	1,400
33	Xiao Hao[a]	21	Single	Tourist	2,000	Guilin	Escort	2,800

[a] Domestic trafficked victim
[b] Included a referral fee

from Changde (Hunan) who was a domestic trafficked victim, described to us how she began to engage in prostitution in Kuala Lumpur:

> Here in Kuala Lumpur, my company will drive us to where customers are —their hotels or their homes. Generally, the company will show a customer two girls and ask him to choose one. If he is not satisfied, then the company will show him two more girls. If there are three or four customers, the company will send about five girls to let them choose. We must go to the company every day. Customers pay the company at least $60 per session. I get $30 no matter how much the customers pay the company. In addition, the daily rent is $18, and the "turning light on" fee $9. [The first customer is $3, the second is $6, and the third $9. After the third, no need to pay any more.] This is the introduction fee. We will not be "shining" without their [the company] "light" or introduction. If we don't have them [the company and its introductions], customers are not going to find us. This means we do not make any money from the first customer of the day [the $30 from the first customer will cover the daily $18 rent and the $9 "turning the light on" fee]. (25)

There are also Chinese women working on the streets in Kuala Lumpur, and they are mostly married or divorced women in their thirties or forties. Besides Chinese women, there are also Indian and Indonesian women working on the outskirts of these particular areas. Ah Xue, a 37-year-old divorced woman from Hubei Province characterized her journey to Malaysia this way:

> When I was in Fuqing [Fujian], I met a woman who came back from Malaysia. She helped me find a travel agency which applied for a Malay visa and booked an air ticket for me. I applied for a Chinese passport myself. The woman told me explicitly what I would do after I came to Malaysia. She told me that it was easy to make money in Malaysia; you could make $25 to $40 a day. She was also a street prostitute in Kuala Lumpur who looked for customers on the streets on her own.
>
> On the first day of my arrival, my coworkers introduced a client to me for overnight service. I did not know how much to charge him, so I charged him only $50. The client said the price was low. I kept the whole $50, nobody divided the money with me. I started to stand on the sidewalk from the second day on, and people approached me and asked how much. After that, we go to hotels around here, do it right after entering the room, and leave immediately after doing it. (17)

Women in Malaysia made an average of $2,536 a month—more than those in Thailand ($1,110), but somewhat less than those in Macau ($3,145) and Hong Kong ($2,856), and significantly less than those in Taiwan ($7,218).

Singapore

The commercial sex business in Singapore is highly diversified. During the late nineteenth and early twentieth centuries, women from China and Japan were brought to Singapore to meet the demands of many groups of male laborers there.[22] Nowadays, women from Thailand, Malaysia, Burma, India, Indonesia, and China can be found working in any one of the red-light districts there.[23] According to a media report in August 2004, after a two-day sweep of the city's red-light districts, police in Singapore detained 220 women, of whom 133 were from China. The media in Singapore have accused the Chinese women of moving into residential areas to target retired men, in addition to staking out housing blocks.

We interviewed fifteen *xiaojies* in Singapore (see Table 4.6). About half of them were in their thirties, and about the same proportion of them were married or divorced. We met a 17-year-old subject, the youngest in our sample of 164 *xiaojies*, on the street of a red-light district in Singapore. Eleven of the women said they arrived in Singapore as tourists, and three with business visas. It cost them between $625 to $12,500 for their travel.

Jiao Jiao, the 17-year-old street walker from Dongfeng (Jilin), explained how she came to Singapore:

> Later, I met another chickenhead in Macau and he urged me to go to Singapore. With his help, I went to Changchun [Jilin] to apply for a Chinese passport and then a visa to Singapore. He charged me $12,500 for the trip to Singapore. If I want to come here again after this trip, he will help me again but won't charge me any money except the visa application fee.
>
> I came here with a tourist visa. It is valid for two months, but when I got here, the Singapore authorities only allowed me to stay for a month. So I must go back to China in a month and then come back again if I want to.
>
> Here, I work from evening to about 6 or 7 in the morning. I solicit business on the street, and then walk to the hotel across the street to have sex; it's very simple. I charge $66 for a 30-minute session, and the hotel charges $7 for the room. I give a local chickenhead $7 per client. I can make more money here than in Macau. I normally see about 7 to 8 customers a day. Singapore is better than Macau because it is quicker here; often a session is over in 20 minutes. Besides, here you can work 24 hours a day if you want.[24] (11)

Table 4.6. Xiaojies in Singapore (N = 15)

Case no.	Name	Age	Marital status	Visa	Travel fee ($)	Began to sell sex in	Current venue	Monthly income ($)
1	Yang Yang	25	Single	Business	3,750	Singapore	Street—with chickenhead	5,800
2	Ah Dong	30	Married	Missing	9,756	Shenzhen	Street—with chickenhead	Missing
3	Chu Chu	26	Divorced	Tourist	1,875	Singapore	KTV	2,400
4	Ah Jin	45	Widowed	Tourist	1,625	Singapore	Restaurant	2,200
5	Xiao Huan	35	Single	Tourist	750	Dalian	KTV	2,000
6	Rong Rong	33	Divorced	Tourist	1,250	Singapore	Street—with chickenhead	3,674
7	Ah Chun	35	Separated	Tourist	625	Thailand	Restaurant	660
8	Ding Ling	23	Single	Tourist	1,875	Beijing	Massage parlor	1,800
9	Meng Meng	28	Single	Business	Missing	Hong Kong	Nightclub	10,000
10	Qian Qian	34	Divorced	Tourist	1,250	Shenzhen	Massage parlor	6,000
11	Jiao Jiao[a]	17	Single	Tourist	12,500	Shenzhen	Street—with chickenhead	11,000
12	Xiao Ting	20	Single	Tourist	1,875	Singapore	Street—with chickenhead	2,500
13	Xiao Wang	34	Married	Tourist	1,060	Singapore	KTV	5,400
14	Ah Lian	35	Divorced	Tourist	1,375	Singapore	Street—with chickenhead	3,600
15	Xiao Hui	25	Single	Business	4,375	Singapore	Street—with chickenhead	7,200

[a] Transnational trafficked victim due to being a minor

Besides the streets, many Chinese women also work in KTVs (karaoke TV lounges) in Singapore. Chu Chu, a 26-year-old divorced woman from Harbin (Heilongjiang) explained how she arrived in Singapore and what had happened to her since then:

> After I graduated from college, I worked as an elementary school teacher until I got here. A friend who had returned from Singapore told me how easy it was to make money in Singapore, so I came. I gave her my passport photo and other materials, and she found someone to help me obtain the necessary travel documents. I did not meet that person. After a month, I was on my way to Singapore. I flew from Harbin to Shanghai, and then to Singapore. I came with a tourist visa, and it allowed me to stay for 28 days. It cost me $1,875 for the trip and I paid the entire fee before I left China.
>
> Once I landed here, I went to the XX KTV (name omitted) to take a look. I went in and walked around for a little while and it scared the hell out of me. There were plenty of Chinese girls in there, and once customers walk in, the girls would be jumping all over the customers trying to remove their clothes. The girls all wear only bras and short skirts and they all sit on the laps of the customers. And then they will start doing all kinds of things right there. It was like watching an X-rated movie. That's why I decided to go to work for another KTV. Right now, I work at two stores, one in the afternoon and another in the evening. (3)

The fifteen female subjects in Singapore were making an average of $4,588 a month, ranging from $660 to $11,000. A subject's level of income was not associated with the type of sex venue in which she was working; some street-walkers may make more than hostesses in high-end KTVs. As a result, it is not possible to rank a woman's status (or earning power) in the sex business simply by considering where she works.

Indonesia

Indonesia, like Malaysia, is a Muslim country with a large number of ethnic Chinese who play a key role in the local economy. Not only are Indonesian women active in the sex sectors of neighboring countries such as Singapore and Malaysia, there are also many Indonesian girls and women in the local sex industry. Batam, an island about 30 kilometers south of Singapore, has a booming sex industry that mainly caters to visitors from Singapore and Malaysia.[25] Freelance writer Moammar Emka, in his book on commercial sex in Jakarta, described in detail the many sex venues there, and concluded that "it is a myth that Indonesia is a prudish society."[26] Most women from China stay in Jakarta or Surabaya, even though it is believed that almost every Indonesian town has a certain number of Chinese prostitutes.

In Indonesia, we interviewed eighteen *xiaojies*. All the interviews were conducted in Jakarta, the capital (see Table 4.7).

Thirteen subjects were single at the time of the interviews, and most of them were in their twenties and came from Hunan, Sichuan, or northeast China. At least half of them arrived in Indonesia with so-called work visas. For example, Judy, a 21-year-old woman from Henyang (Hunan) explained how she came to Indonesia:

> I worked in Guangzhou after dropping out of high school. I was 18 at that time. I worked as a secretary for a company, and my monthly income was a little more than $125. I wanted to go to Japan, but I came to Indonesia instead after my visa application to Japan was rejected. I found this company [which assisted me to come here] with the help of my elder sister and her friend. They told me I can make between $1,250 to $2,500 a month here. I knew before I came here that I would *zuotai*. I did that occasionally when I was in China, but I did not *chutai*.
>
> The people who are involved in helping women go overseas advertise their services all over the city of Guangzhou. My sister brought me to this company. This company used to help women go to Japan. Now, it specializes in moving women to Indonesia. This company cooperates closely with an Indonesian company, and helps the Indonesian company recruit girls in China. They told me a lot. For example, how much I should pay them, that I need to sign a contract, and how much I would make in a month. With a work visa, you can stay for two months and then apply for an extension of two more months. (37)

Most participants in Indonesia worked in a KTV or a spa. Unlike the women we interviewed in the other two non-Chinese societies, Thailand and Malaysia, Chinese women in Indonesia seemed to be more embedded in the mainstream Indonesian sex business. The KTVs and spas where our subjects in Indonesia worked were venues that catered to both Indonesian Chinese and ethnic Indonesians, and very often these venues were staffed with Chinese, Indonesian, and women from other countries. As a result, the potential for Chinese women to continue to expand their network in Indonesia is significantly greater than in Thailand and Malaysia.

Table 4.7. Xiaojies in Indonesia (N=18)

Case no.	Name	Age	Marital status	Visa	Travel fee ($)	Began to sell sex in	Current venue	Monthly income ($)
34	Ah Xiang	37	Divorced	Business	1,625	Jakarta	Restaurant	Missing
35	Xiao Ke	40	Divorced	Missing	500	Jakarta	Nightclub	1,350
36	Ah Fang	22	Single	Missing	1,250	Xiamen	Spa	3,000
37	Judy	21	Single	Work visa	1,250	Guangzhou	KTV	2,000
38	Hung Hung	25	Single	Work visa	1,500	Guangzhou	KTV	1,250
39	Wang Fei	27	Single	Tourist	Missing	Jakarta	KTV	Missing
40	Candy	27	Married	Work visa	1,500	Jakarta	Spa	950
41	Su Su	26	Married	Work visa	1,500	Jakarta	Spa	950
42	Sun Hung	28	Single	Work visa	1,500	Nagoya, Japan	KTV	1,500
43	Fei Fei[a]	21	Single	Work visa	1,437	Changde	Spa	3,000
44	Xin Xin	22	Single	Work visa	Missing	Kuala Lumpur	Spa	3,000
45	Gui Gui[a]	25	Single	Missing	3,500	Jilin	Spa	6,000
46	Lin Yu	20	Single	Missing	1,875	Jakarta	Spa	2,300
47	Xiao Fen	23	Single	Work visa	1,097	Jakarta	Spa	2,000
48	Liu Li[a]	34	Divorced	Tourist	6,250	Beijing	Spa	2,000
49	Wang Fang	33	Single	Tourist	450	Haikuo	KTV	Missing
50	Dan Dan	31	Single	Tourist	1,250	Baoan, Guangdong	KTV	1,500
51	Xiao Dai	24	Single	Work visa	400	Chengdu	Spa	2,700

[a] Domestic trafficked victim

Los Angeles

Chinese women in prostitution in the United States began as soon as the first wave of Chinese immigrants arrived in the 1850s. By the late nineteenth century, authorities claimed that San Francisco's Chinatown was a major commercial sex center frequented by both white and Chinese men.[27] Scores of police officers testified at the 1877 U.S. Senate hearings on Chinese immigration that hundreds of Chinese women were imported into California to work as prostitutes in a community overrun with brothels.[28] The predicaments of these women were vividly described in the biographies of Donaldina Cameron, a missionary who spent most of her life rescuing Chinese prostitutes from the hands of the tongs—community-based adult organizations that controlled gambling, prostitution, and the opium trade.[29]

Prior to the mid-1980s, most Asian prostitutes in the United States were believed to be Korean women who had entered the country through fraudulent marriages to U.S. soldiers stationed in South Korea.[30] Then in the mid-1980s, there was an increase in the number of Taiwanese prostitutes working in the United States.[31] However, after the Immigration and Naturalization Service (INS) dismantled a Taiwanese prostitution ring in 1986, it tightened up on the issuance of tourist visas to young Taiwanese women, and the number of Taiwanese prostitutes declined. This void was, however, soon filled by Chinese women from Malaysia and China.

Currently, there are Asian sex venues in almost every American city, large and small. Women from South Korea, Thailand, Japan, Taiwan, Malaysia, and China are considered to be the more prominent groups, and they are almost always working only in indoor sex markets. A predominant venue is a massage parlor located inside a single family house in a residential area or a business office hidden inside a small commercial building. Over the past three decades, the media often reported police raids of Asian sex establishments in San Francisco, Los Angeles, Las Vegas, Atlanta, Dallas, Houston, Chicago, Washington, D.C., Philadelphia, Atlantic City, Boston, and New York. According to a U.S. government report, of the estimated 45,000 to 50,000 women and children trafficked into the United States every year, approximately 30,000 were estimated to be from Southeast Asia, especially China, Thailand, and Vietnam.[32]

Many Chinese massage parlors, hair salons, clubs, and hostess bars in Los Angeles and the surrounding areas (i.e., Monterey Park, San Gabriel, Rosemead, Alhambra, Rowland Heights) are operating as fronts for commercial sex. Many brothels (called "houses" by our subjects in Los Angeles) also place their ads in the local Chinese newspapers. The Asian sex market in the greater Los Angeles area was once dominated by females from South Korea and Taiwan. As more and more men and women from China have been arriving in Los Angeles since the late 1980s, however, the number of Chinese women in the area's sex business has also significantly increased.

Sixteen Chinese women were interviewed in Los Angeles County, most of them working in San Gabriel, Monterey Park, Rosemead, and Rowland Heights (see Table 4.8). Compared to the subjects in Asia, subjects in Los Angeles were older (with an average age of 37.6), more likely to be married or divorced, and predominantly from the northeastern provinces of China. Chinese people in Los Angeles often joke about how old prostitutes from China are; a Chinese lawyer told a reporter that he once represented an arrested Chinese woman who was 74.[33] Most women arrive in the United States with a tourist visa, a business visa, or as the spouse of a U.S. citizen.

Joey, a 36-year-old married woman with a 10-year-old daughter explained how she arrived in the United States and later entered prostitution:

In China, government officials are so corrupt, there is no hope for ordinary people. But I just happened to know a document procurer who said he can help me come to America, so I came. This company first helped me go to Europe and Japan as a tourist. After I had those records, there was a chance that I would be able to get a U.S. visa. If you have never been overseas, it is not possible for you to come here because U.S. officials would think that you are not going to go back once you are in the U.S. It took about a year to obtain the U.S. visa. When I went to the U.S. Embassy for an interview, there were altogether three of us. The other two were men: one was the director of a factory and the other, the deputy director of that factory. I was their secretary. In fact, it was all fake. We said we were going to Las Vegas to participate in a business exhibition. We flew from Shanghai to Los Angeles, and then we did show up briefly at the exhibition in Las Vegas. A man in Los Angeles who was working for the company in China helped in the process. I came to the U.S. with a business visa. Altogether it cost me more than $30,000 to come to America, including the expenses for the trips to Japan and Europe. After my business visa expired in three months, I found a church to help me to apply for political asylum—I said that I was persecuted in China because I was a Christian. I am expecting to receive my green card anytime now.

After I arrived in Los Angeles, I stayed in a "family hotel." At first, I worked as a busgirl in a restaurant. I worked for seven days and I quit because, one, it was hard work, and two, the men in the kitchen were sexually harassing me all the time. I can't work under such circumstances! After

Table 4.8. Xiaojies in Los Angeles (N = 16)

Case no.	Name	Age	Marital status	Visa	Travel fee ($)	Began to sell sex in	Current venue	Monthly income ($)
118	Na Na	28	Single	Tourist	40,000	Los Angeles	Home	6,600
119	Joey	36	Married	Business	30,000	Los Angeles	House	8,000
120	Mei Juan	46	Divorced	Missing	Missing	Los Angeles	Hotel	Missing
121	Kelly	38	Divorced	Marriage	N/A	Los Angeles	House	10,000
122	Lisa	50	Married	Business	N/A	Los Angeles	House	3,000
123	Ming Ming	33	Divorced	Tourist	20,000	Los Angeles	House	12,000
124	Angel	36	Single	F5 (Family sponsored)	N/A	Los Angeles	House	13,500
125	Sarah	34	Married	Marriage	N/A	Los Angeles	Massage parlor	4,500
126	Helen	34	Single	Business	30,000	Beijing	House	8,800
127	Anna	42	Married	Business	N/A	Los Angeles	House	13,000
128	Tina	44	Divorced	Marriage	N/A	Los Angeles	House	4,000
129	Laura	38	Single	Student	N/A	Los Angeles	House	7,000
130	Niko	39	Divorce	Business	18,750	Los Angeles	House	4,000
131	Mandy	Missing	Divorced	Family visit	7,500	Los Angeles	House	5,000
132	Linda	35	Married	Business	6,875	Los Angeles	House	12,500
133	Wang Jing	31	Married	Fake marriage	60,000	Los Angeles	House	5,500

I quit the job at the restaurant, I called a massage parlor. I said I would like to do pure massage, but the female owner asked me to go over to her place first. After I got there, she told me if I do only massage, I am not going to make much money and then she began to talk me into doing more. After I worked there for a few days, I began to do "full set" (119).

Na Na, a 28-year-old college graduate from Dalian (in China's northeast Liaoning Province) who entered the United States as a tourist, described how she paid about $40,000 to come to America:

At one point, a friend came back from the United States and I asked her how she went there. She said a company helped her, and then she introduced me to people from that company. They said I was too young to go to the United States. They can only help people who are 35 or above. At that point, I was only 25 or 26. Later on, they said if I really want to go, they still can help me but I need to pay significantly more than other people. They charge most people $26,500, but I must pay an extra $13,500 because they must change all the information in my household registration and come up with an entire new set of personal information. All the new documents will show that I am more than 30. That's how I was able to come to the United States. The company is also located in Dalian. (118)

Of all the subjects in Los Angeles who had to pay someone to help them go to America, Wang Jing, a 31-year-old married woman from Fuzhou (Fujian), paid the most: $60,000. She said she came to the United States in 1999 after a fraudulent marriage with an American citizen, and at the time of the interview she was a permanent resident.

Some of the subjects in Los Angeles arrived in the United States as legal immigrants and so they did not have to pay anyone to create fake documents or marriages. For example, Angel, a 36-year-old single woman from Dalian (Liaoning), came to the United States after her sister, a U.S. citizen, sponsored her as an immigrant:

After I graduated from a two-year college, I started a small advertisement company and I made quite a lot of money. I had a boyfriend for a few years but we split up later. Before I came here, I sold my business and came here with more than $200,000. My sister helped me to immigrate to America. After I arrived in LA, I opened a restaurant and invested more than $100,000. When my partner, the chef, left, the business went downhill. I sold the restaurant and I lost about $60,000. At that point, I became very nervous about my financial situation, and when I saw a newspaper advertisement claiming I can make $20,000 a month, I went to work in a house. (124)

Kelly, a 38-year-old woman from Beijing, told us how she arrived in the United States after her divorce in China:

After I graduated from college, I worked as a teacher at an elementary school and made about $350 a month. I married when I was 22 and gave birth many years later. My husband was a neighbor. After we married, we found out we have very different personalities. Not long after our child was born, we divorced. He had the child and I had the house. Later, my ex-husband and my daughter immigrated to the United States and lived in Los Angeles. At that point, I realized I also wanted to leave China, so I found a white man via the internet. He was in his 50s and lived in Irvine [Orange County]. After we chatted for a while over the internet, he came to Beijing to visit me and very soon we were married. I did not like him at all, but in order to come to America, I married him. I lived with him for more than a year, and then we broke up. (121)

Unlike women we interviewed in Asia, only one in the Los Angeles sample was a *xiaojie* before arriving in the United States. However, like women in Taiwan who were predominantly working for one type of business, namely an escort service, almost all the subjects in Los Angeles were also employed in one type of sex venue, in the LA case, a house or brothel. A house is simply an apartment, a townhouse, or a single-family house that has been converted into a brothel.

New York

New York City has long been the base of Chinese gangs and organized crime in America[34] and it also has the largest Chinatown in North America.[35] Since the late 1980s, tens of thousands of Fujianese smuggled from China into the United States settled in New York City.[36] The Asian sex business in New York City has always been dominated by South Korean women catering to both Asian and American customers. But as the Chinese are now the fastest growing Asian group in the United States, Chinese commercial sex in this country is also expanding rapidly. Many sex establishments involving Chinese women—in the forms of massage parlors, nightclubs, karaoke lounges, and brothels—have been set up in New York City and New Jersey, and some of them are becoming increasingly aggressive in marketing their services to the public.

We interviewed sixteen Chinese women in New York City and northern New Jersey (see Table 4.9).

Like the subjects in Los Angeles, women we interviewed in New York/New Jersey were on average older than those in Asia; all of them in their thirties or forties and even fifties, and only one had never been married. This could be due to the fact that young women in China, unless they are coming to the United States as students or as legal immigrants, are unlikely to obtain a U.S. visa. Older women can claim that they are key employees of a private company or senior officials of a government unit and apply for a business visa to come to America. Or they can say that they wish to come to the United States to visit their adult children or relatives. Ah Zhen, a 48-year-old married woman from Shenyang (Liaoning) arrived in the United States with a family visit visa, at a cost of $21,000. According to her:

> I hoped that I could come here to make more money so that I could buy a house and a car for my son when he got married. I asked an agency to apply for a visa for me and I got the visa very soon. I applied for a family visa which means that I had a son in the U.S. and I would visit him, even though my only son is in China. I went to the American embassy in Beijing for an interview. The interviewer was a white man who spoke Chinese. He did not ask me anything except whether I had been abroad before. I told him that I had been in Europe. He asked me why there was no stamp on my passport if I had been there. I told him that I used an official passport when I went to Europe. Then he asked whether my son had been back to China. I did not understand until he asked me this question three times. I told him that my son had not come back since he went to America. One month later I got the visa. I flew to Los Angeles and the agency arranged to have someone meet me at the airport and help me go to New York. (108)

Ah Jiao, a 38-year-old married woman from Tianjin who was working at a massage parlor in New Jersey at the time of the interview, described how she entered the United States as a tourist and then simply left her group:

> I wanted to come to the U.S. since 2002, but I did not have the money to pay for the trip and so it was just a dream. Later, my sister loaned me the money. I applied for a passport in 2002 when I began to think about going overseas. A travel agency in Tianjin said they could help, but they required that I have records of going abroad twice. Therefore I went abroad twice in

Table 4.9. Xiaojies in New York and New Jersey (N = 16)

Case no.	Name	Age	Marital status	Visa	Travel fee ($)	Began to sell sex in	Current venue	Monthly income ($)
102	Lily	36	Married	Business	6,250	New York	Massage parlor	6,000
103	Cheryl	35	Separated	Business	N/A	New York	Hotel	15,000
104	Mona	34	Divorced	Marriage	N/A	New Jersey	Massage parlor	5,000
105	Ah Jiao	38	Married	Tourist	26,250	Tianjin	Massage parlor	5,000
106	Cindy	34	Married	Business	7,500	New York	Massage parlor	6,000
107	Mei Ling	38	Married	Business	15,000	New Jersey	Massage parlor	Missing
108	Ah Zhen	48	Married	Family visit	21,000	New York	Home	7,000
109	Mary	33	Divorced	Business	N/A	New York	Massage parlor	5,000
110	Jenny	45	Married	Business	20,000	New Jersey	Massage parlor	5,000
111	Yao Qian	55	Married	Family visit	15,000	New York	Massage parlor	4,000
112	Bo Bo	38	Divorced	Business	18,750	New Jersey	Massage parlor	4,000
113	Ying Hong	37	Single	Business	11,250	New York	Home	5,800
114	Eva	43	Divorced	Business	25,000	New York	Home	4,500
115	Ellen	32	Divorced	Tourist	7,500	Dongguang	Brothel	5,000
116	Mi Mi	33	Married	Student	2,500	New York	Brothel	6,000
117	Jia Jia	41	Married	Smuggled via Mexico	73,000	New York	Home	4,500

order to come here. It cost me more than $1,250 to go to Europe and also cost me a lot of money to go to Singapore and Malaysia. It cost me an extra $400 in order to have a particular stamp on my passport.

Then the travel agency applied for a business visa for me to come to the U.S., but it was rejected; then the agency applied for a tourist visa for me and it was issued. There were more than 20 people on the tour going to the U.S., three of them (including me) deciding not to go back to China after arriving in the U.S. (105)

Mi Mi, a 33-year-old married woman with a bachelor's degree in engineering explained how she arrived in America with an F-1 student visa and then became involved in commercial sex not long after:

> I found a company that told me they could get me out of China very quickly. Of course, I needed to take the GRE and TOEFL exams myself, even though I need not have very high scores. They helped me find a school in the U.S. where I could learn English and take a preparatory course. It was agreed by both sides that for their service, I will pay them $2,500. I must buy the air ticket myself and pay the tuition out of my own pocket. I came with an F-1 student visa and now it has expired. I attended the school for only one semester and I paid quite a lot of money for tuition.
>
> At school, I came to know quite a few Chinese students and they all wore name-brand clothes and acted like they were very rich. I pretty much know what their profession was. After quitting school, I worked in a restaurant and made about $2,000 a month. The job was hard and humiliating. So I decided to become a *xiaojie*. (116)

Jia Jia, a 41-year-old married woman from Fuzhou (Fujian), arrived in America in August 2006 like many other Fuzhounese, by crossing the U.S.-Mexican border:

> I had been trying to come to the U.S. since 1996. I tried and failed three times. The first time I was turned back in Beijing. The second time I was arrested in Korea and sent back to China. The third time I was trying to go to Bangkok via Burma, but I was arrested in Jinghong, Yunnan Province. You can say I waited for ten years to get here. This time, I entered the U.S. via Mexico climbing mountains. At one point, I was hidden inside a truck with a Chinese man, and we could not even move. And the engine was right beneath us, and it was hot as hell. We were tortured for more

than seven hours like that. Later, we walked and climbed mountains. I will never forget that experience. I traveled for fifty days to get here because I was stuck in Venezuela for more than a month. Now, I am applying for political asylum. (117)

The majority of the women we interviewed in the New York metropolitan area entered the United States with a business visa. Ying Hong, a 37-year-old single woman from Shenyang (Liaoning), explained how she came to the United States:

> I came here with an official Chinese passport and a business visa. The people who organized the delegation added a few extra members and then they sold these extra quotas to others who want to come to the U.S. I did not buy my slot directly from the delegation organizer; if I had done that, it would have been a lot cheaper. In fact, the slot had gone through several intermediaries. I agreed that I would pay $11,250, and that the entire payment will be made once I obtain all the travel documents.
>
> There were almost twenty members in the delegation. We flew from Beijing to Los Angeles, and then to other American cities before landing in New York. Once in New York, I left a note with the head of the delegation that I would go back to China on my own later. It was necessary because I did not want him to go looking for me. I didn't want him to report the incident to the police, either. Now I am a visa overstayer. (113)

Shenzhen, China

We originally did not plan to interview any subjects in China, but after we had completed all the interviews in the other nine sites, we decided to interview some subjects there to give us a better understanding of prostitution and sex trafficking in China itself. This might, we thought, help explain why so many Chinese women were going overseas to work in commercial sex. Eventually we traveled to Shenzhen, a major urban center bordering Hong Kong in the coastal area of southeast China. There we interviewed a number of *xiaojies*, sex ring operators, and law enforcement authorities. Shenzhen was chosen not only because it has one of the largest sex sectors in China, but also because many Chinese women working overseas either go through Shenzhen to go abroad or they used to work in Shenzhen before going overseas. Moreover, many of these women use Shenzhen as a temporary stopping off place while they are juggling between work (abroad), rest (Shenzhen), and family (usually a hometown in the rural hinterland). We also went to Changan, a city about a hundred miles from Shenzhen, because it has been reported that prostitution is even more open and rampant there than in Shenzhen. We also interviewed a couple of other women in Fuzhou while we were there to interview an experienced *xiaojie* who had already been to Taiwan six times.

With an average age of just over 24, the women we interviewed in China were significantly younger than the women we interviewed in the overseas sites. Moreover, women in China were predominantly single. And with an average income of $1,250 a month, they made a lot less than the women who were overseas, even though they were younger (see Table 4.10).

In Shenzhen, as in many urban centers in China, there are a number of open-air sex markets. One such market, called the XXX Village (name omitted), is conveniently located just a minute's walk from the Luohu Checkpoint, where many men from Hong Kong can go to buy sex and return to work or home in a few hours.[37] The village is dotted with hair salons (*falang*) where sexual transactions are conducted on the premises. There is also a block deep inside the village where large numbers of young women, female pimps, and sex buyers can be seen sizing up one another, talking to one another, and going to a nearby rental house for paid sex. The young women there charge about $14 per date; the women's share is generally $10 and the pimp gets $4.

Another open-air sex market is located in the downtown area of Shenzhen, only several blocks away from the above-mentioned village. This one is more expensive; women here charge $27 to $40 per session. Like the women in the village, women in the downtown area also do not solicit business on their own; there are many male and female pimps who are sourcing clients for these women. According to Shirley, a 20-year-old single woman from Nanchang (Sichuan):

> I had many pimps, more than 20. There are so many that I do not know for sure how many people are soliciting clients for me. At any rate, if I see you [a pimp], and you see me, and if we think we are both alright, we exchange phone numbers and if you have business, you call me. It's as simple as that. Everyday, approximately between 8 and 10 in the evening I will be arriving in this intersection. Then I will be standing there with other girls and the pimps. When men pass by, we girls won't approach them; the pimps will do the solicitation for us. Even if men want to talk to us, we won't pay attention to them because the pimps will come up to talk to the men right away. Our relationships with the pimps are not that good; we argue often because of money. They do not keep their word. (160)

Table 4.10. Xiaojies in China (N = 15)

Case no.	Name	Age	Marital status	Interview site	Began to sell sex in	Current venue	Monthly income ($)
150	Xiao Meng	18	Single	Shenzhen	Shenzhen	Brothel	860
151	Cai Hung	24	Single	Shenzhen	Shenzhen	Sauna	800
152	Ah Xia	35	Divorced	Shenzhen	Changchun	Falang	Missing
153	Cola	25	Single	Shenzhen	Shenzhen	Falang	Missing
154	Shuang Shuang[a]	27	Single	Shenzhen	Harbin	Sauna	Missing
155	Ah Yi[b]	19	Single	Shenzhen	Ningbo	Sauna	2,200
156	Jing Jing	30	Single	Shenzhen	Shenzhen	Sauna	1,000
157	Rosa	21	Single	Shenzhen	Shenzhen	Street—with mommy	587[c]
158	Julie[a]	21	Single	Shenzhen	Haikuo	Street—with mommy	1,470
159	Sha Sha	31	Single	Shenzhen	Fuzhou	KTV	1,760
160	Shirley	20	Single	Shenzhen	Shenzhen	Street—with mommy	950
161	Hua Hua	23	Single	Changan	Changan	Sauna	1,600
162	Lan Lan	21	Single	Changan	Changan	Sauna	1,700
163	Tian Tian	31	Single	Fuzhou	Yingkuo, Liaoling	KTV	Missing
164	Winnie	22	Single	Fuzhou	Fuzhou	KTV	800

[a] Domestic trafficked victim
[b] Controlled by a chickenhead
[c] Part-time
Mean age, 24.5; percent single, 87; mean monthly income, $1,247

Besides walking the street, *xiaojies* in Shenzhen may also work in the many indoor venues called *xiuxianhuisuo* (recreation clubs), *xiuxianzhongxin* (recreation centers) or *shuiliaoguan* (water therapy clubs), saunas, or spas where men go to have a bath, a massage, and if they like, sex. In Changan, there are places called "sauna stores" and they are somewhat different from "recreation centers." According to the *xiaojies* we talked to in Changan, "sauna establishments" are more expensive than "recreation centers" because workers in the sauna places are required to serve their customers in a more elaborate way, similar to the high-end sauna establishments in Macau. Lan Lan, a 21-year-old single woman from Nanchong (Sichuan Province) explained how the place where she was working operated:

> Not long ago, I went to work in a sauna with my ex-boyfriend's sister. We know that working in a sauna venue is very challenging, but to make more money, we were willing to sacrifice. The room cost $25, and the service fee is $53, $66, $80, or $106. Services are all the same, it is just that different groups of girls are charging different prices. The tall ones with good features and big breasts are the ones who can ask for $106. In our place, only 3 to 4 are in the $106 range. When a customer comes in, a mommy will bring three girls for him to choose from. I was trained for nine days before they let me start working. During the training period, I was disgusted everyday. I can't eat, and I was vomiting all the time. That's because we have to learn all kinds of services, including all the licking and blowing of a man's entire body. (162)

Besides providing sex services in *falangs* or brothels, seeing clients in hotels, or working in the sauna/spa establishments, many women in China also work in nightclubs or KTVs as *sanpei xiaojie* (hostesses)—literally young women who accompany men in three ways—alcohol consumption, dancing, and singing. Some hostesses offer sexual services inside or outside the premises for an additional fee.[38]

Whatever their individual differences, in each of the sites we studied there was clearly a culture of tolerance for commercial sex. Whatever the legal proscriptions and the official postures with respect to those proscriptions, there was an underground business in sex that had to be more or less clandestine, depending upon the particular political and enforcement contingencies. The legal status of commercial sex (what is permitted and where); the presence of potential buyers (businessmen, military, etc.); having tourist attractions; the national and local law enforcement policies and practices (how vigorously the laws are enforced and whether there is corruption, etc.); the

society's governing moral philosophy and traditions (two sites are predominantly Muslim); and the specific nature of and venues for commercial sex
—all play a role in shaping the culture of tolerance in these cities. As can be
discerned from the stories of the women we interviewed, other factors that
may come into play include geography, history, traditions, laws, language,
and many other influences. But perhaps most importantly, the normalization
of commercial sex exemplified in these sites makes it an acceptable option
for women seeking to better their economic condition.

5

The Sex Markets

When Chinese women go overseas to engage in prostitution, there are a number of ways for them to make money. They can, for example, work independently, meaning they do not have to rely on anyone else. Although at first blush this may seem improbable, given that they are in a foreign country and engaging in an illicit activity, the women with whom we spoke describe how this is indeed possible.

In this chapter, we will expand upon the theme of the cultural and economic aspects of prostitution. Again relying upon the words and experiences of the *xiaojies* themselves, we want to portray and illustrate specifically how the various commercial sex venues operate. We especially want to reiterate that, with some few exceptions such as in the case of child prostitution or pornography, we believe that it is via these particular venues that the profits from commercial sex are largely accrued. If the end goal of sex trafficking is profit, which we think is undeniable, we should see some connection between sex trafficking and these various venues.

Women interviewed in this study, whether independent or self-employed, typically work in one of the following four settings.

- On the street. In this venue, a woman solicits business on the street, and then provides sexual services in her apartment, or a nearby hotel, or at the customer's place. A Chinese woman working overseas is unlikely to engage in specific sexual transactions in a public place, a car, or outdoors because of the fear of detection and arrest. Although being a streetwalker is by definition being publicly exposed, a woman must be very careful and subtle in soliciting customers so as not to attract unwanted attention. We found streetwalkers to be most likely in the streets of old residential areas of Hong Kong and Macau, and in the Chinatowns of Kuala Lumpur and Singapore.

- Restaurants and other public places. Here a woman solicits customers in a restaurant, a tea shop, a bar, or a food court by approaching men and asking them if they want her companionship. While drinking or eating, the woman plays the role of a hostess and tries to create a lively and pleasant atmosphere. Paid sex after the drink or the meal may or may not follow, but the woman receives or expects to receive a tip in any event. This form of approach occurs especially in the restaurants and tea shops in the red-light district of Singapore, at a food court in Kuala Lumpur, and in the Chinatown of Bangkok.

- Hotels. A woman rents a hotel room, solicits business in the hotel lobby, and then sells sex in her room. Neither the women nor the hotel management advertise the availability of sex services. Instead, through word of mouth, local people (and in some places repeat foreign visitors) know which hotels to go to if they want to buy sex. This is the kind of street knowledge (knowing where commercial sex is available) to which we referred earlier, and it is a critical link in the demand/supply chain. In this type of arrangement, there are no formal agreements between the hotel management and the women. In essence, hotel management cares only that the women pay for their room; beyond that the women are free to work as they please. Although somewhat similar to the home-based women (to be discussed later), the hotel-based women do not have as much autonomy. This particular kind of hotel-based commercial sex is particularly prevalent in certain hotels in Macau and Malaysia.

- At home. A woman rents a place (an apartment, a townhouse, or a single-family house), advertises her business in a newspaper or on the internet, answers the phone herself, and provides sexual services in her home. Unlike the independent street prostitutes mentioned above, she does not venture out of her place to seek clients. She takes care of every aspect of her business herself, and her only major expense is the rent and advertisement fee. This type of business is called a "one-woman apartment" in Hong Kong, a "house" in Los Angeles, and an "apartment" in New York.

Of the 149 overseas Chinese women we interviewed, 36 (24%) identified themselves as independent and self-employed *xiaojies*. Of these 36 women, 4 worked the streets, 16 solicited their business in restaurants, 8 waited for clients in hotel lobbies, and 8 worked from their homes or apartments. Our data demonstrate that selling sex overseas does not have to be particularly organized, and indeed can be simply a series of one-to-one interactions. Further, women can enter and exit certain sex markets at will without having to gain the approval or assistance of criminals or anyone else. Under those circumstances, these women are unlikely to be exploited or victimized by operators in the local sex business, not least because they have little or no contact with any sex ring operators or local criminals in the destination country.

If she does not choose to work alone, a woman can work in collaboration with a mommy who will solicit business for her or with a local chickenhead who will look after her. This type of arrangement is a kind of partnership. There are two such types of partnerships, the first being one in which a mommy is the solicitor: To avoid being arrested for seeking customers on the street, some women may ask one or more mommies to recruit customers for them. The mommy will charge a customer according to her judgment of how rich and anxious for sex the customer is, and the woman who provides the sexual services will get only a standard fee. She may, however, keep any tips. This type of arrangement exists, for example, on the streets of Hong Kong's tourist areas and in certain restaurants in Jakarta.

In the second type of partnership, a local man agrees to act as a protector from the police and difficult customers. This local man, working in concert with other local men who play the same role, will keep an eye out for the police, and will make sure that the woman he is working with is in and out of a hotel within a certain time when she is with a customer. The women decide how much they will charge their customers per session; they need only to pay the local man a certain amount of money per transaction or per day. This form is most prevalent on the streets of Hong Kong and Singapore.

In yet a third form, the women work for a group of people or an establishment as employees. In this type of arrangement, a woman is most likely to be working for a nightclub/KTV/flower hall, a sauna/spa/massage parlor, a brothel/apartment/house/*falang*, or an escort agency. In the nightclub, KTV, or flower hall venues, which are indoors, women are called hostesses or "public relations officers," and they drink, sing, chat, or dance with customers in private rooms. Some customers may also want these women to take drugs with them. In some of these venues, customers are allowed to have sex with the hostesses without having to leave the establishment.[1] More often, though, the customer is required to take the hostess out if he wants sexual services. Chinese women are most likely to work in this fashion in nightclubs in Malaysia and Indonesia, in nightclubs and KTV lounges in Singapore, and in the flower halls in Thailand.

The saunas or spas are places where men go to have a bath, a sauna, and a massage; but most men want to buy sex as well. The size of the establishment and the prices they charge vary significantly. Some massage parlors in New York may have only two female workers at any given time, whereas the saunas in Macau and the spas in Jakarta might have more than a hundred. Prices can range from $50 to $250 per visit.

The massage parlors are actually usually a simpler and smaller version of the sauna or spa. A customer can take a bath and have a massage in one of these parlors, but he can also buy sex if he wants. The massage parlors have only a few women, and the facilities are usually sparsely decorated and furnished.

The brothels, apartments, or houses, unlike the venues described above, do not provide any entertainment or massages. Their only commodity is sex. And unlike the self-employed, home-based brothels, these locations normally have two or more women working at any given time. This particular form is called a *malan* (horse barn) or brothel in Hong Kong and Macau, an apartment in New York, a house in Los Angeles, and a *falang* (hair salon) in China.

The final venue form is the escort service. Here an escort agency delivers women to wherever the customers are—mostly to hotels or motels where they are staying, or to a flat operated by a pimp who has connections to the escort agency, or to the customer's home. Chinese women in Taiwan, Malaysia, and New York are relatively active in the escort service business.

Why do Chinese women work in such a variety of different sex markets? According to the interviews we had with our subjects, where a woman works depends on many factors. First, women are most likely to work at the very venue where the returned *xiaojie* who helped them to go overseas is working. For a woman to go somewhere else to work is not impossible, but it can be difficult. Second, younger women are more likely to work for a sauna/spa (where the average age was 24), or for an escort agency (with an average age of 25). Older women are more likely to solicit business in restaurants on their own (where the average age was 37), or to work from their own places (average age 38). According to our respondents, other criteria include having a "pretty face" (more likely to work in nightclubs or KTVs); a "good figure" (more likely to work in saunas and spas); and "good social and verbal skills" (more likely to work for a nightclub or a KTV). Those women who prefer to keep things simple are more likely to work in a brothel. If a woman does not like drinking or using drugs, then it is almost impossible for her to survive in a nightclub or a KTV lounge because the hostesses are expected to drink or use drugs quite heavily.

The Independent

The Independent: Street-Based

According to Ronald Weitzer, a sociology professor, "in street prostitution, the initial transaction occurs in a public place (a sidewalk, park, truck stop), while the sex act takes place in either a public or private setting (alley, park, vehicle, hotel, etc.)"[2] In many major cities in Asia, Chinese women can be seen soliciting business on the streets. The obvious nature of this soliciting varies from one location to another. In some places, the police generally look the other way unless there is a specific complaint to which they may respond. Street prostitution is tolerated in some city neighborhoods, but not others. In some places, the police are paid to look away. In most places with streetwalkers, the pimps keep an eye out for the police.

Some of the women with whom we spoke had been assisted by someone (for a fee) when they were trying to go overseas and some were not, but when they arrived in the destination country, their entry into prostitution was not aided by a third party. For example, when Chinese women arrive in Kuala Lumpur with their friends who are already involved in commercial sex there, they rent a room in Kuala Lumpur's Chinatown and then solicit business on the street near where they live. They are not employed by anyone; nor do they need to pay protection money to local men or share their income with anyone. Ah Juan, a 28-year-old married Sichuanese with a 4-year-old son back in China, described how it works: "I solicit business in this street. After I strike a deal with a client, we go to a nearby hotel to have sex. Customers pay $6 for a hotel room and pay me $14 to $23. I keep all the money the customers pay me. The service is simple and quick. I have about 10 customers a day. I start to work around 10 a.m. and work until 11 to 12 p.m." (21).

These self-employed women are able to keep all the money the customers pay them; the downside is that they have to solicit their business on their own and have to do all the negotiations themselves. Very often, these negotiations are time-consuming and frustrating. For example, a conversation we overheard between a potential customer and a woman went like this:

> MAN: Is it true that one session means one hour?
> WOMAN: Yes!

MAN: Can I do it twice within an hour?
WOMAN: No, unless if you pay extra.
MAN: Forget about it. (He walked away.)

Another potential customer, a Chinese Malay, carried out the following dialogue with a woman:

MAN: Do you provide overnight service?
WOMAN: Yes, but when do you want to start and when is it going to end?
MAN: We can go now [about 7 p.m.], and you will return tomorrow morning.
WOMAN: What time in the morning?
MAN: Well, I can't tell you exactly when, it's going to end in the morning.
WOMAN: Ok, but you need to pay me first.
MAN: I will pay you when we get to my place.
WOMAN: No, that's not possible.
MAN: Goodbye.

At the time when we were conducting our fieldwork in 2007 and 2008, there were also women from China working on the streets of Chinatowns in Bangkok, Singapore, and Jakarta. Like the street prostitutes in Kuala Lumpur's Chinatown, the women in the Chinese communities of Bangkok, Singapore, and Jakarta appeared to be self-employed. As a result of police crackdowns, however, the number of prostitutes on the street was relatively small in these places, and the women there were also very cautious. Police crackdowns appear to be rather haphazard. If there are complaints, or embarrassing incidents, or certain political developments, then the police may pay attention and clean up the streets for a while. All those in the commercial sex business know that these crackdowns are usually temporary, an occupational hazard but not a permanent one.

Streetwalkers are often depicted in the prostitution literature as being homeless drug addicts who provide sex services in cars and parks to a rather violent group of men.[3] Ronald Weitzer characterized street prostitutes as follows:

Many street prostitutes are runways who end up in a new locale with no resources and little recourse but to engage in some kind of criminal activity—whether theft, drug dealing, or selling sex. Many street workers, both runaways and others, experience abysmal working conditions and are involved in "survival sex." They sell sex out of dire necessity or to support a drug habit. Many use addictive drugs; work and live in crime-ridden areas; are socially isolated and disconnected from support services, risk contracting and transmitting sexual diseases; are exploited and abused by pimps, and are vulnerable to being assaulted, robbed, raped, or killed on the streets.[4]

From our research, this characterization of street prostitutes does not fit the majority of the Chinese women who solicit business in the streets of Asian cities. Most of the street women we met in Asia were adult women who did not use drugs. Their descriptions and our perceptions of their involvement in commercial sex did not make it out to be as risky and difficult as one, including us initially, might think. There are certainly risks—of arrest or from difficult customers—but the women considered these to be risks worth taking in terms of the economic payoffs. This is evidence of the "bounded" rational choices made by the women, to which we referred earlier.

The Independent: Restaurant-Based

As well as on the streets, a self-employed woman who sells sex may also solicit business in public places such as restaurants and bars. For example, some of the restaurants in Bangkok's Chinatown are frequented by men and women who go there to buy or sell sex. In general, these restaurants are small, rather dirty, and do not have particularly good food. The male customers are mostly retired Chinese Thais who belong to a particular network. Zhao Tong, a 24-year-old divorced woman from Harbin recalled what happened after her arrival in Bangkok:

> Three days after I got here, the person who picked us [a group of women] up at the airport took us to work at XXX [a restaurant in Bangkok's Chinatown, name omitted]. We were shocked to find out how shabby the place was and how old the customers were. But now that we were here, we might as well work and try to make some money to go home. I did not *chutai*, just *zuotai*. Two months later, someone took us to XXX KTV [name omitted] to work and we felt much better after we began to work there. (64)

When our respondents said they "went to work" in these restaurants in Bangkok's Chinatown, they were not really employed by these restaurants to entertain customers, nor were there private rooms, as in the nightclubs and KTV lounges, for men and women to engage in intimate interactions. When local Chinese men go to these restaurants, they expect to encounter women from China, and so they are in general willing to buy these women lunch or dinner and to tip them after the eating, drinking, and chatting are over. If a man and a woman are both interested in engaging in a commercial sexual transaction, they will go to a nearby hotel. Most of the women told us they were reluctant to engage in fleeting sexual transactions with male customers in these restaurants because they were more interested in finding stable "boyfriends" who could support them on a regular basis. The male customers in these restaurants usually belong to a close network of people who know each other and thus they will gossip about the women. The customers are often old and not very attractive, and according to our respondents, tend to be cheap.

Besides the restaurants in Bangkok, some of the restaurants and roadside tea shops in Singapore, Jakarta, and Kuala Lumpur are also points of contact for local Chinese men and women from China. For example, some men go to a food court in Kuala Lumpur explicitly for the purpose of buying sex, and they are most likely to be seen wandering around its periphery. Those who want to eat first and maybe purchase sex only if they meet someone they really like, will find a table, order food, and then wait for a woman to approach them.

Most self-employed women, especially those who work the streets or work out of their hotel rooms or homes told us that they preferred the kind of workplace where they can engage in sexual intercourse with their clients right after the initial encounter, without having to accompany them in drinking, eating, or singing. Rong Rong, a 33-year-old divorcee from Chongqing with an 8-year old son, explained why she stopped working at a nightclub and instead worked the streets of Singapore's Chinatown:

> My classmate brought me to the nightclub where she was working. I worked for twenty days at the nightclub and then came over here to Chinatown to work the streets. I did not like the nightclub because I was not free; walking the streets allows you the freedom to decide when to work. Besides, in the nightclub, customers touch you everywhere, and it gets very dirty. I can't stand it. Instead of having a man moving his fingers all over my body in a nightclub, I would rather go to a hotel and have sex with him. I make about the same amount of money [about $140 to $200 a day] as I did working in a nightclub or walking the streets. (6)

The Independent: Hotel-Based

Many Chinese women also provide sexual services in the cheap, small hotels that dot the back streets of Asian cities. For example, in an old section of

Macau that is only several blocks away from the newly-built, American-owned hotels and casinos such as the Wynn and the Sands, there are many small hotels that are essentially brothels. Women from the mainland, after crossing the border at the Gongbei Checkpoint, simply take a taxi to one of these hotels, check in, and then start working right away by soliciting business in the hotel lobby. Most customers are local men, but men from China, Hong Kong, and Taiwan, as well as Koreans, Japanese, and even Westerners, may show up at these hotels to buy sex. According to Yin Yin, a 24-year-old from Changde (Hunan):

> All the rooms in this hotel are occupied by us. My room is the smallest, but others are not that much bigger than mine. The rent is $40 a day. If a man picks me, I will bring him to my room to provide sex. The maximum amount of time a customer has is 30 minutes per session. (86)[5]

Because these women live and work in the same hotel, and because they are working for themselves, it is up to them to decide how many hours they want to work and when. Xiao Tao, a 20-year-old from Changde (Hunan Province) told us:

> I get up at 10 in the morning and go outside [of my room] at 11 to wait for clients. I will call delivery when I am hungry; we do not leave the hotel. I stop working at 2 a.m. I won't see clients even if they knock on my door after I go to sleep. Some girls only sleep two hours a day. They wait for business most of the time. They are very aggressive. (85)

Yin Yin, the subject quoted above, said she worked from 3 in the afternoon to 6 in the morning. Other subjects said they worked only during the day to avoid the police. A 24-year-old woman from Huangmei (Hubei) said: "I go downstairs around 8 or 9 a.m. and stop working at 4 p.m. or 5 p.m. Police are most likely to come around between 5 p.m. and 10 p.m., and that's why I work only during the daytime" (99).

Subjects in those small Macau hotels rarely ventured outside the hotels when they were not working. This was mainly to keep themselves out of trouble with the police and other potential sources of trouble such as local thugs. The PRC women normally come directly to the hotel after they enter Macau, and they stay inside the hotel until they return to China or go to a country in Southeast Asia. Every day, they sit in the hotel lobby or stairway and wait for business. While waiting, most of them engage in conversation among themselves, but a few just sit there quietly. Those who are not under pressure to make more money may take it easy, and prefer playing mahjong with the other girls instead of working.

Most subjects indicated that they provided only straight sex and nothing else. If a customer asks for oral sex, then he must pay extra. Some subjects, however, told us that they would provide oral sex without charging extra so that the customer will visit them again. They also told us that this has to be done in a very discreet way; because if their fellow sex workers find out about this, they will be ostracized for breaking an informal rule that no oral sex should be provided without an extra charge. Xiao Tan, a 24-year-old woman from Changde, explained how she maintained a steady group of regular clients:

> I have some regular clients because I help my clients to have a shower, while other girls won't. I do not rush my customers; and I treat my customers very well. One time, a client smoked a cigarette after entering a woman's room. This woman became angry and asked him: "What do you want to do? Smoke or have sex?" The man turned around and left. All of us tried to stop him, but he left. I am patient with my clients, I also try to find a way to make them happy, especially during intercourse. In addition, if a customer asks me to *chuixiao* [play the flute or provide oral sex], I will *chuixiao* even when he refuses to pay more money, in order to keep this person as my regular customer. But other girls will charge $3 to $7 more and if a client says no, they will refuse to *chuixiao*. (84)

When we were in Malaysia, we noticed that Chinese women were also working out of certain hotels there. The most troublesome, at least from the Malaysian authorities' point of view, was the congregation of Chinese *xiaojies* in the Genting, a casino resort near Kuala Lumpur.[6] Xiao Tan, the woman quoted above, recalled how she used to work in the Genting:

> I went to Malaysia one time after I had been in Macau, and stayed there for one month in a hotel close to the Genting Casino. I solicited patrons inside the casino. I charged $58 per session and sometimes I earned as much as $860 a day. Eleven days later, the employees of the casino blacklisted me for soliciting clients and did not allow me to enter the casino. I assumed that I could not make money any more in Malaysia, but actually I could solicit business outside the casino. Of course, business and tips were not as good as before when I solicited customers inside the casino. (84)

The Independent: Home-Based

The third group of independent *xiaojie* are the home-based. A Chinese woman, after arriving in a foreign country or in a special administrative region such as Hong Kong or Macau, may rent a house, an apartment, or a room in a residential area in order to provide sex services. Some not only work there but also live there, whereas others who prefer to separate the two spheres (for safety or privacy reasons, or both) will rent another place to stay after work.

In Macau, many Chinese women work out of apartment buildings located in the old residential areas. These areas are dominated by newcomers from mainland China and by local blue-collar workers. The following observation is illustrative of the situation in Macau:

> This respondent was soliciting business out of an old building whose entrance was facing a back alley. She waved to me and said: "Why don't you come upstairs for a massage? It costs only $7." I climbed the dark stairway and followed her to her place, which was on the second floor of an old and poorly maintained building. Her apartment was very small. There was a living room and a bathroom. On a table in the living room, there were four rice cookers, Hunan-flavor sausages, and preserved vegetables in bottles. There was no kitchen in the unit and they used a rice cooker to cook food for themselves. There were five rooms in the unit, occupied by five women. The rent was $7 each day per room. Mainland women come and go because they can only stay for fourteen days. All the rooms were very small and this respondent's room had no window. According to her, her room was originally the kitchen.

Many of the women we interviewed in Los Angeles and New York were independent *xiaojies* working out of their own places. Most of them had worked in a third-party managed massage parlor or brothel before they began to operate their own businesses. According to a woman in Los Angeles:

> I rented this place for $1,600 a month. I use one bedroom for business and another for me to sleep at night. If business is good, I will call other women to come help me. So you can say my place is also a "house." In this apartment complex, there are many "houses." I charge $100 per visit. (Joey, 36, married with a 10-year-old daughter) (119)

Na Na, a 28-year-old college graduate from Dalian (Liaoning), explained how she managed her business:

A friend rented this place for $1,600 a month, and I pay half of the rent. I put an ad in the newspapers, I charge $120 per trick, and I keep all of it. Every day, I come to this place around 2 p.m. I live in another place. I do not have a car; so I rely on a limousine service to move back and forth between this place and my home. Normally, I have one to two dates a day. When business is good, I might have three or four customers a day. I am very cautious. If I think the caller is difficult, I would rather not do business with him. Besides, I only advertise my services in the Chinese newspapers and do business with only Chinese clients. (118)

In sum, contrary to public perceptions based largely upon media coverage and official publications, not all women who engage in commercial sex overseas do so in third-party managed sex venues, nor are they controlled by sex traffickers or sex ring operators. As illustrated above, many of the women we interviewed were independently self-employed, either by working the streets, working out of their hotel rooms or apartments, or by soliciting business inside or around certain restaurants. They do everything on their own: placing ads online or in newspapers, answering the phone and giving directions, soliciting business on the streets, in hotel lobbies, restaurants, or bars by themselves, and then providing sexual services. They are not only not managed by a third party, but their business is also not controlled by the hotels, restaurants, and bars where they solicit business. Why might that be the case? A possible explanation is that these particular hotels and restaurants and so on, do not attract much "legitimate" business. They are small, shabby, dirty, and generally unattractive. Thus, having women who engage in paid sex as customers is a primary source of income for them. Without the women and their clients, these establishments probably could not survive. In some hotels, the only rooms rented are to these women. It is for this reason that the managements do not make other demands on the women.

Women in our sample who were working independently overseas, be they street-based, restaurant-based, hotel-based, or home-based, were very similar to the Dominican women in Sosua studied by anthropology professor Denise Brennan, the author of a book on sex tourism in the Dominican Republic. According to Brennan, "Dominican women are not trafficked into Sosua's trade but usually are drawn to it through social networks of family and female friends who work or have worked in it. The absence of pimps in Sosua is critical to sex workers' lives. Without them, Sosuan sex workers keep all their earnings, essentially working freelance. They decide how many hours they will work, with whom, and for what price."[7]

Partnerships

For our respondents, the second approach to engaging in commercial sex involves establishing a partnership with a mommy or a chickenhead. As mentioned, a mommy is a locally hired woman who solicits business for the women who sell sex. She may or may not be a former *xiaojie* herself. She is the one who approaches potential customers on the street or in a public place, finds out whether they are interested in buying sex, and if so, strikes a deal. The mommy pays the woman who provides the sexual service a pre-agreed amount of money, regardless of how much the mommy charges a customer. It is the mommy who takes the risk of being arrested and goes through the trouble of dealing with strangers and negotiating with potential clients. A mommy working in this fashion is highly unlikely to play any role in the actual movement of the women from China to their overseas destinations. A chickenhead, on the other hand, can either help a woman go overseas or provide protection to a woman in the destination country. Either way, the chickenhead takes a cut of the woman's earnings.

Unlike the independent, self-employed women described above, the women who work in partnerships with a mommy or a chickenhead may not be in a position to decide how much they charge their clients, nor do they get to keep all the money their clients pay for their services. Thirty-three of our subjects out of 149 (22%) worked with a mommy (N = 19) or a chickenhead (N = 14).

Working with a Mommy

While we were conducting fieldwork in Asia and the United States between January 2007 and August 2008, we noticed that certain streetwalkers in Hong Kong, Jakarta, Macau, and Shenzhen relied on one or more women to find customers for them. These women, the so-called mommies, often solicit business in a park, in front of a hotel, inside a restaurant, or on the streets. For example, some of the women we interviewed in Hong Kong remarked that, besides earning tips in various nightclubs through hostessing, they also relied on several street-based mommies to find men who would like to buy sex:

> A few days after I got here, I met Wendy [a street mommy] near a park. She told me and other girls that, besides *zuotai* and *chutai* at various night-clubs, we should also entertain the customers she refers to us. We agreed. (Chun Chun, 24, single, both a streetwalker and a hostess, from Chong-qing) (78)

We also interviewed this same Wendy while she was soliciting business in a small park near a tourist area. She recalled how she got into this business:

> What can I do in Hong Kong? I know I can push a cart and sell *dim sum* [a type of Chinese dish usually served in a small steamer basket] in a restaurant or work as a cleaning lady in a hotel. The income is meager, the work is laborious, and you are bullied. Who would want that kind of job? Therefore I choose to be a mommy. Although it is risky, it is also an easy job and you are free. On average, I can make more than $140 a day. You can make more than $2,700 a month even if you do not work every day. The most you can earn by selling *dim sum* or working in a hotel is $800 to $930 a month.
>
> I propose a price once I have a potential customer. No matter how much I ask, girls can only have $53. This work is relatively easy. I come out around 8 to 9 p.m. and stop work at 1 to 2 a.m. I make money by taking risks, but those girls are jealous of me and view me as an enemy. They make $53 for each customer; or $27 if they have a chickenhead. If my asking price is $133, I make $80. Of course, the girls are not happy. Fuck them, these bitches only make $13 per session in China. It is already a good deal that they make $27 or $53 in Hong Kong, why are they complaining? They do not have any risk, I take all the risks. Of course, I should take a lot.

In Jakarta, we also saw several women hanging out at a fast food restaurant located within a complex near the new Chinatown, and they all relied on a mommy to find clients for them.

Working for or with a Chickenhead

A chickenhead, usually a male, is someone who plays one or more of the following roles: (1) (a man in China) helps a woman to go overseas and engage in prostitution; (2) (a man overseas) manages a woman's commercial sex work in a foreign country; and (3) (a man overseas) acts as a woman's protector in the destination country. In general, women we interviewed in Macau working out of hotels were affiliated with the first type of chickenhead, respondents in Hong Kong who worked the streets were associated with the second type, and streetwalkers in a red-light district of Singapore were linked to the third type.

CHICKENHEAD AS A PARTNER

As mentioned above, among the hotel-based women we interviewed in Macau, some were independents who went to Macau on their own and were working for themselves and keeping all their earnings. Others, however, were brought to Macau by their boyfriend pimps ("romantic chickenheads") or by "business chickenheads." If they were affiliated with a romantic chicken-head, they gave him all their earnings; if they were associated with a business chickenhead, they paid this person a certain amount of money before they could terminate the partnership.

It might be argued that these sorts of arrangements come dangerously close to meeting the definition of debt bondage, and if that is the case we might be seeing sex trafficking. The chickenheads have fronted a certain sum of money to pay for the women's travel overseas. The women then engage in commercial sex and repay the chickenheads. Is this debt bondage? Well, it depends. If the sum of repayment demanded is greater than the original debt, then probably yes. If the amount repaid is the same as the amount of the original debt and there is no further financial obligation, then probably not. What about the boyfriend situation? This is even more sticky, because although the payment to the romantic chickenhead may exceed—even far exceed—any initial investment by him, the woman as girlfriend is ostensibly giving him her money out of love. This certainly could be exploitation, but would probably not meet the legal definition of debt bondage. We will come back to this issue in chapter 10 when we discuss the many ways to define sex trafficking.

Hotel XXX (name omitted) is the oldest and best known hotel and ca-sino in Macau. As a five-star establishment situated in the heart of the city, it attracts a large number of visitors every day and symbolizes the booming gambling industry of Macau, with revenues that surpassed Las Vegas for the first time in 2007. However, in our view the hotel is also one of the largest brothels in Macau, where at any given time dozens of Chinese women can be seen soliciting business on the ground floor of the hotel.[8] After one of these women strikes a deal with a customer, she takes him to her room on the fifth or sixth floor of the hotel to have sex. After the sexual transaction is completed, which normally takes no more than twenty minutes, she comes downstairs and immediately begins looking for the next customer. Accord-ing to a security guard at the hotel, the hotel management, the chickenheads, and the women all work together to promote the sex trade within the hotel:

> Once a girl rents a room in our hotel, she can solicit business in the base-ment. We [the security guards] will make sure women who are not staying in our hotel will not walk the basement of the hotel. There is a manager in our hotel who is in charge of the so-called *xiaojiefang* [miss room]. He

screens the women who are qualified for these rooms. Only those who are pretty can stay in this hotel's *xiaojiefang*.

The hotel must control "traffic flow" and keep the hotel in a "normal appearance." First, we must make sure there are no more than thirty girls in the basement at any given time. There is a person responsible for monitoring the number of women. This person will notify security guards if there are more than thirty women. The security guards will then ask some women not to walk around but to sit in the restaurant in the basement. This is one way to keep things under control.

Chickenheads from China are good to us because this is our turf and we do not create problems for them. That's because we receive benefits from them. To be honest with you, I do not get any cash from anyone; some of my colleagues may, I don't know. However, when my manager and I visit Zhuhai, the chickenheads there treat us to everything—food, drinks, and women.

CHICKENHEAD AS A MANAGER

Some of the street prostitutes we interviewed in Hong Kong were associated with chickenheads who acted as "business managers." These chickenheads brought the respondents to Hong Kong, helped them to hook up with one or more street mommies who would solicit business for them, and provided a place for the respondents to stay. As the following quote illustrates, we do not believe these business arrangements constitute debt bondage. Xiao Zheng, a 23-year-old single woman from Liuzhou (Guangxi) explained how she and her chickenhead worked together:

> We agreed that he would apply for a Thai visa for me, accompany me to Hong Kong, provide me food and a room, introduce me to mommies, and take half of the $53 the mommies give me for each customer. He doesn't take advantage of me, nor ask me how much in tips I make, and he is kind of polite. The bottom line is, he is relying on me to make money, and that's why he can't be rude to me. All the chickenheads maintain a good relationship with the mommies and the mommies will tell the chickenheads how many customers we see a day. (83)

CHICKENHEAD AS A PROTECTOR

Chickenheads in a red-light district of Singapore mainly play the role of protector. This particular area is controlled by several criminal gangs and members of these gangs have become the key players in the business of protection. As protectors, these gang members are responsible for watching the streets and alerting the streetwalkers if the police are coming; protecting the women from victimization by male customers; and protecting their turf so that women from other places will not intrude on their territory. According to a streetwalker we interviewed in this red-light district: "They told us that every *lorong* [lane] here is protected by somebody, so we can only walk this *lorong* and shouldn't go over to other *lorongs*" (1).

None of the women we interviewed in the red-light district told us that they were mistreated by their local chickenheads:

> We charge between $33 to $40 per session. Everyone of us pays a chicken-head $13 a day, no matter how many customers we have. We do not pay them if we do not work. This is their turf. We should give them money if we make money on their turf. They treat us very well, respect us very much, and they never take advantage of us. (Ah Lian, 35, divorced with a 6-year-old son, from Xinhui, Guangdong) (14)

Yang Yang, a streetwalker we met on Lorong 14 who charged $46 per session, believed that the groups of people running the red-light district are not highly organized: "Every *lorong* belongs to a separate group of people. Some play the role of chickenheads and some are look-outs. They can't be considered an organization. I only had contact with three men and they are all Singaporeans. They treat us all right. They don't take advantage of us because, if they do, it won't be easy for them to lead us because we would not follow their orders" (1).

According to a former gang member who used to work as a look-out in a red-light district in Singapore: "I worked from 6 p.m. to 6 a.m. everyday, and I was paid $66 per shift. It was hard work because even if I wanted to take a leak, I needed to ask someone to cover me. There was one lookout on either end of a *lorong*, mainly to watch out for police."

The Employed

Here we turn to the working arrangements and conditions of those women who were employed by a commercial sex establishment. As employees, these subjects worked in one of the indoor sex venues previously described. Eighty out of the 149 subjects (54%) we interviewed who were working outside China belonged to this group: 23 subjects worked in a nightclub/KTV/flower hall arrangement, 12 in a sauna/spa, 13 in a massage parlor, 13 in a brothel, and 19 in an escort business.

Nightclubs and KTVs

There are many adult entertainment centers in Asia that are called night-clubs, or KTVs, or flower halls. When a group of male customers walks into one of these establishments, they are brought to a private room, a mommy introduces her girls (called hostesses or public relation officers) to the cus-tomers, food and drinks are served, and then the male customers and the female hostesses engage in drinking, singing, and just talking. The hostesses will do whatever they can to make the customers happy, knowing that their income depends on tips from the customers and on the likelihood of cus-tomers taking them out for sex.[9]

Meng Meng, 28, a college graduate from Beijing, described what it was like to be a hostess in one of Singapore's high-end nightclubs:

> XXX [name omitted] is a first-class nightclub and the customers are also of high class. They are all businessmen and most of them come here to dis-cuss business. After the customers settle into a room, a mommy will take a few girls to their room for them to select. Whoever is chosen will sit their table. During happy hours, we normally will go around to various tables, and receive tips in the amount of $33 per table. In the evenings we may or may not go around to the tables, it depends. In the evenings, we will earn $66 to $100 tips per table. If we go out with customers, we get $200, but we need to give $33 to our mommy. There are more than a hundred girls working in this nightclub. (9)

In general, all these sorts of entertainment venues are places men go to have a good time. Unlike brothels where a sexual transaction is the norm rather than the exception, these particular venues are, at least on paper, places where customers go simply to drink, sing, dance, and talk with host-esses. Sexual transactions are therefore the exception rather than the norm. It is also true, however, that these venues are quite diverse, not only in terms of size and price, but also in terms of the kinds of services provided.[10] Some of the well-established and well-known nightclubs in Asia are basically large brothels. For example, the manager of a well-known nightclub in Macau ex-plained how his place operated:

> Ours is a so-called "uniform nightclub."[11] Our girls must select one of the four or five uniforms we provide and wear them when they come to work. Girls, managers, and mommies have no salary, and their income depends on the girls to *zuotai* and *chuchang* [going out].[12] The price for going out

is $130, girls pay the company $40 afterwards. We all rely on *chuchang* because *zuotai* makes much less money.

The same is true with some of the KTVs. In the high-end KTVs, where the customers are mostly upper-class businessmen, physical contact between hostesses and clients is very limited. On the other hand, there are low-end KTVs where customers and hostesses are often involved in very intimate acts, even including sexual intercourse.

> I now work at XXX [name omitted], which is a KTV. We sit in the lounge and mommy will introduce us to the customers when they arrive. If we are selected, we go to a private room with customers to drink and sing. There are also bedrooms inside the KTV where we can have sex.[13] (Wang Fang, 33, single, KTV hostess, Jakarta) (49)
>
> In the nightclubs, customers pay $66 per hostess for sitting their table; the girl gets $53 and the house takes $13. We can sit only one or two tables a night. Customers also pay us tips. There are private rooms in the nightclub. There is a corner in the private rooms and people can have sex in the corner. (Xiao Ya, 20, single, freelancing as a hostess at various nightclubs in Hong Kong) (75)

In Bangkok, besides the nightclubs, there were also other types of indoor entertainment such as the KTVs and flower halls. Zhao Tong, a 24-year-old woman from Harbin (Heilongjiang), explained the differences between KTVs and flower halls:

> XXX [name omitted] is a KTV and it does not have a big lounge, only private rooms. When customers come, mommies bring the girls out for customers to choose. Each "hour" lasts 40 minutes and it cost $8 per "hour." The girls get about $3 per "hour." Before customers leave, they must also pay at least $15 as tips per hostess. For *chutai*, customers must buy 10 "hours" [pay the house $80], pay the girl $140, sometimes as high as $285 or $570. The girl must pay the mommy $30 afterward.
>
> XXX [name omitted] is a *guahuating* [flower hall]; there is a big lounge, no private rooms. When customers enter, the mommy brings the hostesses out for customers to choose. The girls *zuotai* once chosen by customers, they primarily earn flower money by singing songs. The flower money [tip] ranges from $10, $15, to about $1,000. Some hang as high as $1,500, but they all are hung by a "husband." The most that regular customers hang is $60 to $90. There is no "hour" money or tips at a *guahuating*. (64)

For the women who were working for a nightclub, a KTV, or a flower hall, going out with a customer or not was the major decision that needed to be made, at least at the beginning of their employment. Going out or not was a critical move because it not only affected their immediate level of income, but also their reputation, any future income, their chances of finding a "husband," and their relationships with a mommy and the management. Sun Hung, 28, single, from Guangzhou (Guangdong), was a KTV hostess in Jakarta at the time of the interview, and she explained the "politics of going out" this way:

> Some of the girls here do not *chujie* for a very good reason.[14] Even though a girl can make two to three hundred dollars per outing, she is also going to have a hard time finding customers to sit tables as time goes by. If a girl already goes out with a particular customer, how can she have the face to sit the table of the same customer when he comes again? Besides, men normally would not want to have a woman they had already slept with to sit their tables! (42)

Sauna and Spa

While nightclubs and KTVs are places for men to drink and sing, saunas and spas are geared toward baths and massages. These too, however, have become fronts for commercial sexual transactions. Many saunas and spas in Asia are well established business enterprises with strong ties to the local authorities, and may be located in a large hotel or have their own commercial building. Different saunas and spas operate differently and hire women from different countries. In others, the owners hire only women from a particular country, such as China, Vietnam, or Thailand. For example, there is a sauna in Macau that is staffed only with Chinese masseuses, even though all the waitresses are Indonesian women.

Our respondents who were working in a sauna or a spa told us they preferred working in this type of venue because they can get involved in sexual transactions with their clients without having to go through the talking, drinking, and singing that are required in a nightclub or a KTV during the initial encounter between a male client and a female hostess. Even if a hostess tries her best to please a customer, at the end of the evening there is no guarantee that the customer is going to ask the hostess out for sex, leading to great frustration for the women who cannot make real money unless they often go out with their customers. In addition, many subjects we talked to indicated that working in a sauna or a spa saved them a lot of money because they do not have to spend on makeup, clothes, and other personal items to impress their clients like women in the nightclubs and KTVs. However, there are also many downsides to working in these particular venues, the worst of which is the types of services (complicated and humiliating) that have to be provided, especially in the upscale saunas and spas that charge about $200 per session.

In Indonesia, an establishment that operates very much like a sauna in Hong Kong or Macau and charges very much the same amount of money for sexual services is often called a spa. The cashier of a well-established, upscale spa in Jakarta explained to us about the price and the service as follows:

> Our entrance fee is $12, and it will allow you to use all the facilities inside the spa. If you want to *jinfan* [enter a room with a masseuse to have sex], then you must pay $150. If you *jinfan*, you need not pay the $12 entrance fee. We've got five to ten Chinese women at any given time, plus women from Indonesia, Thailand, and Malaysia. The price for *jingfan* is the same for all the women here, regardless of where they are from. Every evening, around 8 or 9, all our women will be in the pool wearing only bikinis to let customers inspect and select.

Other spas in Jakarta, however, have different entrance fees and prices for women from different countries. For example, one spa charged $5 as an entrance fee and the women were both imports and locals. The imports were from China, Thailand, Uzbekistan, and Spain, and they all charged $150 per session. The Indonesians were divided into three groups, charging $35, $80, and $100 respectively. The imports and the locals had their own mommies. Another spa we visited had one room for Russians and Thai, the second room was all Indonesians, and the third all Chinese. Again, all foreign women charged their customers $150 and there were three prices for Indonesians: $50, $80, and $100. Even though different spas may be staffed and operated differently, according to our respondents, many of the spas in Jakarta actually belonged to the same group of owners who coordinated their activities, and the person with the highest stake in the business was often the one who was the least known.

Massage Parlor

Massage parlors, like saunas and spas, are places for people to go have a massage and relax. Many massage parlors in Asia and the United States, however, including both licensed and unlicensed, are involved in providing so-called "half set" (hand job) or "full set" (sexual intercourse) services. As we mentioned previously, in general massage parlors are smaller and cheaper than saunas and spas. They are often owned and run by former prostitutes and have two or three masseuses. Among our subjects, thirteen (9%) of them worked in massage parlors: nine in New York, two in Singapore, and one each in Los Angeles and Taiwan.

The two masseuses we interviewed in Singapore worked for two separate massage parlors in a major red-light district. According to one of these respondents:

> I have been working in this massage parlor for a year and a half. After a customer comes in, we massage his back first. After he turns over, he may ask for special service, either hand job or sexual intercourse. Most of them prefer hand jobs. Prices are for massage $30, hand job $50, intercourse $100. For massage service [or entrance fee], the owner will take $20 out of $30. Whatever a customer gives us for extra service all belongs to us. (Qian Qian, 34, divorced twice, has a 5-year-old son, from Nanjing) (10)

In the New York metropolitan area, there are quite a few Chinese massage parlors that cater to either Chinese or American customers or both. Mona, a 34-year-old divorced woman from Baicheng (Jilin) told us how she became a masseuse in a wealthy town in New Jersey:

> Well, I just checked the ads in the *Star Ledger* [a local newspaper] and called an Asian massage parlor. The ad was for customers, but I figured I can just call and see whether the place needed workers. The place I called was located somewhere in Bergen County [in northern New Jersey], and sure enough, the owner spoke Chinese and she was willing to meet me. So, I went for an interview. The store charged a $50 entrance fee and our share was $10. We provided massage to the customers and also "happy ending" [hand job]. If a customer wanted, we also provided sex service. All the tips a customer gave us belonged to us. (104)

According to our field interviews with masseuses and massage parlor owners, most of the women working in the massage parlors live in Flushing (in the Queens borough of New York City), populated by large numbers of Chinese (from China and Taiwan) and by Korean immigrants.[15] Normally, the massage parlor owner will pick up her girls in Flushing in the morning and drop them off back there in the evening. Most massage parlors open around 10 in the morning and close by 8 in the evening. According to the respondents, like restaurants, they have two peak hours, one around noon (when customers can come during their lunchtime) and another around 6 p.m. when their clients are done working and on their way home.

In the United States, besides the above mentioned "ambiguous" massage parlors in the tristate area of New York, New Jersey, and Connecticut, there are also sex venues outside the tristate area that operate like brothels, but call themselves "massage parlors" as well. These venues are "unambiguous" in the sense that they do not normally provide massages nor hand jobs, but only sexual intercourse. Moreover, these places tend to have more women working than do the massage parlors in the tristate area.

Brothel

It is not easy to differentiate between a brothel and a massage parlor, except to say that a brothel normally does not pretend to be a place for a massage, and it provides only full service. It is also somewhat different from a sauna and a spa; workers in a brothel normally do not provide a variety of sexual services such as women in saunas and spas do. Miao Miao, a 24-year-old single woman from Liuzhou (Guangxi) who was working for a brothel in Macau at the time of the interview, told us of her experiences:

> I worked as a streetwalker around the ferry terminal when I was in Macau the first time. I brought clients to my apartment nearby. Now I do not solicit on the street anymore because "walking the street" are awful words and streetwalkers are presumably very cheap women. This is why I now work in this establishment (a brothel located inside a high-rise apartment). I do not want to work at saunas either because you have to provide many kinds of services that are not what human beings can possibly do, it is disgusting. I simply can't do that. (90)

In Los Angeles, respondents who were working in brothel-like venues called the places "houses." Angel, a 36-year-old woman from Dalian (in China's northeast Liaoning Province), recounted her experience in the Los Angeles commercial sex scene:

> At the beginning, I worked as an in-house *xiaojie*. After two months, I bought a car and began to rotate among houses. You get more business if

you work for more than one house, so you can make more money. I also used to work in a house that catered to foreigners and Mexicans. It was easier to work in that house because foreigners were not picky about us and they paid more. However, it was also risky to work there, because the chance of being arrested is higher. After a while, I opened my own house, mainly because it did not take much to start a house. All you need is a few thousand dollars; you rent a place and put an advertisement in the newspapers. My plan was that I would open a house, but I would do it myself, and only if I could not handle the business myself, I would call someone to come over to help me. (124)

Like "houses" in Los Angeles, brothels in New York also charge between $100 to $120 per client and the money is similarly distributed between the brothel owner and the women. Ellen, a 32-year-old divorced woman from Zhuzhou (Hunan), explained her experience with a brothel in New York:

Yesterday, I had four customers. We have two women [including the subject] working here. When a customer comes in, he selects one of us, and then goes upstairs to have sex. We will massage the customer a little while, then offer a blow job, and then intercourse. We insist all the customers wear condoms. After that, the customer can take a shower before he leaves. All these things take place within 45 minutes. Our boss is a man and he is not here most of the time. He just comes every day to cook for us or buy take-out food for us and then leaves. He is nice to us, and he provides free food and lodging. We can go out whenever we want, and he won't take advantage of us sexually. We charge a customer $100 per visit, and the girls get $70. The other $30 will go to the boss. Sometimes, customers may give us $10 or $20 tips. (115)

Escort Agency

Nineteen out of the 149 respondents (13%) we interviewed outside China said that they worked as escorts: 14 in Taiwan and 5 in Malaysia. There were two reasons why we interviewed so many escorts in these two countries: first, our contacts in Taiwan introduced us to some escort agency owners who made the arrangements for us to interview their female employees; and second, there are just many more Chinese women in Taiwan and Malaysia who work in the escort business. In fact, in Taiwan the vast majority of the women from China work for an escort agency. This is because the Taiwanese authorities have been very aggressive in preventing Chinese women from penetrating into their other sex markets such as nightclubs, KTVs, and massage parlors.

The way things typically work is, after a woman from China arrives in Taiwan through a fraudulent marriage scheme, the person who arranged her trip to Taiwan—her agent—hooks her up with an escort agency. That agency assigns a jockey (driver) for the woman, and the jockey then delivers the woman to her clients' places for sex.

When we were in Taiwan doing field observation, an escort agency owner (Ah Qiang) showed us around one evening. Some observations follow:

> Ah Qiang took me to a motel. That motel provides a room for Ah Qiang's jockeys to relax while they were waiting for their women to complete their sexual transactions in the motel. Inside the room, there was a sofa set and a TV, and there was a bathroom. One of Ah Qiang's jockeys was in the room when we arrived, and he was waiting for a girl who was with a client. Ah Qiang said that he had a good relationship with the owner of this motel. This is why the motel provided him a room and a CCTV monitor was installed in this room so that Ah Qiang and his drivers could see what is going on at the entrance. The motel registers the room where his girl meets a client as a regular customer room [meaning, the customer is staying overnight], and not as an hour room [meaning, the room is rented to someone who only wants to spend a couple of hours in the room]. If the police come, they do not check the rooms occupied by regular customers; only the hour rooms.

Ah Qiang explained the logistics of delivering women to various spots:

> This is how we do things routinely. We send a woman to an auntie's [a pimp's] location once we receive his or her call. We call the auntie's location the "store." Most stores are apartments with two or three rooms, rented by the aunties. Men go to these stores if they want to meet mainland Chinese women and the aunties call us when they have business. The aunties normally come out of the apartments to meet the women and take them upstairs to meet the clients. Then we drive around the area to see whether there are any unusual things going on around the building just to make us feel safe.

According to a massage parlor owner in New York, women from China are not as active as Chinese women from other parts of the world in the New York escort market, and she explained why:

Here in New York there are also large numbers of women from Taiwan, Hong Kong, Malaysia, and Singapore who are engaged in paid sex. They tend to be younger and prettier—especially those from Hong Kong and Taiwan—than the women from China because being young is not a problem for them when they apply for an American visa. That's why so many women from these areas are involved in take-out sex services. Take-out means these girls are delivered to the customers' places by a limousine arranged by an escort agency owner. Only a young and pretty woman can enter the take-out business because if she is not sufficiently young and pretty, a customer will reject her when she shows up at the customer's place.

The research literature on sex work has typically described escort services as follows:

> In an effort to avoid legal prosecution, escorts often frame their services as providing dinner or travel companions or dates for corporate functions. While sex is often implied or assumed to be included in the services on offer, escorts and escort agencies typically avoid any explicit mention of sex for sale. . . . Escort agencies seek to lend an aura of sophistication and glamour to their services, and escorts are often portrayed as providers of "high-class" companionship.[16]

But the Chinese escorts we interviewed, and the fieldwork we conducted tell us a rather different story. According to our subjects and our observations, women who are employed in escort agencies are no more likely to act as companions or dates—referred to as providing "girlfriend experience"— to their clients, than are women in other types of sex markets. Here again is an example that many of the generalizations about the different types of commercial sex markets in the literature on prostitution are not borne out by our research. This does not mean that the existing literature has gotten it all wrong, but rather that certain previously accepted conclusions may have to be rethought.

Table 5.1 illustrates the distribution of our female subjects in the various sex markets. Our data suggest that a substantial number of *xiaojies* are working independently or in simple cooperation with another party, and thus need not work for anyone else. Our data also show that these independent workers are not confined to working only on the streets. The latter is also true with the women who were working as partners together with a third party, or who were being employed by a third party.

Table 5.1. Type of Sex Market, by Type of Arrangement (N = 149)

	Market arrangement			
	Independent	Partnership	Employed	Total
Independent: street	4	0	0	4
Indepdendent: hotel	8	0	0	8
Independent: home	8	0	0	8
Independent: restaurant	16	0	0	16
Partnership: mommy	0	19	0	19
Partnership: chickenhead	0	14	0	14
Employed: nightclub/KTV	0	0	23	23
Employed: sauna/spa	0	0	12	12
Employed: massage parlors	0	0	13	13
Employed: brothel	0	0	13	13
Employed: escort	0	0	19	19
Total	36	33	80	149

Mistress

Women employed in nightclubs, KTVs, and flower halls are supposedly "hostesses" or "public relations officers" who only drink and sing with customers. To protect their reputations and to increase their opportunity to *zoutai*, these hostesses sometimes claim that they do not *chutai*, meaning they are not really prostitutes. This is something the women working in other types of venues cannot claim. Because they can deny they sell sex, many women working in the nightclubs and so on, can look for a "husband" —a man (often a former client) who as the "husband" is willing to provide a monthly stipend and perhaps other types of financial assistance to a woman with the explicit understanding that the woman will provide sexual favors (or at least get together regularly) in return.[17] This was especially true for the women we interviewed in Thailand and Indonesia, simply because many respondents there could not make much money just through the tips they received as hostesses.

Establishing the above type of relationship with a client is called *bao* (cover or contract). Very often it can be a tricky relationship because the woman is in it only for the man's money, and the man is paying only under the condition that the woman does not continue to work in the sex business, or at least does not go out with other customers. Sometimes, the problem is with the man, who typically does not want to maintain a relationship with one woman for long. Other times, one party may fall in love with the other party and become entangled in a web of love, money and loyalty, as this respondent's story illustrates:

When I was here last time, I met a Beijing man who is currently my "boy-friend." He works at a ship company and he is married. I met him when I was working at a flower hall. I was one of the hostesses for him and his friends. One of his friends said something that offended me and I cried. The next day, he and his friend took me to dinner and his friend apologized to me. I had sex with him [the married man] afterward.

I like him, although I know that we *xiaojies* should not be entangled in a romantic relationship with a client. In the past, when I heard that a woman who sold sex was falling in love with a customer, I could not understand how that could happen. But now I myself am romantically involved with a customer. I know that the two of us do not have a future, but people often have feelings for one another, right? To be honest with you, it does not pay to be with him. He pays me only $700 or $800 a month, and I have to spend so much time on him. I believe that he is capable of giving me more money. I do not know how much he really loves me. (Zhao Tong, 24, divorced, from Harbin, a flower hall hostess in Bangkok) (64)

Other respondents, however, were happy simply to terminate this kind of relationship after a while, mainly because their "husbands" were too old, were unattractive, or were not wealthy enough for them. Ah Yu, 40, divorced with a 16-year-old daughter, recalled how she was *bao* with a man for about a month while working as a restaurant-based freelancer in Bangkok:

Once I got here, I went to work at a restaurant as a freelancer the following day. While sitting in the restaurant, I was crying most of the time. I made about $8 in tips that day. About twenty days later, I met an old man—he was 74—who said he wanted to *bao* me. He agreed to pay my rent [$120 a month], to buy me a cell phone, to take me out to dinner often, and to give me a monthly stipend. I did not like him, so after a month of being with him I told him not to come see me and we broke up. (57)

Some subjects, especially the younger ones, were reluctant to be *bao* simply because they did not want to be restricted by their "husbands," and they were confident that because of their youth they could make enough money by going out with customers occasionally. Dong Dong, 26, married with an infant son, had this to say about "husbands":

To tell you the truth, I am easily contented. I am not greedy, and so far I have never let any men to *bao* me. There were men who want to *bao* me, but I don't want to treat anybody like an emperor and act like a slave. I would rather make less money but enjoy the freedom and not be dictated to by one man. A woman in her thirties or forties may need a man to support her so that she does not need to work that hard. I am still young, and I know I can make money on my own. (53)

We have presented here a considerable amount of detail about the sex markets involving Chinese women. We see that often the particular sex venue in which a woman ends up has much to do with the nature of her social network. While being an independent *xiaojie* provides freedom of choice and control over one's schedule and customers, working with a partner (a mommy or a chickenhead) also has its benefits. The presence of a partner tells a lot about how the business, once it is organized with some level of differentiation in roles and labor, produces greater profits or at least stable incomes for all. In this negotiated business environment, women maximize their income while minimizing hassles and risks. Mommies and chickenheads are risk managers who serve as buffers and sales staff to recruit and screen customers. From the myriad of market factors there has to arise some hierarchical arrangement and predictable patterns for how the business can be profitably sustained. The women we interviewed demonstrated high levels of agency in realizing their material ambition, while navigating the complex world of prostitution and confronting one type of problem or another.

Our findings presented so far clearly suggest that the sex industry involving Chinese women is diverse. The oppression paradigm that defines prostitution solely as inherently exploitative and harmful to workers does not reflect this diversity. Instead, as already proposed by Weitzer, "victimization, exploitation, choice, job satisfaction, self-esteem, and other dimensions . . . differ depending on type of sex work, geographical location, and other structural and organizational conditions."[18] An alternative paradigm proposed by Weitzer—the polymorphous paradigm—"holds that a constellation of occupational arrangements, power relations, and worker experiences exists within the arena of paid sexual services and performances. This paradigm is sensitive to complexities and to the structural conditions resulting in the uneven distribution of agency and subordination."[19]

Our results support this conclusion.

6

The Traffickers

A "trafficker" can be a recruiter, a transporter, a pimp, a sex venue owner, or anyone else who plays a role in the business of transnational prostitution. Thus, the word "trafficker" is normally used in the sex trafficking literature to refer to all the actors who are involved in the recruitment of women in the countries of origin, their transportation across national borders, and the facilitation and management of the women in whatever commercial sex venues they become engaged. In this chapter, we will describe all the people we interviewed in this study who would fit this broad definition of being "traffickers." We will examine their backgrounds, their motivations, their roles and functions in the sex business, and the nature of their relationships with the women who sell sex. We will also look at whether, and to what extent, organized crime groups seem to be involved in the transnational sex trade.

Chickenheads

Chinese often use the word *ji* (chicken) to refer to women who sell sex, so men or male pimps who are in charge of the "chickens" are called *jitou* (chickenheads). As discussed in chapter 3, some of our subjects were "turned out" by chickenheads when they first entered prostitution in China. Overseas, only women in Hong Kong, Macau, and Singapore told us that they were either brought overseas by a chickenhead, or that they were working with, or for a chickenhead whom they met abroad. Liu Yan, a 36-year-old woman from Harbin (Heilongjiang Province, located in northeast China) recounted how she was helped by a chickenhead to go to work in Hong Kong, and how she eventually got rid of him with the help of another man:

> I applied for a business visa on my own for my first trip to Hong Kong. After arriving in Shenzhen, I was brought to Hong Kong by a chickenhead. He had helped many girls go to Hong Kong. In Hong Kong, he introduced several mommies to me, gave me food, and allowed me to sleep in his place for free. In return, I agreed to give him half of what I earned, excluding tips. I found the arrangement to be unfair because he just brought me here; I applied for the visa on my own. Food and lodging do not cost him much anyway. So I left him and went to another area to solicit business on my own. Later, this chickenhead threatened me. He said I would not be allowed to make money in Hong Kong if I ran away from him. I found a "daddy" who was a native Hong Kong man to talk to my chickenhead. My "daddy" found the chickenhead and warned him: "I can make it hard for you to make a living in Hong Kong. Leave XXX [the subject] alone; she is my woman now." The chickenhead backed off, so I returned to the area where I used to work and the "daddy" became my protector and my pimp. I get $53 per customer he refers to me; he decides how much to charge a customer, I get $53 regardless of how much he charges. If a mommy introduces me to a customer, I will only receive $40 because my "daddy" will take the other $13. At any rate, this is better than sharing the money half and half with that chickenhead. (82)

Many women we interviewed in Macau, especially those who were seeing clients in small hotels, admitted that they had their own chickenheads, even though some of them preferred to call these men their "boyfriends" or "husbands." Zhao Yan, a 24-year-old single woman from Yongzhou (Hunan Province), told us of her experience with a chickenhead:

> I met a Hunanese man when I was working at a massage parlor in Changsa [the capital of Hunan Province]. I was very happy when we were together. He was not working, so I supported him. I often stopped working for a

while and went on vacations with him. I went back to work after using up all the money. Later, he said it was easier to make money in Shenzhen and took me there. He made the arrangements for me to work in a nightclub in Shenzhen. I made about $1,200 a month and I spent the money with my boyfriend. He did not work in Shenzhen and depended on me.

In Shenzhen, he had many friends who brought their girlfriends to Macau and therefore he suggested that we should also go to Macau. I did not object because I was fine as long as he was happy. He applied for all the documents for me and accompanied me to Macau. He also brought me to this hotel.

My boyfriend went back to Shenzhen a few days after we arrived here. He came over to Macau occasionally and I gave him all the money I made. But we broke up in the first half of this year because he started to fool around with women in Shenzhen. Now I realize that I was exploited by him; he spent at least $28,000 of my money over these years. People used to tell me that I was taken advantage of by him, but how could I have believed them at the time when I was so madly in love with him? (100)

Several subjects we interviewed in Macau told us a very similar story: Selling sex in the interior of China, they met someone they liked and that someone began to live off their earnings. Soon, that man would suggest that they should go to a city in the coastal areas because there was more money to be made. But after working for a while in this or that city, the man would eventually bring the woman over to Hong Kong or Macau. Our impression is that these men plotted this scenario from the outset, and it was just a matter of time before the women ended up working as prostitutes overseas. According to our subjects, as many as 80 percent of the women working out of the small hotels of Macau were being controlled by their chickenheads.

Interestingly, the women in Macau categorized chickenheads into "business chickenheads" and "romantic chickenheads." Zhao Yan, the above-cited woman who wasted many years of her earnings on a man who broke her heart, said: "Most chickenheads who come from the three northeastern provinces [Heilongjiang, Jilin, and Liaoning] have no emotional attachment to their women and tell the women in advance how much they should pay for help in going overseas. The chickenheads' fees ranged from $4,200 to $5,500; but were sometimes as low as $1,400 to $2,800. They are the business chickenheads. The Hunanese chickenheads, on the other hand, are different from the northeastern chickenheads. They maintain a romantic relationship with their women and do not require the women to pay them for the trip. These are the romantic chickenheads" (100).

In the descriptions of these relationships we can begin to see the undertones of exploitation and coercion, and thus sex trafficking. The stories that follow relate this in particularly blatant fashion. Most of the women we talked to had nothing good to say about their chickenheads. They saw these men as cold-blooded predators whose main purpose was to squeeze as much money as possible from the women—some of whom were unfortunate enough to fall in love with their exploiters.

We interviewed a streetwalker in Macau who was affiliated with a chickenhead, but was clearly not at all naïve about the affiliation. According to the woman, a 29-year-old divorcee from Dalian (Liaoning):

> My chickenhead is in his forties. He has three women working for him. One woman has a sexual relationship with him, but I am not that woman. My relationship with him is all business. Most chickenheads have only one woman working for them, and if that's the case, they [the chickenhead and the woman] may present themselves as husband and wife wherever they go. Some women are willing to make money for their chickenheads, and call their chickenheads "husband" all the time. Who is really a husband? These chickenheads all have wives! Some women are beaten up by their so-called husband or boyfriend and yet they will kneel down to apologize. I really do not understand what is wrong with these women, but I think there must be something wrong with their brains. In fact, I figure most women here are not that smart; they really look dumb. They allow these chickenheads to manipulate and exploit them and yet they can't see the problem. (91)

According to the manager of an expensive spa in Macau, Chinese women working in the upscale spas there may also be exploited by chickenheads.

> The women in this spa trust me because I always stand on their side when they have any problem with their chickenheads. After a chickenhead brings a girl in and I think she is qualified to work here, we discuss how to divide the money. I ask the chickenhead how much the girl must pay him for bringing her to Macau. If he says $14,000, I will ask him to take the girl and leave. How could you ask for so much money? It will force a woman to have to work very hard to make that kind of money. The most I can accept is $8,000. Personally, I think a reasonable fee a chickenhead should charge a girl for bringing her to Macau is between $2,700 to $4,000. If a

chickenhead is unhappy with how I conduct this business, I will not only refuse to let the girl work in my place, but will also notify other sauna venues, especially those having the same owner, not to hire this girl. If that happens, the chickenhead will not be able to make a living in Macau.

Many of the subjects who were soliciting business in some of the hotels in Macau said they had witnessed a chickenhead using violence against the women that worked for him, especially when the woman was not making money. Yin Yin, a 24-year-old single woman we interviewed in a small hotel in Macau, told us: "We used to have a girl working here who was from northeast China. She was quite chubby, so she did not have a lot of business. Her chickenhead grabbed her by the hair and struck her head against the wall. When she came down to work, we saw that there were cuts and bruises all over her body" (86). Yan Yan, the woman who herself was heavily exploited by her chickenhead, said: "Once, there was a northeastern girl here who was not pretty enough to have any business. Her chickenhead hit her, wouldn't let her sleep, and forced her to work 24 hours a day. Every day, she was waiting for business in the lobby with blackened eyes" (87).

We believe these cases could clearly be defined as sex trafficking victims. Keeping in mind that we did not interview the women being described, these cases illustrate the point that even women who go overseas to engage in commercial sex by choice can end up being victimized as a consequence of their choices. Here, the chickenheads are willing to treat "their" women well only if and when the women are making good money for them. Women who willingly go overseas, but then do not make a lot of money because they are deemed unattractive are the most likely to be subjected to physical and psychological abuse by their chickenheads. We know that at least in China, Hong Kong, and Macau, there are a number of married men who work as full-time pimps. They befriend women who may or may not already be working in commercial sex, and act as boyfriends or lovers for a while before they try to move the women to a coastal city, and eventually out of China, to either enter or to continue to work in the sex business. These chickenheads are mostly working on their own, but there are also many networks among them.

The so-called business chickenheads and pretend boyfriends described above are sex traffickers. They are not simply the kind of business partners discussed earlier. Through force, fraud, and/or coercion they take advantage of the naiveté and lack of sophistication of some Chinese women in order to exploit them for financial gain. This more subtle, or at least less blatant form of victimization has received much less attention in the overall discussion of sex trafficking, that has tended to focus on kidnapping and sex slaves.

Agents

While conducting fieldwork in Taiwan and Indonesia, we ran into men and women who called themselves "agents," or who were identified as such by our female subjects. Respondents in Taiwan used the Chinese word *jingji* to refer to this group of people, and the subjects in Indonesia actually used the English word "agent." In fact, agents in Taiwan and Indonesia were very different, even though they were referred to by the same name.

In Taiwan

A *jingji* in Taiwan is someone who "owns" a woman because he or she has fronted the money to bring her to Taiwan. After the woman arrives in Taiwan, she is obliged to go to work and repay this agent a certain amount of money (usually about $6,250).[1] The agent places the woman with an escort agency. Most of the women we talked to in Taiwan claimed that they were not controlled by their agents. Zhao Shuang, a 26-year-old single woman from Inner Mongolia, said: "Now I have more freedom than before I paid off the debt. However, I am not saying I was completely controlled before. At the very least, I had my travel documents with me during that time" (139). Xiao Cai, a 22-year-old single woman from Guangxi Province, told us that she was being treated very well by her agent: "I am free. I am able to go wherever I want. Sometimes, I go shopping, or my boss and I will go sightseeing. When I am in a bad mood, my boss will drive me around for a spin. I like going out in a car late at night and I will be in a good mood" (140).

After we interviewed Xiao Cai, without her agent being present, we also talked to the agent, a man who appeared to be in his fifties, and who talked and dressed like a typical Taiwanese man from a rural area. He told us in a serious tone that he was doing a good deed because it was impossible for these women to make much money in China. Moreover, he said he treated them very well. He would buy cherries if they wanted to eat cherries (cherries may cost more than $10 a pound in Taiwan); and he did not force them to work if they did not feel well. He went on to describe all the uncertainties associated with his work as an agent:

> After I invest so much money to bring a woman here, many things could go wrong. First, the girl may change her mind and decide not to come to Taiwan. During the waiting period, usually about six months, she may find a good job, meet a boyfriend, or simply change her mind for no reason. I get nothing back if she does not come and I cannot go to China and

force her to come. Second, after we have gone through the difficult application process, she does not get the approval from the Taiwanese authorities and therefore cannot enter Taiwan. Third, even though she may arrive in Taiwan, she flees soon after. Fourth, she is not healthy and thus cannot work on a regular basis. Fifth, she does not work hard. Finally, she is arrested soon after her arrival. If one of these things happens, then I will lose money.

In Indonesia

Unlike the *jingji* in Taiwan, agents in Indonesia do not "own" any women. Instead, as the word "agent" actually implies, they represent the women in various affairs, including helping women to come to Indonesia, finding places for them to work, acting as go-betweens for them when interacting with the employers, making sure that the women they represent are happy with the working conditions and the income, and helping them change venues if the original arrangement does not work out. Agents in Indonesia are more like "labor brokers." A Chinese *xiaojie* in Indonesia may have had an agent in China who persuaded her to go to Indonesia and helped her to obtain travel documents. The agent in Indonesia may have a working relationship with the agent in China, and will be mainly responsible for the woman's job placement in Indonesia. Because of the strong demand for Chinese prostitutes in Indonesia, and also because of the short supply, recruiters or agents in China often act very aggressively in the recruitment process. Ah Xiang, a 37-year-old divorcee from Wuhan (Hubei Province) recounted what happened when she arrived in Jakarta in 2007 with the help of a Taiwanese agent who was in China:

> I went to the nightclub the second day after I got here. The manager took one look at me and told me right away that I may not be suitable to work in his nightclub. He said the Taiwanese recruiter overestimated me, meaning that I am not young or pretty enough to work in a nightclub. He asked me to work at a KTV instead. I cannot work at that KTV because it's a place where "blunt" deals are made, that is, girls have to provide sex to customers inside the KTV. I could not accept it. So I asked the company to give me back my passport and I will work on my own and will repay what I owe to the company.[2] (34)

Other subjects told us that they were asked by their agents to pay more than the agreed upon transportation fee after they arrived in Indonesia.

Liu Li, a 34-year-old divorcee from Leshan (Sichuan), said: "My classmate introduced me to an agent who charged me $4,200 for the trip. My classmate also asked me to pay her $700 as a referral fee. After arriving here, the agent asked me to pay him an additional $2,000" (48).

We were able to interview three agents in Jakarta. One was a woman from China who told us how hard she had to work: "I must keep my cell phones on all the time. I am working almost every night and work until dawn, and that's because my clients [*xiaojies*] are also working during this time. As an agent, my work routine is not much different from a *xiaojie*." Another agent, a young man from Hong Kong, explained how he and his company were recruiting women to work in the overseas sex business:

> I have been in Indonesia for five months; the company in Indonesia has been in operation for five years. The company's headquarters are in Hong Kong. We can go back to Hong Kong for vacation once every six months. The company has business in Malaysia, Indonesia, United Kingdom, Japan, and some of the countries in the Middle East, but we are most active in Malaysia and Indonesia.
>
> We have people in Shenzhen, Guangzhou, Zhuhai, Zhongshan, and Dongguan[3] who recruit girls to come to Indonesia. They will go around various entertainment establishments in the downtown areas of those cities and look for potential candidates. We also do the recruitment in Indonesia. One of my main responsibilities is to make contacts with Chinese girls here and ask them if they have friends or relatives in China who would want to come here. If they do, I will ask them to give me the phone number of her friend or relative. I will call the person in China and if we have a good conversation on the phone, our partners in China will contact her, and help her to apply for travel documents, sign a contract, etc.
>
> Before we bring a woman here, we will discuss with her every term and condition. For example, which kind of venue they will work; what they will do; how much customers pay; how the money will be divided; how to pay us back for the documents' fee and airline ticket fee, etc. For those who have never been a *xiaojie*, we emphasize that their work is not just drinking or talking with customers.
>
> My income mainly depends on recruiting women. If I can recruit ten women every six months, the compensation will be higher than my salary as an agent. My minimum salary is about $1,500. But I can make more than $1,000 if I recruit one girl. Therefore I spend a lot of time looking for Chinese women in Indonesia who can refer me to girls in China.

Taking care of these girls is another responsibility. I go to every spa before I go home every night to see whether these girls *chutai*. I will send text messages to them to make sure they are fine before I go to sleep around 3 or 4 in the morning. If they do not reply, I will send another message again the next morning to make sure they are back in their dorm. On their off day, I take them shopping or help them send money to China. In any event, I have to help them with a lot of things.

We have to rely on Chinese women who are already here to refer their friends and neighbors to us. If they are not happy with us, how can we ask them to introduce other women to us? Besides, there is a Chinese embassy here and they can complain to the embassy if they are upset about us. How can we do business if they often go to their embassy and complain about us?

Agreeing to let us observe firsthand how agents in Jakarta work, Ah Lam, an agent, invited one of the authors to spend time with him one evening. He picked the author up around 6 p.m. that day and we went to a roadside food vendor to buy a large amount of fried food. Ah Lam said the women working in a KTV we would be visiting specifically asked him to bring along certain kinds of fried food. Not long after, we arrived in a mid-level KTV and were greeted by about thirty Chinese hostesses waiting for customers in a lounge. In the KTV, there were also about fifty Indonesian hostesses sitting in a separate area. The Chinese women were all very excited to see their agent, especially when they saw him with so many bags of their favorite fried food. The women complained to Ah Lam that business was slow and they were not making much money. Two mommies also came over to talk to Ah Lam. The Chinese hostesses appeared to be in very different moods: some were joking and smiling with others, and some just sat there quietly all by themselves and played with their cell phones. A few women asked Ah Lam if they could go somewhere else to work.

After about an hour in that KTV, we left to go to another KTV. This time, we walked into the manager's office and Ah Lam and the manager sat down to go over various money issues. They discussed a number of the hostesses' earnings, and finally the manager gave Ah Lam a stack of cash.[4] After that, we went to two more KTVs. Around 3 in the morning, Ah Lum drove the author back to his hotel. At that point, Ah Lam's cell phone rang and a KTV hostess said she had been hospitalized after taking drugs with a group of customers, and she asked him whether he could come to see her. Ah Lam sighed, and said he would be there in thirty minutes.

Escort Agency Owner

As discussed previously, some of our subjects worked for escort agencies in Taiwan, Malaysia, and New York. In Taiwan, we interviewed two escort agency owners, both referred to us by law enforcement officials there. The first subject, Boss Zhang, was a man in his forties, the owner of one of the top escort agencies in Taiwan. He showed up for the interview in a shiny black Mercedes-Benz.

> I have been in this business for twenty years. Right now, there are about a dozen Chinese women working in my agency and all of them are high-class escorts who charge a minimum of $230 per session. We screen our escorts carefully and select only one out of ten who want to join us. Besides running this escort agency, I am also the agent of two Chinese women.[5]
>
> We pay our women and their agents every ten days. A woman must repay her agent a $6,250 smuggling fee. They can pay it off in one month, but girls at our escort agency need forty days because we provide service only to rich clients and so our customer base is small. However, by the time they go back to China six months later, they may have earned as much as $60,000.

The second escort agency owner was a 36-year-old male, married with a ten-month-old baby girl. His wife had also operated an escort agency before their marriage, but her women were all from Korea. The two came to know each other after they were involved in a business dispute. The owner, Ah Qiang, described his experiences with both the recruitment and management of *xiaojies* from China:

> I became involved in the recruitment of Chinese *xiaojies* in 1998. I went to the rural areas of Fujian Province and signed up those who were already engaged in commercial sex and brought them over to Taiwan through fake marriages. You have to be very familiar with the process if you want to successfully bring a Chinese woman to Taiwan by means of fraudulent marriage. First, you need to find the right man to play the role of the fake husband who will then go to China to meet the potential "wife" for the first time. After he returns to Taiwan, he needs to call her very often. Next, he goes to China for the second time to marry his "wife." You must have a lot of photos, genuine or fake, to prove that the two are married; you also need to prepare the "wife" on how to answer all the questions asked by the Taiwanese authorities. Once a girl arrives in Taiwan, you need to train

her, buy her clothes, a cell phone, and the other things she needs to go to work. I need to spend about $5,000 to bring a girl to Taiwan, but charge her $6,250 for the trip. We tell the girls what they will do in Taiwan. We do not force or deceive them. The profit of this business is not that high, so there is no reason to force a girl to be a prostitute. Moreover, she can call the police anytime if we deceive her. Besides, more than 80 percent have been *xiaojies* in China.

Jockeys

In Hong Kong, Taiwan, and Malaysia there are male facilitators who are called *mafu* or jockeys. In Hong Kong, a *mafu* delivers a girl to a sex venue or a hotel on foot, and in Taiwan and Malaysia, by car. According to a *mafu* in Taiwan:

There are a few rules a good jockey must follow. First, a jockey must protect his woman. After he drops off his woman for a sex appointment, he must make sure that she enters the premises safely. Furthermore, he must watch what is going on outside the premises. Moreover, while driving the woman around, he must know how to deal with road checks by the police. A good jockey must prevent his *xiaojie* from being arrested during a road check. If the *xiaojie* is detained by the authorities during a road check, her jockey is fully responsible. If she is arrested in a sting operation, that's another story.

Second, a jockey must react quickly and take the right measures when something goes wrong. Once, I was stopped on the road by a group of police officers. I immediately called a friend, also a police officer. When the cops were questioning me, I intentionally dragged out my answers until my friend came. He talked to the cops and soon the woman and I were released.

One main thing that a jockey must avoid is having sex with his woman. He will be beaten up and fired if the woman's agent finds out about this. Most Chinese women will not get into a sexual relationship with their jockeys unless the jockey started it. Another taboo is if the jockey persuades a *xiaojie* to work for another escort company.

My daily income is about $80, this is what a *xiaojie* pays me. The escort company does not pay me. I pay for the expenses of car and gas. So my net daily income is a little more than $30. It is comparatively dangerous to drive for Chinese women. We must wait nearby while these women are seeing clients.

In Taiwan, many taxi drivers are recruited to work as jockeys and utilize their taxis to deliver Chinese women to various places to meet clients. However, when authorities in Taiwan began to scrutinize the taxi industry for its role in the sex trade, the escort agency owners started hiring drivers with private cars.

In Taiwan, a person can be an agent, an escort agency owner, and a jockey at the same time; or one can switch from one role to another in response to law enforcement reactions or market demands. As a result, we should be mindful that the roles of the facilitators or intermediaries in the sex trade are extremely fluid and most of the participants in the business can perform most of these roles if needed.

Fake Husbands

A *jialaogong* (fake husband) is someone hired by an agent to go to China, marry a Chinese woman, and then help her travel to the fake husband's (and the agent's) home country (in this case Taiwan) for the explicit purpose of engaging in prostitution. The agent pays for all the expenses, including the fake husband's flight, hotel, wedding banquet, and so on; and the woman has to repay her agent about $6,250 for getting her out of China and into Taiwan. The woman is also responsible for paying the fake husband about $1,000 a month during her stay in Taiwan, which is normally between six months to two years. In fact, once the woman arrives in Taiwan, there is little interaction between her and the fake husband, as she is immediately sent by the agent to work for an escort agency.

According to various reports in the Taiwanese media, agents normally look for the unemployed, the handicapped, or army veterans to engage in these fraudulent marriages with Chinese women. These men are willing to become fake husbands simply because they find the $1,000 monthly stipend very appealing and relatively easy to earn.

Figure 6.1 illustrates the social organization of the transnational sex operation in Taiwan. An agent makes the arrangements for a woman in China to marry a man (fake husband) from Taiwan and then take the woman to Taiwan. The agent then puts the woman to work with an escort agency. The escort agency owner arranges a driver (jockey) to deliver the woman to various sex appointments set up by a female pimp (auntie) or a "store owner" (a person using a rented apartment or studio for the explicit purpose of offering a place for sexual transactions between *xiaojies* and customers). Under this arrangement, the "store owner" takes a major cut of the fees from the customers.

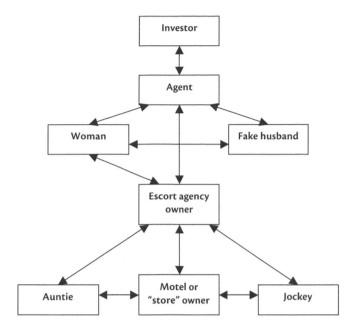

Figure 6.1. Social organization of transnational commercial sex in Taiwan

Mommy

The mommies, mostly women who may or may not have previously engaged in commercial sex themselves, solicit business for their girls. They do this by either approaching strangers on the streets or introducing the girls to customers in the nightclubs or KTVs. As mentioned in chapter 5, we met Wendy in Hong Kong; she was a street-based mommy who was seeking clients in a tourist area there. We also interviewed a mommy in a cheap dance hall in Hong Kong. Stella, that mommy, was in her late forties. She told us: "I became a *xiaojie* when I was 18. I did not attend school at all. I was a teenager when I moved to Hong Kong from Macau. I was married and had children. Now, I have several *xiaojies* under my supervision."

A mommy in Bangkok who also worked for a few years in Indonesia explained how difficult it was to be a mommy, even though she was making good money: "Actually, to be a mommy is hard work. Every day, I drink until I get very drunk, and throw up after I return home. I thought I was going to have my heart spit out. Although I was making lots of money, every day after work I just ate a bowl of instant noodles and went to sleep. How could I be able to live a happy life like this?"

We also talked to a mommy who was working for a large KTV establishment in Jakarta. The woman, Jessy, was in her forties and we met at the fancy restaurant of the KTV lounge where she was working. While talking to us, Jessy was also busy eating her dinner (around 10 p.m.) and answering her two cell phones that were constantly ringing. Dressed in a business suit, she seemed to be living a frantic life.

Brothel Keeper

In addition to the recruiters and transporters, brothel keepers are the third most often mentioned "sex traffickers" in the media and government reports. It is believed that for a woman to go overseas to engage in prostitution, someone must have first recruited her, and then another person must have transported her overseas, and finally someone (a sex venue owner) must have harbored and employed her in the destination country. Because brothel keepers are believed to be one of the principal actors who control and exploit these women for prolonged periods of time (from months to years) before they discard or resell the women, they are often considered to be among the worst of all the actors in sex trafficking.

While we were in Los Angeles, we had a long talk with Sam, a house owner who was originally from China. A stocky man in his forties, wearing short pants and a T-shirt most of the time, Sam shared with us his views on the sex business:

> My net profit is three to four thousand a month at most. As a housekeeper, I definitely do not make more than a *xiaojie*. My rent is $1,800 a month, and if you add to the rent all the other expenses, my daily operating cost is about $100. My business is very slow for the past few months and this is the worst of times for me. I had a girlfriend before and she answered the phone and so business was much better than now. Because I am answering the phone myself, many callers are reluctant to come. If one out of every five or six callers come, that's already quite good.[6]
>
> This is just a kind of exchange; a very fair exchange. In my opinion, my business is like a matchmaking business; I provide a venue for a man and a woman to get involved in a trade. Both sides get what he or she wants, and I am just making some money as a middleman. The man must get what he wants, otherwise there are going to be a lot of problems in this society. I often tell my *xiaojies* they should see themselves as medical doctors and their clients, patients. These women are treating their patients, it is that simple.

We also interviewed a young couple in Los Angeles who were running a house together. The female keeper, a thirty-something woman, said she was from Shenyang (Liaoning) and the man (a tall man also in his thirties) said he was a boyfriend of the woman. According to the couple:

> Our house is a small house, so we do not have our own regular girls. I myself do not see clients, so we are not making much. Our rent is a little more than $2,000 a month, and if we deduct all the expenses plus rent, we net about $2,000 to $3,000 a month. Some house keepers also see clients, and they certainly make much more because they can keep the whole $120 per date. With us, a client pays $120 per date, the girl gets $80 and we keep $40. How much money can we make like this? Of course, I can make $2,000 to $3,000 a month working in a restaurant, but running a house is an easy job because I don't have to be home every day.

Another keeper of a house we interviewed in Los Angeles was herself a former *xiaojie*, and we suspected, was still selling sex if a client insisted on seeing her or when business was good and she could not find enough women to meet the demand. We spent quite a few days in her house talking to her on and off on several occasions while interviewing women who were seeing clients in her house. We found the owner after we called a phone number from an ad in the local Chinese newspapers. The owner answered the phone and when we asked her about the price, she said $120.[7] Mei Mei, the owner, who is a young, petite woman with a pleasant personality, recalled how she became involved in prostitution and how she became a house owner later:

> In China, I was married, and then divorced. I came here as the wife of a Chinese man who was granted political asylum in the United States. In his application, he put me down as his wife. I knew the man's sister very well and they charged me $30,000 for their help. After I got here, I worked in a restaurant for a few days. Later, I found a job as a telephone operator at a house. After three months, I felt like I was not making enough money and when the boss also urged me to *xiahai* ["going down to the sea"], I did. At that house, I saw about five or six clients a day, and I made more than $10,000 a month.
>
> About a year later, I opened my own house. That house was also located in this area and I had about two or three in-house women working for me. Business was very good, and I was willing to take the risk of letting in all kinds of customers. Anyone who called was told the directions to my house. However, I am applying for citizenship next year and I don't want

to be arrested, and that's why I moved here and keep a very low profile. I now have only one in-house woman [a Korean], and if I need to, I call other women.

In addition to the keepers of houses in Los Angeles, we also interviewed a few massage parlor owners in New York and New Jersey. A woman from China who had many years of experience as a massage parlor owner on the East Coast described what her role as an owner was, and how the massage parlors catered to different groups of customers:

> You don't have to have any special qualifications to be a massage parlor owner. All you need is to be able to speak some English and that's because it is the owner's job to screen the customers when they call to ask about the place. Of course, most of these parlors do not have a phone installed; the owner can use a cell phone and answer the phone from any place. Those places that cater to only white Americans will refuse to give directions to people who speak English with a Chinese accent or who only speak Chinese. Of course, there are also many stores that only cater to Chinese customers. It's just that these two types of stores run their ads in very different places.

A Chinese lawyer in New York who had represented several massage parlor owners in court told us what he knew about these owners:

> Most owners are ordinary people; there is nothing special about them. They are not members of the underworld. Besides, anybody can become an owner. It is a very simple operation, at least here in New York City's Chinatown. A person can rent an apartment, hire a few women, place an ad in the newspaper, answer phone calls, and that's it. There is no need to decorate the apartment at all. Of course, the establishments in the suburban areas could be somewhat different because there you might have to have a sauna and shower facilities.

Big Business Owner

Of course, the chickenheads, agents, mommies, brothel owners, escort agency owners, jockeys, and fake husbands are well-known commercial sex entrepreneurs, but one should also understand that there are many big business owners who are facilitators, and have directly and greatly benefited from the existence of large numbers of *xiaojies* in or around their business establishments. For example, many nightclubs, KTVs, and hotels located in our research sites are actually owned by a small network of wealthy businessmen who are well-connected to the local and central authorities. This is an example of the role of corruption in supporting the commercial sex business in particular jurisdictions. The same is true with the hotel chains in Singapore. All the hotels in the main red-light district belong to one or more major hotel chains, and according to a local small-time hoodlum who used to work as a lookout man there:

> Hotels in this red-light district make a lot of money mainly because of the presence of these Chinese women. These hotels charge $6 to $8 per session. So these hotels will let the girls go inside and hide for a while when police come into the area. The chickenheads definitely get some benefit from these hotels, but we do not know exactly how. It is possible that hotel owners are the main bosses behind the whole business. They finance the chickenheads to recruit *xiaojies* from China because all of them will benefit from this business.

A Chinese Malay who used to work as an agent in Jakarta concurred: "In this sex business, you rarely see the investors. We only see the people who are involved in the day-to-day operations." A Chinese Indonesian businessman who used to be a regular customer of the various sex establishments in Jakarta said:

> All the KTVs and spas you see here in Jakarta were opened only as recently as 2002. Here, several spas are actually owned by a group of bosses. For example, if I want to open a spa, I will find a group of investors as partners; then one of us will run the spa on a daily basis. The rest of us will remain behind the scenes. If this first spa is a success, then we will open a second spa, and pick another partner to be the front man of the new spa. The smaller partners are usually picked to run the spas; the big partners always prefer to keep a low profile.

The Role of Organized Crime

As we indicated at the outset, many observers of human trafficking have claimed that organized crime groups are active in the promotion of the transnational movement of women for commercial sex.[8] For example, in a chapter on the relationship between the global sex trade and organized crime, Sarah Shannon, an expert on international security, concluded: "One of the most important actors in the world of illicit sex is organized crime. Mafia groups are an essential part of the structure that controls this market and their involvement takes many forms."[9] Donna Hughes, a leading international researcher on human trafficking, argued that organized crime groups are behind the trafficking of women from the former Soviet Union to Western Europe and the United States for prostitution.[10] Sociologist Kathryn Farr, in her book *Sex Trafficking*, concluded: "Because of its profit potential, a number of well-established organized crime groups—most notably the Russian mafia, the Japanese Yakuza, and the Chinese Triads—have become heavily involved in sex trafficking. Newer organized crime groups, such as those in Albania, Ukraine, and Nigeria, have become active sex traffickers as well."[11]

As Maggy Lee noted in her edited book on human trafficking: "Human trafficking has been conceptualized within a framework of organized crime. The role of criminally sophisticated, transnational organized crime groups as a driving force behind the highly profitable trade of smuggling and trafficking unauthorized migrants or asylum seekers has been commented upon widely."[12] According to Lee, a sociology professor, the United Nations and many governments around the world, including the United Kingdom and the United States, have institutionalized the "trafficking-as-organized crime" approach. From the point of view of Louise Shelley, a leading expert on transnational crime and terrorism, human trafficking is indeed transnational organized crime and it is tightly linked to all other forms of transnational organized crime such as human smuggling, drug trafficking, and money laundering: "The tardiness [with] . . . which the international community had responded to this problem has made many organized criminals switch to this area of criminal activity from other forms of transnational crime. Some crime groups traffic in human beings at the same time that they engage in other criminal activity."[13]

Some observers have claimed that not only are organized crime figures involved in human trafficking, but human traffickers are also engaged in other forms of transnational criminal activities (such as drug trafficking) as well.[14] In proposing that there are basically two types of human trafficking groups, the United Nations Office on Drug and Crime (UNODC) claimed that there is a thin line between human trafficking, organized crime, and other forms of cross-border crimes.[15] A 2010 UNODC paper on the topic concluded that there was probably even more diversity than previously recognized:

> It became clear from the review of the existing literature and from consultations with experts, that the key players on the criminal markets of trafficking in persons and smuggling of migrants can be organized in a

large variety of ways. The global landscape of organized crime, whether it is in smuggling of migrants or trafficking in persons, drugs, weapons, etc. has changed. The overall common ground in this respect is that not only there exists an enormous diversity in the landscape of organized criminal involvement in both phenomena but that overall there is an enormous diversity as to the different actors active in these markets. The actors involved may be organized criminal groups, individual traffickers or smugglers, or even friends and family of migrants or trafficking victims.[16]

As far as the trafficking of Chinese victims is concerned, a 2000 report prepared by Amy O'Neill Richard of the U.S. Department of State suggested that "The Sun Yee On Triad, Wo Hop To Triad, the United Bamboo Gang, and Fuk Ching Gang are all believed to be involved in alien smuggling to the US, and it is likely that their activities include trafficking."[17] Louise Shelley, in her most recent book *Human Trafficking*, pointed out that "Asian trafficking has many distinctive features apart from its sheer scale and diversity. Organized crime groups, particularly the *yakuza* and *triads*, as well as the less known Thai, Korean, and Indian crime groups, are key actors in the smuggling and trafficking of human beings. Trade in people is a more important part of their commercial activity than other major international crime groups."[18]

But many scholars have also argued otherwise.[19] For example, Yiu Kong Chu, an expert on the Hong Kong triads (who are generally regarded as the most sophisticated and dangerous organized crime entity in that part of the world) wrote: "It is quite clear that Chinese criminals in China and different parts of Southeast Asia countries collaborate to bring a large number of Chinese women to the destination country for prostitution. It should be noted that these syndicate members are not necessarily triads and usually have nothing to do with Hong Kong triads."[20]

In terms of our own research, the majority of the people we interviewed do not believe that members of traditional organized crime groups play a major role in the transnational movement of Chinese women for commercial sex.[21] There are indeed triads in Hong Kong and Macau,[21] organized gangs and local *jiaotou* groups in Taiwan,[22] *jao pho* in Thailand,[23] Chinese gangs in Singapore and Malaysia, and street gangs and tongs in the United States,[24] but our sources deny that members of these various groups are involved in the transnational movement of Chinese women for commercial sex, either as individuals or as groups.

Persons we spoke with who were facilitators in the business told us they did not see organized crime involvement. By way of explanation, a manager of a spa in Macau said: "Local gangs in Macau do not get involved in the prostitution business. Their main business is gambling. They don't pay much attention to the small profits from prostitution. As a result, there is not much contact between the local gangs and the chickenheads; the two groups are minding their own business without much interaction." A security guard at a five-star hotel in Macau concurred: "The triads such as the 14K or the Shuifang do not get involved in this business. They mainly depend on gambling to make money. Gambling is actually big business here in Macau. Chickenheads are all mainland people." Ah Qiang, the escort agency owner in Taiwan who is cited earlier in this chapter, explained why organized crime groups in Taiwan rarely get involved in the sex trade:

> Why do gangs not get involved in the Chinese women sex trade? It is because this is not a business with a lot of profit. The gangs look down on this type of business. In addition, you must be patient to do this business. You need to coax the women. Gang members tend to either beat them or spoil them. These are not solutions. It is impossible for them to run the business with patience and hard work.

A subject we interviewed in a prison in Taiwan who was doing time for sex trafficking also said: "Outsiders often think that people who are involved in this business are all gangsters. In fact, all the agents and jockeys I know are family men. They go home after work; they don't fool around."

Of course, not all the people we interviewed agreed that organized crime groups do not get into the action. Sammi, the mommy we interviewed in Bangkok, said that at one point most of the Chinese nightclubs in a particular area in Bangkok were owned and operated by the Taiwan-based Bamboo United and Four Seas, and, she said, these organized gangs were engaged in a power struggle with the 14K (a triad group from Hong Kong). However, it was not clear how these organized crime groups were connected to the movement of women from China to Thailand. A jockey we interviewed in Taiwan also told us that he once worked for an escort agency owner who was a midlevel leader of the United Bamboo. But, the jockey also stressed that the gang leader was running the escort service operation with his girlfriend and a group of nongang people and the operation was not part of his gang's business. Our key informants in Singapore also told us that the local gangs were active in some of the red-light districts in Singapore by either running the sex venues or providing protection to the girls walking the streets. Thus, there is no denying that in certain sites members of certain organized crime groups were involved in the sex trade as individuals, but they were not the key players.

Government officials we talked to also agreed with most of the "actives" when it came to the connection between the sex trade and organized crime. An official with the Ministry of Home Affairs of Singapore bluntly commented: "The men who are offering protection to the women in the red-light district are just a bunch of petty criminals, and I wouldn't call them members of a crime syndicate. To do so would be giving them too much credit." A high-ranking police officer with the Royal Malaysia Police likewise argued that this business is certainly organized, but it is not being controlled by organized crime. Indonesian National Police officials who we interviewed in Jakarta said that "syndicates" recruit Chinese women and bring them to Indonesia, but by syndicates they seemed to mean just a few individuals working with others in China. In fact, these officials said they had no indication that traditional organized crime was involved. Organized crime in Indonesia, they said, was into drug trafficking, money laundering, illegal logging, and terrorism—not human trafficking. However, it is also important to point out that one of the police officers in Hong Kong told us that a former 14K leader was active in the transportation of women from China to Hong Kong and that was the main reason for the implementation of Operation Fire Lily in 2002, a major police operation targeted at PRC *xiaojies* in Hong Kong.

In New York City, we asked members of the Human Trafficking Task Force of the New York Police Department whether any of the people who were bringing mainland Chinese women into the U.S. were members of organized crime groups or had anything to do with organized crime, and their answer was no. This was the same answer that we got from two female attorneys from the New York Eastern District office who are charged with investigating and prosecuting human trafficking cases. They both said that sex trafficking is organized, with a "small o," but is not organized crime, as with a "big O!"

In the end, it may be that our female subjects might be in the best position to tell us whether there seems to be a connection between organized crime groups and the transnational sex trade. They were the ones who could tell us a lot about the very people who had facilitated their movement and recruitment (coerced or otherwise) into prostitution. The experiences they described were almost exclusively with chickenheads, agents, brothel owners, escort agency owners, jockeys, and so on and practically none of them mentioned the words "gangs" or "organized crime" in their descriptions of these facilitators and operators.

Consequently, we think it is safe to conclude that even if some of these operators/facilitators might have been members of a gang or of an organized crime group, it does not seem to matter much because such membership is irrelevant in this particular context. By this we mean that they are operating

in this specific instance as individual criminal entrepreneurs, and not on be-
half of any criminal gang. The recruitment, transportation, and marketing of
these Chinese women obviously require a level of organization. But what our
data suggest is more akin to this being a crime that is organized rather than
organized crime.

Roles and Functions in Transnational Prostitution

From the above discussion, it is clear that when a Chinese woman goes overseas to engage in commercial sex, she may need one or more of the following
five types of assistance, depending on how easy or difficult it is to travel to the
destination country and how the sex industry in that country is structured:
financing the trip, obtaining travel documents, transportation, job referral,
and client referral. Some women can travel overseas and engage in paid sex
without anyone offering any of the above assistance, or with just a minimum
of help from a returned *xiaojie*. These women are most likely to be destined
for Hong Kong, Macau, or Thailand. In an exception to this, we found that
some women in Macau are being assisted by chickenheads. Some women
need all or nearly all of the various forms of assistance, and these women
are most likely to be found in Taiwan, Singapore, Malaysia, and Indonesia.
Women in the United States are unique in the sense that they need help
mainly to procure travel documents but not much else. Here we should keep
in mind that the Chinese women with whom we spoke in the U.S. had not
entered the country with the intention of entering into prostitution.

Table 6.1 lists the many actors in the transnational Chinese sex business,
the sites where they are more active, their functions, and their approximate
monthly income. They are the key players in providing all kinds of assistance
to (or engaging in exploitation of) women from China. These different roles
emerged in their particular geocultural environment to help sustain the sex
trade that employs a large number of Chinese women and in response to
market constraints and risk management. These actors or facilitators managed sex rings of various sizes, and seemed to thrive in their uniquely carved
out market niches, providing services to customers from diverse backgrounds and to the women who sell sex. The actors constitute a powerful informal enterprise that drives much of the underground economy for a large
number of Chinese women.

Our female subjects in Hong Kong and Macau did complain considerably about the chickenheads they encountered in the two research sites, and
some of the women we interviewed in Indonesia were not very happy with
their employers (the companies). The reasons for their complaints varied,

Table 6.1. Actors in the Transnational Chinese Sex Trade

Actor	Gender	Active in	Functions	Approximate monthly income ($)
Chickenhead	Male	Hong Kong and Macau	Transport, protect, and manage the girls	Not sure
Agent (as "owner")	Both	Taiwan	Invest money and orchestrate the movement of women	$5,000 per woman
Agent (as labor broker)	Both	Indonesia	Act as labor agent	$2,000 to $4,000
Mommy	Female	Hong Kong, Thailand, Malaysia, Indonesia	Function as an intermediary between the women and the clients	As high as $5,000
Brothel keeper (or house or massage parlor owner)	Both	Hong Kong, Los Angeles, New York	Operate a brothel (or a house or a massage parlor)	From a few thousands to $25,000
Jockey	Male	Hong Kong, Taiwan, Malaysia	Deliver the girls to the customers	$80 a day
Fake husband	Male	Taiwan	Travel to China, engage in fake marriage, and bring a woman overseas	$1,000
Auntie	Both	Taiwan	Refer customers to various sex venues	$30 to $45 per referral
Manager	Male	Hong Kong, Macau, Thailand, Malaysia, Indonesia	Manage a nightclub or KTV and be responsible for recruiting customers	Not sure

but the women were upset mainly because the chickenheads took away most of their money (and sometimes could be violent) and the companies took away their travel documents. On the other hand, the women rarely complained about the rest of the actors, to the extent that they even interacted with them. The issue of these actors' level of financial exploitation and control of the women will be discussed in chapter 10, but we think it is important for law enforcement authorities to understand that, at least within the Chinese context, women who sell sex are more likely to view only two types of players—the chickenheads in Hong Kong and Macau and the companies in Indonesia—as victimizers or exploiters, and not all the individuals associated with them.

7

Supply and Demand

Follow the Money

One of the weaknesses of much of the study of sex trafficking has been the lack of information and discussion about its financial aspects. An exception is the generally accepted estimate that human trafficking is a $32 billion-a-year business.[1] Suffice it to say that there is great deal of estimation that goes into substantiating that claim. There are many components to the "business," with many players involved. These components are mostly clandestine and the money transactions are in cash with no record keeping. Moreover, the cash changing hands is in different currencies. For all these reasons and more, we should be very cautious about accepting any financial estimates. That includes our own caveated discussion that follows.

The fact is that researchers know very little about the specific fees women from sending countries have to pay to go overseas; and yet the common conclusion is that these fees are exorbitant and that the interest attached is so high that it takes many years for the women to repay their debts. This is the basis for the conclusions that are generally reached about debt bondedness. We also have little data on specifically how much money these women are making overseas; but again the generally accepted conclusion is that they usually earn little or nothing, and that they often end up returning home empty-handed.[2]

In this chapter, we describe what we have learned about this issue from our interviews with 350 respondents who have knowledge with respect to Chinese women in this regard. In particular, we learn how much our respondents paid facilitators for the chance to go abroad, how much they charged their clients per sexual transaction, how many transactions they had on average, and how the money from the clients was distributed among the women and the various collaborators and employers. Harking back to the critically important role of economics as the dominant push factor in the transnational movement of women for commercial sex, we believe that these sort of data shed light on the economic aspects of the global sex trade, and thus help us better understand the force behind the massive movement of women across international borders.

Sticking with the economics of commercial sex, but shifting to the demand side of the equation, we then look at those whose money is driving the whole commercial sex business, namely, its clientele. Most of the work on prostitution and sex trafficking has focused on the women who sell sex, and on the (typically) male traffickers who force women to engage in prostitution. A number of experts have, however, argued that the men who buy sex should not be overlooked in any examination of prostitution and sex trafficking.[3] We did not conduct any formal interviews with buyers of sex in our research, but we did talk to a number of them informally. In addition, we asked our female subjects about their clients, and thereby learned a lot about the men who bought sex from them. In this chapter, we will examine who these clients are; we will look at client violence, which has been said to be a major concern for *xiaojies*; and at the nature of the relationships between buyers and sellers in the sex business.

We want to make clear at the outset of our discussion of specific money issues that all the monetary calculations we will present are just that—calculations. They are rough estimates; but they are the best estimates possible given the nature of the information available. For example, nearly all the figures in American dollars have been converted from foreign currencies, and because of the fluctuations in exchange rates the U.S. dollar amounts we present had to be ballpark estimates.[4] The conversion also accounts for why the amounts cited are often seemingly very specific, e.g., $106 or $67 or $221. Second, when we calculated the female subjects' daily or monthly incomes, we did not have information about money they may have received in tips. We know that some women, especially those who work in nightclubs and KTVs, rely substantially on tips. For these women, our estimates are going to understate their possible incomes. We have also not included in our estimates the regular stipends some women receive from their "husbands," again resulting in a lower estimate than might actually be the case.

The two greatest "fudge factors" here are first, the fact that most of the women we interviewed were not very good at remembering how much they made, either because they live a chaotic life and/or because it is simply not easy to keep a record of their earnings to begin with. Second, when we refer to the women's "monthly salaries," these are our estimates based upon multiplying what they said they made a day by the number of days they said they worked a month. It is important to reiterate that our estimates of earnings are, if anything, understated. In all probability the women made more, and possibly considerably more, than we have estimated.

Road Fee

Many respondents used the words *lufei* (road fee) or *shouxufei* (processing fee) to refer to the money they had to pay to go overseas. Of the 149 Chinese women we interviewed outside of China, 146 answered our questions about a road fee, and 99 (68%) said they had paid someone to help them get out of China (see Table 7.1). The other 47 (32%) said they did not have to pay anyone, even though they did spend some money to obtain travel documents such as a passport or visa, and to buy a plane or train ticket.

Table 7.1 shows that subjects in different sites were in different situations in terms of paying someone for their overseas travel. For example, subjects in Hong Kong and Macau rarely had to pay (only one out of five), simply because Chinese citizens can make the arrangements to travel to Hong Kong and Macau without outside help. A substantial portion of our subjects in Thailand (35%) also did not have to pay anyone to go to there. Many of the subjects in Los Angeles (47%) and some in New York (19%) did not pay because they came as legal immigrants or with an F-1 (student) or B-2 (business) visa—a visa they obtained without having to spend any money. On the other hand, almost all the subjects in Taiwan (94%), Malaysia (89%), Singapore (93%), and Indonesia (89%) said they had to pay someone to help them leave China.

Table 7.1 also indicates the amount of money our subjects paid for their travel. For those ninety-nine subjects who did pay someone, the average road fee was just over $7,000, but the makeup of charges was significantly

Table 7.1. Road Fee, by Research Site (N = 149) *

Site	N	Number of subjects who paid	Percentage who paid	Average amount ($)
Hong Kong	15	3	20	903
Macau	18	4	24	9,750
Taiwan	16	14	94	6,405
Thailand	17	11	65	1,315
Malaysia	18	16	89	1,074
Singapore	15	14	93	3,138
Indonesia	18	16	89	1,680
Los Angeles	16	8	53	26,640
New York	16	13	81	19,346
Total	149	99	68	7,055

* Three missing observations

different depending on the site. The three subjects in Hong Kong paid an average of only about $900, compared to almost $27,000 for the eight subjects in Los Angeles. Subjects in Thailand, Malaysia, and Indonesia also did not pay a lot—roughly $1,000. For Taiwan, the average road fee was over $6,000, and it was one of the more expensive places to go among our research sites in Asia. Ah Qiang, the escort agency owner mentioned earlier, explained why this relatively large amount of money was needed to bring someone from China to Taiwan, using the fake marriage method:

> In the past, it took only forty-five days for the "bride" in China to come to Taiwan. At that time, the fake husband had to go to China only once [visit and marry]. Now, the fake husband needs to go to China three times: first, he goes to China as a member of a tour group for three days [this is the cheapest way to visit China], second, he goes to China to marry, and third, he goes to China to bring his "wife" back to Taiwan. Sometimes, both the agent and the fake husband's parents also need to go to China to arrange things to make it more convincing to the Taiwanese authorities. So, it costs a lot of money. Once the "wife" comes, the agent pays the fake husband about $1,000 as the first monthly payment; pays her rent [the total amount of one month rent plus deposit is about $500]; and buys two sets of nice clothes and makeup.

Most of the women we interviewed in Taiwan did not think that the amount of money they owed their agents was unreasonable. As mentioned in chapter 4, the $6,000 road fee to Taiwan was so taken for granted by both sides that it was not even discussed when the two sides met to discuss traveling to Taiwan.

Even though only 24 percent of the women we interviewed in Macau had to pay someone to get there, the four women who did pay had to spend an average of almost $10,000 for the trip. The explanation for this high fee is that for these four women, their trips to Macau and/or their initiations into commercial sex in Macau were arranged by a chickenhead.

In sum, as illustrated in Table 7.1, not all the Chinese women had to pay someone to go overseas, because some of them were able to obtain the necessary travel documents on their own or with the help of a returned *xiaojie* who helped them for nothing. The odds of paying or not paying seem to depend on the person, the helper, and the destination. We also see that for the majority of the women, the road fee was not as exorbitant as generally suggested in the writings and commentary on human trafficking. Most women paid one or two thousand dollars for their trips, and consequently they did not have to work all that long to repay the money.

It is also the case that many women were able to pay for their trip with their own savings, or were able to borrow the relatively small amount of money from friends and relatives. Our data in fact show that this was exactly what happened with most of our subjects. Table 7.2 shows that 36 (38%) of the subjects who paid someone for their trip, paid with their own money. Another 25 subjects (26%) said they borrowed the money from their friends or relatives. Only 34 (36%) subjects owed money to someone who was not an acquaintance.

All the subjects in Taiwan arrived there with debts to various agents, but none of the women we interviewed in the United States, even though they had to pay significantly more than did the subjects in Asia, were under debt bondage. Moreover, when we asked the 34 subjects who arrived overseas

Table 7.2. *How the Road Fee Was Paid, by Research Site* ($N = 99$)

Site	Own money	Borrowed money	Debt to a sex ring operator	Total
Hong Kong	2 (67%)	1 (33%)	0 (0%)	3
Macau	1 (25%)	0 (0%)	3 (75%)	4
Taiwan	0 (0%)	0 (0%)	15 (100%)	15
Thailand	4 (36%)	6 (55%)	1 (9%)	11
Malaysia	6 (46%)	3 (23%)	4 (31%)	13
Singapore	8 (57%)	3 (21%)	3 (21%)	14
Indonesia	7 (44%)	1 (6%)	8 (50%)	16
Los Angeles	2 (29%)	5 (71%)	0 (0%)	7
New York	6 (50%)	6 (50%)	0 (0%)	12
Total	36 (38%)	25 (26%)	34 (36%)	95*

* Four missing observations

owing money to sex ring operators whether they were still under debt bond-age at the time of the interviews, only 13 said they were. This means the other 21 subjects had already cleared their debts by the time we interviewed them. This is a very different picture than that presented by, for example, Human Rights Watch.[5] Referring to the experience of Thai women in Japan, Human Rights Watch concluded that most Thai women who were working in the Japanese sex business took anywhere from several months to two years to repay their debts.

Our findings suggest that perhaps we need to reexamine some of the as-sumptions about sex trafficking and debt bondage. For example, according to an excerpt from the book *Sex Slaves* by Louise Brown:

> Debt bondage is the name given to this system. It is a widespread prac-tice throughout the global sex industry and is common in Asia. At its best it can be seen as a way a girl can secure an advance upon her earnings. At worst it is akin to sexual slavery because the brothel and club owners manipulate the debt. The debt is not fixed and it expands at the whim of the brothel owner or manager. In essence debt bondage is used to force women to become prostitutes and to make them accept customers and comply with sexual acts that they would otherwise refuse.[6]

Contrary to this common perception, none of our subjects said that they had been asked to pay interest on their debts. This could be in part because of the relatively short period of time that was needed to repay their travel ex-penses (normally between ten and twenty days)—perhaps making it less of an issue.[7] We did not find many travel expense-related disputes between the women and their various intermediaries.

We asked those who owed money to sex ring operators whether they had encountered any problems when they tried to clear their debts, and most said their debtors handled the repayments in good faith. According to Yang Yang, a 25-year-old single woman from Shenyang who was working the streets of a red-light area in Singapore: "So far, I gave them all the money I had earned here, about $2,000, as a road fee. They won't cheat me; after I repay them the entire $4,200, they will stop collecting money from me. Every time I pay them, they record the transaction. I also keep a separate record. I never heard about them having any money-related disputes with any women here" (1).

When it came to the road fee, most subjects were quite rational and even fatalistic about it. Of course, some women were not happy with the road fee, especially when they found out later that they had been charged significantly more than other women. This unhappiness is of course exacerbated if they are also having a hard time making money overseas. Despite the fact that some subjects were not happy because they thought they had been duped into paying more than others, none of our subjects said they had experienced anything like what has been described in much of the antitrafficking literature. For example, according to Donna Hughes: "Women are held in debt bondage in which they must repay their purchase price, travel expenses and all other expenses charged to them, which can be considerable, before they are allowed to leave. A woman may be sold from one pimp to another at which time her debt to be repaid starts all over again."[8] None of our subjects said anything about a purchase price, or about being sold to another debtor after they had repaid their road fee to one debtor.

Charges and Earnings

In most descriptions of sex trafficking, there is an assumption that when women go overseas to sell sex, especially if they have been tricked or coerced, they are going to be exploited by pimps and brothel owners under the debt bondage system. One of the most frequently mentioned types of exploitation is monetary, as Louise Brown has asserted in her book *Sex Slaves*: "We can guarantee that the women who are held in sexual slavery see very little of this [money]."[9] "Women in sexual slavery receive nothing, or, at best, a pitiful fraction of the income that the brothel owners collect from the sale of their sexual labour."[10] Our data do not support this conclusion.

In the main, what we find is that there are two ways a *xiaojie* makes money. She has sex with a customer and the customer pays her for the sexual services. These sexual transactions can take place in a hotel, a nightclub or a KTV, a sauna or a spa, a massage parlor, a brothel, or an apartment. Or she can drink, sing, dance, and chat with a customer or a group of customers as a hostess in a nightclub, a KTV, or a flower hall, and then receive tips from her customers.

As shown in Table 7.3, customers paid our respondents an average of $96 per session for sexual transactions and $38 per table (not per customer) for hostessing. Subjects in Macau were paid, on average, as low as $30 per sexual transaction, whereas respondents in Indonesia were paid as much as $145. Of course, most of our subjects in Macau were women providing quick sex out of cheap hotels, whereas most of our subjects in Indonesia were working for upscale spas where a variety of sexual services must be provided before sexual intercourse. As a result, the overall payment is significantly different. But the price difference reflects the nature of the sex service rather than the nature of the sex business in Macau and Indonesia. If, for example, we had interviewed more women working in the upscale spas of Macau, we clearly

Table 7.3. Charges, Earnings, and Percentage Retained, by Research Site
$(N=149)$

Site	Per session (sexual transaction)			Per table (hostessing)		
	Customer pays (charges in $)	Subject gets (earnings in $)	% retained	Customer pays (charges in $)	Subject gets (earnings in $)	% retained
Hong Kong	77	54	63	50	35	70
Macau	30	27	97	N/A	N/A	N/A
Taiwan	135	57	43	N/A	N/A	N/A
Thailand	130	93	75	12	8	66
Malaysia	43	39	78	34	28	82
Singapore	82	72	92	Missing	42	N/A
Indonesia	145	75	55	65	45	69
Los Angeles	116	86	74	N/A	N/A	N/A
New York	129	102	80	N/A	N/A	N/A
Total	96	66	74	38	27	71

might have had a different finding. Lest one question the $96 per transaction figure, we would point out that this is very close to the average charge of $94 per client for trafficked victims recorded in the Counter-Trafficking Module Database of the International Organization for Migration (IOM).[11]

Another key issue addressed in Table 7.3 is the percentage of the charges that actually went to the respondents, to the women themselves. On average, our respondents received an average of $66 per commercial sexual transaction, which is equivalent to about three-fourths of the money that the customers paid. Respondents in Taiwan received only 43 percent of the payment, whereas respondents in Macau obtained as much as 97 percent of the payment.

Our data suggest that the majority of the women who went overseas to engage in commercial sex were not, contrary to what is often asserted in the trafficking literature, subjected to grossly unfair treatment at the hands of those who helped them to sell sex. We think the reasons for this are twofold. First, as mentioned above, many women engage in prostitution as independent entrepreneurs, so there are no pimps or brothel keepers to take advantage of them, and they are able to pocket most if not all the money their customers paid. Second, the people who are intermediaries or facilitators know quite well that they must rely on these women to do a profitable business. It is not good business practice to take an unreasonable share of the profits if they want the women to continue to work for them, or better yet, want them to help recruit friends and others into the business.

Our findings are very much in accord with findings from some other studies. For example, when demographer Gavin Jones and his colleagues at the National University of Singapore conducted a study of the sex sector in Indonesia and examined the earnings of Indonesian women, they found that:

> In most brothels, the sex worker received half of the fee paid by the client. . . . On the other hand, customers frequently paid a tip directly to the woman, and this was not shared with the pimp or brothel manager. . . . This finding suggests that the sex industry workers were relatively well-off compared to workers outside the industry with the same level of education and social background.[12]

Likewise, according to Thai demographer Wathinee Boonchalaksi and her colleague Philip Guest, in Thailand "it was possible for a prostitute to receive between 50 and 60 percent of the money paid by a client, but to do so, she had to work regularly."[13] On the other hand, the IOM data mentioned above showed that victims in their data base normally received only about 16 percent of the money they charged their customers; but this finding was based upon only 72 valid cases out of a sample of 4,559.[14]

Table 7.4 shows charges, earnings, and percentage retained by types of working arrangements. As may be expected, independent workers charged less per sexual transaction ($63), but they also received almost all the money (97%). Women who worked with a partner, be it a mommy or a chicken-head, charged $20 more than the independent workers for an average of $84, but actually received only $62—just $2 more than the independent workers. Women who worked in the organized commercial sex sectors charged the most—an average of $117 per sexual transaction—and received slightly more ($72) than women working elsewhere.

Table 7.5 illustrates the charges, earnings, and percentages retained by sex venue. As described above, the first four types of venue were all independent

Table 7.4. Charges, Earnings, and Percentage Retained, by Type of Working Arrangement (N=149)

	Per session (sexual transaction)			Per table (hostessing)		
Arrangement	Customer pays (charges in $)	Subject gets (earnings in $)	% retained	Customer pays (charges in $)	Subject gets (earnings in $)	% retained
Independent	63	60	97	19	14	74
Partnership	84	62	79	67	53	79
Employed	117	71	61	37	28	76
Total	96	66	74	38	27	71

Table 7.5. Charges, Earnings, and Percentage Retained, by Sex Venue (N = 149)

Venue	Customer pays (charges in $)	Subject gets (earnings in $)	% retained
Independent: street	23	23	100
Independent: hotel	65	65	100
Independent: home	81	81	100
Independent: restaurant	63	56	93
Partnership: mommy	115	77	65
Partnership: chickenhead	43	41	98
Employed: nightclub/KTV	154	108	74
Employed: sauna/spa	133	67	48
Employed: massage parlor	120	84	71
Employed: brothel	55	38	72
Employed: escort	120	50	42
Total	96	66	74

(Column group header: Per session (sexual transaction))

modes of operations—women soliciting business on the street, out of a hotel, from their homes, or in a restaurant. These women kept whatever their customers paid them because they were operating on their own.

Subjects who were working in conjunction with a mommy or a chickenhead had to pay these partners. According to our data, women with mommies charged their customers an average of $115 per session, but kept only $77 (65%).[15] Women with chickenheads charged their customers $43 per session, and were able to keep 98 percent of that money ($41).

Women who were involved in organized prostitution and worked for a sex ring operator also had to give up a certain portion of the money their customers paid. As shown in Table 7.5, customers paid an average of $154 per sexual transaction to women who were working in nightclubs and KTVs, $133 to subjects in the sauna or spa sector, $120 to respondents in the massage parlor, $55 to women in the brothels, and $120 for those who worked in the escort business. Subjects in the sauna/spa sector (mainly in Indonesia) and the escort business (primarily in Taiwan and Malaysia) were the most heavily exploited, because they got only 48 percent (sauna/spa) or 42 percent (escort) of what their customers paid.

The bottom line income of the independent workers was reduced by whatever living expenses they had to pay. For example, Xiao Ju, a 23-year-old from Jinzhou whom we interviewed in a small hotel in Macau, said: "I charge $27 per session and I keep all the money. However, I have to pay for my room every day. I share a room with another girl. The room costs $43 a day if there is only one occupant. If there are two occupants, it costs more than $60 a day. That's why me and my roommate are paying more than $30 a day per person" (94). Yin Yin, a 24-year-old from Changde, worked out of another small hotel only a block away from Xiao Ju's hotel, and the two hotels were owned by the same owner and managed by the same manager. Even though the women in the two hotels charged a different price per sexual transaction ($27 in Xiao Ju's hotel and $13 in Yin Yin's), the room costs were about the same for both hotels. According to Yin Yin, she also had to pay extra if she asked for extra towels and/or a change of bedsheets more than once a day:

> Besides the $41 a day hotel room fee, I keep all the money I make. The room costs $45 on weekends. The hotel would change our bedsheets and towels only once a day; if we want to have extra services, the hotel charges us $1.30 for changing bedsheets and $.67 for changing towels. I do not need to pay the police, hotel employees, or the local thugs. I think the hotel charges us too much for rooms. We must see at least three clients a day; otherwise, we will lose money on that day. (86)

Monthly Income

As indicated previously, the monthly income estimates have a number of caveats: accuracy of subject's earnings estimates; number and amount of any tips; how many days and weeks they actually work in any given time period, and so on. But based upon what the women told us about how much they charge their customers per session, how much of the money belongs to them, approximately how many clients they see a day, and how many days they normally work a month, we have calculated their approximate monthly earnings. We believe this is a useful exercise because it provides a benchmark, rough as it is, against which to compare the monthly income possibilities if the women had stayed in China working in jobs other than the commercial sex business.

Table 7.6 shows that our subjects made an average of $188 a day for about an average of just over $4,000 a month. For a woman who might have been making $100 to $200 a month in the legitimate job sector in China, $4,000 a month (tax free) is certainly a very attractive income. None of this is to suggest that our respondents were getting rich from being prostitutes, regardless of the kind of sex venue in which they were involved.

Table 7.6 indicates that women in Los Angeles were making the most, about $7,800 a month, and this monthly income was almost seven times the amount of money a woman in Thailand made, which was about $1,100 a month. Wang Jing, a 31-year-old woman from Fuzhou with a brand new

Table 7.6. Income, by Research Site (N = 149)

Site	Daily earnings ($)	Monthly earnings ($)
Hong Kong	130	2,856
Macau	142	3,145
Taiwan	367	7,218
Thailand	53	1,110
Malaysia	120	2,537
Singapore	207	4,588
Indonesia	112	2,233
Los Angeles	345	7,827
New York	285	5,987
Total	188	4,026

BMW X5, reiterated how much she was making in Los Angeles when she became a prostitute at the age of 23:

> I began to work in a house a few days after I got here because my friend kicked me out of her apartment (she thought I was flirting with her boy-friend) and I owed my parents $60,000 for the fake marriage to come here. I worked in that house for nine months, and I made a lot of money. At that time, I could have as much business as I wanted; one day I saw twenty-two men. That's because I was young then; many women were in their forties. After those twenty-two sessions, I did not even have the strength to apply the brake when I drove home. Those nine months, I sent home $105,000. (133)

Taiwan ranked second in income where respondents averaged about $7,200 a month, followed by subjects in New York with an average monthly income of almost $6,000. Bing Bing, a 25-year-old single woman from Changchun who was working as an escort in Taiwan, recalled how much she had made on her first trip to Taiwan:

> When I was in Taiwan for the first time, I worked for seven months before I was arrested and was ordered by the authorities to return to China. During those seven months, after clearing the debt [road fee] of $6,250, I went home with about $42,000. Normally, I made about $7,200 to $7,800 a month, but sometimes as high as $9,400. I am very frugal; I do not do drugs or gamble. When I go shopping or eating, I need not spend my own money anyway because there will always be men eager to pay. I can basically save all my earnings. (144)

Xiao Xiao, a 32-year-old woman from Yuncheng who had been to Taiwan six times between 1998 and 2008, explained why she repeatedly returned to Taiwan despite being deported many times: "After staying for six months during my first trip to Taiwan, I made about $12,500 after repaying the road fee. In China, how the hell am I going to make this kind of money in six months?" (149).

The amount of money a woman from China can make in a particular destination is a good indicator of the desirability of that country. According to a tour guide in Bangkok who is very familiar with the sex trade in Southeast Asia: "For Chinese women, the number one destination is the United States, followed by Japan. If they cannot go to these two countries, they want to go to Taiwan, Singapore, Macau, and Hong Kong. Further down the line is Malaysia. They go to Indonesia or Thailand only if they have no other choices. You can say Thailand is their last choice."

Money Management

At the time of the interviews, few of our subjects sounded like they were in excellent financial shape, even though some of them had entered the profession years before and had made good money for a number of years. Some did not have much money because they gave all or most of their earnings to their boyfriends or chickenheads. According to Xiao Ya, a 20-year-old single woman from Chongqing who was in Hong Kong for the second time when we interviewed her in a brothel:

I made more than $1,300 during my first trip [for seven days] and I gave all the money to the man who took me to Guangdong. He is 23, not handsome, but I like him. He told me that after one more year, I don't have to work anymore. He used to have a girlfriend who was also a *xiaojie*. Many people warned me that he is not dependable, including my mother. But I won't listen to them. My female boss [the brothel owner] also told me not to give him all my money. But I do. I hope he won't cheat on me. (75)

Some said they spent all their money whenever they returned to China. Xiao Qian, a 22-year-old hotel-based *xiaojie* who had been to Macau more than five times, said:

It is hard to say how much I make here in Macau. All I can say is that each time when I go back to China after working in Macau for fourteen days, I bring home about $1,000 after deducting all the expenses. So far, I don't even have 10,000 yuan [$1,200] in savings yet. Each time when I am back in Zhuhai, I will eat, drink, play, shop, and use Ketamine powder [a popular drug in China]. I will spend all my money before I return to Macau. Besides, I also send money to my family regularly, about $140 a month. (88)

Some were fond of gambling and thus did not hold on to their earnings. In Macau, we interviewed a woman who was turning tricks out of a dilapidated housing project for $8 a trick, and who told us:

During my first trip here, I made about $2,600. Before I went back to China, I visited the Sands Casino and lost $2,000. As a result, I brought home only $600. This is my second trip to Macau. I went to another casino the day before yesterday, just a few days before returning to China, and I lost $1,600. I lost all the money I made over the past several days plus the money I brought from China. It upset me so much that I did not work yesterday. (97)

Some subjects were at least somewhat better and smarter when it came to managing their money. Linda, a 35-year-old married woman from Beijing whom we interviewed in a house in Los Angeles, said she spent all her savings buying an apartment in Beijing:

I just bought a house in Beijing; it's a duplex apartment. I bought it for more than $150,000. Now the apartment needs to be decorated, and I thought it was going to cost about $75,000. But my family in Beijing is telling me that it will cost another $150,000 to decorate the house, and that's why I am working like hell now.[16] (132)

Kelly, a 38-year-old divorcee from Beijing whom we interviewed inside a house in Monterey Park, California, explained how she allocated her money: "Recently, I bought a new BMW. It cost me more than $50,000. I drive it only when I go shopping or sightseeing; when I am working, I drive my old car. This way, I don't attract people's attention. I am saving money to buy a house [in which to live]. I also plan to open my own house [for the sex business] next year" (121).

A former massage parlor owner we interviewed in New York had her own observations about how Chinese xiaojies handle their money:

Most of these women are not very generous. They try to save as much as they can. However, there are things that they are willing to spend their money on, and those are gambling, drugs, and men. They go to Atlantic City, Foxwoods, and mahjong clubs in New York to gamble. It is not unusual to see these women lose up to $10,000 in a single visit to one of these places. Some of them use drugs. The one thing most of them do is spend money on their men. These are men who shamelessly exploit these girls. This group of men is also active in drug use. The other thing these women are willing to spend their money on is expensive handbags by LV, Gucci, and Chanel.

In sum, when we asked women why they had such low savings after working so many years, some of them shrugged and said: "Well, easy come, easy go." It is perhaps not surprising to see a kind of financial shortsightedness among them. Even though some women speak of saving and investing for the future, most are very now-oriented. They live in the present, trading off their youthful attractiveness as long as they can. They have to know it will not last, but seem torn between preparing for the day when they will be old former prostitutes, and living life to the fullest in the moment.

The Clients

Most of our attention so far has been on the supply side of the commercial sex equation—on the *xiaojies*, the various facilitators, the sex ring operators, and so on. Now we want to look briefly at the demand side, at the clientele. We should acknowledge that demand is more than just that from clients. For example, it can be argued that the supply/demand picture may not be as clear-cut and simple as it might first appear, because sex operators, for instance, can be part of both the supply and the demand. The continuing requirement for new blood on the part of the brothel owners, massage parlor owners, and so on, is very much a part of the demand side of the commercial sex business. That said, our focus here will be on the clients—the men who pay for sex and thus create the profits that drive the business.

As we have already indicated with respect to much of the prevailing thinking, research, and writing about sex trafficking, there has been a concerted effort to simplify and to promulgate a particular point of view. In this instance, the goal seems to have been to paint the men who buy sex (seemingly all of them) as exploiters and abusers of sex trafficking victims. Again, we think it is useful and enlightening to step back and see just what the most knowledgeable persons—those directly involved—have to say about this.

That there is another point of view to the abuser/exploiter picture has already been reflected in some of the work done by others. For example, Galma Jahic, an expert on prostitution and sex trafficking in Bosnia and Herzegovina, challenges the notion that sex trafficking victims make the "best" prostitutes. She writes that although a "very small minority" of customers may have a particular interest in trafficking victims "perhaps for sadistic reasons . . . [in most cases] customer demand is not particularly for trafficking victims per se, but for certain types of sex workers. . . . In the majority of cases, customers are simply after sex workers with a preference for cheaper . . . more docile, and more eager to please sex service providers, or sex workers who are from a different country or from a different ethnic background—exotic."[17]

Jahic cites studies by Jordan,[18] Martilla,[19] and Plumridge et al.,[20] all pointing to the same conclusion. And that conclusion is that the men who buy sex want to believe that the women are also enjoying the sexual experience. There is, in other words, a body of research that finds that the "demand is not just for sex, but for a fully emotionally responsive woman to have sex with."[21] Rather than just paying for sex, Jahic says, "men are actually paying for an approximation or an illusion of a real intimate relationship, one where pressures on men assigned by their gender roles are significantly reduced."[22]

Our data suggest that the majority of our female subjects were engaged in providing sex services to mainly Chinese men, even though they were working outside China. Hong Kong, Macau, Taiwan, and Singapore are all Chinese societies, so the majority of the sex buyers there are naturally most likely to be ethnic Chinese. The other research sites—Thailand, Malaysia, Indonesia, and the United States—are not Chinese societies, and yet most of the subjects we interviewed in these sites said their clients were also mainly Chinese, be they overseas Chinese or Chinese nationals who were visiting, working, or conducting business there.

In Hong Kong, the majority of the men who bought sex from our subjects were local Hong Kong males. Only those subjects who solicited business (with or without the help of a mommy) in tourist areas were likely to have an opportunity to meet non-Chinese clients. Foreigners in Hong Kong can find Chinese women through a website in which the photos, prices, approximate locations, and contact numbers of hundreds of women (95% from China and the other 5% from Taiwan, Korea, Japan, Eastern European countries, and local women) are listed in Chinese and English.

Our female respondents in Hong Kong were divided when they were asked about their experiences with their clients; some said Hong Kong men were nice, others said sex buyers in Hong Kong were obnoxious. For example,

Su Ting, a 23-year-old single woman who worked as a nightclub hostess and a streetwalker, was not very happy with the men she met in Hong Kong:

> I sit one or two tables a day in the nightclubs. Hong Kong people are weird, probably because they are stressed. Some customers asked me to go up to a mountain or go to a beach to have sex. On one occasion, I agreed to go to a beach with a man, but I became scared after we got there and I came back without having sex. Some customers ask us to use ketamine with them, but I do not entertain this type of customer. Some girls are willing to do so because a tip for hostessing this type of table is $106 instead of $66. I think Hong Kong people look down on us. Some customers are really hard to please. It seemed like they wanted to get back as much as they can. They won't let you take their money easily. (76)

Women we interviewed in the smaller hotels of Macau were also not pleased with their clients who were predominantly lower-class local people, migrant laborers from China, or chickenheads from northeast China. "I see an average of about ten clients a day. My clients are mainly local people or laborers from the mainland. A few of them are from Hong Kong. The quality of my clients is really bad. It seems that they must get enough back after paying me $14," said Xiao Tao, a 20-year-old petite woman from Changde who was selling sex in a hotel in Macau (85). Yin Yin, another hotel-based *xiaojie*, complained: "Men from the northeast and Fujian Province are difficult to please. Northeasterners are forceful when they have sex, and often won't release after more than half an hour" (86). Zhang Li, a 24-year-old single woman from Huangmei who we interviewed in another small hotel, agreed: "We especially do not like people from northeastern China. If they want me, I tell them that another woman is working in my room and so I can't see them. I had a customer not long ago. He did not look like a northeasterner at all, so I went upstairs with him and only after we entered my room did I realize I had made a mistake. He may have taken some kind of drug in advance and he could not ejaculate even after half an hour. I asked him to pay me $14 and go. My regular charge was $28. But he said that he would not leave until he got release and money was not a concern for him. After that, he still could not ejaculate after an hour or so. I told him to go and I will not charge him any money. He left and paid me nothing" (99).

Like women working out of the smaller hotels, women in apartment-based brothels in Macau also charge $14 for "pure sex" (sexual intercourse) and $20 for "full service" (oral sex first and sexual intercourse later). Subjects who worked inside those apartment brothels in Macau were also disappointed with clients who were mostly from China:

> Most customers are from China, and mainly from Fujian Province. We do not like them and do not want to do business with them. Some customers are local people. Few are from Hong Kong or Taiwan. Fujianese customers often do not pay after having sex and they are rude. Drunk people are the kinds of customers with whom I least want to do business. They cannot ejaculate even after a long time. They will not pay if they do not release even though I have served them for more than one hour. (Xiao Song, a 24-year-old single woman from Shashi, Hubei) (98)

A woman who was soliciting business on a street in Macau was significantly more positive than those women who were turning tricks for $14 or $28 in the hotels.

> My customers are mainly from Hong Kong, Taiwan, and the mainland; very few local men. Men from the mainland would bargain. I ask for $66 and they would say $53. Clients from Hong Kong and Taiwan would not cut my price. My clients are not bad; they won't force me to do anything. A few days ago, I had a customer from the mainland. He said he would pay me $266 if he does not have to wear a condom. I said no way. Then he said he can increase it to $360. I still said no. He did not insist after that. (Ah Qin, a 29-year-old divorced woman from Dalian) (91)

Those who were selling sex in five-star hotels, and charging more than a $100 per session, were impressed with the generosity of their clients. Shan Shan, a 24-year-old single woman from Changsha, said: "My clients are mostly from Hong Kong and Taiwan. Recently, there are more and more Shanghainese. Our customers are rarely local people. All my clients are very nice. People who come here to gamble are all very generous. It is normal that they would give you $1,000 or more if they have a good time with you" (92).

Most of the women we interviewed in Taiwan also told us that their clients were generally nice, but a few thought Taiwanese men were, in their words, sick. According to Co Co, a 28-year-old woman from Henyang who was working as an escort in Taiwan, "they like to remove their condoms when I am not paying attention and they want to ejaculate inside my body" (136). Zhao Shuang, a young woman from Hulunbeier (Inner Mongolia) whom we interviewed in Taiwan, was of the view that "some customers became abnormal after watching so many x-rated movies. It seems to them," she said, "that they are entitled to humiliate you as long as they are paying you" (139). Xiao Cai, a 22-year-old escort in Taiwan who came from Guangxi Province, agreed that most of her clients were pleasant , but once in a while she became very upset with some of them:

> Ninety percent of the customers are good, but sometimes I run into bad customers. One time, I had a customer whom I already had sex with for two or three times. He treated me very well in the past. But that day, right after I entered his hotel room, he took off my clothes and had sex with me. After being a prostitute for a while, we need to apply lubricant before having sex. Otherwise, it is painful during sex. But on that occasion, not only did I not use any lubricant, but he did not wear a condom either. I complained to my boss and my boss argued with him. The result was he paid me an extra $50. (140)

Women we interviewed in Thailand were in general not very happy to have sex with local men, especially those of Chaozhou origins who belong to a tight network. According to Dong Dong, a 26-year-old married woman who left China for Bangkok a month after she gave birth to her son, "My clients at the restaurants or flower halls are mainly Chinese Thai or PRC Chinese. We try our best not to go out with Chaozhou men and that's because they are regular customers and they all belong to a close network. They will tell everybody after they have sex with one of us. So, we only drink tea and sing with them" (53). Ah Chan, a 38-year-old divorcee from Shenyang also did not like going out with the local Chaozhou men, although for different reasons:

> When I was working at XXX [a nightclub, name omitted] and XXX [a flower hall, name omitted], I sat tables and sang songs to earn flower money [tips]. I *chutai* if I had opportunities. But most of them were people from outside of Thailand. I seldom *chutai* with the old men [of Chaozhou origin] at XXX [a restaurant, name omitted] because they only pay you $9 to $15. Customers at XXX [the flower hall mentioned above] could pay you as much as $142. Besides, the old men at that restaurant don't have normal sex with you because they can't; they like to do all kinds of things to torture you. (62)

But not all the women we interviewed were unhappy with their clients; and in fact some of them told us how they fell in love with men who were their clients. Dong Dong, the above quoted married woman from Songchi was very excited when she talked about her recent love affair with a client:

> A few days ago, a friend asked me to refer a woman [a *xiaojie*] to his friend, so I took a fellow villager to meet this man. He was not satisfied with my fellow villager. He gave her $28 and let her go. I told him that I would refer another woman to him. But he said that I need not refer anyone to him anymore because he had found what he wants. When I came out with him, he asked me to let him come to my place. I was unable to dissuade him and took him home. We talked for three hours at my place and then had sex. I totally forgot that he was my client, even though he paid me afterward. The next night, he came to my home with grapes that I liked. We talked and then had sex. He went to Guangzhou on the third day and will not be back in one month. His wife is in Guangzhou. I miss him badly. I have an emotional attachment to him. This is the happiest event I have had in Thailand. (53)

Women we interviewed in Malaysia said most of their clients were Chinese Malay, and only rarely ethnic Malay. "We do not like to see Malaysians because, first, we cannot communicate with them; second, they have body odor, and we do not like that," said Yi Ning, a 33-year-old divorced woman from Chongqing who was working as a KTV hostess. (18) Xiao Feng, a 33-year-old married woman from Jinzhou who was soliciting business near a restaurant in Kuala Lumpur, said this about her clients:

> All kinds of people patronize us, but most of them are retired Chinese Malay. They are not bad, but I did meet two bad customers. One of them wanted to have sex with me for the second time right after we did it for the first time. He said if I said no, he will beat me up. I asked him to wash himself first, and when he was in the bathroom, I dashed outside and asked for help from the girls next door. He chased me out. He wouldn't leave me alone even after I gave him back his money. Only when another girl came up with a customer, did he leave. Another customer in his forties looked honest, so I did not ask him to pay me in advance. After sex, he looked at his wallet and said that he did not have enough money. He had only $10 (he should pay me $28) and I had to take what he had. (22)

Other subjects in Malaysia said that although they were not terrorized or exploited by their clients, they often felt like they were being commodified by men. Here are a few examples:

Most of my clients are old men. They do not force me to do anything, but they hurt me with their words. For example, a customer once asked me to refer another *xiaojie* to him right after having sex with me. They are completely oblivious to how we feel; they see us only as something they can buy. (Lu Lu, 35-year-old, married, from Shashi, Hubei, a restaurant-based *xiaojie* in Kuala Lumpur) (28)

In this line of work, customers are nice to us in a superficial way. I can tell that they look down on us by the way they act and talk. (Li Min, 26-year-old, single, from Mulan, Heilongjiang, an escort in Kuala Lumpur) (29)

In general, most of the women we interviewed in Singapore also had only nice things to say about their customers. According to Qian Qian, a 34-year-old from Nanjing who was twice divorced and was working as a masseuse in Singapore: "I have six to seven customers a day. Most of them are local residents or drivers. Singaporeans are nice. Very often a man passes by our parlor and if I ask him whether he would like to have a massage, he will say: 'No, but if you haven't yet eaten, I can go buy you lunch.' Some customers will not express any dissatisfaction even if they do not like you after you serve them; they will just select another woman when they come next time" (10).

Rong Rong, a 33-year-old divorced woman from Chongqing who was soliciting business on the street of Singapore's Chinatown, told us she rarely had any problems with Singaporean men, but once in a while she was humiliated.

Here in Singapore, even if you are a streetwalker, people normally don't look at you for the second time. However, yesterday an old man approached me on the streets and said he wanted to "go out" with me. And then he asked me to walk in front of him. So I did and after walking for a while, I turned around and he was nowhere to be found. So I walked back to where I met him, and saw him standing on the roadside with a bunch of old men chatting and laughing. I asked him what was going on and he smiled at me and said: "Well, I just asked you to walk in front of me, I did not say anything about wanting to do anything with you." (6)

Female subjects we interviewed in Indonesia said the majority of their clients were Chinese Indonesians. Fei Fei, a 21-year-old single woman from Hunan Province, said the following about her customers:

Most of the customers are Chinese Indonesians. There are also some dark Indonesian clients, but I do not like them. Customers are in general not bad. They do not force us to do anything. Anyway, this is a legitimate spa. We have security people here and customers would not behave unreasonably here. (43)

Many women we interviewed in Los Angeles worked in sex venues called "houses" that catered only to Asian men. Linda, a Los Angeles-based, 35-year-old married woman from Beijing who had worked in a number of cities in America, compared customers in various American cities this way:

Clients in New York are worse than Los Angeles; they are rude. I have also been to San Francisco before, in fact I just got back from San Francisco. Customers there are the best, and customers there pay $150 per session, and I get $100. Some of the good owners in San Francisco will let the girls keep $110 per session, plus the customers there often give us tips. I also have been to San Jose. No matter where we go, our clients are mostly Chinese. (132)

Wang Jing, a 31-year-old married woman from Fuzhou we interviewed in Los Angeles, told us why she preferred to deal exclusively with Chinese clients:

I never have foreign clients. First of all, it is dangerous because they could be cops. Secondly, we have a different body structure and it is not good to have sex with them because it's like you plug something into something that is not a match. Thirdly, they have sex with you and it is just an exchange. With Chinese clients, there are some relationships besides the pure exchange. Chinese clients will bring you gifts during Chinese holidays, or they will buy you something if they go out of town. It is a different feeling. (133)

Unlike the two subjects in Los Angeles, a woman we interviewed in New Jersey who was seeing mostly white clients had no qualms about it. Mona, a 34-year-old divorced woman who was working in a massage parlor in a wealthy New Jersey town told us this: "I see maybe two to three customers a day. All of them are very nice and they give good tips. Where else can you earn $100 in tips providing a hand job? Most of them are white and many of them are regular customers. They never force us to do anything we do not want to do (well, there is also the question of how much they are willing to pay) and I have not encountered any sick clients here" (104).

On the other hand, a woman working in a massage parlor in a substantially less affluent New Jersey town had a very different opinion about the mostly white clients she met there:

> On average, I see four to five customers a day. Most customers are foreigners and some of them are mean. They are tall and often ask us to do what we do not want to do. For example, he may press your head with force and require you to do that. We are worried that they will report to the police [about our business] if we do not do as they ask. You have to know that what concerns us the most is that our customers might call the police. We do not have to be concerned about the routine police inspection. But once a customer calls the police, we would be in big trouble. Some Americans also want to have sex from the back, but we usually do not consent. It is already a deep humiliation to sell our bodies, how much more people can ask us to do! (Cindy, 34, from Harbin, Heilongjiang Province, divorced and married for the second time, had a 10-year-old daughter) (106)

Ying Hong, a 37-year-old single woman from Shenyang, who was seeing clients in her apartment in New Jersey, had the following to say about her customers:

> Most of my customers are Chinese living in a nearby town. I also have a few white customers who are all referred by other white customers. Men here are much better than those in Flushing [Queens]. That's why I don't mind working here, even though business here is slower than in Flushing. Most customers are normal: they come, they make love, and they leave. Only a few of them are abnormal: they like to wear high heel shoes and a blouse and walk back and forth in front of me. I also had a Chinese man who graduated from Beijing University and is now pursuing a Ph.D. degree here. He said his former girl friend taught him many kinky sex acts. He is crazy about drinking urine when he visits me. (113)

Other subjects also told us that some of their clients were very unusual. A woman who was working as an operator and a cashier, and also moonlighting as a masseuse at a massage parlor in New Jersey told us:

> There was a medical doctor who recently lost his wife and he comes to us regularly to cry. He asked for me once and we went into a room and he cried and I cried with him. I did not have to do anything else. There are also customers who come here and do nothing but give a nice massage to a

girl, and after the massage, peel an apple for the girl to eat. In the process, he pays $50 to the house and $100 to the girl. I don't understand what's wrong with these people.

A white man in New Jersey who said he frequently visited Asian massage parlors had this to say about the women working in these venues:

A few years ago, I read the *Star Ledger* and there were all kinds of ads for massage. I picked a phone number and made a call, and the woman who answered the phone told me it will cost $50 per session. I told myself, what's the big deal, $50 for a massage, so I went. Once you walk into the place, you are done. These Chinese women will treat you like a king, so submissive and so willing to please you by all means. It is not all about sex; it is the kind of feeling that you are welcomed, liked, and treated well. I mean, most of the men who go there are married and they are having some kinds of problems with their wives. There, you forget all the problems in your families for a short period of time. They will tell you all the nice things about you, like you are handsome, you are nice, you are generous, and so on and so forth.

Many American customers fall in love with the Chinese women. After you go there a few times, you will try to take out a girl you like. However, they are not going to say yes right away because they will try to bring you back to the parlor again and again. After you become a frequent customer, then they will agree to go out with you. Even so, it is not going to be free to be their boyfriend. She will ask you to pay her rent, buy her a car, or do something to please her. Then you become the Lucky 5. Lucky 5 because you are not going to be the only boyfriend; she is close to four or five men all at the same time and you are just one of the men she is seeing. Many Lucky 5s do not know this, they think they are the LUCKY ONE.

In brief, most of our subjects were selling sex to overseas Chinese who were born outside China or PRC nationals visiting or working overseas. Almost none of them were offering sexual services to non-Chinese clients exclusively. It is difficult to generalize about how our subjects felt about their clients, because their views varied by sex venue, research site, and client background. However, it is safe to say that the women were not particularly unhappy with their clients, regardless of venue, site, and client background. Most subjects said the majority of their clients were pleasant, that they were "normal," and that the sexual transactions between them and their clients were generally quick, straightforward, and businesslike. It is also true, however, that some of the women occasionally ran into difficult clients, and the encounters with those clients often upset them for long periods.

Abuses in the Sex Trade

In the literature on prostitution and sex trafficking, one of the most frequently discussed issues is how client violence is a key component of the sex business, and how women who engage in commercial sex, especially street prostitution, are highly vulnerable to physical violence inflicted upon them by their clients.[23] This point relates to our earlier discussion of prostitutes being willing sex partners. If a woman, whether or not she is a trafficking victim, is reluctant to see a client or is not very accommodating in serving a client, this may lead to physical abuse and violence. But as witness the discussion that follows, violence is not the only problem the women face.

Our subjects spoke at length about some of the problems they may confront when interacting with their clients. These problems can be categorized as (1) condom use, (2) refusal to pay, (3) verbal abuse, (4) physical assault, and (5) robbery.

Condom Use

According to Louise Brown and others who have written about prostitution and sex trafficking, the vast majority of women who engage in paid sex have no say in whether their clients wear a condom or not. For example, Brown argued in her book *Sex Slaves* that prostitutes "are unable to demand that the client use a condom."[24] Despite the widely accepted view that prostitutes are not in a position to demand that their customers wear condoms, our subjects told us that they always asked their customers to wear a condom, and that if they refused, the women said they in turn simply responded by saying, "no condom, no sex." Some of the men might be willing to pay more for unprotected sex, but the subjects said they were never swayed by this extra amount of money. In any event, most of the male clients wore condoms as a natural thing to do to protect themselves. A chef we interviewed in Los Angeles explained: "Even if a prostitute said I can do it without a condom, I won't. That's too dangerous!" Even those who were initially opposed to wearing a condom usually changed their minds once the women asked them to do so. But as mentioned above, a very small number of men did try to remove their condoms while the sexual activity was taking place, and this very much upset our subjects.

A very small number of women said they were indeed forced to have sex with clients who refused to wear a condom. Li Min, a 26-year-old single woman from Mulan (Heilongjiang Province) who was working as an escort in Kuala Lumpur, told us:

> Our clients are diverse: Singaporeans, Hongkongers, Taiwanese, Americans, and British. One time, I had sex with an Indian who did not use a condom and I could not refuse him. I felt like I was raped. He was very tall, and he originally asked for overnight service. I was lying on the bed and he came over and forced himself on me without wearing a condom. I asked him to put on a condom, but he just ignored me. I called my company after he raped me and the company sent a driver and took me away. I saw a doctor and took some medicine right after that. (29)

Refusal to Pay

Our subjects were more likely to run into a customer who refused to pay as opposed to one who refused to wear a condom. Kelly, a 38-year-old woman who was divorced twice and was working for a "house" in Monterey Park, California, recalled a very unpleasant and even terrifying incident: "Once, I was with a guy in his home who looked like an Albanian, and he had fun with me for three hours and did not pay me a penny. I protested, and he stuck a gun to my head and yelled. After that, I never see clients in their homes anymore" (121). This sort of incident reinforces the point that consenting prostitutes can still be victimized.

Some customers were willing to pay, but not at the full price as agreed upon; usually because they thought they were being overcharged. A man in his thirties who was running a house in Los Angeles with his "girlfriend" explained how this could happen:

> These people [clients who are laborers] make less than $120 a day, but when they visit us, they have to pay $120. They may feel upset because the girls are charging more in thirty minutes than what they make in a day. We never encounter any violent clients, only clients who refuse to pay the full charge. We won't force a client to pay in full if the girl who sees him does not insist, and that's because you don't want to upset your clients in this type of business.

Most of our subjects were not very willing to compromise when their customers refused to pay, or tried to pay a lesser amount. From their viewpoint, once a man enters a room with them, they must be paid regardless of what happens afterward. Most of them did not intend to stay in the same work-place for a long time, or expect customers to revisit them in the future, so they did not really care much about alienating their customers.

Verbal Abuse

Many female subjects said what hurt them the most was not outright hostility from their clients, but the derogatory remarks these clients sometimes made about them. Dong Dong, a 26-year-old married woman we interviewed in Bangkok, explained: "After sex, my clients often ask me whether women like me still have any real feelings. They wonder whether everything for us is just a matter of exchange between money and flesh. Whenever a customer asks me this question, it really hurts me."(53) Most female subjects thought their clients simply saw them as whores, and as whores they are not someone the clients would trust or respect.

Physical Assault

When asked whether they had ever been subjected to customer violence, only 12 out of 147 subjects (8%) said they had. Of the abused subjects, one in Kuala Lumpur said she was raped and the other in Los Angeles said she was almost raped. Our data suggest that younger women were more likely to be victims of such violence than are older women; women in Macau, Taiwan, New York, and Los Angeles were more vulnerable to client assault than were those in Thailand and Malaysia (none of the women we interviewed in Hong Kong, Singapore, and Indonesia were ever physically attacked by their clients). Women who were involved in organized prostitution were more likely to experience client violence than were those who were independent *xiaojies*. Women who saw clients in hotels, regardless of whether they were operating out of a hotel as independent *xiaojies* or working as escorts for an out-call agency, were more vulnerable to violence than women who worked in other sex venues.

Yan Yan, a 20-year-old single woman from Changde in Hunan Province who was seeing clients in her hotel room in Macau, described one such violent incident:

I was assaulted by a client before. Once, I ran into a customer who was from northeast China. He asked me to wash my face right after he stepped into my room because he did not like my heavy makeup. I refused to wash, and he mumbled a few words about my bad attitude. After sex, he asked me whether it was possible for him not to pay me. I said hell, no. I also said if he won't pay, I will call the police. He said go ahead, so I picked up the phone. He then hit me. I was deeply hurt by what he did. After the police came, he paid me $28[the normal price per session] and left. (87)

Another young woman working out of a small hotel in Macau recalled how a seemingly routine act of selling or buying sex could turn ugly very quickly:

A few days ago, a man walked in pretty drunk. Initially, it went well; the two of us were talking and laughing when we went upstairs to my room. However, when we began to have sex, he kept sucking my breasts. Some women do not care about this, but I would not let people kiss my breasts for only $14 [the price per session]. He stopped after I told him not to. But not long after, he bites my breasts. I was annoyed, and said: "What is wrong with you!" Of course, he was not happy and did not ejaculate even after twenty minutes. I told him that time was up, and if he wanted to continue, he had to pay for another session. He said fine. But he still could not ejaculate after another twenty minutes and he blamed my bad attitude for all this. I said forget about it and wanted to leave, but he pushed me back on the bed. Later, when he sucked my breasts again, I patted his shoulder so that he will stop. I did not intend to hit him, but he thought that I was hitting him and so he slapped me. So I got up, dressed, and was about to leave. He wouldn't let me leave or pay me. When I tried to call someone, he threw both my cell phone and the room phone to the floor. Anyway, all hell broke out for a while. Eventually, he threw down $35 and left. (96)

Some subjects said they were able to escape from their clients before they were assaulted. Joey, a 36-year-old married woman from Beijing, was operating her own house in Los Angeles when we interviewed her, and she recalled this incident:

When I was working for several houses, I met a man who was very drunk. He wouldn't ejaculate after a long time, so I told him I can't go on like this. He said I came here to fuck you, how can you say you cannot stand it anymore. I said you should not say something that hurts my dignity, and he said women like us had no dignity to speak of. And then he was about to hit me, so I rushed out of the room to avoid being assaulted. (119)

At least three subjects said that they hit their clients, not the other way around. Asked whether she was ever assaulted by her clients, Angie, a 37-year-old divorced woman from Yiyang who was working in Hong Kong at the time of the interview, replied with a smirk: "No clients have ever hit me; only I hit them [upon their request]" (80).

We do not know how many working women from China were murdered overseas by their clients, but we have to believe that this is a very rare occurrence. Subjects in Malaysia, Indonesia, and Singapore did separately mention an instance in which a *xiaojie* from China was killed, but they were not sure who actually committed the murder or what the circumstances were.

In sum, our data echo the observation of John Lowman and Chris Atchison of Simon Frazer University after they conducted a survey of men who buy sex in Vancouver, Canada: "Much of the literature on the frequency and nature of sex buyer violence appears to be empirically overestimated and theoretically underspecified."[25] A study by Martin Monto, a sociology professor, also concluded that only a small minority of customers assault prostitutes.[26]

Robbery

Some of the women we interviewed told us that they had been robbed at their workplaces. Jia Jia, a 41-year-old married woman from Fuzhou who was smuggled into the United States for the price of $73,000, was selling sex out of her one-bedroom apartment in Flushing, Queens, as an independent *xiaojie*:

> Over the past twelve months, I was robbed three or four times. When I was robbed the first time, my place had been opened for only a month. A young Wenzhounese walked in and after he was sure I was all by myself, called his partners and let them in. Altogether, there were four of them, and they took away $500 and two cell phones. They also ransacked my place. Not long after that, I was robbed by a group of Fuzhounese. After the first incident, I became smarter; I didn't keep a lot of cash in my place. As a result, the Fuzhounese did not find much money, and so they forced me to have sex with them for free. I did not dare call the police. (117)

Women we interviewed in Los Angeles were concerned that they would be robbed by either Mexican or Vietnamese men. Many women there said they preferred to do business with only Chinese clients, mainly because Chinese men were less likely to rob them. Because of the large numbers of immigrants from Mexico and Vietnam in the Los Angeles area, it was not easy for

Chinese women there to completely avoid these two ethnic groups. Linda, a 35-year-old married woman with a college degree from Beijing, talked about the risks of dealing with Mexicans and Vietnamese:

> I was robbed once in another house. The house owner wasn't there; I was working with another woman. Two Mexicans came in, and then they immediately pulled out their guns. They took all our money and left. We also do not want to do business with Vietnamese. Once a Vietnam-ese shows up, he will spread the word about our place in the Vietnamese community. Sooner or later, those young Vietnamese who are in need of money will come to rob us. (132)

Robberies were not restricted to the United States; some women in some of the Asian sites also had been robbed. For example, Ah Lian, a streetwalker in a red-light district of Singapore, described how she was victimized:

> Once, I was victimized by a man. He asked me to go with him to another hotel several blocks away after he complained that the hotel across the street where I was standing was not good enough. Once we entered that hotel room, he flashed a badge and said that he was a cop. He said if I did not want to be arrested, I must pay him. I gave him all the money I had; it was more than $270. I realized later that I was deceived because Singapore police never ask for money. (14)

Violence or Pleasure?

Contrary to popular belief, client violence was not a major concern for the vast majority of our subjects. When asked what concerned them the most while working, violence, including rape, was not mentioned at all. Only 3 out of 149 subjects said they were concerned about meeting "bad customers," but by "bad customers" they did not mean "violent customers." Some subjects even preferred to see themselves as perpetrators of some physical altercation than as victims. For example, Chen Cui, a 22-year-old hotel-based *xiaojie* in Macau, was dead serious when she described how she treated some of her customers: "I do not do anything to cope with being a *xiaojie*; you can say I have no bad habits. One way to balance myself is that if I come across a not-so-good customer, I will lash out at him" (96). Another subject, a 32-year-old woman from Shanxi Province who had been an escort in Taiwan for many years, explained why her clients are more "vulnerable" than she is when the two cross paths:

When we are with our clients, it is more likely that we mistreat our clients, not that our clients mistreat us. What can they do against us? The worst they can do is to rape us! Once we walk into a room with them, they've got to pay us, no matter whether they are pleased or not. Whether they are pleased or not depends on our mood. If we are in a good mood, we can let them "fly"; otherwise, if we act like we are "dying" and have no response to whatever a client does, how can he be "happy"? If we are in a good mood we will cooperate, we will act, and let a client feel like he is making love with his girlfriend, even though it is nothing but an illusion we have created. (149)

The above subject's comments reflect our earlier point about willing versus unwilling sex partners. We also found that the majority of the men who buy sex were not interested in unusual sex acts, nor were they very difficult to please. Many women we interviewed told us that the transactions between them and their clients were relatively straightforward and routine: they enter a room, undress, and then have sex. Very often, a transaction is completed within a few minutes, and there is very little time for a client to do anything else besides having straight sex and then leaving. Teela Sanders, a British sociologist, conducted face-to-face interviews with thirty-seven men who bought sex, and she concluded that "clients are usually not interested in bizarre sexual acts, do not act violently and generally stick to the conditions of the commercial contract."[27] In her study, Sanders argued that men who bought sex were paying for pleasure, and "referring to sexual services as pleasure recognizes the possibilities that not all sex work is damaging, coerced or against the sex workers' will."[28] Even though Sanders's subjects were predominantly middle-class, professional men, we think paying for pleasure can also be applicable to working-class men who buy sex.

From this discussion of money and clients, we get the sense of the normalization of commercial sex as described in the introductory chapter. These are sexual transactions, but are also very clearly business transactions. There are fixed fees and going rates for certain kinds of services. Both the customers and the service providers seem to go to considerable lengths to keep what they are doing within the realm of normality. Neither party wants to see themselves as deviants. Ambiguity about what is normal and what is deviant with respect to commercial sex should perhaps not be surprising, since the larger subject of sexual practices is itself subject to considerable differences of opinion about what is "normal" and what is "abnormal."

8

Response and Rescue

How the System Works

The Trafficking Victims Protection Act (TVPA) was signed into law by President Bill Clinton on October 28, 2000. That law was aimed at accomplishing "Three Ps" (prosecuting traffickers, protecting victims, and preventing human trafficking) as well as a victim-centered "Three Rs" (rescue, rehabilitation, and reintegration). To carry out the U.S. response to the problem of human trafficking, the U.S. Department of State established the Office to Monitor and Combat Trafficking in Persons (GTIP Office). In accordance with TVPA, the Department of State is required to submit to the U.S. Congress an annual report (the Trafficking in Persons Report) on foreign governments' efforts to eliminate severe forms of trafficking in persons. That report groups and ranks all the countries in tiers based upon the extent of their effort to fight against human trafficking. The tiers are as follows:[1]

Tier 1
Countries whose governments fully comply with the Trafficking Victims Protection Act's (TVPA) minimum standards.

Tier 2

Countries whose governments do not fully comply with the TVPA's minimum standards, but are making significant efforts to bring themselves into
compliance with those standards.

Tier 2 Watch List

Countries whose governments do not fully comply with the TVPA's minimum standards, but are making significant efforts to bring themselves into
compliance with those standards, AND

The absolute number of victims of severe forms of trafficking is very significant or is significantly increasing; or

There is a failure to provide evidence of increasing efforts to combat severe
forms of trafficking in persons from the previous year; or

The determination that a country is making significant efforts to bring themselves into compliance with minimum standards was based on commit-
ments by the country to take additional future steps over the next year.[2]

Tier 3

Countries whose governments do not fully comply with the minimum standards and are not making significant efforts to do so.

The report is a tool for the U.S. government to "name and shame" foreign
governments in the hope that they will prosecute traffickers, protect victims,
and prevent human trafficking.[3] Pursuant to the TVPA, the U.S. government
may withhold foreign assistance that is neither humanitarian nor trade-re-
lated to countries in Tier 3.

In the United States, 46 states had enacted antitrafficking laws as of 2012,
and many state-level agencies were formed to carry out the "Three Ps" and
"Three Rs" approach to human trafficking. The U.S. State Department also
supports a number of NGOs (non-governmental organizations) worldwide
to rescue and assist trafficked victims and to prevent human trafficking.
Thus, a considerable effort has been mounted since 2000—both in the U.S.
and worldwide—to combat human trafficking and to rescue and assist trafficking victims.

Official and NGO Responses

Under pressure from the U.S. government, authorities in Asia began to pay
attention to the existence of large numbers of foreign prostitutes within their
jurisdictions. Most countries reacted to U.S. pressure by passing antitraffick-

ing laws, prosecuting traffickers, and cracking down on street prostitution, in hopes that their rankings in the TIP reports would move up.

Hong Kong

According to the 2009 TIP Report: "The Hong Kong Special Administrative Region (HKSAR) of the People's Republic of China is a destination and transit territory for men and women from mainland China, Thailand, the Philippines, Indonesia, and elsewhere in Southeast Asia trafficked for the purposes of forced labor and commercial exploitation."[4] When the TIP Report first came out in 2001, Hong Kong was placed in Tier 1 and remained there for eight consecutive years (see Figure 8.1). But Hong Kong fell to Tier 2 in 2009 and 2010 because of problems associated with the exploitation of foreign domestic workers in the territory, and because it failed to investigate, prosecute, or convict any trafficking offenders during the reporting periods.

According to the TIP reports, Hong Kong does not have specific antitrafficking laws, but the reports conclude that its immigration ordinance, crimes ordinance, and other relevant laws adequately prohibit trafficking offenses. A high-ranking officer with the Organized Crime and Triad Bureau (OCTB), Hong Kong Police, explained: "We've got four ordinances that deal with prostitution. If someone brings a woman into Hong Kong for the purpose of commercial sex, even if the woman comes knowingly and voluntarily, the person who brings her here could be sentenced to up to ten years. There are three more sex-related crimes for which an indictment could lead to a maximum of ten to fourteen years, like living off a sex worker, facilitating sex work, etc."[5]

In response to the large numbers of women seemingly working on the streets of Hong Kong, the authorities there have conducted numerous crackdowns. An example of one of these major law enforcement responses was Operation Fire Lily. According to another senior officer with the OCTB, Hong Kong Police:

> We conducted that major operation—Operation Fire Lily—in 2002 because we received intelligence that a huge syndicate was bringing in hundreds of mainland Chinese women into Hong Kong to work in the sex industry. The syndicate was headed by a former 14K member and his wife and the group had about 12 core members. Most of the core members were originally from China. When we arrested the group members, we also nabbed about 80 mainland women. In the year 2004, we arrested about 10,000 mainland women for prostitution. In 2005, it dropped to about

Figure 8.1. TIP tier ranking by year

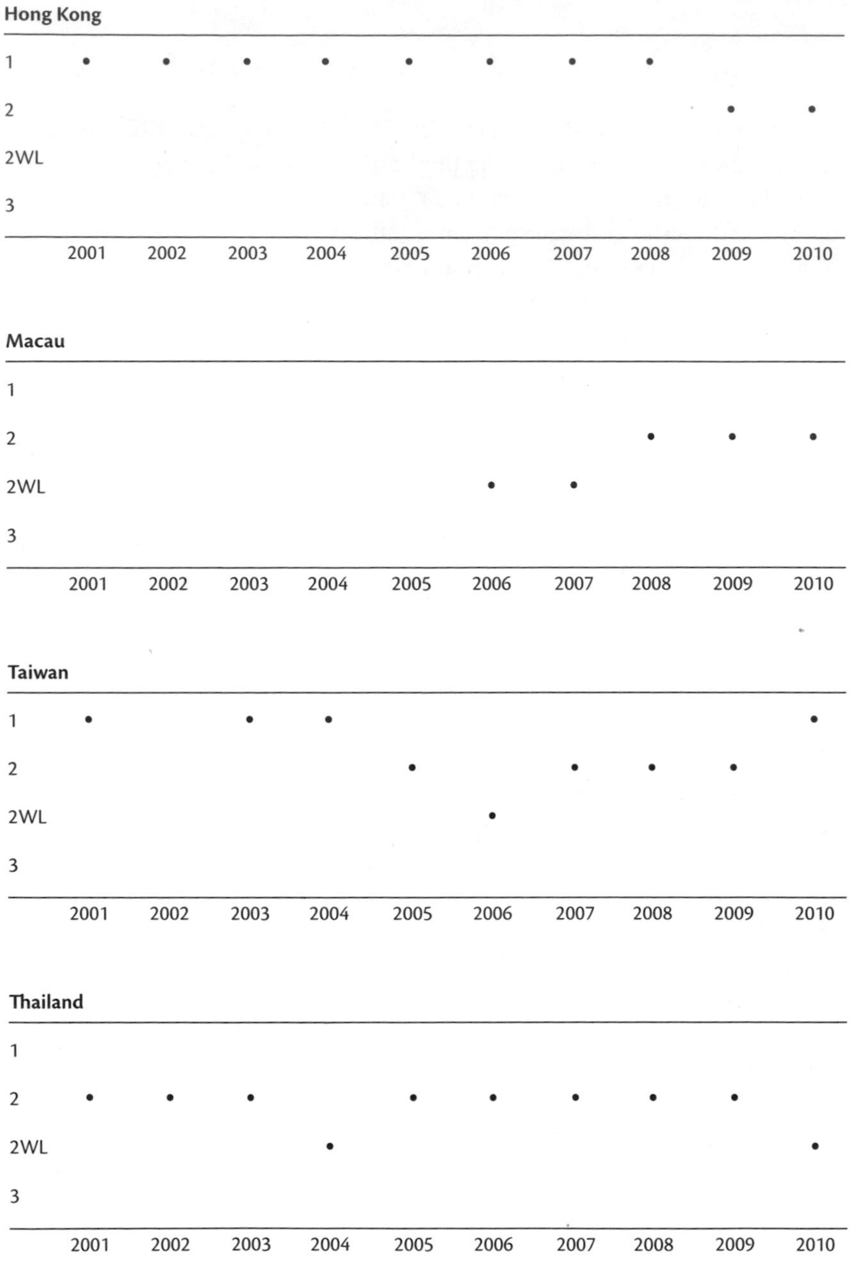

Hong Kong

	2001	2002	2003	2004	2005	2006	2007	2008	2009	2010
1	•	•	•	•	•	•	•	•		
2									•	•
2WL										
3										

Macau

	2001	2002	2003	2004	2005	2006	2007	2008	2009	2010
1										
2								•	•	•
2WL						•	•			
3										

Taiwan

	2001	2002	2003	2004	2005	2006	2007	2008	2009	2010
1	•		•	•						•
2					•		•	•	•	
2WL						•				
3										

Thailand

	2001	2002	2003	2004	2005	2006	2007	2008	2009	2010
1										
2	•	•	•		•	•	•	•	•	
2WL			•							•
3										

Malaysia

	2001	2002	2003	2004	2005	2006	2007	2008	2009	2010
1										
2		•	•	•	•					
2WL						•		•		•
3	•						•		•	

Singapore

	2001	2002	2003	2004	2005	2006	2007	2008	2009	2010
1						•				
2	•	•		•	•		•	•	•	
2WL										•
3										

Indonesia

	2001	2002	2003	2004	2005	2006	2007	2008	2009	2010
1										
2			•	•	•		•	•	•	•
2WL						•				
3	•	•								

China

	2001	2002	2003	2004	2005	2006	2007	2008	2009	2010
1										
2	•	•	•	•						
2WL					•	•	•	•	•	•
3										

8,000, and last year it was about 5,000. We believe there are fewer and fewer mainland women coming here for sex work because they know that there is a good chance of being arrested and sent back to China.

Our own observations lend credence to the officer's conclusion. When we arrived in Hong Kong in December 2006 and went to an area to find streetwalkers willing to participate in this research project, we did not see any. This was a dramatic contrast to what we saw in 2003. Then there were hundreds of Chinese women aggressively soliciting business within sight of passersby and store owners. According to several high-ranking officers with the Immigration Department, one of the reasons for the decline has to do with Hong Kong's tough policy against PRC (mainland) women working in the sex businesses of Hong Kong:

> Prostitution is not illegal here, but PRC ladies are visitors and they are not allowed to work here. If we arrest a PRC lady in the process, she will be imprisoned for at least three months before being deported. If we do not have hard evidence but we suspect they are involved in prostitution, we ask them to leave and we will stamp their travel documents indicating that they are being deported and we will not allow them to return to Hong Kong for two to five years.

These officers also pointed out that the sex industry of Hong Kong is shrinking because many Hong Kong men are instead going to mainland China to buy sex:

> The sex industry in Hong Kong is in decline now because it is very convenient for Hong Kong people to go to China for sex. It is much more expensive to buy sex in Hong Kong. Besides, when you go into a nightclub in Hong Kong, there are only twenty or so girls there. In China, it's not only cheaper but also every nightclub has hundreds of girls for the customers to choose from. Moreover, in going to these sex venues in Hong Kong you might end up bumping into an acquaintance. In China, nobody knows who you are. That's why all the big nightclubs in Hong Kong are going out of business, one after another.

In Hong Kong, women from mainland China are also constrained in their ability to work in the mainstream sex venues because most well-established venues are unwilling to take the risk of being penalized for hiring mainland women. According to the officers cited above:

For PRC women, there are not many venues for them to go to work be-cause most establishments would not want to risk their license to hire PRC women. All the well-established nightclubs and saunas are highly unlikely to hire PRC ladies; some of the small ones in the more remote areas might do so. As a result, most PRC women pretend to be customers when they are soliciting clients in those nightclubs in Tsim Sha Tsui; they are not for-mally employed by the nightclubs. Otherwise, they either walk the streets or work in the one-woman apartments.

Several websites in Hong Kong have become instrumental in helping cli-ents locate Chinese *xiaojies*. It seems that the police crackdowns have only pushed the women off the streets, but not actually out of the sex business.

None of the officials we talked to in Hong Kong considered mainland Chinese women who were selling sex in Hong Kong to be trafficking victims. Instead, they said that in the vast majority of cases these women came to Hong Kong voluntarily and willingly entered prostitution. According to their estimates, only 1 or 2 percent of the PRC women in the Hong Kong sex sector actually fit the definition of being trafficked victims.

Action for REACH OUT and Zi Teng are the two major organizations providing help to prostitutes in Hong Kong. According to an administrator of Action for REACH OUT:

> This organization is funded mainly by the Hong Kong horse racing club. They provide almost half of the funds. Since we consider sex work as work, it is not possible for us to receive any money from the U.S. Department of State or USAID,
>
> We do a lot of outreach. We will send our people to various sex ven-ues, mostly KTV/nightclubs and the streets to distribute pamphlets on safe sex and human rights. Most venues will allow our workers to go in and hand out the pamphlets to their sex workers. We rarely go to the sauna places, though. Sometimes our workers will talk to the girls on the streets, unless their pimps say we cannot do so. We will urge the girls to contact us should they need help. We also provide HIV/AIDS tests to sex workers and we do about ten tests a week. We also just started a clinic.

According to Zi Teng's website, it is "a non-governmental organization formed by people of different working experiences. They are social work-ers, labor activists, researchers specializing in women's studies and church workers, etc. who care and are concerned about the interests and basic rights of women. We believe that all women, regardless of their profession, social class, religion, or race, have the same basic human rights, that they are equal and entitled to fair and equal treatment in the legal and judicial system, that nobody should be oppressed against, that all people should live with dignity."

When we interviewed workers from Zi Teng, it was obvious that their number one priority is to fight for the rights of sex workers, and they are very critical of the way the police in Hong Kong are treating local and foreign prostitutes. They are also skeptical of the true benevolence of the US/TVPA antitrafficking paradigm, and believe that rescuers and advocates under that particular banner of antitrafficking are actually doing more harm than good in helping trafficking victims. This view is reflective of the ideological differences existing with respect to sex trafficking policy and practices.

Macau

From the U.S. government standpoint, authorities in Macau are not doing their best to deal with the problem of human trafficking or to cooperate with the United States. As a result, Macau was relegated to the Tier 2 Watch List in 2006 and 2007, but was moved up to Tier 2 in 2008, 2009, and 2010 after the Macau Legislative Assembly passed an antitrafficking law in June 2008 (see Figure 8.1). According to the 2009 TIP Report: "Macau is primarily a destination for the trafficking of women and girls from the Chinese mainland, Mongolia, Russia, Philippines, Thailand, Vietnam, Burma, and Central Asia for the purpose of commercial sexual exploitation."[6]

Because Macau relies heavily on revenue from the casino industry to keep its economy afloat, it would not be surprising if the authorities in Macau were not very aggressive in stopping women from China and other countries from selling sex there. There are many nightclubs and sauna establishments in Macau where men can buy sex and women can sell their bodies without much interference from the authorities. The Macau authorities are, however, concerned about the congregation of Chinese, Eastern European, and Russian women in front of the hotels that are right in the heart of Macau, and where many desirable hotel customers and other visitors are present. As a result, when we were in Macau collecting data, we witnessed police officers in uniform and detectives in plainclothes arresting a number of young white women (believed to be from the former Soviet Union or Eastern Europe) who were loitering around a big hotel.

According to an official at the U.S. Consulate General's Office in Hong Kong and Macau, U.S. authorities are more concerned with human trafficking in Macau than in Hong Kong. He estimated that 80 to 85 percent of all the women who engage in commercial sex in Macau are from mainland

China, and that 10 to 15 percent of these PRC women could be trafficking victims. In 2008, the U.S. government was not happy when the Macau authorities deported three underage masseuses arrested inside a spa back to China without offering them any help or treatment.

Taiwan

There is no formal diplomatic tie between the U.S. and Taiwan, but the American Institute in Taiwan (AIT) serves as the de facto U.S. embassy there. The TIP reports placed Taiwan in Tier 1 between 2001 and 2004, but moved the island down to Tier 2 in 2005 and further down to the Tier 2 Watch List in 2006. Taiwan was moved back to Tier 2 in 2007, 2008, and 2009, and by 2010 it had again reached Tier 1 (see Figure 8.1). The 2009 TIP Report characterized the situation in Taiwan as follows: "Taiwan is primarily a destination for men, women, and children trafficked for the purposes of forced labor and commercial sexual exploitation. To a far lesser extent, it is a source of women trafficked to Japan, Australia, the UK, and the United States for sexual exploitation and forced labor, as well as a transit area for People's Republic of China (PRC) citizens seeking to enter the United States illegally, some of whom may become victims of debt bondage and forced prostitution."[7]

In 2003, after six Chinese women were killed in the process of being smuggled into Taiwan by boat (the so-called Miaoli Incident), the authorities in Taiwan began to pay more attention to the penetration of women from China into the Taiwanese commercial sex business.[8] When the GTIP Office downgraded Taiwan from Tier 1 to Tier 2 and then later to the Tier 2 Watch List, Taiwanese officials responded by not only making it very difficult for boat captains to smuggle Chinese women into Taiwan, but also by monitoring marriages between Taiwanese citizens and PRC nationals to prevent Chinese women from entering Taiwan by means of fake marriages. One mechanism employed was to interview the newly arrived Chinese brides at the international airports in Taipei and Kaohsiung. In January 2009 the Legislative Yuan of Taiwan passed a new antitrafficking law.

Thailand

The 2009 TIP Report characterized human trafficking in Thailand as follows: "Thailand is a source, transit, and destination country for men, women, and children trafficked for the purposes of forced labor and commercial sexual exploitation. Thailand's relative prosperity attracts migrants from neighboring countries and from as far away as Russia and Fiji who flee conditions of poverty and, in the case of Burma, military repression."[9]

Thailand was on Tier 2 between 2001 and 2009, with the exception that in 2004 the country fell to the Tier 2 Watch List because Thai authorities deported many Cambodians without checking to verify if they were trafficking victims. Thailand's antitrafficking law went into effect in June 2008. However, in 2010 Thailand again fell to the Tier 2 Watch List because few victims were identified and not many traffickers were convicted (see Figure 8.1). American officials we talked to in Bangkok were mostly unaware of and unconcerned about mainland Chinese women engaging in commercial sex in Thailand. According to an official in the U.S. Embassy in Bangkok: "The ICE office in Thailand is responsible for five countries: Thailand, Myanmar, Laos, Cambodia, and Vietnam. For us, when it comes to PRC nationals, we are more concerned with the smuggling of them into the U.S. via Thailand and not much about the presence of PRC women in the sex industry in Thailand. We have never had any dealings with PRC women in Thailand. We think the Chinese are significantly less likely to be trafficked than women and girls from, say, Cambodia, Laos, Myanmar, and Vietnam."

Many NGOs maintain a strong presence in Thailand and many have their regional offices set up in Bangkok. Employees at the International Organization for Migration office in Bangkok said they did not have much experience dealing with trafficking victims from mainland China. According to a worker with the Human Trafficking Division of IOM in Bangkok:

> Here in Thailand, the three countries with the most trafficked victims are Laos [mostly sex trafficking victims], Myanmar [mostly labor trafficking victims but a substantial number of them are sex trafficking victims], and Cambodia [mostly forced beggars]. There are not many sex trafficking victims or labor trafficking victims from Indonesia in Thailand. We also have some sex trafficking victims from Vietnam and the former Soviet Union. We do not deal with domestic human trafficking, but we are involved in helping Thai sex trafficking victims return home. Thai police and immigration officers are becoming more and more aware of the problem of human trafficking. In the past, they were very ignorant, but recently, they try to determine if an arrested foreign woman who engages in commercial sex is a victim of human trafficking.

Besides the IOM and the International Labor Organization, the Asia Foundation in Bangkok is also concerned with human trafficking. According to an administrator of the foundation: "We are running a human trafficking project and it is mainly concerned with the trafficking of Burmese and hill tribe women from Yunnan, China. We focus on prosecution instead of prevention and protection. We have also established a multidisciplinary team (MDT) that consists of social workers, police officers, NGOs, medical doctors, and prosecutors to work collectively as a team. We receive our human trafficking-related funding from USAID. Thai police officers are more concerned with illegal migrant workers than with trafficked victims. But one of the main reasons for this is that police officers are receiving bribes from sex ring operators to turn a blind eye to commercial sex."

Malaysia

Of the eight special regions or countries in Asia that were sites in our study, Malaysia and Indonesia are the only two that have ever been ranked in Tier 3 in the TIP reports. Malaysia was relegated to Tier 3 in the first TIP Report in 2001, moved up to Tier 2 in the following four years between 2002 and 2005, but got downgraded to the Tier 2 Watch List in 2006 and then to Tier 3 in 2007. The country bounced back to the Tier 2 Watch List in 2008, but then again fell back to Tier 3 in 2009, only to be moved up to the Tier 2 Watch List again in 2010 (see Figure 8.1). According to the 2009 TIP Report:

> Malaysia is a destination and, to a lesser extent, a source and transit country for women and children trafficked for the purpose of commercial sexual exploitation, and for men, women, and children trafficked for the purpose of forced labor. Malaysia is mainly a destination country for men, women, and children who migrate willingly from Indonesia, Nepal, Thailand, the People's Republic of China (PRC), the Philippines, Burma, Cambodia, Bangladesh, Pakistan, India, and Vietnam for work—usually legal, contractual labor—and are subsequently subjected to conditions of involuntary servitude in the domestic, agricultural, food service, construction, plantation, industrial, and fisheries sectors. Some foreign women and girls are also victims of commercial sexual exploitation.[10]

According to an official with the U.S. Embassy in Kuala Lumpur, the human trafficking problem in Malaysia is essentially a labor trafficking issue, especially with the exploitation of Indonesian migrant workers by ethnic Malay, Chinese Malay, and Indian Malay employers.[11]

According to U.S. officials in Malaysia, even though the Malay government and the Malay people were quite upset when they learned that the TIP Report had ranked their country in Tier 3, the Malay authorities were simply not doing what they should be doing, nor did they admit they had a problem. Malay officials we talked to were indeed not happy with the way their country was rated in the TIP reports. A high-ranking official with the Criminal Investigation Department of the Royal Malaysia Police had this to say:

> We don't think it is fair for the U.S. State Department to put us on Tier 3 in their TIP report because we are doing our very best to fight human trafficking. We think we are doing much better than other countries that are on the Tier 2 Watch List or higher. I also do not see the exploitation and control of Indonesian migrant workers as a trafficking issue. Most of them are smuggled into Malaysia of their own will or are self-smuggled, and they are later exploited by their agents and their employers in Malaysia. I can't see this as human trafficking.

This same official also thought that most Chinese women were in Malaysia of their own free will, and that they knew what they would be doing in Malaysia before they left China. He pointed out that, even though the number of arrests involving PRC women is the highest among all nationalities, the number of rescued PRC women is lower than for Indonesians because PRC women are highly unlikely to have been trafficked.

In Malaysia, we interviewed workers from two NGOs: the PT Foundation and Tenaganita (meaning women's force). The PT Foundation is a community-based organization providing information, education, and care services relating to HIV/AIDS and sexuality. It was first founded in 1987 under the name "Pink Triangle," to provide telephone counseling about HIV/AIDS and sexuality. In response to the needs and concerns of the community, it has expanded its services and changed its name to the PT Foundation. Today, the PT Foundation works with people living with HIV/AIDS, drug users, sex workers, transsexual, and homosexual men and women. According to a worker at the foundation: "Most sex workers in Malaysia are ethnic Malay, Indians, and Chinese Malay. There are also many Indonesians, and they are probably the second largest group after the ethnic Malay. Most sex workers here are not young; the young ones normally go overseas to make more money. Our main activities involve the operation of a drop-in center and doing outreach. We do not deal with foreigners, only domestic people. We also do not deal with trafficking victims, regardless of their nationalities. If we encounter foreigners, we refer them to Tenaganita."

According to an administrator of Tenaganita, "Our main mandate is to protect workers' rights, including the rights of migrant and domestic workers. A year ago we started a shelter for trafficked victims. Last year, we had about 25 victims and now 13. Most of them are Indonesians, and the majority of them are abused workers. We have one or two sex trafficking victims from Vietnam and Cambodia. We never had any Chinese women in our shelter, or ever had any referred to us. When the police here come into contact with Chinese women in police raids, the women will say they don't want to be rescued, they want to go back to work. The police point of view is, as far as Chinese women are concerned, they are not trafficking victims but willing participants in commercial sex." She went on to explain how uncertain funding was for the shelter: "For our shelter, we receive money from the U.S. government via IOM [the International Organization for Migration]. IOM said we will continue to receive support after the first year, but they are now saying there is no money. The U.S. embassy is now supporting us on a short-term basis until we get the money from IOM. Because we are a domestic organization, we could not receive money directly from the U.S. government, only through an international NGO like the IOM or the ILO [the International Labor Organization]."

Singapore

According to the 2009 TIP Report:

> Singapore is a destination country for women and girls trafficked for the purpose of commercial sexual exploitation. Some women from Thailand and the Philippines who travel to Singapore voluntarily for prostitution or work are subsequently deceived or coerced into sexual servitude. Some foreign domestic workers are subject to conditions that may be indicative of labor trafficking, including physical or sexual abuse, confiscation of travel documents, confinement, inadequate food, rest, or accommodation, deceptions about wages or conditions of work, and improper withholding of pay. Some Singaporean men travel to countries in the region for child sex tourism.[12]

For the nine years between 2001 and 2009, the TIP reports placed Singapore on Tier 2, with the exception that it was moved up to Tier 1 in 2006. However, in 2010 the country was demoted to the Tier 2 Watch List for the first time because of the lack of efforts to identify victims and prosecute traffickers (see Figure 8.1). As described to us, most women (including those from the PRC) come to Singapore on social or work passes. The former passes are good for up to ninety days, and the length of the latter is determined by the nature of the work contract. In neither of these cases is the entry hidden or illegal.

We found it particularly interesting that the officials with whom we spoke at the U.S. embassy sharply disagreed with the TIP assessment of the human trafficking situation in Singapore. These U.S. officials said that human trafficking in general is not a problem in Singapore. They strongly disagreed with the TIPs definition of cases, examples, and situations that have been used to illustrate alleged instances of trafficking. Further, they criticized the TIP office as having preconceived notions and assumptions that distort its objectivity, among other things. However, the same officials did point out that the government of Singapore generally downplays its crime problems in order to protect the city's image. With respect to commercial sex, they said that it was child sex tourism and child pornography that were the big problems in the region.

Representatives of the Singapore National Police and the Ministry of Home Affairs with whom we spoke likewise told us that the trafficking of PRC women for paid sex was not an issue of concern in Singapore. They admitted that some women do indeed come to Singapore to work as prostitutes (using the social passes referred to above). Prostitution, they said, is not legal, but neither is it criminalized. This means that soliciting prostitution in public places is a crime, but sex among consenting adults—even if involving payment—is not.

Because of pressure from the U.S. government, Singapore authorities had conducted numerous crackdowns in some of the red-light districts there. When arrests are made, it is usually pimps and handlers who are arrested —the prostitutes are not charged. These pimps, the police said, are usually low-level operatives who are generally not associated with traditional organized crime.

Local law enforcement officials indicated that there had been only a handful (fewer than five) criminal cases in the previous three years (2004–2006) involving the sexual exploitation of women, and that none of those involved women from China. It is their view that PRC women are not being forced, coerced, or deceived into commercial sex, but that instead they come freely with their approved passes. They did say that known prostitutes in the PRC would not be approved for such a social visit pass.

Indonesia

When the TIP Report first came out in 2001, Indonesia was placed in Tier 3 status, and remained so the following year, before being moved up to Tier

2 in 2003. Since then it has fluctuated between Tier 2 and Tier 2 Watch List (see Figure 8.1). According to the 2009 TIP Report:

> Indonesia is a major source of women, children, and men trafficked for the purposes of forced labor and commercial sexual exploitation. To a far lesser extent, it is a destination and transit country for foreign trafficking victims. The greatest threat of trafficking facing Indonesian men and women is that posed by conditions of forced labor and debt bondage in more developed Asian countries—particularly Malaysia, Singapore, and Japan—and the Middle East, particularly Saudi Arabia, according to IOM data. Indonesian women and girls are also trafficked to Malaysia and Singapore for forced prostitution and throughout Indonesia for both forced prostitution and forced labor.[13]

Indonesian officials we talked to were not happy with the way their government was handling the arrival of Chinese women in Indonesia. For example, a senior officer with the Directorate General of Immigration (DGIM) bluntly asserted: "We passed the anti-trafficking law because we were forced to by the Americans. Now, with this law, we are basically further victimizing these PRC women because we arrest them, deport them, make their lives here miserable, and deprive them of the opportunity to make a living."

U.S. officials in the U.S. embassy in Jakarta, like other American officials in other sites, said they were not very familiar with the problem of PRC women engaging in commercial sex in their host country. Some complained that since they have to work on at least four reports every year (TIP, human rights, religious freedom, and child labor), there is often a blurring of the material in these reports.

A representative who works with an affiliate of the AFL/CIO in Jakarta said the new Indonesian antitrafficking law is stronger than the UN protocol requirements in some respects, but would benefit from the addition of provisions for assisting cooperating witnesses and providing alternatives to the deportation of victims. She said that although prostitution is not illegal, pimping is, and that prostitution is largely contained to certain areas where there are karaoke bars, massage parlors, and brothels. The police, she said, occasionally conduct show raids to pick up prostitutes and transport them to rehabilitation centers where they are held for three months for vocational training and moral reeducation.

This representative indicated that there are overseas women working in the commercial sex business, including some from China; but the database is so weak that there are no real accurate numbers. The most pressing aspect of human trafficking in Indonesia, according to her, is that involving Indonesian nationals in domestic work, overseas jobs, and the like.

Finally, on the political front, this same representative said that her agency receives funding from the U.S. State Department, and thus has to "officially" accept U.S. policy with respect to prostitution and sex trafficking. She said the Indonesian president claims that human trafficking is a major priority, but that the primary cabinet level agencies dealing with it are not the "power" agencies. In particular, she characterized the Indonesian immigration department as "clueless."

We then spoke with three members (including the head) of the twenty-person unit of the Indonesian National Police which has been designated to handle human trafficking nationwide. They told us that indeed Chinese women come to Indonesia to work in karaoke lounges, massage parlors, and the like, but that they make up only a very small portion of the sex business in Indonesia. There had been no criminal cases involving Chinese women at the time of our interview.

According to the police, when women are picked up for prostitution they are divided into two categories, either misdemeanants or victims, depending upon whether they appear to be freelancing on their own or are being exploited by someone else. The misdemeanant types are sentenced. The victims are sent to rehabilitation if they are local, and deported if they are not. The biggest complaint of these officials was that they are vastly underresourced, given that they have only twenty people to cover the entire country.

China

China, like Indonesia, has not been positively assessed by the TIP reports over the past nine years. During the first four years (2001–2004), China was in Tier 2 and then it was moved down to the Tier 2 Watch List in 2005 and remained there for the next five years (see Figure 8.1). The 2009 TIP Report characterized the problem of human trafficking in China as follows:

> The People's Republic of China (PRC) is a source, transit, and destination country for men, women, and children trafficked for the purposes of forced labor and sexual exploitation. Although the majority of trafficking in the PRC occurs within the country's borders, there is also considerable trafficking of PRC citizens to Africa, other parts of Asia, Europe, Latin America, the Middle East, and North America. Women are lured through false promises of legitimate employment and forced into commercial sexual exploitation largely in Taiwan, Thailand, Malaysia, and Japan. PRC

women and men are smuggled throughout the world at great personal financial cost and then forced into commercial sexual exploitation or exploitative labor to repay debts to traffickers.[14]

Most Chinese officials we talked to argued that their country is just a source country when it comes to human smuggling and trafficking, and is not a destination or transit country. Although prostitution is rampant in China, most government officials there are very sensitive about this issue and it is almost impossible to get a candid assessment of the problem from Chinese officials if the interviews are conducted formally. As a result, we relied on informal interviews arranged by an intermediary.

Based on our informal conversations with many public security and government officials, it appears that prostitution is a viable occupation that can boost the entertainment and service industries, and provide jobs to millions of young women who would otherwise have no other options for making money. Local governments without exception turn a blind eye and only respond reluctantly to occasional pressure from Beijing to crack down on pornography and prostitution. One interview with a local police station chief was quite revealing about the social organization of the sex industry in China:

> If you want to obtain a sauna permit, you might have to bribe up to 3 million yuan with the help of a *baishoutao* [white glove or a middleman]. Most high-ranking government officials are not going to accept your bribe if you do not know such an intermediary. If you are going to apply for a permit in this city, not only does the mayor have to approve it, but also officials at the provincial public security department. There is a network among sauna establishment owners, and people from this network will put pressure on the mayor not to issue too many permits to restrict competition. This business is a chain relationship: sauna establishment owners, mayor, provincial leaders, all the way up to leaders in Beijing. After the mayor takes the bribes, he surely must kick up some of the money to the provincial leaders. There is no way a police station chief is going to go into a sauna establishment and look for trouble. If I do not handle these places right, not only will I lose my job, but my boss—the city police commissioner—could also be fired. All we can do is to go after those *falang* [hair salons] that are operating without permits. Those *falangs* are in the open, and not only can these places be seen by the public, but they also have an impact on the public.

In a group interview with several police officers from a large and booming business district near Shenzhen that has the reputation of being a "heaven" for Hong Kong men, the officers claimed that since transnational human trafficking is under the jurisdiction of the border police, they were not familiar with the problem. None of the police officers had any experience with domestic human trafficking either; they had only heard about it some years ago. The officers argued that prostitution was widespread when the local economy was developing in the 1990s, but now that the district's economy is well-established the number of prostitutes in their jurisdiction has decreased significantly, and the women have moved to other less-developed areas.

In another group discussion with several police officers in Fuzhou, these officers also argued that women in China are rarely being forced into prostitution. From their viewpoint, many women are willing to pick up commercial sex simply because selling sex is lucrative. According to those officers, China passed a law in 2005 that requires arrested prostitutes to be automatically detained for a maximum of fifteen days instead of simply being fined. Because most *xiaojies* were quite capable of paying the fine if arrested, the mandatory detention policy has had a major deterrent effect on women who sell sex.

In China, the All-China Women's Federation is the most influential women's organization. Founded in April 1949, this nationwide organization was founded to unite women from all ethnic groups and all walks of life to fight for women's further emancipation and the protection of women's rights and interests. The Federation is not, however, very active on human trafficking issues; instead several small organizations were established in the border regions to deal with the problem of Vietnamese and North Korean women who were being trafficked into China for sexual exploitation or forced marriage.

Table 8.1 shows that all the countries or special regions included in our study received a Tier 2 or lower status in the 2010 TIP Report, with the exception of Taiwan. Of the eight sites in Asia, the Hong Kong rankings from 2000 to 2010 were considered the best, with an average ranking of 1.20. Hong Kong is followed by Taiwan with an average ranking of 1.61, and Singapore ranked third with an average ranking of 1.94. Malaysia received the worst rankings with an average ranking of 2.45. Under pressure from the United States, five out of the eight sites have implemented antitrafficking laws in their jurisdictions. As to the results, many American authorities told us they were not sure how serious these governments are in enforcing the law, going after traffickers, and protecting victims.

New York Metropolitan Region

Just for the sake of comparison, we can look at the U.S. domestic situation, for example in New York and northern New Jersey. We interviewed three

Table 8.1. TIP Tier Ranking of the Research Sites

Site	Ranking in 2010	Overall ranking among the sites	Average ranking over the years	Number of years being ranked	Year antitrafficking law was implemented
Hong Kong	2	1	1.20	10	No such law
Macau	2	5	2.20	5	2008
Taiwan	1	2	1.61	9	2009
Thailand	2WL	4	2.10	10	2008
Malaysia	2WL	8	2.45	10	2007
Singapore	2WL	3	1.94	9	No such law
Indonesia	2	6	2.25	10	2007
China	2WL	7	2.30	10	No such law

members of the New York City Human Trafficking Task Force—the coordinator, an NYPD lieutenant, and a sergeant. This thirty-five-person unit has responsibility for training, providing information, and generally increasing awareness in the NYPD of the human trafficking problem. They told us that there were indeed women from overseas working in the sex businesses in NYC; as far as Asian women are concerned, most are from Korea, but there are some from China as well. As of 2007, the task force had handled eight cases involving Chinese women in the two years of its existence. In general, most of the women are smuggled (not trafficked) into the U.S., and according to these officials they come for prostitution in order to make as much money as they can. The Chinese women work mostly in massage parlors.

When we asked the task force members explicitly if the women from China come with the intention or knowledge that they are going to be engaged in paid sex, they said yes. They said that none of the women are initially being forced, coerced, or deceived into commercial sex; however, some may later have their documents withheld, be threatened, or be subjected to debt bondage. They believe the women are being exploited in at least some cases, but see them as being both victims and willing accomplices.

Asked to characterize the smugglers and traffickers, these officials said they are not members of organized crime, and do not really have anything to do with organized crime.

Finally, the task force representatives said their current strategies for arresting and prosecuting smugglers and traffickers were not working very well, in part because the different boroughs of NYC have different policies. Because there is no secure facility for the housing and detention of trafficking victims, they said victims often disappear, making it impossible to prosecute the traffickers. This, they said, leads to a great deal of frustration among law enforcement agencies. They also said that language barriers are a serious problem, as well as the fact that victims do not trust law enforcement.

We also interviewed two assistant U. S. attorneys from the Eastern District of New York (Brooklyn). They described the Chinese women coming to New York as originating mostly from rural villages, and as being young, uneducated, and unsophisticated. Although they did not think that human trafficking was being controlled by organized crime or indeed had anything to do with organized crime, they did see the same individuals in the trafficking business—beginning with the local recruiters—working together over a period of time, which is an indicator of a crime that is organized.

Asked about what the women know before coming to the U.S., they said that some women know that they will be engaging in commercial sex, but in some of these cases the women get more than they bargained for—meaning, less money, more demands, harsher conditions, and the like. As to the motives of the women, the attorneys described a case in which Asian prostitutes were recorded discussing the amounts of money made, and how and where in the city they could make the most money. But in other cases, they said, women are indeed deceived or misled.

We asked the two female prosecutors generally about the use of force, fraud, and/or coercion in the situations with which they were familiar. They said that yes women from mainland China were being exploited in some cases, but not all. They likewise said some of the women were being controlled in some instances, and that violence and physical abuse were used to control them. Asked about coercion, they said it operates in very subtle ways. The women do not speak English; they do not trust law enforcement authorities; and, they believe that the smugglers and traffickers are in cahoots with law enforcement. These are all reasons keeping possible victims from seeking help from authorities.

We interviewed three representatives of NGOs in the NYC area: the director of an agency providing human trafficking information and a referral hotline, the director of the human rights program, Vital Voices Global Partnership, and a director of refugee resettlement and human trafficking in Newark, New Jersey. Although they had only limited experience with the smuggling or trafficking of Chinese women, they did offer some relevant observations from that experience. For example, the director from Vital Voices (herself a Chinese woman) said: "I met some smuggled Chinese. When I talked to them, I was shocked because they thought sex work is a good [meaning, fast] way of 'making money,' and this is true even for minors." Similarly, the Newark director said that she was surprised that some victims who they help go back to prostitution after being granted T-visas, even though they may have been initially forced into prostitution. They do so, she said, because they can make a lot of money in prostitution. Those women were not necessarily prostitutes in their countries of origin.

The picture we see here is not all that different from that in the Asian cities. Chinese women are involved in paid sex and some of those women may be victims, but certainly not all, nor even a majority. The driving force is clearly money, and the people running the operations are not seen to be members of or involved with organized crime.

The principal approach of the police in response to crime is to make arrests. Let's see what the experience of our subjects has been with this approach for dealing with prostitution.

Arrests

As mentioned earlier, most of our subjects were very concerned about being arrested while working as sex workers overseas. They were concerned because the arrests might lead their families in China to find out that they were engaged in prostitution abroad. As a result, a few subjects were somewhat upset about even being asked about past arrests, because they thought that it was bad luck.

Women we interviewed in Hong Kong were particularly worried about being arrested because of the proximity of Hong Kong to China; there was a good chance that whatever was being reported in the media in Hong Kong might be seen or read by people in China. Even more important, if a woman is arrested for prostitution in Hong Kong, the authorities there usually add a comment on the woman's travel documents that she has been engaged in prostitution. This practice undoubtedly causes women to try to avoid being arrested in Hong Kong to the greatest extent possible. Chun Chun, a 24-year-old single woman from Chongqing who was selling sex in a tourist area in Hong Kong with the help of a street mommy, described how concerned she was about the police:

> I am afraid of being arrested. Every day, my heart is jumping when I go to work, especially when I am dealing with *kuaican* ["fast food" or quickie] clients near a park located in a tourist area. If a customer brings me to an expensive hotel, I feel fine. But if he takes me to a cheap, hourly hotel, I am really worried about police inspections and therefore I usually finish up my job in ten minutes and leave. (78)

Mei Fang, a woman we interviewed in a *falang* in Shenzhen who had been to Hong Kong many times, told us how she was arrested and deported the last time she was in Hong Kong:

It was not my lucky day that day. On that trip, I had been there for six days and was ready to return to China because my travel permit was a seven-day permit. But I met a villager that night and she suggested that I go back to China with her the next day. So I did not leave that night and we went out for dinner. The restaurant was on Temple Street in Jordan. We were stopped by the police. After inspecting our documents, the police demanded that we get into the police car. One officer said that it was a red-light district we were in and that we were *xiaojies*. I became mad upon hearing this and yelled at them: "How can you prove that we are *xiaojies*? I do not even know what a red-light district is. How can you bully us Chinese people like this? You all have mothers and sisters. Do you call them *xiaojies* without evidence?" The police officer responded: "Well, if you do not admit that you are a prostitute, which means we won't be able to deport you tomorrow, that's fine with us. We will gather evidence that you are a prostitute, but it may take one day, or seven days, or even one month. While we are collecting evidence, you will be detained in Hong Kong. It's up to you." Once we heard that we might be locked up for a month in Hong Kong, we had no choice but to give in and admit that we were *xiaojies*. The next morning we were sent back to China. They took our fingerprints and our travel pass was stamped with a seal that was in English and we did not know what it meant. But we knew that we won't be able to enter Hong Kong for two years. When we passed through Chinese customs, the mainland police saw the seal and just muttered the words: "Oh, you were deported." (73)

Our subjects in Macau were also very concerned about being arrested, even though Macau authorities were in general not as aggressive as the Hong Kong authorities when it came to cracking down on prostitution. According to women selling sex in the smaller hotels in Macau, the police did come to inspect often, but as long as the girls were in their rooms they would not be bothered. In Macau if a mainland woman is arrested for prostitution for the first time, she is usually freed after a brief interrogation:

I was once arrested and released after questioning because that was the first time. If a woman is arrested for prostitution for the second time, her travel documents will be confiscated and she will be sent back to China, but no fine. The police arrest those hanging around in the hotel lobbies without asking any questions; it is obvious what we are doing there. Police will come to this hotel several times a year. (Yin Yin, 24, single, from Changde, Hunan) (86)

In Macau, when police show up at the hotels known for prostitution and attempt to arrest the women loitering in the hotel lobby or stairways, the women may flee to avoid being arrested. In the process, they put their lives at risk if they take extreme measures to evade the police. C C, a 31-year-old woman from Wushun who was selling sex in a hotel in Macau, recalled an unfortunate incident:

> At one point, the police came to this hotel. A woman who had been arrested once was so scared that she crawled out of the window and tried to make use of the air-conditioning machine and jumped to the floor below. Unfortunately, she fell to the ground from the third floor. We never saw her after that. I guess that she must be paralyzed, or at least crippled. (101)

Early in the 2000s, Thai authorities also became concerned with the appearance of large numbers of women from China on the streets or in the sex establishments of Yawarat (Bangkok's Chinatown, one of the largest in Southeast Asia) or KTVs or flower halls located outside Chinatown—all catering to Chinese men. Thai authorities were particularly aggressive in stopping and arresting Chinese women in Yawarat, and many subjects in Bangkok told us of their frequent encounters with the police.

Dubbed as "little dragon ladies" by the media in Malaysia, Chinese *xiaojies* in Malaysia were also a concern for the local authorities. Ah Shuang, a 42-year-old divorced woman from Dalian who was a streetwalker in Jalan Pedaling—Kuala Lumpur's Chinatown—told us of an encounter with the Malay police:

> I was released just two days ago. Soon after I began to work at Cichang Street [the main commercial street of Jalan Pedaling where hundreds of street vendors are located], someone knocked on my door. I opened the door and a man told me in Chinese that he wanted to inspect my passport. The cleaning woman told me not to be afraid because he was a police officer. I gave him my passport. Anyway, my visa was not expired and I was home alone. Soon after that, the police brought two other handcuffed Chinese women upstairs. I was handcuffed along with them and we were brought to a detention center near Jalan Bazar. We were detained for

fourteen days. We slept on the cement floor when we were in the detention center; the quilt they gave us was very thin. We ate the same tasteless meal every day. It smelled very bad in the detention area. There are many Chinese women in the detention center and there are always new detainees. They were all very young, looked like in their twenties. Among the three of us who were arrested together, one woman had a local boyfriend. He came and tried to get his woman released on bail. But the police said he could not bail out only one, all three of us had to be bailed out at the same time. The bail was about $570 each, and I had only $400. I did not have enough money nor did I want to post bail. But that man wanted to take his girlfriend out, so he helped me by paying the extra $170. He did not ask me to sign any IOU. (24)

Yang Fei, a domestic trafficking victim who was working voluntarily as an escort in Kuala Lumpur at the time of the interview, also recounted her experience with the Malay police: "Once I was arrested when I was in a hotel with a customer. I was detained for three days and fined $800. I paid the fine on my own; the company [escort agency] won't pay for us" (25).

Because the U.S. authorities estimate that the majority of the sex trafficking victims in the United States come from source countries in Asia, police crackdowns on prostitution in America often target Asian massage parlors, especially venues dominated by women from China, Korea, and Thailand. For example, authorities in San Francisco conducted Operation Gilded Cage in 2005, in which hundreds of federal and local law enforcers raided 11 massage parlors in the Bay Area and arrested 27 suspects and more than 100 women. The massage parlors were spread out around San Francisco, from North Beach to the Tenderloin to the Excelsior district. Authorities in Southern California also conducted a similar operation and arrested 18 people believed to be involved in smuggling hundreds of South Korean women into the United States to engage in prostitution. Agents there also detained 46 women working in Santa Monica, the Koreantown area of Los Angeles, and Redondo Beach.

Chinese-owned houses or brothels in Los Angeles are situated mainly in the areas surrounding San Gabriel and Rowland Heights. Because of frequent police crackdowns, Chinese women we interviewed in Los Angeles told us some of the precautionary measures they took to avoid being arrested. For example, Joey, a 36-year-old married woman who owned a house and was seeing clients in her house told us how she tried to protect herself from the police:

The one thing that concerns me the most is the police. Every day when I answer the phone, I am very nervous. That's why I have three cell phones. The first one is the number in the newspaper ad, and I am always very careful whenever I am talking on that phone. After a customer comes for the first time, and if I like him, I will give him my business card with the second cell phone number on it. I am always very comfortable talking to anyone on this phone. The third one is an old cell phone. I am still using it because I don't want to lose contact with my old customers. (119)

Even though Chinese *xiaojies* in Asia and the United States are often subjected to police crackdowns, we believe that independent streetwalkers are more likely to be targeted than those who are involved in organized, indoor prostitution. There are two reasons for this. First, independent streetwalkers normally do not pay protection to the police, so they are more vulnerable to police suppression. And second, streetwalkers are more likely to attract the attention of the general public and the media, so the police are eager to remove these women from the street. If they work indoors, it is more discreet, and as a result they are less likely to be bothered by the authorities.

Corruption

In most sex trafficking materials, official corruption is often mentioned as one of the main facilitators in the emergence and dramatic expansion of transnational commercial sex and sex trafficking. The police in source, transit, and destination countries are believed to play a role in all stages of sex trafficking, facilitating the outflow of women from source countries, enabling the movement of victims through various transit countries, and protecting sex venues in destination countries. Sometimes the police are found to be directly involved in investing in and operating sex establishments in destination countries.

It is no secret in Taiwan that some of the members of the police force are either protecting or are otherwise involved in the operation of the sex venues in their jurisdictions. An agent we interviewed inside a prison in Taiwan told us of his experience with the police:

Once I brought three girls to a store to buy cosmetics. Someone must have tipped off the police, so we were stopped inside that store. One of the girls' visas had expired, so all four of us were brought to a police station. After the police interrogated us separately, one of the girls told the police that I am the agent. When the police asked me whether I am an agent or not, I asked for permission to call my lawyer. I told my lawyer my situation and asked him to find a way to buy me out of this predicament. After my lawyer talked to the police, he said I needed to pay $4,600. After I paid, the police destroyed all the interrogation notes and we were let go. I need to pay the police in my jurisdiction more than $3,000 a month. Often, I also have to pay their bills in various entertainment venues. That's why I must spend at least $9,375 to $12,500 a month on police.

Moreover, the police there have also been found to be involved in the kidnapping of *xiaojies* from China for ransom. Another agent, also interviewed inside a prison, told us this story:

In Taiwan, there are certainly bad cops. Some of my girls were arrested when they were meeting their clients in small hotels, and then the cops called me and asked for money. I asked how much and they say $1,500 to $1,800. I dared not call in other police; I just paid quietly. I also know that there are cops involved in this business—it's just that they aren't directly involved in the operation. They just invest in their friends' business.

Our female subjects in different sites often mentioned how they were approached by the police for money. Ah Hua, a 32-year-old married woman from Hunan Province who was working in Bangkok, told us about her experience with the Thai police: "I was stopped three times and I was fined each time. When you are walking in Chinatown and you are stopped by the cops, you need to pay about $60 to $150. The Thai police just want money. They will release you if you give them money" (54). Our subjects in Thailand also told us that they have to pay a "protection fee" to the police. According to these subjects, the venues where they worked always deduct 40 baht ($1.20) per transaction between the girls and their clients, regardless of how much a woman charges a customer for a transaction. This money, called a "protection fee" by all parties involved, is given to the police by the venue owners on a monthly basis.

Women we interviewed in Malaysia also claimed that they were routinely asked to pay if and when they were stopped by the Malay police: "I was stopped once when I stepped out of a bar with a customer. I paid the police $140 and I was let go" (Ah Hung, 36, married with a 14-year-old daughter and a 9-year-old son, from Nangping, Fujian, an independent *xiaojie* soliciting business in a bar area in Kuala Lumpur) (16). According to Xiao Hao, a

21-year-old single woman from Yongfu, her escort company had a "diplo-mat" to deal with the police:

> Yesterday, our car was stopped by the police in front of a hotel. There were four girls and a driver. Later, the police brought us to an isolated place and asked for $1,150. The company sent a "diplomat" to negotiate with the police. Eventually, we paid the police about $600 and they let us go. Since the company did not talk to us about the payment, it could mean they are going to pay for it. I was scared to death. (33)

Of all the research sites, Indonesia seemed to be the worst in terms of po-lice corruption. The majority of the subjects there said whenever they were stopped by the police, they had to pay.

> One day I took a tricycle home after work and was stopped by a policeman. He wanted to see my passport. While I showed him my passport, he used another hand to signal to me that I should give him money. I gave him some money and he let me go. A few days ago, about thirty women living in this complex were stopped by the police on their way home, and all of them had to pay before the police let them go. (Ah Xiang, 37, divorced, from Wuhan, Hubei, independent *xiaojie* in Jakarta) (34)

People we interviewed in the United States also told us that police com-plicity in the sex business is an open secret. Most subjects believe that with-out police protection it is highly unlikely that a massage parlor that is offer-ing sexual services can remain open for a prolonged period of time, because it does not take that long for the local police to find out about it. A man who visited massage parlors on a regular basis, said: "Let me tell you this, there are cops behind every massage parlor in New Jersey; either the cops are pro-tecting the parlors, or they are directly involved in the operation by investing money in it. As a result, if there is a pending crackdown on the parlors, the cops will tip off those establishments they are protecting or have a stake in. The massage parlors that are tipped off will simply close their doors for a few days."

See No Evil

Most government officials and police officers we interviewed told us frankly that prostitution is not a top priority for their governments or departments.

Most also do not believe that Chinese women working in their jurisdictions are trafficking victims. Because of pressure from the U.S. government, the United Nations, and the European Union, however, many Asian countries have been compelled to follow the example of the United States by passing antitrafficking laws, going after human traffickers and sex venue owners, and treating foreign women who engage in commercial sex as victims rather than as prostitutes or illegal migrants. The main purpose of such efforts is to receive a good ranking in the U.S. government's annual TIP report; but there is not much actual concern about eliminating prostitution or dismantling sex ring networks. As a result, since 2000 prostitution in Asia has gone further underground—out of sight but certainly not out of existence.

In *Temporarily Yours*, Elizabeth Bernstein argued that sexual commerce in postindustrial cities has been transformed from predominantly street prostitution to "a brave new world of commercially available intimate encounters that are subjectively normalized for sex workers and clients alike."[15] Bernstein also pointed out that one of the main effects of recent law enforcement efforts against commercial sex has been to push sexual transactions from outdoors to indoors:

> What is arguably most remarkable about the disparate array of legal strategies that Europeans and North Americans have implemented in recent years is how singular they have been in effect: The overarching trend has been toward the elimination of prostitution from city streets, coupled with the state-facilitated (or de facto tolerated) flourishing of the indoor and online sectors of the sex trade. Despite their seeming differences, the common focus of state interventions has been on eliminating the visible manifestations of poverty and deviance (both racial and national) from urban spaces, rather than the exchange of sex for money per se.[16]

Commercial sex and commercial sex work—irrespective of the politically correct euphemisms that may be applied to it—continues to thrive everywhere we looked. Both demand and supply are strong. Government efforts against prostitution and sex trafficking, promulgated principally by developed countries, may be yet another example of what happens when governments attempt to insert themselves into the realm of moral behavior. History tells us that legislating morality is almost always problematical. But not surprisingly, here as elsewhere ignoring the lessons of history seems to be the order of the day.

In our discussions with various responders and rescuers, several themes emerge from or are reiterated in our discussions with others. One is that the issue of sex trafficking and its connections to prostitution are much more complex and nuanced than has been recognized in much of the discussion to this point. There is indeed exploitation and victimization of some women, but it is not of the nature and magnitude that some experts have been led and have led us to believe. Economics clearly plays a dominant role in both producing the pool of potentially vulnerable women and in attracting the various facilitators and other players to the commercial sex business. The latter is aided and abetted by various governments and businesses because it is very profitable. This is just one example of the hypocrisy that seems to characterize so many aspects of this subject.

Hypocritical (in so many words) is how many officials in other countries describe the U.S. policies and practices with respect to human trafficking. Because it is the "800 pound gorilla," the U.S. is able to hold other countries to account according to standards it does not itself meet. One result in some countries is lip service to the U.S. standards promulgated in the TVPA and the TIPs report. Laws and policies are adopted but are only slightly related to the actual practices on the ground. Interestingly, respondents in the U.S. describe a similar phenomenon as well. That phenomenon might best be described as a circumstance in which ideology and a kind of politicized morality have seemingly outrun the facts and evidence. This will be taken up in our concluding chapter.

9

The Reality and the Myths

A Critical Analysis of Sex Trafficking

According to the prevailing trafficking paradigm as described in chapter 1, sex trafficking can be divided into the following stages: (1) the *recruitment* of potential victims by recruiters, (2) the *transportation* of victims by traffickers, (3) the *selling* of victims to brothel owners by stakeholders, be they recruiters, traffickers, or human traders who pay for the traveling expenses of victims or buy victims from traffickers, (4) the *control* of victims, (5) the subsequent *victimization* of victims by sex ring operators, (6) the use of *debt bondage* as a form of control, and (7) the *exploitation* of victims, primarily in financial terms. Let us examine what our subjects had to say about these processes, based on their own experiences and observations. Keep in mind that we are only talking about *transnational* sex trafficking. As mentioned before, about 10 percent of our female subjects were trafficked domestically in China. But we are not focusing on their domestic experience, only their overseas experiences.

Recruitment

According to Kathleen Barry, author of *The Prostitution of Sexuality*, traffickers usually recruit girls and women mainly through three methods: purchase, deception, or abduction (including force and coercion).[1] Were our female subjects recruited in these ways?

Purchase

None of our female subjects said they had been sold into prostitution, nor did they know anyone who entered prostitution because they had been purchased by someone. In fact, none of them had even heard that women could be purchased for the purpose of putting them to work in commercial sex. In China, girls and women are traded for the purpose of adoption or marriage, but not for the sex trade.

Deception

In much of the discourse on trafficking, the most frequently mentioned recruiting method is deception. A recruiter is said to approach a woman who is interested in going overseas to engage in legitimate work, and tells her that she can work as a nanny, a waitress, or a model in a foreign country. The potential pay is painted as being very attractive. Alternatively, a woman is promised that she can marry a man when she arrives in the destination country. Selling sex is not mentioned at all, and thus it is the last thing in the mind of the woman being recruited. Only after she has arrived in the destination country does the recruiter tell her that she must work in a sex venue to repay the debt she owes because of the cost of her travel documents, airplane ticket, and other expenditures.

The vast majority of our subjects, be they sex ring operators, law enforcement authorities, or *xiaojies*, said they did not think that women are usually deceived into going overseas to engage in commercial sex. The owner of an escort agency in Taiwan explained why: "We will not force, deceive, or coerce women to sell sex. We also tell the agents to give their women more freedom. It is impossible to force a girl to sleep with a client. Besides, it is impossible to control a person in Taiwan; they can call the police anytime." The manager of a legitimate massage parlor in Kuala Lumpur concurred: "I believe all mainland women know what they will do after they arrive; all of them are willing to come because they have no jobs and make no money in China. They are highly unlikely to be deceived."

A mommy who was soliciting business for Chinese women in a tourist area of Hong Kong also expressed her doubts about the use of deception in recruitment: "I never met a girl who was deceived or heard that some girls were deceived. Some girls may be deceived in the sense that they were charged more for travel expenses or were told that they will make more than they actually can. I believe all of them know what they will do overseas. If someone tells you she did not, she is lying."

An agent who was serving time in a prison in Taiwan blamed the media for a misconception that most women are being forced or deceived into prostitution:

> These women want to make money, so they come to Taiwan. It is all about supply and demand. Everyone is involved in it voluntarily, including those who come by boats. Why the hell are we saying this is trafficking? Maybe these are stories made up by reporters. I read in the newspapers about how certain women in China are transported to Taiwan after they have been drugged; that's bullshit. I hope you academics are not going to copy the reporters and say that Chinese women are being deceived and being traded; it does not happen.

Likewise, all the government authorities and law enforcers we interviewed in Asia, including American officials working there, suggested that deception was by and large not involved in the transnational movement of Chinese women.

We asked our female subjects via three separate questions whether they were forced, deceived, or coerced into selling sex overseas; only one of them answered yes to any one of these three questions, even though some of them (again about 10%) said they had been forced, deceived, or coerced into prostitution back in China. We also asked them whether they had ever met a Chinese woman who said she was forced, deceived, or coerced into prostitution abroad, and only 3 out of 148 (2%) said they had. Li Na, a 30-year-old single woman from Shanzhi who was working as an independent freelance *xiaojie* in Malacca and Kuala Lumpur, said: "I met a girl when I was here the last time. She said she did not know she would be a *xiaojie* before arriving here. But she also said now that she's here and she owed people money, she had no choice but to do it. Where could she go? It makes no difference even if you call the police. Police here are all corrupt" (31).

When asked why they or other women were not likely to be deceived into prostitution, the women offered the following reasons. First, they said they were not children who could be easily deceived:

How in the world could a person be so dumb as to be deceived to come to the United States to work as a prostitute? We are not kids! Besides, we all have some education and there is so much information on the internet where you can learn a lot about the outside world. (Niko, 39, divorced, from Qingdao, a house prostitute in Los Angeles) (130)

The second reason offered by our subjects was that even if initially deceived, a person can easily escape, and that was why (they said) nobody would use this method to recruit a woman: "I did not meet anyone like this in Guangdong Province, not to mention Hong Kong. If a woman was deceived and brought here, isn't it very easy to escape in a place like Hong Kong? How can a person be under control here?" (Chun Chun, 24, single, from Chongqing, a mommy-assisted streetwalker in Hong Kong) (78).

The third reason mentioned was that, if they were deceived, they could go after those who had deceived them upon their return to China. Under such circumstances, a recruiter in China was said to be highly unlikely to use deception in the process because he or she would know that there could be repercussions.

Our subjects also suggested that since many women were already selling sex in China, it was not possible to deceive these experienced *xiaojies* into engaging in prostitution overseas without their knowledge. Ah Xue, 37, divorced with a 14-year-old daughter, an independent streetwalker in the Chinatown of Kuala Lumpur, reasoned: "Among the more than ten women working on this street, only one or two are like me who worked for a government unit in China. Most of them were *xiaojies* back in China. If they claim that they were deceived, they are lying. When we fellow sisters are together, who would dare to say that she was deceived?" (17).

Some of our subjects also mentioned that women from rural China were unlikely to be deceived because these women, contrary to the assumption that rural people are eager to trust strangers, were actually very suspicious: "We all know what this is all about before we come. Rural girls are particularly less likely to be deceived because they are extremely cautious. They very often suspect what people's motivations are, so it is almost impossible to deceive them" (Ah Dong, 30, married, from Chongqing, a streetwalker in Singapore) (2).

Other subjects made another point about how unlikely it was to deceive a person into traveling overseas, especially when the destination country was so far away from the source country:

How can anyone deceive a woman to come to the United States? Don't forget, to bring a person to America, you need to go to the American

embassy, fill out a lot of forms, go through many processes, and you must
obtain a visa. How can someone deceive someone like this? (Joey, 36, married, from Beijing, a house prostitute in Los Angeles) (119)

Some subjects suggested that if there was any deception involved, it was
not about the nature of the work but rather something else: "If there is any
deception, it is that they [the recruiters or the facilitators] trick you into paying a higher document fee or they lied and said that you can make much
more money than you actually do" (Xiao Yao, 37, divorced, from Wuxi, Jiang-
shu, a nightclub hostess in Bangkok) (58).

Other subjects said they were not told exactly what they would be doing
overseas, but they all knew what they were getting into, even though they
were not *xiaojies* back home: "When I was in China, the woman who helped
me to come here did not tell me explicitly what I would be doing in Thailand,
but I understood what she was saying" (Zhao Tong, 24, divorced, from Harbin, Heilongjiang, a flower hall hostess in Bangkok) (64).

On the other hand, the women we interviewed did admit that they knew
quite a few women from the rural hinterlands of China who had been deceived by their boyfriends or chickenheads into working in the sex business
in China—especially in the coastal areas. As mentioned above, a small proportion of our female subjects said they were forced, deceived, or coerced
into prostitution in China.

When asked why there is a public perception that many women are deceived into prostitution, two women offered the following explanations:

When a woman from China is arrested for prostitution here, she is not
going to admit that she entered this line of work willingly; she has to save
face. (Bing Bing, 25, single, from Changchun, Jilin, an escort in Taipei) (144)

Everyone knows that you need to sleep with men to make money. Only
those who did not make money in Malaysia will go back and say that they
did not anticipate that they needed to sleep with clients; they refused to do
so and that's why they did not make money and went back to China. Let
them go to hell! They went back to China empty-handed simply because
no men wanted them. And because of them, people in my hometown village know what we are doing in Malaysia. (Ah Hung, 36, married, from
Nanping, Fujian, a freelance woman soliciting business in a bar area in
Kuala Lumpur) (16)

From our interviews, it was clear that our subjects were not subjected to
deception, and that before they left China they all knew that they would be

going overseas to engage in paid sex. A very small number of subjects said they had not been told that they would have to sleep with men, but they said they knew that this could be part of their jobs as hostesses.

Abduction, Force, or Coercion

According to some antitrafficking advocates, abduction, force, or coercion are often adopted by traffickers to pressure children or young women to engage in paid sex. These advocates assume that prostitution is not a profession that women willingly enter, so drastic measures must have been used by traffickers to ensure victims' cooperation. But literally, none of the women we interviewed said they had been subjected to abduction, force, or coercion in the process of entering the commercial sex business overseas. One subject gave the following explanation as to why not: "We left our hometown so many years ago and have had so much social experience, it is not possible for anyone to force us to do what we don't want to do" (Ah Dong, 30, married, from Chongqing, a streetwalker in Singapore) (2).

Other subjects thought it was impossible for anyone to force anyone to sell sex because, if so, a woman who was forced or coerced could always escape. Fang Fang, a 31-year-old single woman from Guilin (Guangxi) who was working as an escort in Taiwan, explained: "Who can coerce me into doing this? If it happens, I will report it to the police once I step out of the airplane, and the worst that can happen to me is that I will be sent back to China. I can't have sex with men against my will!" (137). Jiao Jiao, a 17-year-old street-walker from Dongfeng, Jilin, who was working as a streetwalker in Singapore, agreed: "It is impossible. Even if one is being forced, she has two legs, why doesn't she escape? How could it be possible that a person is controlled for a long time and forced to have sex with customers every day?"[2] (11).

Other subjects suggested that forced prostitution was, for them, simply unimaginable. Others thought that the main reason for the absence of forced prostitution was because criminals were not so stupid as to commit such a serious crime: "In Singapore, forcing someone into prostitution is a serious crime, so they won't dare to do this" (Yang Yang, 25, single, from Shenyang, Liaoning, a streetwalker in Singapore) (1). A very small number of women we interviewed suggested that, since selling sex was such an easy job for them, it was inconceivable that they had to be forced into it.

Na Na, a 28-year-old single woman from Dalian, Liaoning, who was working as an independent *xiaojie* out of an apartment complex in Los Angeles, told us how older women would tell the younger ones to lie if arrested: "It is not possible to deceive or force someone to enter this line of work. If a woman says she is being deceived or forced, it must be a lie. She must have been coached by other women about what to tell the police if she is arrested. Other women have told me this. I can assure you that there are no trafficked victims in Los Angeles, just many willing prostitutes here" (118).

Some subjects thought that this practice of forcing women to go overseas to engage in commercial sex did exist, but that it was many years ago: "It may have happened a long time ago. What age is it now? Nowadays, it is impossible to force a woman to work as a prostitute" (Ah Ping, 36, married, from Jinzhou, Hubei, a freelance woman soliciting business in restaurants around Bangkok's Chinatown) (52).

Most law enforcers we interviewed in Asia also believed that women from China were highly unlikely to have been forced into prostitution overseas. A Hong Kong police officer who is also an expert on triad organizations, explained why:

> It is not true that there are forced prostitutes. If a mainland woman is forced, the Hong Kong jockey [pimp] will send the woman back to the mainland and the mainland agent will either return the money or send another woman to Hong Kong. There are many women who want to be *xiaojies* in Hong Kong; it is not necessary to force women to be prostitutes in Hong Kong. If they are forced, how could they carry out their job-related activities well? How could they make their clients happy? Furthermore, Hong Kong is so small and crowded, how can you have complete control of a person?

Robyn Emerton, a human rights scholar who conducted a study of Chinese women in the Hong Kong sex sector, concluded: "I have not found any reports of women being abducted or forcefully taken from their homes and brought to Hong Kong for the purpose of prostitution."[3]

The manager of an expensive spa in Macau explained to us that forced prostitution is not a good business practice because it is practically impossible to run a sex business employing women against their will:

> Mainland women come to Macau willingly, and most of them have been engaged in commercial sex before they came. Macau is a free society. If a woman is forced to be a prostitute, she can flee and call the police anytime. It is also impossible to hide a girl in a secret place and provide sex service only to regular customers. Clients must see the *xiaojies* first before they make a decision to buy the service or not. No man would be willing to go with a stranger to a strange place just to have a look at a prostitute.

Yiu Kong Chu, a professor at the University of Hong Kong who is an expert on organized crime, explained why it is so incomprehensible for sex ring operators in China and Hong Kong to dupe women into prostitution: "If a woman is reluctant to go to Hong Kong for sex work, a chickenhead [trafficker] is highly unlikely to force, coerce, or cheat her into it because the woman could become a major headache for everyone involved after she arrives in Hong Kong. What if the woman does not cooperate? What if the woman tries to run away? What if she calls the police? I mean, no sex operator in his or her right mind wants to deal with such a woman. Most women know what they are going to do when they arrive in Hong Kong."

In sum, our findings demonstrate that among those we interviewed, purchase, deception, and abduction or force were not the prevalent methods used by recruiters and facilitators when they talked to women who were interested in working overseas. Are our findings with respect to force and coercion unique? No, if anything they are quite in line with the findings from a number of other studies.[4]

Previous research has also found that cooperating migrants are much more likely to get across national borders than are abducted and kidnapped victims who may try to get attention. This is why, in the view of many who have looked at this issue, the element of coercion is often not present at the beginning of the trafficking process.[5]

Transportation

According to the official view of human trafficking and the U.S. and UN definitions of trafficking, after a girl or a woman is recruited in a source country through force, fraud, or coercion, she is usually transported abroad by one or more traffickers. After paying the recruiter a certain sum of money, the trafficker obtains travel documents (usually a passport and a visa) for the victim, and personally brings the victim to a destination country, sometimes through one or more transit countries. In this process, the trafficker may bribe government officials in the sending, transit, and receiving countries if necessary. Once the victim arrives in the destination country, the trafficker then sells her to a brothel owner for a substantial amount of money. Many commentators have indicated, as did Kathleen Barry in the earlier quote, that organized crime groups (e.g., the Japanese Yakuza, the Hong Kong triads, the Russian Mafiya, Albanian organized gangs, etc.) play a key role in the transportation of women across international borders.[6]

Of the 149 women we interviewed in overseas locations, almost all of them had arrived with genuine documents; only one said she was smuggled into the United States via Mexico, and four said they flew to their destination countries using fake documents. Bribery of officials in the source country (China) and the destination countries for the purpose of exit and entry was almost never mentioned by our subjects. This, by the way, is significantly different from the experiences of illegal Chinese immigrants who were smuggled into the United States.[7] In the Chinese smuggling scenario, the smugglers and the smuggled migrants often used bribery to facilitate their transnational movements.

Further, unlike what has often been depicted in the trafficking literature, none of our subjects were transported overseas by a "trafficker." When we asked who had brought them abroad, many said they had traveled alone (31%), or were accompanied by a returned *xiaojie* (25%), or were with other females who, like them, were going to the same destination country for the first time (15%). Other subjects mentioned that they had gone overseas as members of a business or official delegation (8%, and mostly to the United States), or as wives of fake husbands through fraudulent marriages (4%, mostly to Taiwan), or were accompanied by their husbands/boyfriends/chickenheads (5%, mostly to Hong Kong or Macau). It is clear that the "trafficker" (or transporter) so prominently mentioned in the human trafficking discussion, and so often put forward by authorities as the prime target in the war against human trafficking, does not come up as a key figure in our subjects' cross-border movements. If the kinds of "traffickers" who have been typically described do not actually exist, or they exist but are not as prominent as has been claimed, then it would seem that the assumption that organized crime figures are key traffickers would also seem to be unfounded. This was indeed the conclusion of, among others, Joanna Busza and her colleagues at the London School of Hygiene and Tropical Medicine when they argued that intermediaries should not be automatically labeled as "traffickers," because "for many of these migrants, movement across international borders depended on assistance from intermediaries, often family members. . . . Classifying such assistance as 'trafficking' simplifies a much deeper cultural reality."[8]

Sale

Of all the activities alleged to be associated with sex trafficking—recruitment, transportation, sale, debt bondage, control, violence, exploitation—the sale of a human being as a commodity is probably the most sinister and horrifying, and it is this aspect that has particularly caught the public imagination and view of human trafficking. Again, according to most of the literature on sex trafficking, not only can a girl or a woman be sold once she arrives in a destination country, but the buyer can resell her again after exploiting her for a certain period of time, normally when the victim is about to clear the debt she owes to the buyer.[9] After she leaves the first buyer without a penny for herself, the victim is then said to have to start all over again with the second buyer. That is why, according to this view, victims are characterized as commodities that can be used and reused again and again by numerous buyers. When the victims are too old or too sick to be sold again, they are killed or discarded. The following is a good illustration of how Moldovans are said to be traded like commodities in the Italian sex industry.

> The owner of the nightclub told Tatyana that she owed him four thousand euros for the cost of buying her and he would return her to Moldova after she slept with four hundred men. She slept with the required four hundred men in under two months, netting approximately twelve thousand euros for her owner and nothing for herself. The owner did not free Tatyana. Instead, he sold her to a protector who forced her to work on the streets.[10]

With one exception, none of our subjects said they had been traded by their helpers in China or their employers in the destination countries. Xiao Xiao, a 32-year-old escort in Taiwan, said her agent sold her to another agent after he was convinced that she might try to escape without repaying him the road fee of $6,250. Xiao Xiao had been to Taiwan many times and the agent who sold her thought that she was too experienced and too familiar with Taiwan to remain working for him. Otherwise, agents in Taiwan did not import women for the purpose of trading them, but rather to place them in an escort agency to make money. After a woman had repaid her debt, she continued to work for her agent and made money for both herself and the agent. The agents thus prefer to keep their women because they can continue to take a cut of their earnings. The same is true with subjects in the other research sites; they might go overseas under debt to someone in the destination country, but with the exception of one very unique case, none was sold or resold.

Control

After a sex trafficking victim has been recruited, transported, and sold, according to the popular view, a brothel or an escort agency owner who buys her maintains complete control to prevent her from escaping. This view promulgates the following scenario as being typical: the brothel owner takes away her travel documents, locks her up in a room, and watches her closely all the time. She works and sleeps in her room, and is never allowed to leave. For those who are not cooperative, there is even the further possibility that they are chained when they are not seeing clients. Those who attempt to escape are beaten or even killed, often in front of other girls so as to set an example.

From our discussion in the earlier chapters, it is clear that the vast majority of our subjects were not under this sort of control when we interviewed them. We explicitly asked them whether they were being controlled by their employers or debtors. Of the 149 subjects (excluding the 15 subjects in China), 127 (85%) said they were free, and 22 (15%) said they were not free. Looking at this situation in the context of other factors we have considered suggests the following. First, the level of control varies by research sites. Seventy-two percent of the women in Indonesia said they were not free, while none of the women in Singapore, Los Angeles, and New York said they were being controlled. Second, whether a subject was controlled or not was related to whether she still owed a debt. Only 12 percent of those who did not owe money said they were controlled, whereas 43 percent of those in debt said they were not free. Third, 97 percent of the independent and 97 percent of the partnership *xiaojies* said they were free to move around as compared to 75 percent of the employed *xiaojies*. Finally, women working in saunas and spas were most likely to say that their movements were restricted, followed by escort agencies (26%) and nightclubs/KTVs (22%). Women working along with mommies and chickenheads were as free as those working independently. In sum, the majority of the women who said they did not feel free were in Indonesia, and the main reason they said this was because they were required to turn in their travel documents to their employers. The opportunity to work independently in Indonesia was, unlike in the other research sites, very limited. Those who worked in saunas and spas in Jakarta were monitored closely by their employers and were required to stay in the dormitories located within the compound of their workplaces. As a result, their movements were limited.

Asked why she felt she was not free, a subject working in Jakarta gave the following reasons:

> I do not have much freedom. We must ask for approval to take a leave if we do not want to work and we can only ask for a sick leave. In addition, the company takes away our passport and visa; we only have the copies. We can only stay in our dorms if we are off duty because they don't

allow us to go out with our customers. We will be fined 50 hours ($300) if the company finds out that we go out with a customer. We also have to sign a contract with the company before we start working, which says that we must work at least four months for the company. This means we cannot quit if we want to. (Judy, 21, single, from Henyang, Hunan, a KTV hostess)[11] (37)

In contrast, Yang Yang, 25 and single, from Shenyang, who arrived in Singapore with the help of people to whom she owed $3,750, explained why she was free to move around while working in a red-light district as a streetwalker: "I am absolutely free. All my travel documents are in my hands. They are not afraid that I will run away, and that's because they know where I live in Shenyang. Neither will I flee just because I owe them $3,750; it is not that difficult to make this amount of money here. Besides, where could I go in Singapore after I leave them?" (1).

An agent in Taiwan who was serving time for his role in the sex trade said he normally did not control his girls at all: "These women are completely free; they can go shopping or take a walk. We also won't take hold of their travel documents. There is no management of these women whatsoever. The only problem is when they want to go somewhere and they don't know how to get there, they need someone to take them there and so they must rely on us. They can also give their cell phone numbers to their customers, and sometimes their customers will take them out for shopping or dining."

Li Yin, 24 and single, who was working as an escort in Kuala Lumpur, said she felt she was living a relatively free life, even though she lived in a place provided by her escort agency and she needed a ride no matter whether she was working or not: "I would say that we are relatively free. The company does not control or monitor our every move. Like on our days off, they give us a ride to a shopping mall and then leave us there. We set a time for them to pick us up" (27).

Victimization

Regardless of whether women are controlled or not, there is a perception in the trafficking coverage that women are significantly vulnerable to victimization when they go overseas to sell sex. Forms of victimization are categorized as violence (physical and sexual) by their clients or handlers, being forced to have unsafe sex, being coerced to see an extreme number of clients every day, and being denied any right to select customers.

Violence

We have already discussed the rarity of client violence; thus we will only examine violence by sex ring operators here. In the course of discussing the transnational movement of women for the purpose of commercial sex, some antitrafficking advocates, NGOs, and researchers have argued that many innocent victims go through a relatively similar experience: they are procured or recruited, transported or trafficked, seasoned or violently coerced, prostituted or pimped, exploited or victimized, resold or retrafficked, and finally discarded or killed. For example, Kathleen Barry described the importance of procuring and pimping in the process of men prostituting women:

> Together, pimping and procuring are perhaps the most ruthless displays of male power and sexual dominance. . . . Procuring is a strategy, a tactic for acquiring women and turning them into prostitution; pimping keeps them there. Procuring today involves "convincing" a woman to be a prostitute through cunning, fraud, and/or physical force, taking her against her will or knowledge and putting her into prostitution.[12]

If a woman resists becoming a prostitute after being recruited and trafficked, then she is said to be in need of seasoning. According to Barry: "Seasoning is meant to break its victim's will, reduce her ego, and separate her from her previous life. All procuring strategies include some form of seasoning."[13] And if a woman continues to put up a fight after being seasoned, then it is highly likely that she will be killed, perhaps by beheading, as suggested by Donna Hughes, a University of Rhode Island professor of women's studies: "In two reported cases, women who resisted were killed as an example to other women. In Istanbul, Turkey, two Ukrainian women were thrown off a balcony and killed, while six of their Russian friends watched. In Serbia, a Ukrainian woman who resisted was beheaded in public."[14]

In dramatic contrast to this picture, our interviews with *xiaojies* and sex entrepreneurs disclosed just one violent incident, and that was between an agent in Taiwan and a Chinese woman. The agent, who was in prison at the time of the interview, explained why he was arrested:

> This is my first arrest after so many years as an agent. That's because a girl of mine got mixed up with a jockey and she moved into the jockey's house. This is something I am very much against. Besides, the jockey was taking her out for fun all day long and she did not pay much attention to her

work anymore. Worse, sometimes the two of them worked together to take a "case" [seeing clients] without my knowledge, like I did not even exist. After I found out about that, I beat them up with a stick. They called the police, and that's how I got in here.

Because none of the women we interviewed said they were being forced into prostitution, the need to use violence to coerce them becomes moot. However, as the above incident demonstrates, the question might arise as to what happens if there is a conflict or an argument between a subject and her employer or handler? Would they then be subjected to violence under such circumstances? According to the respondents, with the exception of some chickenheads, conflicts between them and their facilitators were rare. Even when a dispute between a woman and a facilitator developed, the woman, not the facilitator, often got the upper hand. Xiao Dai, a 24-year-old single from Leshan told us this story:

Last time when I was in Jakarta, I worked at XXX [a spa, name omitted] and after working there for a month, some girls wanted to go home. The company refused to return our passports because they wanted us to work for a few more months. We told the company: "We do not owe you any money and yet you won't let us go home." We also told them we would go to the Chinese embassy here if they won't return our passports. Once they learned this, they gave our passports back to us. (51)

An agent we interviewed in Taiwan explained why, even if there are problems between a woman and her agent, it is unlikely the agent will use violence: "If I am not happy with a woman, the most I can do is to ask her to go home. If I mistreat her, I am afraid that she might go to the police."

Besides the issue of physical violence, there is also the matter of sexual violence. If an employer or a facilitator is a male, how likely is it that these males are going to take advantage of, coerce, or even rape the women who work for them? In our interviews and conversations with the women and the sex ring operators, some women said they did have sex with their agents, escort agency owners, jockeys, fake husbands, or chickenheads, but it was not common. The majority of such sexual relationships, according to the women, were the result of mutual consent rather than being forced or coerced.

We suspect that actor-on-sex worker violence is not as common as reported in the media and most of the antitrafficking literature. It is thus not surprising that Laura Agustin, author of *Sex at the Margins*, would find that "'rescue' raids by police and NGOs often fail because arrested workers refuse to denounce anyone. Critics conclude that workers are afraid of reprisals, but it could be that they have nothing to denounce."[15]

Unsafe Sex

Unsafe sex is another form of victimization. We discussed the issue of being forced to engage in unsafe sex earlier. According to our subjects, it was standard procedure in their daily work that their clients had to use condoms. They also said that they did not engage in certain sex acts such as anal sex, nor would they allow clients to kiss them. The women we interviewed said they were very cautious about their health, and they would not take a risk even if some clients were willing to pay them more for unsafe sex. Only a small number of subjects (N = 9) said they were concerned about being infected with sexually transmitted diseases. Most subjects were worried about being arrested or not having enough business.

Too Many Clients

In many discussions of sex trafficking, the victimization of women is often underscored by the notion that women who are trafficked often end up serving dozens of men on a daily basis. If they work ten hours a day, many observers assume, and a session lasts half an hour, then they must be seeing twenty men a day. But is business really so brisk that women are actually required to have sex with that many men nonstop?

The women we interviewed did not complain at all about this particular problem. If anything, they complained that business was much slower than expected and thus they were disappointed with their earnings. When asked whether they were bothered by having to have sex with so many men, the common answer was: "No! Many of us are actually unhappy simply because there is not enough work" (Kelly, 38, divorced, from Beijing, a house prostitute in Los Angeles) (121). Another subject made the same point: "Sometimes, we would cry and feel depressed, and that's simply because business is slow and we are not making good money, not because we engage in paid sex" (Yang Yang, 25, single, a streetwalker in Singapore) (1).

Our aggregate data support this subject's point: when asked how many clients they saw in a day on average, 86 percent of them said six clients or fewer a day. Almost half of the subjects had three clients or fewer a day on average. Only 14 percent said they saw six or more clients a day, with the highest being an average of twelve clients a day. Table 9.1 shows the average

Table 9.1. Average Sessions (or Number of Clients)
Per Day, by Research Site (N = 149)

Site	Sessions per day
Hong Kong	3.45
Macau	5.72
Taiwan	6.75
Thailand	2.00
Malaysia	4.33
Singapore	4.58
Indonesia	1.47
Los Angeles	4.27
New York	3.12
Total	4.17

Table 9.2. Average Sessions (or Number of Clients)
Per Day, by Sex Venue

Venue	Sessions per day
Independent: street	6.25
Independent: hotel	4.71
Independent: home	4.12
Independent: restaurant	2.83
Partnership: mommy	3.83
Partnership: chickenhead	5.77
Employed: nightclub/KTV	1.75
Employed: sauna/spa	2.08
Employed: massage parlor	3.31
Employed: brothel	4.27
Employed: escort	6.60
Total	4.17

sessions per day by research site, and it is clear that women working as escorts in Taiwan were the ones with the most clients per day (almost seven) and subjects in Thailand and Indonesia (mostly independent *xiaojies*, hostesses in nightclubs/KTVs, or masseuses in saunas and spas) had the fewest (barely two clients a day). See Table 9.2 for average sessions per day by sex venues or markets. It should be pointed out that those subjects who were working as hostesses in restaurants, nightclubs, KTVs, and flower halls may make money mainly through sitting tables and those who were working as masseuses may rely on providing massages and half-service (hand jobs) for a substantial amount of their income.

For many female subjects who had to spend money for the opportunity to work a few weeks overseas, or who had to see at least three clients a day to simply cover their hotel room costs, having only a few clients was certainly not enough, especially if they then had to idle away their time for a few months in China before they could undertake another overseas trip.

Can't Refuse a Client

Another type of victimization often discussed in the media and the sex trafficking literature is that women working in overseas sex businesses are not able to select their client—they must see anyone who walks in the door. This again was not the experience of most of our subjects—they did have the right to select clients and they often screened their clients for potential trouble. For example, Rong Rong, a 33-year-old divorced woman from Chongqing who was an independent streetwalker in Singapore's Chinatown, said: "I have about six to seven clients a day. Most of them are local men, but I also have customers from Taiwan, Hong Kong, and Korea. I don't do business with foreigners. Most of my customers are nice and polite, and they are regular customers. To protect myself, I also won't do business with young customers, because they are more likely to be undercover cops" (6). As an independent *xiaojie* who did not owe any money, it is conceivable that she was indeed free to choose customers, but what about those who owed money or who worked for a sex establishment?

Yang Yang, a streetwalker working in Singapore under the protection of local chickenheads who owed $3,750 for the trip to Singapore, told us she could decide who to see and not to see: "Most of my customers are Singaporeans, and some of them are from Hong Kong, Taiwan, or China. I won't do business with black people [Indians]. If an Indian approaches me and asks me how much, I will say $70, just to scare him away. My fee is actually $50" (1). Clearly racism plays a role in the sex industry, just as it does in all aspects of society.

We believe that subjects who are working as hostesses in a nightclub/KTV or as masseuses in a sauna/spa/massage parlor are less likely to be able to select clients because they work for third-party-managed or organized sex venues. In these arrangements, once a woman has been selected by a client after an elaborate selection procedure (as previously discussed), it is not possible for the woman to refuse the client.

Debt Bondage

Again contrary to the common perception, the majority of our subjects (77%) did not owe money to someone in the trafficking or sex business for their overseas trips. Instead, they did not have to pay someone or used their savings or borrowed money from their friends or relatives to finance their travel. Among the 34 subjects who had owed money to someone who was not a friend or relative, only 13 said they were still in debt at the time of the interviews. This means the rest had cleared their debts within a relatively short period of time. The fact that so many of them were able to clear their debts within a few weeks or months tells us that (1) the amount of money our subjects owed for their trips was not as high as generally believed; (2) the women did not have to pay interest on their debts; and (3) the people who fronted the money for the women to travel did not arbitrarily increase the amount of the debt after the women had arrived overseas.

Exploitation

Financial exploitation is another assumed characteristic of sex trafficking. When women are transported across international borders to engage in prostitution, they are believed to be heavily exploited by their handlers or facilitators. It is claimed that traffickers charge exorbitant fees for travel documents and that the women receive only a very small portion of the money their clients give them, or maybe even nothing at all. Sex establishment owners also are said to charge these women outrageous sums of money for food, lodging, cosmetics, dresses, fines, and for a variety of other reasons. Consequently, or so the story goes, after all these expenses are deducted from their meager share, there is almost nothing left for them to keep.

We discussed previously how much money clients paid our subjects per session, how much the subjects received, and approximately how much they made in a month. Our data suggest that the women we interviewed were receiving on average about three-fourths of the money the clients paid; it would thus seem difficult to label this as financial exploitation.

Lin Lean Lim, the editor of the book *The Sex Sector: The Economic and Social Bases of Prostitution in Southeast Asia*, concluded that "[m]ost of the commercial sex workers [in Indonesia, Malaysia, Philippines, and Thailand] get to keep only a portion of their earnings, but many tend to view deductions, such as payments to pimps or other intermediaries, as the costs involved in their jobs rather than as real 'exploitation.'"[16]

Of course, defining what is exploitation is not an easy task because it can be very subjective. But in the interviews with our subjects, most of them did not express unhappiness with the way the money paid by their customers was being distributed between them and their employers. An executive director of an outreach program for prostitutes in Hong Kong concurs with our conclusion: "I don't think sex workers in Hong Kong are heavily exploited. We think most of the time the pimps or the owners keep their word and pay their sex workers as promised." As we pointed out previously, many women we interviewed were independent *xiaojies* who actually kept all the money their clients paid them.

O'Connell Davidson, a University of Leicester's sociologist, had earlier posed some key questions on this issue: "Just how exploitative does an employment relation have to be before we can say that a person has been recruited and transported 'for purposes of exploitation'? And exactly how deceived does a worker have to be about the nature and terms of the employment prior to migrating before s/he can properly be described as a 'victim of trafficking'?"[17] As with the many other notions of conventional wisdom about sex trafficking, the answers to these questions are not so obvious.

Lack of Fit

Table 9.3 clearly shows what we conclude is the lack of fit between the generally accepted antitrafficking paradigm's characterization of sex trafficking (U.S. and UN provisions) and the actual experiences of our subjects. It seems apparent that the transnational movement of Chinese women for the sex trade does not have the characteristics of sex trafficking as defined by the U.S. government, the United Nations, and other bodies. Our subjects did not view themselves as trafficked victims who were being forced, deceived, or coerced. Is it possible, as some scholars and critics seem to suggest, that these women are too naïve or ignorant to be able to comprehend the fact that they are victims? To help answer this question, we asked government officials, service providers, sex ring operators, and other key informants their perceptions of the Chinese women who were selling sex overseas.

Of all the officials, agency personnel, facilitators, and informants that we interviewed in Asia, only one, who was working for the U.S. embassy in Jakarta, argued that the transnational movement of Chinese women is indeed sex trafficking. According to that American official, the reason is quite simple: "For us, if there is debt bondage, it is human trafficking. Also, if a person's travel documents are controlled by others, that's human trafficking." Following this definition, almost all the Chinese *xiaojies* in Jakarta can be labeled trafficking victims because, as mentioned above, their travel documents are indeed kept by their employers.

Other officials, however, even in Jakarta as well as elsewhere, did not see the overall problem as one of sex trafficking. An American official with the U.S. embassy in one of our research sites was relatively blunt in his comments

Table 9.3. Comparing Female Subjects' Experiences with the Antitrafficking Paradigm's Characterization of Sex Trafficking

	Antitrafficking paradigm's characterization of the situation	Subjects' depictions of their experiences
Recruitment		
Recruiter	Stranger or trafficked victim	Most could not even be considered as having been recruited; some were helped by a returned *xiaojie* or a document vendor
Methods		
Purchase	Very prevalent	Not even heard about it
Deception	The most popular method	Almost no deception
Abduction	Some	None
Transportation	Transported by traffickers, many being smuggled	31% traveled on their own 25% with a returned sex worker 15% with other women Only a few were smuggled
Sale	Traffickers sell victims to brothel owners; victims may be traded again later	No buying and selling, except one
Control	All the victims are tightly controlled Victims' travel documents are seized by their victimizers	Only 15% said they were not free Only women in Indonesia said their employers were in possession of their documents
Victimization		
Violence	It's the norm	Almost none
Unsafe sex	Victims have no say	Clients were always required to wear condoms
Number of clients	Too many	Too few
Client selection	None	Most of them did; not an issue
Debt bondage	Almost all victims are under debt bondage, and the debt is not easy to repay	Only 23% were under debt to a sex ring operator when they left China; average road fee was $7,055, and it took most subjects not more than 20 days to clear
Exploitation	Victims receive very little or no money	Received about 74% of what their clients paid

about the U.S. Department of State and its GTIP Office in its dealings with human trafficking:

> When they [the GTIP officials] came, we had meetings, and at the meetings I told them that these women are not trafficked victims, but they did not want to listen to this. We also tell the person in our embassy who prepares the country report our observations in the field, but he still writes what he wants. Most U.S. embassies in Asia are encountering the same problem. That is, people who write the TIP Report and the agents with the FBI or Homeland Security do not have the same opinion about sex trafficking.

Not one Asian official we interviewed thought that the transnational movement of Chinese women for prostitution is a form of sex trafficking. We realize that some readers might say, of course! What would you expect these officials to say? We too might be skeptical except for the fact that their perceptions are very much in line with those of almost everyone else we interviewed. A retired antitriad police officer in Hong Kong explained this thinking, although he also asserted that domestic sex trafficking did indeed exist in mainland China:

> Nobody is forced, deceived, or coerced; they are willing to work as street-walkers here in Hong Kong. The bottom line is, there are so many women in the mainland who want to engage in commercial sex in Hong Kong; there is no problem to find voluntary participants. So, there is no need to force those who are not willing. It may be possible that a few women were forced or deceived into the sex trade in Hong Kong a few years back. Now, however, it is increasingly unlikely. Having said this, domestic trafficking does exist in mainland China. Some women in rural areas are deceived into traveling to Shenzhen to get involved in the sex business.

A police officer with the Special Branch, Royal Malaysia Police, also believed that Chinese women in Malaysia had not been trafficked: "I don't think PRC women are being trafficked to Malaysia. They come voluntarily, they know what they are up to, and they come because they want to make money. When we arrest them, they will say they were trafficked because this way they will be sent home faster. Otherwise, they will have to spend more time in our detention center."

An official with the Singapore Ministry of Home Affairs also insisted that sex trafficking is a myth that applies not only to Chinese women but also to women from Thailand, Malaysia, and Indonesia: "There are no trafficked victims in Singapore. All these women come to Singapore knowing what they will be doing and come willingly. Over the past three years, we did not have one trafficking case to be investigated. We only arrested a few men who were relying on prostitutes to make a living."

Indonesian officials also indicated that they did not view the arrival of women from the PRC in Indonesia to engage in paid sex as sex trafficking. According to a high-ranking immigration official: "We do not see the arrival of PRC women in Indonesia as human trafficking because we believe these women come voluntarily and they know what they are going to do in Indonesia before they leave China. In the past, we arrested many Chinese women for prostitution, and they told us that they came here to make money and they were not forced, deceived, or coerced into prostitution. We arrested them because they were not authorized to work as prostitutes in Indonesia."

Some service providers in Asia had a very broad definition of sex trafficking—such that force, fraud, or coercion were not required for them to define a woman as a trafficking victim. This position is best characterized by a service provider in Kuala Lumpur: "From our standpoint, anyone who comes here with the help of others, whose income is exploited, who is not free to move around, who is in debt bondage, whose documents are confiscated by others, they are trafficked victims, even if they know what they will be doing here and they come voluntarily." Even if we were to grant this, it still does not define as victims the women who are not helped by others, not exploited financially, are free to move around, do not owe money, and are in possession of their travel documents. This was true of most of the women with whom we talked.

We also interviewed an immigration lawyer in New York whose clients include large numbers of *xiaojies* from China. The lawyer said he often helps his clients to post bail when they are arrested for prostitution. According to him:

> I never met a Chinese woman who was being trafficked into the United States for commercial sex, nor did I ever hear about this. In fact, most of the Chinese *xiaojies* in America are married women in their thirties or forties who entered prostitution only after they arrived here. They did not come here for the purpose of prostitution either. It is just that, after they got here, they found out that it was not easy to make a living, and that paid sex could allow them to make a lot of money.

We posed these same questions to sex ring operators, and they, perhaps less surprisingly, also denied the existence of forced prostitution or sex trafficking. A key figure in the Kuala Lumpur commercial sex business and the owner of a major escort agency was very blunt when he said: "There is no such thing as a trafficked woman! If you force a woman and she does not cooperate, how can you do business? If it exists, the women fabricated the idea of trafficking after being arrested, so that people would have sympathy for them."

Other sex entrepreneurs we interviewed were equally certain that women from China could not be considered trafficking victims. A phone operator for a massage parlor in New Jersey, herself a former *xiaojie*, had the following to say about commercial sex:

> I have never met anyone who was trafficked into this country or being controlled and exploited by sex ring operators. There is no such thing as a Chinese woman owing money to a human trafficker. In my opinion, this is a very fair business. Nobody owes anybody anything. Two consenting adults come together and they are involved in a fair transaction, that's all. Both parties get what they want out of the deal, unlike in many other transactions, where the more powerful side gets the money and provides nothing in return. Take lawyers and doctors, for example. They charge you lots of money but often do not provide service or provide only lousy service.

A man who was locked up for importing Chinese women to Taiwan for commercial sex thought that the sex trade is actually a business with a strong demand and that all the people engaged—*xiaojies*, sex ring operators, and customers—are all getting what they want and, as a result, this should not be considered a serious crime:

> I don't think there is anything wrong with this business, even though I know people generally see this business in a very negative way. In my opinion, I am helping these women to make money; we are all in it together to make money and I am not exploiting them. Besides, there is a demand for this kind of service in our society. Customers come looking for this type of service on their own; nobody forces them to spend money on this. In sum, this business is about all kinds of people getting what they want out of it; it is not a serious crime by any means. Up until now, I have always seen it this way.

Are our findings perhaps unique to Chinese women and the particular sex venues in which they work? Seemingly not. In a very different part of the world, Denise Brennan conducted an ethnographic study of the sex trade in

Sosua, a small town on the north coast of the Dominican Republic that has been a popular vacation spot for male European sex tourists since the early 1990s. According to Brennan:

> Dominican women are not coerced into Sosua's trade but rather end up there through networks of female family members and friends who have worked there. Without pimps, sex workers keep all their earnings; they are essentially working freelance. They can choose the bars and nightclubs in which to hang out, the number of hours they work, the clients with whom they will work, and the amount of money to charge. There has been considerable debate over whether sex work can be anything but exploitative. The stories of Dominican women in Sosua help demonstrate that there is a wide range of experiences within the sex trade, some of them beneficial, others tragic.[18]

Likewise, in her study on sexual commerce in postindustrial culture, sociologist Elizabeth Bernstein also concluded that women engage in paid sex for a variety of reasons, not as a consequence of force, fraud, or coercion:

> For the overwhelming majority of female migrants, it is not brute force, pure deceit, or random abduction that propels them to engage in sexual labor, but rather the desire for economic, social, and geographic mobility; the potentially pleasurable aspects of being an object of affection and desire; and the allure of flexible schedules and instant cash.[19]

Our conclusions echo those of Kamala Kempadoo in her book, *Trafficking and Prostitution Reconsidered*, where she offers criticism of what has been the dominant trafficking paradigm. We cannot state it any better than this:

> Many of the claims made about trafficking are unsubstantiated and undocumented, and are based on sensationalist reports, hyperbole, and conceptual confusions, a problem that extends to wider international discourse on transnational crime. The "non-empirical basis for many of the media, police and political responses," the packaging of news as entertainment, the imprecision that creeps into concepts due to overuse, the exaggerations and "guesstimates," and unreliable evaluative information, plague many studies and claims about transnational criminal activity.[20]

10

The Politics of Prostitution and Sex Trafficking

According to sociologist Kevin Bales, who has written widely about what he deems contemporary human slavery, at any given time some twenty-seven million people are enslaved. One piece of this slavery—human trafficking —is said to generate $32 billion in profits annually.[1] These are huge and impressive numbers. In fact, according to some antitrafficking advocates, human trafficking is the second most lucrative transnational crime, trailing only drug trafficking. The U.S. government spends tens of millions of dollars every year to assist foreign governments and nongovernmental organizations in helping eliminate human trafficking. The expenditure totaled about $375 million between 2001 and 2005.[2] The criminal justice system has also been mobilized to combat this modern form of slavery.[3] Publications of all kinds on human trafficking have also become ubiquitous, as have meetings and conferences on the subject.

The Unanswered Question

Despite the attention and resources, there remain a number of unanswered, or at least not completely answered, questions. And good answers to these questions are key to the ultimate success of preventing and combating human trafficking.

The first question or set of questions is just how big the problem of human trafficking is. How many victims are there? And how does anyone know that? At the heart of this question and its answer is the reality that big problems demand big solutions, and big solutions require big resources. When the big problem includes sex and violence, the victimization of young innocents, and mafia figures, it has key ingredients for attracting media and political attention. The converse is also true. Little problems—those that are not sensationalized—get little attention and few resources. Therefore, in order to compete successfully in the public policy arena where there are scarce funds, advocates and special interests have to think big and speak loudly.[4] This brings us to the numbers.

As attention began to galvanize on the trafficking issue in the mid-1990s, an estimate that "4 million people are trafficked annually" appeared. Such organizations as the International Organization for Migration (IOM), the U.S. Agency for International Development (USAID), and the UN were among those that put the 4 million figure on the number of trafficking victims worldwide.[5]

Exactly where this estimate came from and what it was based upon was and remains somewhat of a mystery. It nevertheless captured attention and was repeated in numerous publications, including those of the UN and the U.S. State Department. The repetition both reinforced the four million victims figure, and gave it an aura of authenticity. Similarly, a U.S. report citing various governmental and nongovernmental experts, estimated that there were 700,000 to two million women and children trafficking victims alone, and that some 50,000 of these women and children were being trafficked into the United States each year.[6] These numbers—along with another estimate that human trafficking was a $5 to 7 billion per year business—helped propel both the UN protocol on trafficking and the passage of the U.S. Trafficking Victims Protection Act of 2000.

In the case of the TVPA, substantial funding was attached to the law. For example, in FY 2006, some $30 million was provided for antitrafficking efforts in the United States. These funds are intended to support victims' assistance efforts, and specifically provide benefits—including a special T-visa—for victims in the U.S. There is grant support to develop or expand victims' services programs, and funding for prevention programs, for training, for technical assistance, and for research. As these funds first became available, a host of agencies and organizations at every level geared up to seek the federal dollars to carry out the provisions of the law.[7]

But not for the first time in our public policy history, as specific initiatives began to go into effect the expectations and projections about the numbers of trafficking victims were not met. In fact, there has been a considerable shortfall between the expected numbers of victims and the actual numbers observed.[8] For example, the law stipulates that victims who meet certain criteria (is a victim of a "severe form of trafficking," is physically present in the U.S., is willing to cooperate in the investigation and prosecution of the traffickers unless under 15 years old, and is vulnerable to unusual or severe harm if deported) can be granted T-visas that give them temporary resident status in the United States. The law authorizes the granting of five thousand of these special visas annually. Six years after the law was passed, and after 30,000 T-visas had been authorized, only 729 had actually been issued—with another 645 issued to family members of trafficking victims.[9] Why? Is it a lack of diligence and competence by the police and other authorities, as some have alleged? Is it because the traffickers are so adept at hiding their victims? Or is it just because the numbers were not really ever there?

On the matter of due diligence by law enforcement, there have been many reports that too many times, in too many places authorities do not take human trafficking seriously. This is especially so when it comes to women who engage in commercial sex. We were told by Chinese authorities in 2003, for example, that the mainland Chinese women who were taken to Taiwan were all prostitutes who went to Taiwan simply to make more money. Both the UN and the U.S. State Department have strongly argued that trafficking is not taken sufficiently seriously and is not a priority for many countries. And then, of course, there is the corruption. Law enforcement, border control, and immigration agents who are being paid off are unlikely to take aggressive action against trafficking and traffickers. Whether authorities ignore trafficking cases because they don't take the problem seriously or because they are profiting from it, the bottom line is likely to be underreporting. How much underreporting there is, and how much can be attributed to these causes, we do not know.

Crime reporting in general is largely a matter of individuals, whether victims or witnesses, doing the reporting. Years of study of crime reporting tell us that there is a vast amount of underreporting, mostly resulting from the belief that the authorities will not do anything. In addition, sometimes victims and witnesses do not report crimes because they fear retaliation by the criminals. From what we have learned from some trafficking cases, this seems to be especially true of victims who are coerced and intimidated by their traffickers with threats to themselves and their families.

It seems clear that human trafficking cases have particular characteristics that can make their reporting less likely. Whether due to its low priority, to police corruption, or to an unwillingness of victims and witnesses to come forward, the figures on human trafficking are very likely to be hidden within a large "dark figure" element. That said, there are other reasons why the magnitude of the trafficking problem is itself problematical.

Across the board, shortly after efforts to combat human trafficking got underway—efforts fueled in major part by the severity of the problem pictured in the big numbers noted above—estimates and expectations began to shift. And this shift has consistently been in the direction of downsizing. Before we look at more recent victim estimates, it will be helpful to understand the problems that surround making such estimates in the first place.

One of the difficulties is the fact that the figures are indeed just estimates. As such, they are based upon a variety of assumptions and are thus only as good as their underlying assumptions. Let us look at an example that will illustrate how this estimating process works.

Back in the mid-1990s, an official of a major international agency dealing with migration developed estimates about the numbers of illegal immigrants and the amount of money being made from human smuggling and trafficking.[10] In fact, it was from this effort that the $5 to 7 billion figure cited earlier came.

Jonas Widgren, former Director General of the International Center for Migration Policy Development, based in Vienna, first estimated the number of illegal immigrants trying to enter Europe annually. He did this by taking the number actually arrested (60,000) and multiplied it by five, on the assumption that only one in five illegal immigrants gets caught. This gave him roughly 300,000. In addition, he further estimated that half the known 700,000 asylum seekers to Europe were really ineligibles or fakes—thus another 350,000. Adding these two gave him a total of around 650,000 illegal immigrants coming into Europe every year. It is important to note that any actual trafficking victims would be subsumed in this number, and we do not know what that figure is. Widgren then assumed or estimated that somewhere between 15 and 30 percent of these estimated 650,000 illegals hired smugglers to assist them, and that they paid on average $2,000 to $5,000 each. The resulting $1 billion figure for Europe alone was then ramped up to the $5 to 7 billion estimate worldwide. Without faulting Widgren at all for trying to do his best with the information available to him, one can quickly see the dangers and problems with estimates and assumptions when it comes to human smuggling and trafficking.

And yet as cautious as Widgren and others like him were about what they were projecting, others were not so cautious. Those individuals and organizations that wanted to blow up the problem to highlight their own agendas, for example, latched on to these estimates as justification for why their views should prevail in policymaking and then why they and others like them should receive generous funding to combat this critical problem. Lest one think that we are being overly cynical or harsh in our judgments here, one only need to look at reports of the U.S. Government Accountability Office (GAO) in 2006. That office reached pretty much these same conclusions.

The GAO said that the estimates commonly being offered were not based on hard data but rather on other estimates, or worse, on wild guesses or baseless speculations. Obviously, estimates based upon other estimates are of questionable reliability. Even more critically, the GAO said that trafficking data and estimates had often been developed *for purposes of advocacy* or as a (self-interested) component of a larger project. Similar criticisms have been leveled by others, saying that the sources of the estimates are unclear and possibly exaggerated. This rising criticism has been driven largely by the small number of trafficking victims actually identified both in the U.S. and worldwide.

As the TVPA came up for reauthorization in 2007, this controversy was highlighted. For example, a *Washington Post* story reported the following:

> The debate over the bill comes amid broader questions over how many victims are trafficked into the United States. The government estimated in 1999 that about 50,000 slaves were arriving in the country every year. That estimate was revised downward in 2004 to 14,500 to 17,500 a year. Yet since 2000, and despite 42 Justice Department task forces and more than $150 million in federal dollars to find them, about 1,400 people have been certified as human trafficking victims in this country, a tiny fraction of the original estimates.
>
> The House legislation cites the government's current estimate of up to 17,500 victims a year, but the Justice Department, in a Nov. 9 letter to congressional leaders, "questions the reliability" of the numbers. "Such findings, without a full body of evidence, are counter-productive," the letter says.[11]

What we attempt to do in our study reported here is target venues where we would most likely find sex trafficking victims. From the stories and experiences of these women, we hoped to provide a snapshot that would illustrate and shed some light on these issues. Did we think we would resolve them? Surely not. What we can say is that the women we studied, who would be counted as victims in many of the prevailing estimates, are not really victims in our judgment. From our research, we believe that while the number of sex trafficking victims is certainly not zero, it is questionable that it runs into the millions or even many thousands.

Back to the Issue of Definition

In chapter 1, we made it clear that we were only using the more restrictive definition of sex trafficking—namely, the one applying to severe forms of trafficking in persons, in which a commercial sex act is induced by force, fraud, or coercion. In the United States, a person can be legally considered a trafficked victim only if he or she meets the criteria for severe forms of trafficking, and thus can be eligible to apply for a T-visa and other benefits offered to trafficked victims. However, as mentioned in chapter 1 and the ensuing chapters, many people, including the U.S. TVPA, also loosely define sex trafficking as the recruitment, harboring, transportation, or obtaining of a person for the purpose of a commercial sex act. Others define sex trafficking as debt bondage, financial exploitation, or the denial of freedom of movement by withholding people's travel documents. We think the problem with the global effort to deal with the transnational movement of women for commercial sex is seriously undermined and has failed to gain much momentum mainly because there is no consensus on what sex trafficking is, and because different groups are using different definitions to suit their own interests and agendas.[12] Depending on how strictly or loosely a person defines sex trafficking, he or she might come up with a significantly different estimate of the numbers of trafficked victims.[13] Let us take a look at the prevalence of sex trafficking among our female subjects using a variety of different definitions.

Table 10.1 shows the proportions of our subjects who could be considered transnational trafficking victims depending on how that victimization is defined. Another way of viewing these proportions is to see them as indicators of the possible degree of linkage between commercial sex and sex trafficking. At one extreme, if the definition of a sex trafficking victim is simply a person who is engaged in commercial sex (in our case overseas), then all our female subjects are victims, and there is complete overlap between prostitution and sex trafficking. But as one begins to refine and narrow the definition, the proportion of subjects who would be considered victims declines.

Lest one think that this illustration is just some sort of sleight of hand, we would argue that all definitions of this kind are to some degree arbitrary. This is true even of legal definitions. Someone or somebody decides what the definitional criteria ought to be and then applies them. This is why, for example, criminal laws often define crimes with varying degrees depending upon

Table 10.1. *Definition of Sex Trafficking and Its Prevalence, by Research Site (percentage, N = 149)*

Site	being helped to go overseas to sell sex	who is accompanied overseas to be involved in paid sex	paying someone to be helped to go abroad to sell sex	who is selling sex overseas with the help of sex ring operator(s)	who is under debt to go overseas to engage in paid sex	who is financially exploited while selling sex overseas	whose travel documents are withheld	who is forced, defrauded, or deceived into paid sex or is underage
				A sex trafficking victim is a person ...				
Hong Kong	60	53	20	100	0	29	7	0
Macau	94	72	24	61	17	6	0	0
Taiwan	100	100	94	100	94	93	19	0
Thailand	100	88	65	47	6	0	6	6
Malaysia	95	78	89	56	22	40	6	0
Singapore	100	67	93	80	20	0	7	7
Indonesia	94	72	89	94	44	90	83	0
Los Angeles	93	75	53	81	0	0	0	0
New York	100	56	81	69	0	0	0	0
Total	93	74	68	76	23	26	15	1

certain criteria. In the case of sex trafficking, the definition agreed upon determines the nature and magnitude of the problem, sets out the parameters for policies and practices to combat the problem, and sets the benchmark for resources required to do the job. It is therefore obviously an issue of significant practical and political importance.

According to Table 10.1, a very large proportion (about 93%) of our subjects could be defined as trafficking victims if the definition of a victim is simply any person who arrives in a foreign country with the assistance of another person, regardless of whether the subject pays that other person or not. All the women we interviewed in Taiwan, Thailand, Singapore, and New York said they were helped to go overseas. However, being helped is not equivalent to being recruited, and even though recruitment is often emphasized in the trafficking literature as an important first step in human trafficking, we did not find that this happened with most of our female subjects. Instead, most of our subjects took the initiative in their initial encounters with the person who helped them to go abroad.

If we use the transportation criterion, according to which a person is a trafficking victim if transported (or accompanied) by someone when the person travels abroad, then 74 percent of our subjects fit that definition. Here, the fluctuation in the percentage of victims among the various sites is not as significant as with the payment criterion. Nevertheless, only about half of the subjects in Hong Kong and New York would be labeled as trafficking victims as opposed to all the women in Taiwan.

If we move from being helped (regardless of whether the helper was paid or not) to paying a fee for being helped, then the proportion of so-defined trafficking victims in our sample would decrease from 93 percent to 68 percent. Since paying someone for help to go overseas is an important criterion in the definition of human *smuggling*, 68 percent of our subjects could be categorized as having been smuggled. Here then we see a possible link with human smuggling. If we use this definition, we also find that the percentage of trafficking victims varies considerably among the various sites. Only 20 percent of the subjects in Hong Kong and 24 percent in Macau would be viewed as trafficking victims if we use this form of payment as a criterion, whereas the vast majority of the subjects in Taiwan, Malaysia, Singapore, Indonesia, and New York would be victims under this same definition.

As we move from the help, transportation, and payment criteria to a more narrow definition, the proportion of our subjects who could be considered victims drops dramatically. If we define a trafficking victim as a person who goes overseas under debt to the very person for whom she is going to work (excluding those who borrow money from friends and relatives to pay for their overseas trips), then 23 percent of our female subjects could be viewed as trafficking victims. Under the debt criterion, none of our subjects in Hong Kong, Los Angeles, and New York are trafficking victims, but about 44 percent in Indonesia and about 94 percent in Taiwan could be so viewed.

If we define a sex trafficking victim as a person who is financially exploited, then there is first the problem of determining whether such exploitation has in fact occurred. For our purposes, we used 50 percent as the arbitrary cutoff point, which means that if a woman receives only half or less of what a client pays, then she is being financially exploited. The other half would have gone to the house, a mommy, or to whoever the subject is working for or with. We found that any tips always belong to the women, and therefore we do not take tips into consideration in our calculations. Under this criterion, 26 percent of our subjects would be considered trafficking victims. Applying this financial exploitation criterion, none of our subjects in Thailand, Singapore, Los Angeles, or New York would be victims, whereas 93 percent of the subjects in Taiwan and 90 percent of the women in Indonesia would be victims.

We want to point out that, even though only 6 percent of the subjects in Macau could be considered victims under the financial exploitation criterion, many of them were turning almost all their money over to their romantic or business chickenheads. If we were to bring the chickenhead factor into our calculation, then the percentage of victims in Macau would increase to 50 percent.

If we define a sex trafficking victim as a woman who is not free to move around or quit sex work because her travel documents are being withheld by her employer or debtor, then 15 percent of our subjects could be considered trafficking victims. Under the freedom of movement definition, the percentage of trafficked victims is highest for Indonesia (about 83%), but lowest (0%) for subjects in Macau, Los Angeles, and New York. Again, we do not think the eight subjects in Macau who were associated with chickenheads were free to quit commercial sex if they wanted to, and this must be kept in mind when we calculate the number of victims in Macau using this particular definition.

From our study, it is clear that the seriousness and nature of human trafficking could well be very country-specific. Of all the destination regions or countries for PRC women in our study, Hong Kong and Macau are unique, in the sense that women from China can travel to these two special regions with relative ease. However, the women there are also most vulnerable to the chickenheads—the men who probably best fit the notorious characteristics of the "human trafficker" as depicted in the human trafficking literature.

Taiwan scores high in almost all the definitions we use in Table 10.1 to define sex trafficking, but none of the women in Taiwan can be considered to be trafficking victims under the U.S. TVPA definition of "severe forms of trafficking in persons." Even so, the fact that most of the PRC subjects in Taiwan arrived under debt, are "owned" by an agent, are always engaged in highly organized commercial sex involving many parties (e.g., escort agency owner, jockey, mommy, hotel manager, or massage parlor owner), and are often financially exploited, means we should not downplay the plight of Chinese *xiaojies* in Taiwan.

Chinese women in the Thai sex sector are most likely to be brought overseas by their relatives or neighbors who are returned *xiaojies*, as opposed to agents, brokers, or companies. Thailand scores low on the human trafficking prevalence rate in terms of almost all the definitions we adopted in Table 10.1, and Chinese women there are least likely to be victimized by a sex ring operator. Because of the limited opportunity to make money, however, Thailand is also the least popular destination for Chinese *xiaojies* who are thinking about going overseas.

Malaysia, as a destination country, is somewhat unique in the sense that Chinese women there are equally engaged in both highly organized as well as unorganized commercial sex. Singapore likewise has a variety of sex venues available to Chinese women, but because it is a Chinese society and more developed than Malaysia, most Chinese women prefer to go Singapore rather than Malaysia. The two countries are very similar with respect to the prevalence of sex trafficking, irrespective of the definition used.

Indonesia, like Taiwan, ranks high on most of the sex trafficking prevalence rates shown in Table 10.1. What is different about Indonesia is that while most women there, as in Taiwan, are engaged in highly organized commercial sex, unlike in Taiwan, the women in Indonesia must turn in their travel documents to their employers (the companies) when they are hired, regardless of whether they owe road fees to their employers or not. This agent-as-labor broker system in Indonesia (as opposed to the agent-as-owner system in Taiwan) is unique. It restricts the free movement of the women and increases their vulnerability to financial exploitation.

Even though the United States is the world leader in the global war against prostitution and human trafficking—and perhaps because of that—the problem of sex trafficking involving Chinese women here is less grave in comparison with the Asian research sites. The majority of our U.S. subjects had to pay someone to help them to come to the United States, but none of them were underage, under debt to a sex ring operator, financially exploited, denied freedom of movement, or forced, coerced, or deceived into commercial sex. The United States actually ranks very low on almost all the prevalence rates of sex trafficking based on the definitions outlined. There were no chickenheads, agents-as-owners, agents-as-brokers, escort agency owners, jockeys, mommies, or document-withholding companies uncovered in our research in the United States. The two main types of employers—massage parlor owners and "house" owners—are usually small-time entrepreneurs who are themselves former or current *xiaojies*. They are not all that different from the women the U.S. government is trying to rescue.

Let us consider the percentage of trafficked victims among our subjects under the most strict definition, which is also the definition that creates the most problems for those who are concerned about sex trafficking. According to this narrow definition, a transnational trafficking victim is a person who is forced, deceived, or coerced to go overseas for commercial sex. This definition includes persons who gave their consent but were underage. Accordingly, only 1 percent of our sample of commercial sex providers could be considered to be trafficking victims. One subject (Jiao Jiao) in Singapore fits the definition because she was only 17, and another subject (Dong Dong) was deceived. Dong Dong said her aunt (a real one) who brought her to Thailand had told her back in China that she would be working as a hostess in Bangkok and would not have to sleep with men.

If we take into consideration the chickenhead factor, then the percentage of trafficking victims would increase somewhat. Let us assume the female subjects we interviewed in Hong Kong and Macau who were under the control of their chickenheads and were being financially exploited by having all or most of their earnings taken away—regardless of the fact that these women were not forced, coerced, or deceived into commercial sex—should be considered to be trafficking victims. Under that assumption, 27 percent of our subjects in Hong Kong and 44 percent in Macau would be trafficking victims. In that case, the overall proportion of trafficking victims for the whole sample would increase to 9 percent. This latter percentage for transnational sex trafficking is strikingly similar to our estimated percentage for domestic sex trafficking inside China, which is 10 percent. Because of the geographical proximity of Hong Kong and Macau to China, however, and because these places are now special administrative regions of China where Chinese citizens can travel with relative ease, some could argue that our female subjects in Hong Kong and Macau should more appropriately be categorized as domestic, rather than transnational, trafficking victims.

When asked, and indeed closely questioned in various ways, only one of our subjects (as previously described) indicated that she had been deceived into becoming a prostitute. None claimed to have been forced or coerced. Of

Table 10.2. Possible "Coercive" Factors Experienced, by Research Site (N=149)

Site	None	One	Two	Three	N
Hong Kong	67%	33%	0%	0%	15
Macau	78	22	0	0	18
Taiwan	6	0	81	13	16
Thailand	88	12	0	0	17
Malaysia	67	11	17	5	18
Singapore	73	27	0	0	15
Indonesia	6	33	39	22	18
Los Angeles	100	0	0	0	16
New York	100	0	0	0	16
Total	65	15	15	5	149

the three possible elements of severe sex trafficking—force, fraud, or coercion—let us assume that coercion is perhaps the most subtle and difficult to establish, since it depends a great deal on individual perceptions of potential risk and harm, and on how fearful a person may be. Focusing just on coercion, the aforementioned factors of debt bondage, the withholding of documents, and the restricted freedom described by some of the women might be construed as being coercive. The legal definition of coercion in the TVPA is, however, quite limiting: "Coercion means (a) threats of serious harm to or physical restraint against any person; (b) any scheme, plan or pattern intended to cause a person to believe that failure to perform an act would result in serious harm to or physical restraint against any person; or, (c) the abuse or threatened abuse of the legal process."[14] Granting the previous point about what our individual subjects might have believed in this respect, it is difficult to see the circumstances, as the women described them to us, as meeting this legal definition. That said, Table 10.2 shows the breakdown of these factors (debt, withheld documents, and financial exploitation) by site and the proportion of subjects (35%) who experienced one or more of them.

Only the most broadly encompassing definition of sex trafficking would include these roughly one-third of our subjects as victims. We have described the situations in Taiwan and Indonesia that are largely driving these figures, and we believe that any such conclusion to include all these women as victims would be unfounded. Again, as we have repeatedly pointed out, our findings are only relevant to Chinese women. We are not saying that these findings are applicable to women of other nationalities who may be engaged in commercial sex in the destination countries we studied. For example, there are many women from Mexico and Korea active in the U.S. sex market, but their experiences may be very different from the Chinese *xiaojies*.

We think it would be a great advance in our approaches to understanding and combating sex trafficking to have a common definition upon which all involved could agree. Some might argue that we already have such a definition as spelled out in the TVPA (or perhaps in the UN protocol on human trafficking) but as we have explained, these definitions are viewed by some (or many) as being too limiting to really allow us to address the full scope of the issue. Short of a common definition, perhaps the next best thing is to limit the definitions and to make explicit exactly how sex trafficking victims are being defined in any discussions of the scope and magnitude of the problem and of any antitrafficking policies.

To do otherwise means we will continue to talk past each other and will come up with very different estimates of the magnitude of the problem, since we will be using very different criteria. We also think that it is time for us to understand who the "traffickers" actually are, and figure out who, among these "traffickers," are the real and key perpetrators. This would be helpful not only for people who are engaged in the war against sex trafficking but also for the very women we consider its victims.

The Political/Ideological Battlegrounds

An exchange of views, published in the *New York Times* (July 11, 2008), about U.S. Department of Justice policy positions on sex trafficking, illustrated very starkly some of the political and ideological battleground that has surrounded this issue from the beginning. Former Ambassador John Miller, who headed the State Department's Office to Monitor and Combat Trafficking in Persons from 2002 to 2006, accused the Justice Department of undermining the Bush Administration's efforts to combat sex trafficking. Miller cited what he called a "culture clash" as being behind the department's opposition to certain then newly proposed policies. "This isn't the usual culture clash," wrote Miller, but rather one in which "the feminist, religious and secular groups that help sex trafficking survivors are on one side. . . . [O]n the other are the department's lawyers (most of them male), the Erotic Service Providers Union and the American Civil Liberties Union—this side believes that vast numbers of women engage in prostitution as a 'profession,' by choice."[15]

In response to the Miller accusations, Assistant Attorney General Elisebeth Cook said the department opposed the proposals because they "would divert our focus away from the worst of the worst cases by making all prostitution a federal crime."[16] Ms. Cook said further that the department's position was shared by "dozens" of groups, including law enforcement, women, immigrants, and crime victims.

The code word here is prostitution. Its undercurrents are consent, coercion, and exploitation. Although discussion of prostitution and all the issues surrounding it did not start when attention began to be devoted to the trafficking of persons in the 1990s, it became a major bone of contention during that time. And the debate and dispute continue today. Should prostitution be legal and perhaps regulated? Or should it be criminalized? Should "johns" be punished? Are prostitutes victims? Is prostitution exploitative? Always? Does it involve coercion? Always? Is organized crime involved? These are some of the questions that are elements of the dispute.

A conflation of prostitution and sex trafficking, as exemplified in the exchange quoted above, is at the center of the crossfire. Illustrative are the positions of the Coalition Against Trafficking in Women (CATW) on one side, and a loose affiliation of organizations known as the Human Rights Caucus on the other.[17] The latter is comprised of such other collectives as the Global Alliance Against Trafficking in Women (GAATW) and the Network of Sex Workers Project (NSWP). Just as an aside, one cannot fail to note the large array of initials and acronyms that identify the many groups that have sprung up anew, or that have turned their attention to this hot topic. Together they constitute a small army of lobbyists and special interests. And as such, they have had considerable success in influencing both U.S. and UN policies on human trafficking. For example, under the Trafficking Victims Protection Act reauthorization of 2003 there was a stipulation that no U.S. grant funds may be used to "promote, support or advocate for the legalization of prostitution," and that any recipient of federal funds (ourselves included) must stipulate in writing that they will not engage in any such promotion, support, or advocacy.

CATW and like-minded supporters, including religious groups and antiprostitution organizations, argue that any and all forms of recruitment, transportation, and harboring for prostitution are, by definition, elements of sex trafficking. Prostitution is never consented to, they claim, and thus all prostitutes are by definition victims of trafficking. We have heard Ambassador Miller publicly call "forced" prostitution a redundancy, and to strongly argue against use of the phrase, presumably because it implies there is another kind of prostitution—namely, "unforced."

The United Nations Protocol on human trafficking says that the consent of a victim of trafficking to being exploited is irrelevant if that exploitation is accomplished through the use of any of a number of illegal means. Those means include the threat or use of force or other forms of coercion, abduction, fraud, deception, or abuse of power. The governing legal principle here, as well as in many national laws, is that a person cannot consent to enslavement or forced labor of any kind. So the presence of coercion and so on, and of slavelike conditions, is critical to defining trafficking and who a trafficking victim is.

Many of those on the other side of the forced versus unforced prostitution issue argue that adult women may, and do indeed, consent to engage in prostitution as a form of acceptable labor, and are thus not trafficking victims. In support of the latter argument, there are actually a number of studies that demonstrate that not all prostitutes are trafficked or exploited, but rather that some of them at least are working independently and voluntarily.[18] Further, trafficking victims have been found in some cases to be women who were already prostitutes who decided to move and work elsewhere because they hoped to make more money.[19] Such views are quite unacceptable to, and in fact infuriate, the most rabid of the believers in prostitution as exploitation.

Coercion, rational choice, and the boundaries on such choice as these relate to consent, all come into play here. As we discussed earlier, coercion, along with some form of force and fraud, is one of the legally defining elements in just about all accepted definitions of human trafficking, including sex trafficking. In the reauthorization of the TVPA, as we will see shortly, these elements are significantly readjusted.

Conservative U.S. politicians and some religious groups, as well as a number of other organizations, have worked to get all forms of prostitution under the trafficking umbrella. Accomplishing this would mean that being forced or "volunteering" to be a prostitute become irrelevant. In partial summary of what is admittedly a complex argument supporting this idea, one of the feminist views is that many women find themselves in socioeconomic positions that limit their options. One of the greatest of these limitations is the feminization of poverty. Women suffer disproportionately from being poor. In addition, there are factors like the meaning of shame and control, and the exploitation of female sexuality—that are particularly common in patriarchal societies—and which also severely limit opportunities for women.

Prostitutes are thus always victims, according to those on this side of the debate, and traffickers or controllers simply force their victims, if questioned, to claim to be acting voluntarily. What is interesting from the perspective of a researcher (including ourselves) is that if you believe that, then the words of the women themselves cannot be trusted on this point, because they are obviously being coerced into saying they have voluntarily chosen to engage in commercial sex. This seems to set up a kind of "catch 22" situation that allows the conservative and antiprostitution view to prevail under all circumstances, and enables them to dismiss evidence that might suggest anything to the contrary.

Seemingly in response to this debate and in an attempt to find some middle ground, under one of the reauthorizations of the U.S. TVPA a two-tier definition was created that sort of confuses the issue. "Severe forms of trafficking in persons" include "sex trafficking" in which a commercial sex act is induced by force, fraud, or coercion. However, the TVPA also includes a second tier of "sex trafficking," defined simply as the recruitment, harboring, transportation, or obtaining of a person for the purpose of a commercial sex act.[20] The elements of force, fraud, or coercion are not stipulated as requirements. Another circumstance that may have accounted for this two-tier approach is the fact that a number of other countries, including western European countries, recognize the legitimacy of prostitution as work, and have policies and practices to protect the rights and health of sex workers.

Under the 2008 reauthorization of the TVPA (called the William Wilberforce Act), the two-tier approach is maintained, but with significant modifications. *Aggravated sex trafficking* is defined as the recruitment, enticement, harboring, transporting, providing, or obtaining of a person "knowing that force, fraud, or coercion will be used to cause the person to engage in a commercial sex act." A lesser offense, *sex trafficking*, is defined as simply persuading, inducing, or enticing any individual to engage in prostitution. It is this latter provision that makes all prostitution a form of sex trafficking, and makes all prostitution a federal crime. One of the strongest and most outspoken supporters of these changes has been Donna Hughes, a recognized expert on human trafficking issues. Hughes said:

> Most of the debate and misunderstanding of the Wilberforce Act is centered on the requirement of proving that "force, fraud, and coercion" compelled victims to engage in commercial sex acts. The TVPA "severe form of trafficking" statute requires the use of force, fraud, or coercion on an adult victim, while the Mann Act (the federal law against transporting a person across states lines for purposes of prostitution) does not require the perpetrator to use force, fraud, or coercion. These statutes will be brought together in the criminal code to create two levels of sex trafficking: sex trafficking (without force, fraud, and coercion) and aggravated sex trafficking (with force, fraud, and coercion). . . . When sex trafficking is a federal crime only when there is proof of force, fraud, coercion, or the exploitation of a minor, this encourages states in the U.S. and foreign governments to require high standards of proof for trafficking convictions. This type of law is supported by those favoring the legalization of prostitution.[21]

The two sides in the prostitution debate are obviously motivated by strong ideological beliefs that make them, unfortunately, unlikely to accept evidence contrary to those beliefs. Thus the controversy is only likely to continue. This may be yet another example of what has been termed "symbolic politics."[22] In a nutshell, symbolic politics refers to a policy making situation wherein perceptions trump substance; where the appearance of action, sometimes without actually doing or intending to do anything, becomes paramount in reassuring political constituents. Accomplishing some symbolic purpose, irrespective of the reality, becomes the overarching goal.[23] The dispute about prostitution and sex trafficking may have fallen into this policy trap.

Rethinking Sex Trafficking

In an article entitled *The Social Construction of Sex Trafficking*, sociologist Ronald Weitzer said that:

> Moral crusaders advance claims about both the gravity and incidence of a particular problem. They typically rely on horror stories and "atrocity tales" about victims in which the most shocking exemplars of victimization are described and typified. Casting the problem in highly dramatic terms by recounting the plight of highly traumatized victims is intended to alarm the public and policy makers and justify draconian solutions. At the same time, inflated claims are made about the magnitude of the problem. A key feature of moral crusades is that the imputed scale of a problem (e.g., the number of victims) far exceeds what is warranted by the available evidence. Moreover, crusade leaders consider the problem unambiguous: they are not inclined to acknowledge gray areas and are adamant that a particular evil exists precisely as they depict it.[24]

Weitzer also pointed out that "moral crusades often make grand and unverifiable claims about the nature and prevalence of a particular 'social evil,'" and identified the following as the moral crusades' core claims regarding prostitution and sex trafficking:

1. Prostitution is evil by definition.
2. Violence is omnipresent in prostitution and sex trafficking.
3. Customers and traffickers are the personification of evil.
4. Sex workers lack agency.
5. Prostitution and sex trafficking are inextricably linked.

6. The magnitude of both prostitution and sex trafficking is high and has greatly increased in recent years.

7. Legalization would make the situation far worse than it is at present.[25]

Our research on the transnational movement of Chinese women for commercial sex suggests that the first six claims of this moral crusade are indeed open to debate. First, most of the people we interviewed did not view prostitution as inherently evil. Many *xiaojies* we interviewed in fact saw prostitution as an opportunity for them to make the kind of money they could never make through any other means. They also did not think that people who were helping them to enter this profession or the people who were buying sex from them were evil. Even though they may not like what they are doing, for them prostitution is a fair exchange between a woman who sells sex and a man who buys sex, and thus the sex trade is not much different from any other commercial exchange.

The second claim—that violence is omnipresent in prostitution and sex trafficking—is also not supported by our findings. Client violence was rare, and on the few occasions when it did occur, weapons were not involved. Our data also show that the people who were helping women to sell sex—agents, sex venue owners, jockeys, fake husbands—did not use violence as a means to control or exploit the women. The only exception was in the case of some women who were brought to Macau by their chickenheads, and who may have been subject to physical assaults if the chickenheads thought that their women were not working hard enough.

The third claim—that customers and traffickers are the personification of evil—is also questionable because our female subjects certainly did not see their customers or handlers as being evil. Some of the women we interviewed actually developed intimate relationships with their customers and maintained stable relationships for months, if not years. As suggested by sociology professor Teela Sanders in her book *Paying for Pleasure*: "intimacy is not exempt from the commercial sexual experience, but for some an essential part of the criteria and satisfaction of commercial liaisons."[26] Italian researcher Di Nicola and her colleagues also found that men in Italy, the Netherlands, Romania, and Sweden who bought sex from foreign prostitutes were "likely to be ordinary men (professionals and workers, married and single, high and low educated, young and elderly persons)" and "do not represent a particularly deviant group of individuals."[27]

As far as "traffickers" are concerned, we did not find "evil" traffickers involved in the transnational movement of Chinese women either. Many people helped these women to go overseas—returned women, document procurers, agents, fake husbands, chickenheads, and so on. We did not find the professional or full-time "traffickers" (or transporters) usually depicted in the trafficking literature. Some of our subjects were indeed unhappy with a particular type of facilitator —the chickenhead—but the percentage of women who complained was very small and their complaints were not about an evil being perpetrated on them.

"Seasoning," a term very often mentioned in the trafficking literature to underscore the extreme inhumanity of the traffickers, was not mentioned during our conversations with hundreds of subjects over a two-year period.[28] No instances were recounted of the repeated rapes of women by numerous men until their will to resist had been broken.

The fourth claim is about the lack of agency among women who engage in commercial sex. Prostitutes in general, and foreign prostitutes in particular, are often portrayed in sex trafficking discussions as being helpless, childlike, and passive individuals who must be guided, protected, and instructed about their best interests. Our findings, to the contrary, clearly show that many if not most of the women we interviewed considered themselves (in their words) "ferocious dragons," or part of a *Red Detachment Army* who were going overseas to conquer the world.[29] In fact, they were usually the ones who actively initiated the process of going overseas by aggressively looking for an opportunity to go abroad, regardless of whether they had already engaged in paid sex in China or not. No doubt these women were vulnerable when they were working illegally in a foreign country, but they were also very clear about what they wanted and how to get it. We observed many interactions between these women and their clients or handlers, and we conclude that these women could not be pushed around easily. York University professor Kamala Kempadoo echoed this same view:

> The ability of the concept "victim" to rob the (feminized) individual from any notion of agency and subjectivity, and to ideologically locate the person as helpless and pitiful, has strong implications for how change is imagined and brought about through anti-trafficking interventions. Victims, who by definition are passive and child-like, are deemed incapable of undertaking any action, thus requiring "rescue" or "saving" from their circumstances by others who stand outside of the trafficking process and who, it is believed, know best.[30]

In a study of Thai women in Germany's sex sector, social worker Prapairat Ratanaloan Mix argued that "many Thai women make conscious choices about their future and plan their lives carefully in ways that often work to their benefit. These women have significant control over their lives, well-defined life goals, and substantial knowledge of how to achieve those goals."[31]

We believe the vast majority of the women we interviewed were exercising choice in the sense of the bounded rationality we have described. They relied upon the information available to them; they considered that information in the context of what they might be doing if they went overseas versus what they might be doing if they stayed at home; and they weighed the alternatives as they knew of them. In the end, they "satisficed." In other words, they made a choice that seemed good enough for them under the circumstances. This is a difficult possibility to believe for some who are ideologues on the victimization issue, because it means that not all these women are victims in the sense that some want to paint them.

The claim that prostitution and sex trafficking are inextricably linked is not substantiated by our research. Weitzer pointed out that "there is no evidence that 'most' or even the majority of prostitutes have been trafficked," and our study shows exactly that.[32] There is no question that women from China are selling sex overseas, but it is hard to view them as trafficking victims. We should, however, reiterate that some of the women we interviewed had been domestically trafficked in China—that is, they had been taken, usually under false pretenses, from rural areas to urban centers for commercial sex. But the proportion of such women (about 10%) is significantly lower than what is suggested in the trafficking literature. Even in the case of these women, however, the circumstances (the how and why) under which they ultimately ended up in paid sex overseas did not meet the criteria of sex trafficking.

Neither does the argument cited earlier about the magnitude and trends of prostitution and sex trafficking reflect the reality of our findings. The media in our research sites had often reported that women from China were dominating and overwhelming the local sex businesses, but our research suggests that the actual numbers are substantially lower than what is reported. The same is true with the trends—all the women we talked to believe that the trafficking of women might have existed in the past, but not anymore. They all suggested that, if indeed sex trafficking had ever occurred, it was decreasing, not increasing.

With respect to the impact of the legalization of prostitution on the cross-border movement of women for commercial sex, we can only point out that the crackdowns on prostitution in China have had a displacement effect, in that some women decided to go overseas to avoid being arrested for working in the sex trade in China.

Beyond these claims that might be considered "core" claims, there are other assumptions, claims, and in some cases myths that float around in the discussions and debates over human trafficking in general and sex trafficking in particular. For example, some are of the view that victims are recruited by returned women who are engaged in recruitment solely for the purpose of getting rid of their own sex slave status and moving into management. In other words, a victim becomes a victimizer if she wants to stop being a victim, as in the following statement: "The most common way women are recruited in Ukraine is through a friend or acquaintance, who gains the woman's confidence. An increasing phenomenon is called 'the second wave'. . . . One of the few means of escaping the brutality of being forced to have unwanted sex each day with multiple men is to move from victim to perpetrator. To do this, women who have been trafficked return home to recruit new victims."[33]

Victor Malarek, author of *The Natashas*, also made the same observation about the existence of the "second wave":

> Even more disturbing is the use of trafficked women to lure new victims —the so-called second wave. For many trafficked women, it's the only way of escaping the brutality of being forced to have unwanted sex with a dozen men a day. Their pimps give them the option of returning home if they promise to reel in a number of replacements. And the women are extremely convincing, often pulling up in luxury cars, wearing flashing jewelry and expensive clothes. In no time they're surrounded by envious, naïve teenage girls who readily fall for the grandiloquent tales of life in the golden West.[34]

This may happen, but it was certainly not what happened with the women we interviewed. Most of them were actually not recruited. Instead, they initiated the process of going overseas, and they did so on their own. For those who were helped by a returned woman, the process could not really be considered a "recruitment," and definitely had nothing to do with transforming the returned woman from being a victim to being a manager.

Then there is the belief that organized crime groups dominate the transnational sex trade. Many organized crime groups are simultaneously involved in a variety of transnational criminal activities, including drug trafficking, arms trafficking, money laundering, and allegedly human smuggling and human trafficking as well. According to this line of thinking, in some parts of the world established *mafias* dominate the trade. They have simply added human trafficking to their existing crime portfolios, often transporting women alongside their traditional contraband, such as drugs and arms.

Again, maybe this happens sometimes in some places, although in general there is little or no empirical evidence to support this claim. In fact, our own research shows that the transnational movement of Chinese women for commercial sex has very little to do with Chinese organized crime groups such as the triads in Hong Kong and Macau, or organized gangs in Taiwan, or the mafia-style gangs in China. Chinese gangs in Singapore and Malaysia do play a role in the sex business, but it is only a peripheral role, and the gang members who were engaged in it did so as individuals rather than as operatives of their particular gangs.

With regard to financial exploitation, it is claimed that women who go overseas to engage in commercial sex rarely bring any money home. According to the popular or official view, everyone who plays a role in the sex business is making plenty of money—except the women who actually provide the service. Again to the contrary, it is clear from our study that the majority of our subjects were able to return home with a relatively substantial amount of money—as long as they had not gambled or otherwise frittered it away while overseas.

There is also an understanding that most women start out as smuggled migrants, but then end up being trafficking victims. According to this understanding, a certain number of trafficked women go abroad knowing that they will be working as prostitutes of some sort. But they subsequently become trafficking victims when the situation goes horribly wrong and they find that they are trapped. Again, our study does not support such an assumption. When things went wrong, as they sometimes did, our subjects simply returned to China without being trapped and victimized.

Finally, a belief that many women are retrafficked after they are rescued and sent home is also not supported by our study.[35] Some of our subjects indeed were sent back to China after they were arrested or rescued, and they later did return to the country where they had been rescued. However, they did it on their own initiative and not because they were retrafficked.

It is not our intent to gratuitously criticize the efforts of so many benevolent individuals and organizations who are working to help mistreated and powerless women who were and are being victimized and exploited in a foreign country. We do, however, firmly believe that it is not good practice to build policy on a foundation of unsubstantiated claims, false beliefs, and myths.

One example is the unwillingness of antitrafficking advocates to address the reality that even in cases of true trafficking, sometimes the victims have played an active role in the process by placing themselves in a vulnerable position. They have chosen, even sought out, the opportunity to go overseas.

They have further agreed to engage in commercial sex overseas. The advocates refuse to address this reality because doing so might reduce empathy for the victims. But as a consequence of this refusal, the focus of policy and practice is on helping victims and not on looking for ways to create economic opportunities and alternatives for young women. Admittedly the latter is not easy to do, but it does help move from being simply reactive to being more proactive in coping with the problem.

We tend to agree with Gretchen Soderlund when she observed:

> It is commonly assumed that only the most callous would criticize efforts to free the world's sex slaves from the clutches of organized and brutal trafficking networks. Yet I hope to demonstrate here that those who seek a more humane and equitable world should in fact be the first to interrogate and critique the premises underlying many claims about global sex trafficking, as well as the U.S.-based efforts to "free sex slaves" justified by these claims.[36]

If we can get beyond the shrill special interests and the smoke and mirrors, we might find that there are many advantages to reexamining the current trafficking paradigm and the many assumptions upon which that paradigm is based. If we had a better and more realistic definition of trafficking victims, we would be better able to reconcile the huge gap between the number of estimated and actual rescued victims. Second, we would be able to develop a more efficient strategy in our efforts to investigate and prosecute the people who are assisting women in selling sex because we would have arrived at a better understanding of the relationships between the women and the people around them. Lastly, the various interest groups and government agencies around the world would have a shared focus on the major issues when they come together to discuss transnational commercial sex. Under the current trafficking paradigm, it appears that there is little or no common ground among the various governmental and nongovernmental organizations, and this absence greatly impedes our efforts to engage in a true dialogue. It also impedes the ability to develop and implement a coherent and effective human trafficking policy.

Conclusion

U.S. State Department officials working abroad are responsible for collecting information about human trafficking in the country where they are assigned. They prepare a country report for the State Department's GTIP

Office. Based on these country reports, the GTIP prepares the annual TIP Report. According to a frustrated State Department official in one of our research sites: "We don't do fieldwork like you do. We mainly rely on NGOs and local authorities for information. We also collect newspaper articles." We actually observed another U.S. State Department official desperately pleading with a local government official for any information about sex trafficking in that country.

One of the problems with U.S. efforts in combating sex trafficking is that we have very little reliable information about the phenomenon. The public and public officials learn about sex trafficking from watching movies and TV news, reading newspapers and weekly magazines, and more rarely, digesting government or NGO reports.[37] Few of us ever encounter an actual woman who is engaged in commercial sex, not to mention a woman who is a sex trafficking victim. This means that we learn about the problem from intermediaries, as pointed out by Georgetown University professors Elzbieta Gozdziak and Elizabeth Collett from their review of the research literature on human trafficking in North America:

> Most researchers drew information from newspaper reports and media investigations to compile a picture of trafficking in North America or base their studies on interviews with intermediaries: social service providers, counselors, law enforcement, victim advocates, pro bono attorneys, and others working with trafficking victims. . . . Other research has assessed information from prosecuted cases, often high-profile ones.[38]

If we researchers do talk to women who are engaged in paid sex, it is usually the case that the interviews are conducted in a police station, a jail, or a shelter, where the women have very good reasons to present themselves as being trafficking victims. Having been informed by the media, Hollywood, and various official reports, investigators tend to believe these women's stories when they say that they were not willing participants. Liz Kelly, a British sociologist, made the following point after she critically reviewed the literature on trafficking in persons in Europe:

> While the engagement in research and documentation of international bodies, including at least five United Nations (UN) agencies, is welcome, it does not necessarily ensure a deepening of the knowledge base. Publications may primarily reflect a claims-making process, vying for influence over how the issue is understood and where it is located intellectually, symbolically, and materially.[39]

We believed at the outset of this research that it was time for us to talk to the very women we were studying—the women who engage in commercial sex themselves—to best understand prostitution and sex trafficking and the possible linkage between them. Of course, as we pointed out earlier, this also raises an issue about the credibility of the information we received. Maybe the women lied to us? Maybe—although we very much doubt it.

People usually lie when they have something to gain by doing so, or when they have something to fear from telling the truth. Neither of those conditions existed in our interviews. We interviewed the women in their own natural settings and without the presence of a third party. We promised them nothing except anonymity. We were good listeners who gave them every opportunity to tell us their stories. We did not judge them. We did not threaten them. We did not even try to persuade them if they were reluctant to speak with us. We have told this story in large part through the words of these women.

We likewise believed that it was time to interview the very people who are helping women go overseas to engage in commercial sex. Recruiters and document procurers in source countries, and agents, mommies (or their equivalents), and the owners of sex establishments in destination countries also obviously know a great deal about how the business of commercial sex operates. They were valuable to us, and they too should be a source of information in future studies.

Although we disagree on some (or many) points, we do agree with the argument made by many of those combating sex trafficking that we need to pay much more attention to the demand side—the people who are buying sex. Among the questions to think about are whether supply is simply a response to demand? Or is demand actually created or enhanced by sex ring operators manipulating prices? Or does it depend upon the sex service providers themselves who simply show up in a destination country and make themselves available to potential buyers?

Interestingly, we have not been the only ones who believe in the value of ethnographic research in this area. A handful of ethnographers have recently studied sex trafficking by talking to potential victims in source countries, and (like us) to women who were already engaging in paid sex in destination countries. These interviews too were conducted in natural settings. For example, John Frederick studied the movement of Nepali girls to India;[40] Teresa Sobieszcyk examined how Thai women arrived in Japan to engage in local sex businesses there;[41] Joanna Busza et al. looked at the problem of Vietnamese women in the sex industry of Cambodia;[42] and Natasha Ahmad explored the situation of Bangladeshi women in India's sex sector.[43] Each of these studies also questioned the many assumptions associated with the current trafficking paradigm. HIV prevention researcher Busza and her colleagues made an argument for more such participatory research as follows:

> We do not dispute that in both settings migrants have suffered hardship and abuse, but current "anti-trafficking" approaches do not help their problems. The agendas need to be redrawn so that they reflect the needs of the populations they aim to serve, rather than emotive reactions to sensationalized media coverage. This requires deeper investigation at both local and regional levels, including participatory research to inform interventions from the experiences of the migrants and their communities.[44]

We also recommend the study of women from other major sending countries to see whether their experiences are comparable to those of Chinese women. We think that, for example, the experiences of Nepali women in India, Burmese (Myanmar) women in Thailand, Vietnamese women in Cambodia, Thai women in Japan, Moldovan women in Turkey, and Korean and Mexican women in the United States should be examined. We further recommend that female interviewers interview these women, again in their natural settings and without the presence of a third party, so as to avoid any actual or perceived gender bias.

The world of prostitution and sex trafficking is not a black and white world. There are here all the ambiguities and moral dilemmas that characterize so much of the human condition. A failure to recognize the distinctions and nuances that actually characterize the commercial sex business, whether because of ignorance or politicized moral positions or both, obviously does nothing to help the women who are purportedly the major concern. It also does nothing for the development of coherent and effective practices and policies to combat human trafficking. In the end, continuing to use sex trafficking as a moral battleground is unlikely to result in effective policies and practices at any level.

NOTES

NOTES TO CHAPTER 1

1. Pinyin Romanization is used for most of the Chinese words appearing in this book.
2. Chin, 1999.
3. Keefe, 2009; Zhang, 2007, 2008.
4. David, 2008.
5. U.S. Department of Justice, 2008.
6. Scarpa, 2008.
7. Massey et al., 1993; Zhang, 2007.
8. Kyle and Koslowski, 2001; United Nations Office on Drugs and Crime, 2010.
9. Brown, 2000; Kara, 2009.
10. Gozdziak and Bump, 2008; Zhang, 2009.
11. Doezema, 2010; Kempadoo, 2005; Murray, 1998.
12. Zhang, 2007, p. 122.
13. DeStefano, 2007.
14. Weitzer, 2009, p. 217.
15. Cwikel and Hoban, 2005; Di Nicola, 2007; Gozdziak and Bump, 2008.
16. Zhang, 2009, p. 185.
17. Kelly, 2005.
18. Gozdziak and Bump, 2008.
19. The United Nations Office on Drugs and Crime (2006) ranked China with Albania, Belarus, Bulgaria, Lithuania, Nigeria, the Republic of Moldova, Romania, the Russian Federation, Thailand, and Ukraine as one of the ten major countries where human trafficking originates.
20. Anggraeni, 2006; Constable, 2002; Zarembka, 2002.
21. Konisberg, 2008.
22. Barry, 1995, p. 165.
23. U.S. Department of State, 2008, p. 6.
24. *Bangkok Post*, July 14, 2001, p. 1.
25. *Bangkok Post*, May 23, 2001, p. 11.
26. Kempadoo, 2005.
27. According to DeStefano (2007, p. xx), "the UN protocol came into being a mere two months after President Bill Clinton signed the TVPA and was clearly an American policy initiative . . . to assure consensus among nations about the criminalization of trafficking."
28. United Nations, 2000, p. 2.
29. Human Rights Watch, 2000, p. 2.
30. Malarek, 2003, p. 19.
31. Sage and Kasten, 2006, p. 4.

32. Altink, 1995; Bales, 1999; Batstone, 2007; Bechard, 2005; Crawford, 2010; Farley, 2003; Haugen and Hunter, 2005; Human Rights Watch, 1995; Mam, 2007; Pearson, 2002.

33. Human Rights Watch, 2000, pp. 1–2.

34. Dewey, 2008, p. xi.

35. Agustin, 2008; Bernstein, 2007; Brennan, 2004, 2010; Choo, Jang, and Choi, 2010; Doezema, 2010; Frederick, 2005; Global Alliance Against Trafficking in Women, 2007; Jahic and Finckenauer, 2005; Kelly, 2005; Kempadoo, 2005; Parrenas, 2011; Sanders, 2008; Sanghera, 2005; Schifter-Sikora, 2007; Segrave et al., 2009; Thorbeck, 2002; Weitzer, 2007.

36. Shelley, 2007; Williams, 1999.

37. Kyle and Dale, 2001.

38. Chin, 1999; Finckenauer, 2001.

39. Farr, 2005; Morawska, 2007.

40. Jacobs, 1994.

41. Finckenauer, 2007.

42. Blakey, 1994; Jacobs, 1999, 2006.

43. Jacobs, 1999.

44. Kelly, Chin, and Schatzberg, 1994; Kenney and Finckenauer, 1995.

45. Gambetta, 1993.

46. Finckenauer and Waring, 1998; Varese, 2001.

47. Jacobs, 1999.

48. Chin, 1990; Chu, 2000.

49. Hill, 2003; Kaplan and Dubro, 2003.

50. Chepesiuk, 2003.

51. Finckenauer, 2007.

52. Jahic, 2009.

53. In Taiwan, we interviewed one subject in Chiayi (in southern Taiwan) and four subjects in Taichung (in central Taiwan) in addition to Taipei (the capital in northern Taiwan). In Malaysia, we interviewed three women in Ipoh (two and a half hours' drive from Kuala Lumpur) as well as in Kuala Lumpur. Included in the New York metropolitan area sample were nine women we interviewed in northern New Jersey. And in China, we interviewed two in Changan (a city with a big sex sector and not far from Shenzhen), and two in Fuzhou.

54. Brazil, 2004; Lim, 1998; Lintner, 2002; Yang, 2006.

55. Finckenauer and Chin, 2006.

56. Most of the interviews with authorities in China were conducted informally over dinner, and in a group setting.

57. Ferrell and Hamm, 1998; Miller and Tewksbury, 2001.

58. To protect our subjects, the names of the red-light districts, streets, and venues where they worked are not mentioned in this book.

59. Weitzer, 2010a, p. 19.

60. It is important to note that agents in Taiwan are not the same as agents in Indonesia. In Taiwan, an agent is more like the "owner" of a girl, who has arranged and funded the girl's trip to Taiwan; in turn, the girl must repay the agent the "road fee," and also give the agent a cut of her earnings. In Indonesia, an agent represents a girl and provides her a variety of services for a fee or a share of her earnings. This issue will be discussed in detail in chapter 6.

61. World Health Organization (WHO), 2003, p. 1.

62. Ibid., p. 4.
63. United Nations Inter-Agency Project on Human Trafficking (UNIAP), 2008.
64. World Health Organization (WHO), 2003, p. 16.
65. Gozdziak and Bump, 2008; Gozdziak and Collett, 2005.
66. We indicate the case number of the female subject whenever we quote her. Readers interested in the demographic background of a particular subject can find the information in Tables 4.1 to 4.10 by referring to her case number.
67. Tyldum and Brunovskis, 2005, p. 26.
68. Zhang, 2009, p. 187.
69. Malarek, 2003, pp. 135–136.
70. Global Alliance Against Trafficking in Women, 2007; Kempadoo and Doezema, 1998; Miriam, 2005; Outshoorn, 2004; Stetson, 2004; Weitzer, 2010b.
71. Hyde, 2007; Jeffreys, 2004; Liu, 2010; Zheng, 2008, 2009.
72. Gozdziak and Bump, 2008; Zhang 2009.
73. United Nations Office on Drugs and Crime (UNODC), 2006, p. 6.
74. See Chin, 1990, 1996, 2003; Chin, and Godson 2006; Finckenauer and Chin, 2006; and Hill, 2003 for a discussion of all the groups listed above and other similar organized crime groups.

NOTES TO CHAPTER 2

1. *Xaihai* or "going down to the sea" here refers to entering prostitution, although the term has been widely used in China since the Mao era when someone quits his/her salaried job and becomes an entrepreneur. After "going down to the sea," one must swim constantly to stay afloat and to survive, and it connotes struggle, despair, danger, and uncertainty. Quitting prostitution is called *shangan* ("to swim ashore").
2. Enright, Scott, and Chang, 2005; Gittings, 2005; van Kemenade 1997.
3. Massonnet, 2000.
4. Smith, 1997.
5. The Refugee Act of 1980 makes a person eligible for asylum in the United States if he or she has suffered past persecution or has a well-founded fear of persecution on account of race, religion, nationality, membership in a particular social group, or political opinion (Ignatius, 1993).
6. Chin, 1999.
7. Keefe, 2009.
8. Wang, Chin, and Lin, 1997.
9. Finckenauer and Chin, 2006.
10. Lo, 2009.
11. Lindquist and Piper, 2007, p. 152.
12. Mix, 2002, p. 98.
13. We have given all our subjects who were *xiaojies* or sex ring operators, Chinese or English pseudonyms to protect their identities.
14. The red-light district is packed with brothels and massage parlors staffed by women from Thailand, Malaysia, Myanmar (Burma), Vietnam, and India. Hundreds of Chinese and Indonesian girls and women also solicit business on the streets. Some transvestites from Thailand also walk the streets (Brazil, 2004).
15. Actually, the subject was making about $3,000 a month in Singapore, equivalent to what she would have made in four years in China.

16. Even though prostitution is rampant in China, it is illegal to buy or sell sex there (Hyde, 2007; Jeffreys, 2004; Ren, 1993; Zheng, 2009; Zhou, 2006). Most of the time, Chinese authorities do not pay much attention to prostitution. However, when there is pressure from Beijing or when the local authorities need to generate funds, they go after prostitution zealously to please the authorities in Beijing and/or to fine the arrested clients and prostitutes. Besides paying a fine, some clients and *xiaojies* are publicly humiliated or imprisoned, and our subjects were referring to these occasional harsh measures when they said they went overseas to avoid the Chinese authorities.

17. Many people in China are fascinated with the United States. Some are willing to pay professional smugglers tens of thousands of dollars (almost half a million yuan in a country where most people make about one or two thousand yuan a month) to smuggle them to a country they call *meiguo* or "beautiful country" (Chin, 1999; Zhang, 2008; Zhang and Chin, 2002). The majority of the Chinese women we interviewed in the United States did not arrive here with the intention of getting involved in paid sex, so in this chapter we have not discussed their reasons for going to the United States. Rather, we will discuss those reasons when we discuss the routes and the processes for each research site; because for these subjects, the crucial issue is how they arrived and not why they came in the first place.

18. Agustin, 2008, p. 2.

19. As will be discussed in the following chapter, some Chinese women we interviewed left China with a visa to go to a country in Southeast Asia, but their plan was to engage in prostitution while they were in transit in Hong Kong or Macau. As a result, after they arrived in the country in Southeast Asia for which they had the visa, they stayed for only one or two nights, and then returned to the transit country (Hong Kong or Macau) to continue to work as prostitutes before returning to mainland China.

20. Throughout this book, when we present the monthly income of our subjects, we are certainly underestimating their actual incomes, since our estimation of their monthly incomes is based on how much they charged their customers per session and what their share was of that charge. However, as will be discussed later, customers often pay tips on top of the regular charge, and according to the women themselves the tips always belong entirely to the women, regardless of whether they are working independently or in conjunction with a pimp or a venue owner.

21. Chin, 1999; Kwong, 1997; Zhang, 2008.

NOTES TO CHAPTER 3

1. Brown, 2000.
2. Human Rights Watch, 1995, 2000.
3. Zheng, 2009.
4. Ibid.
5. Foshan is the third largest city of Guangdong Province, behind Guangzhou and Shenzhen. The city, with a population of 5.4 million, is a major manufacturing base in the Pearl River Delta and is famous for its porcelain industry (Enright et al., 2005). This subject was a *xiaojie* in Foshan before she began to work in the Hong Kong sex industry.
6. Chang, 2009.
7. Zheng, 2009.
8. Simon, 1982.

9. Clarke and Cornish, 2001; Miller, 2001.

10. Miller, 2001, p. 26.

11. Liu, 2010.

12. Ibid., p. 245.

13. Sykes and Matza, 1957.

14. Chen, 1971; Zhao, 1973.

15. Hsu, 1967.

16. Ren, 1993.

17. Gilmartin, 1990.

18. Liu, 2010.

19. Merry, 2009, p. 35.

20. Shu and Bian, 2002, pp. 302–303.

21. Brown, 2000, p. 215. See also Hoigard and Finstad 1986; Winick and Kinsie, 1971.

22. Yang, 2006, p. 188.

NOTES TO CHAPTER 4

1. van Kemenade, 1997.

2. Wang et al., 2002.

3. Whitehead and Vittachi, 1997.

4. Laidler et al., 2007, p. 70.

5. Yang, 2006.

6. Whitehead and Vittachi, 1997.

7. For many reasons, monthly incomes presented here are only raw estimates. Most female subjects in our study did not work on a monthly basis, and this was especially true for subjects in Hong Kong who were able to stay for only 7 or 14 days per visit. Moreover, a monthly income was based on three estimates: (1) approximately how much a subject earned per transaction, (2) how many transactions she might have in a day, and (3) the assumption that she worked on average about 22 days a month. The monthly income could, if anything, be underestimated because tips that were given them by customers, which were sometimes substantial, are not included.

8. Liang and Lu, 2010

9. According to a female subject in Macau, prior to January 2006 people from China could stay for one month in Macau on their way to a country in Southeast Asia, then return to China and come back to Macau and stay for another 7 days, before they went to a country in Southeast Asia. On their way back to China, they would go through Macau and stay for another month. Since 2006, however, instead of a month Chinese citizens can stay only 14 days whenever they transit through Macau.

10. Rigger, 1999.

11. Chang, 2002.

12. According to an escort company owner, once a jockey takes a woman from her apartment to see her first customer, normally in the early afternoon, the woman will not return to her apartment until she is done working for that day, usually at dawn. This is to avoid having neighbors see the woman going in and out of her apartment several times a day and thus raising suspicions.

13. Bishop and Robinson, 1998; Jeffrey, 2002; Phongpaichit, Piriyarangsan, and Treerat, 1998; Seabrook, 2001.

14. Altman, 2001.
15. Asia Watch and Women's Rights Project, 1993; Brown, 2000; Jeffrey, 2002; Skrobanek et al., 1997.
16. Phongpaichit and Piriyarangsan, 1994.
17. Brennan, 2004; Kempadoo, 2004.
18. Besides the nightclubs, KTVs, flower halls, and restaurants near Bangkok's Chinatown and Suriwong Boulevard, where many local sex venues are located, Chinese women also seek clients in the back alleys and side streets of Bangkok's Chinatown. Even though we did not formally interview any of these streetwalkers, we did talk to three of them briefly when they tried to solicit business from us. The first woman said she was from Hunan and that she charged $14 per session. The second woman identified herself as someone from Shanghai, and she asked for $11 per session. The one from Hunan said customers must go with her to a nearby hotel that she is familiar with, and that the room cost only $2. We asked her whether she would come to our hotel that was only a few blocks away, and she said absolutely not. All three appeared to be in their forties and did not have much business. There was also another group of Chinese women working in the local sex business that catered to Thai men, and they came from Burma or Myanmar (mostly from the Shan State), northern Thailand, or were ethnic Dai women from China (mostly from Yunnan Province). We did interview two of them (Chun Xiang and Li Qun), and the individual characteristics, sex markets, and working experiences of this group of women were quite different from the majority of our subjects who came from Hunan or northeastern China.
19. The majority of the women we interviewed in the ten research sites indicated that they were interested in finding a rich man to support them on a regular basis. Women we interviewed in Bangkok were especially active in seeking this type of relationship. Women working in nightclubs and karaoke lounges, in general, were more likely to have a *laogong* ("husband") than were women working in sauna/spas, brothels, or escort agencies because the former could more credibly claim that they were not prostitutes, and thus were more likely to be treated as a "wife" by men.
20. *New Straits Times*, 2006.
21. Looi et al., 2007.
22. Warren, 2003.
23. Brazil, 2004; Lim, 2004.
24. In Singapore, many *xiaojies* we interviewed thought that working in Singapore was a plus because they could work anytime they wanted. This is because the red light districts there are open for business 24 hours a day, and the weather in Singapore is warm all year round and thus conducive to open-air commercial sex work.
25. Jones et al., 1998.
26. Emka, 2002, p. ii.
27. Light, 1974.
28. U.S. Senate, [1877] 1978.
29. Martin, 1977; Wilson, 1974.
30. Cohen, 1986.
31. Yang, 1985.
32. Richard, 2000.
33. *World Journal*, March 7, 2008.
34. Chin, 1990, 1996.

35. Zhou, 1992.
36. Chin, 1999.
37. In Shenzhen, a metropolis with more than 10 million people, many districts or areas are still called a "village" or a "city village." At one point, landowners in these villages were allowed to build as many so-called "renting apartments" as they wanted; the congregation of large numbers of migrants from all over China in these poorly constructed and maintained renting apartments has created all kinds of problems for the local authorities. Many *falang* and brothels are located there, and many criminals, drug users, and prostitutes are attracted to these apartments for their low rents and tolerance for dubious activities.
38. Zheng, 2008.

NOTES TO CHAPTER 5

1. Zheng, 2009.
2. Weitzer, 2010b, pp. 7–9.
3. Kurtz et al., 2006; Porter and Bonilla, 2010; Weitzer, 2009.
4. Weitzer, 2010b, p. 9.
5. The hotel is unlikely to find ordinary visitors who are willing to pay $40 a night to stay there. It is located away from the main boulevard where many of the big casinos are situated and the rooms are very small, poorly maintained, and equipped with cheap furniture.
6. The casino is located in Genting Highlands, Pahang, Malaysia. According to an advertisement on its website, the casino's 200,000 square foot gaming space features 3,000 gaming machines and 500 table games. The property has twenty-nine restaurants and six hotels with 8,653 rooms.
7. Brennan, 2010, pp. 311–312.
8. Hotel XXX (name omitted) expanded its business by building a new hotel and casino right across the street from the old building. Both the new and old buildings are in operation now, but Chinese *xiaojies* are active only in the old building. The old building is actually composed of an old wing and a new wing.
9. Zheng, 2009.
10. Yang, 2006.
11. In Asia, some of the nightclubs are divided into "uniform" and "casual dress" establishments. In a "uniform" store, all the hostesses are required to wear a uniform issued to them by the store management. Women working in casual dress are allowed to wear whatever they want to wear when they come to work. Readers should not be fooled by the wording; a "uniform" could be very casual and revealing and "casual dress" could be very classy and conservative. The difference is whether hostesses wear their own clothes to work or must put on the clothes required by their employers. There is a common assumption among customers of these nightclubs that "uniform" hostesses are more aggressive and eager to please their customers than "casual dress" hostesses.
12. Actually, this is a misnomer because a hostess in this nightclub simply goes upstairs to have sex after she is selected by a customer. Many nightclubs and karaoke bars are equipped with private rooms upstairs for sexual transactions. This way, a customer not only saves a room charge but also avoids the problem of being seen with a hostess inside a hotel. Those nightclubs and KTVs not big enough to have their own private rooms may strategically pick a location where there is already a hotel within the same building, explicitly for the purpose of promoting paid sex between their hostesses and the hotel's customers.

13. According to a mommy at the KTV, the price for *dapao* ("fire a big gun" or sexual intercourse) was $150, plus $6 for the room.

14. There are many terms that refer to a hostess in a nightclub, a KTV, or a flower hanging hall leaving her workplace with a customer so that the two can engage in paid sex. It is most often called *chutai* (off stage) as opposed to *zoutai* (on stage). Other terms used are *chuzhong* (outside hour), *chujie* (outside street), and *chuchang* (outside the premises) to depict the same process.

15. Chen, 1992.

16. Koken, Bimbi, and Parsons, 2010, p. 205.

17. The woman in this type of relationship is called *ernai* (second wife) or *xiaomi* (little honey).

18. Weitzer, 2010a, p. 26.

19. Ibid., p. 26.

NOTES TO CHAPTER 6

1. A *jinji* (agent) in Taiwan could also team up with a *jinju* (money man) and the two work together to bring one or more Chinese women to Taiwan for prostitution. In this case, the agent does all the work, but he or she need not invest any money. The *jinju* fronts the money to cover the woman's travel expenses, but he or she does not do anything else.

2. Unlike the experience of our subjects in other research sites, our respondents in Indonesia told us that their employers generally required them to turn in their travel documents before they started to work.

3. All these cities are located in the Pearl River Delta area and are popular destinations for young men and women from the interior provinces of China to look for work. *Xiaojies* from the interior provinces also often migrate to these cities to make more money.

4. One American dollar was equal to about ten thousand rupiah in 2007. When we converted five hundred dollars into rupiah at a money exchange, we left with five million rupiah, a lot of cash to be carried around. When Ah Lam left that KTV, he was carrying a large bag of money that held about 50 million rupiah.

5. An escort agency owner can also import Chinese women to Taiwan and be an agent. Of course, the owner can simply place the Chinese women in his or her own agency to work. A person who starts as an agent may also venture into operating an escort agency and play the role of agent and escort agency owner at the same time. An agent or escort agency owner may also be a jockey (driver). The point here is the roles are very fluid, and one person can perform many roles simultaneously or switch roles.

6. The subject had a previous girlfriend who helped him run the house. After his girlfriend left him, his business went downhill because most callers are reluctant to show up when the person answering the phone is a man. As a result, the subject said he was going to cater to Mexicans instead of Chinese. He said that by doing so he would be running the risk of being noticed by the authorities and risking a subsequent crackdown. But he also could not afford not to do so because he simply did not have enough business with Chinese clients alone.

7. The best way to find out whether a venue provides only a massage or a massage plus sexual services is to ask the person who answers the phone how much the place charges. If that person says the service costs $50 or $60, then there is a good chance the place provides only pure massage or a massage plus a "happy ending." If the person says $100, $120,

or $150, it is obvious that the place is a so-called "full set" parlor that offers sexual inter-course. Many "full set" parlors are reluctant to say over the phone that the service costs $100 or more, worried that the caller might be a police officer. To protect themselves, they may tell a caller the price is $50 or $60. The girls in the massage parlor will not offer full service until a customer has visited the place a few times.

8. Caldwell et al., 1999; Farr, 2005; Richard, 2000; Shannon, 1999; Shelley, 2007, 2010; Sulain-manova, 2006.
9. Shannon, 1999, p. 126.
10. Hughes, 2000.
11. Farr, 2005, p. 94.
12. Lee, 2007, p. 5.
13. Shelley, 2007, p. 134.
14. Bales and Lize, 2005.
15. United Nations Office on Drug and Crime, 2006.
16. United Nations Office on Drug and Crime, 2010, p. 7.
17. Richard, 2000, p. 14.
18. Shelley, 2010, p. 172.
19. Sanghera, 2005; Yang, 2006.
20. Chu, 2005, p. 7.
21. Chu, 2000.
22. Chin, 2003.
23. Finckenauer and Chin, 2006.
24. Chin, 1990, 1996.

NOTES TO CHAPTER 7

1. Kara, 2009.
2. Brown, 2000.
3. Di Nicola et al., 2009.
4. For example, a few years ago, one U.S. dollar equaled more than 8 Chinese yuan or *ren-minbi*, but in the year 2012, a dollar was worth about 6.3 yuan only.
5. Human Rights Watch, 2000.
6. Brown, 2000, p. 16.
7. As mentioned in chapter 3, we observed many Indonesian streetwalkers while we were conducting fieldwork in a red-light district in Singapore. According to a Singaporean man who is very familiar with the sex trade in Singapore, sex ring operators usually charge an Indonesian girl a $670 road fee for bringing her from Indonesia to Singapore. An Indo-nesian girl charges $26 per session and splits the money with her sex ring operator. As a result, the girl normally pays off her travel fee after seeing about 50 clients. If a girl sees 25 men a day, which is not unusual according to the Singaporean man, she pays off her travel fee in two days.
8. Hughes, 2000, p. 633.
9. Brown, 2000, p. 157.
10. Ibid., p. 231.
11. Tommaso et al., 2009. One of the weaknesses of the IOM database is that the number of missing values for certain variables is more than 50 percent. For example, even though the N of the database for female sex trafficking victims is 4,559, there are only 235 valid cases for this particular variable—charge per client.

12. Jones et al., 1998, p. 45.
13. Boonchalaksi and Guest, 1998, p. 155.
14. Tommaso et al., 2009.
15. It is important to note that some customers may offer a tip after the sexual transaction and these tips all belong to the women. Mommies and chickenheads are not supposed to ask the women about tips; if they do ask, and the women refuse to provide any information, these facilitators have no way of knowing the details.
16. In China, a new house is very often just a property with unfinished walls and floors. This way, after the deal is closed the owner is free to finish the floors and the walls with materials and colors he or she likes. Of course, this also requires a home owner to come up with half, or more than half the amount of money he or she paid for the new house in the first place.
17. Jahic, 2009, pp. 53–54.
18. Jordan, 1997.
19. Martilla, 2003.
20. Plumridge et al., 1997.
21. Jahic, 2009, p. 61.
22. Ibid., p. 61.
23. Porter and Bonilla, 2010; Weitzer, 2010b.
24. Brown, 2000, p. 213.
25. Lowman and Atchison, 2006, p. 293.
26. Monto, 2010.
27. Sanders, 2008, p. 112.
28. Ibid., p. 11.

NOTES TO CHAPTER 8
1. U.S. Department of State, 2010, p. 47.
2. Tier 2-Watch List first appeared in the 2004 report.
3. DeStefano, 2007.
4. U.S. Department of State, 2009, p. 152.
5. In Hong Kong, the OCTB plays a more prominent role in the crackdown on prostitution than the immigration department because it has greater manpower and resources.
6. U.S. Department of State, 2009, p. 191.
7. Ibid., p. 274.
8. In August 2003, Taiwan's coast guard spotted two speed boats in the waters off a coastal town of Miaoli County. The smugglers forced all the passengers—26 PRC Chinese women—to jump into the sea and then fled. Six women drowned while the others managed to swim ashore or were rescued. All the young women were believed to have been transported to Taiwan to engage in commercial sex. The two boat captains and the crew were arrested later, and one of the captains was executed by the Taiwanese authorities.
9. U.S. Department of State, 2009, p. 279.
10. Ibid., p. 197.
11. The ambassador of the Indonesian embassy in Kuala Lumpur was once interviewed by an Australian producer of a documentary film about Indonesian migrant workers in Malaysia, and he said that, in general, the Chinese employers beat the Indonesian migrant workers, the Malays refused to pay them fairly, and the Indians raped them.

The Indonesian embassy is operating a shelter for Indonesian trafficking victims which has about 1,000 victims.

12. U.S. Department of State, 2009, pp. 256–257.
13. Ibid., p. 158.
14. Ibid., p. 104.
15. Bernstein, 2007, p. 7.
16. Ibid., p. 164.

NOTES TO CHAPTER 9

1. Barry, 1995.
2. Because of her age, Jiao Jiao is a trafficked victim according to the U.S. and UN definition of sex trafficking. She was the only underage subject in our sample.
3. Emerton, 2001, p. 15.
4. International Organization for Migration 2002, 2003; Vocks and Nijboer, 2000.
5. Schloenhardt, 2001; Tyldum and Brunovskis, 2005.
6. King, 2004; Malarek, 2003; Shelley 2007, 2010.
7. Chin, 1999.
8. Busza et al., 2004, pp. 1369–1370.
9. King, 2004; Skinner, 2008.
10. Kara, 2009, p. 87. According to Kara, he personally conducted the interview with the 18-year-old Tatyana two months after she had escaped from her protector. Her protector had not yet been found, but even if he was arrested and charged, Tatyana said she did not want to testify against him.
11. In Indonesia, the practice of taking away the woman's travel documents and having her sign a contract has been applied to all Chinese women, regardless of whether they owe money to their employers or not.
12. Barry, 1981, pp. 86–87.
13. Ibid., p. 93.
14. Hughes, 2000, p. 637.
15. Agustin, 2008, p. 35.
16. Lim, 1998, p. 17.
17. O'Connell Davidson, 2005, p. 73.
18. Brennan, 2002, p. 155.
19. Bernstein, 2007, p. 184.
20. Kempadoo, 2005, p. xix.

NOTES TO CHAPTER 10

1. Bales, 2007.
2. U.S. Government Accountability Office, 2006.
3. Dimitrova, 2007.
4. Hilgartner and Bosk, 1988.
5. Kelly, 2005.
6. Richard, 2000.
7. Dimitrova, 2007.
8. Stolz, 2010.
9. U.S. Department of State, 2007.
10. See Widgren, 1994.

11. Markon, 2007, p. A05.
12. Global Alliance Against Trafficking in Women, 2007; Gozdziak and Bump, 2008; Zhang, 2009.
13. Cwikel and Hoban, 2005.
14. *William Wilberforce Trafficking Victims Protection Reauthorization Act of 2008* [United States of America] Public Law 110-457, 2008.
15. Miller, 2008, p. A17.
16. Cook, 2008.
17. Aradau, 2008.
18. Agustin, 2006; Ahmad, 2005; Kempadoo, 2004.
19. Skeldon, 2000.
20. U.S. Department of State, 2008.
21. Hughes, 2008, p. 2.
22. Edelman, 1964.
23. Stolz, 2007.
24. Weitzer, 2007, p. 448.
25. Ibid., p. 450.
26. Sanders, 2008, p. 6.
27. Di Nicola et al., 2009, p. 3.
28. Brown, 2000; Sage and Kasten, 2006.
29. The *Red Detachment Army* is a story about the liberation of a peasant girl in Hainan Province and her rise in the Chinese Communist Party.
30. Kempadoo, 2005, p. xxiv.
31. Mix, 2002, p. 86.
32. Weitzer, 2007, p. 455.
33. Hughes, 2000, p. 635.
34. Malarek, 2003, p. 13.
35. See Sanghera (2005) for other dominant assumptions that inform the mainstream trafficking discourse.
36. Soderlund, 2005, p. 67.
37. Piper, 2005.
38. Gozdziak and Collett, 2005, p. 116.
39. Kelly, 2005, p. 236.
40. Frederick, 2005.
41. Sobieszcyk, 2002.
42. Busza et al., 2004.
43. Ahmad, 2005.
44. Busza et al., 2004, p. 1371.

REFERENCES

IN ENGLISH

Agustin, Laura Maria. 2006. "The Disappearing of a Migration Category: Migrants who Sell Sex." *Journal of Ethnic and Migration Studies* 32: 29–47.

———. 2008. *Sex at the Margin: Migration, Labour Markets and the Rescue Industry*. London: Zed Books.

Ahmad, Natasha. 2005. "Trafficked Persons or Economic Migrants? Bangladeshis in India." Pp. 211–228 in *Trafficking and Prostitution Reconsidered: New Perspectives on Migration, Sex Work, and Human Rights*, edited by Kamala Kempadoo. Boulder: Paradigm Publishers.

Altink, Sietske. 1995. *Stolen Lives: Trading Women into Sex and Slavery*. London: Scarlet Press.

Altman, Dennis. 2001. *Global Sex*. Chicago: University of Chicago Press.

Anggraeni, Dewi. 2006. *Dreamseekers: Indonesian Women as Domestic Workers in Asia*. Jakarta: Equinox Publishing.

Aradau, Claudia. 2008. *Rethinking Trafficking in Women: Politics out of Security*. New York: Palgrave MacMillan.

Asia Watch and Women's Rights Project. 1993. *A Modern Form of Slavery: Trafficking of Burmese Women and Girls into Brothels in Thailand*. New York: Human Rights Watch.

Bales, Kevin. 1999. *Disposable People: New Slavery in the Global Economy*. Berkeley: University of California Press.

———. 2007. *Ending Slavery: How We Free Today's Slaves*. Berkeley: University of California Press.

Bales, Kevin, and Steven Lize. 2005. "Trafficking in Persons in the United States. Final Report Submitted to the National Institute of Justice, U.S. Department of Justice, for grant 2001-IJ-CX-0027."

Bangkok Post. 2001. "US Slams Modern-Day Slavery." July 14, p. 1.

———. 2001. "Freeh Urges Europe to Stop Slave Trade." May 23, p. 11.

Barry, Kathleen. 1981. *Female Sexual Slavery*. New York: Avon Books.

———. 1995. *The Prostitution of Sexuality: The Global Exploitation of Women*. New York: NYU Press.

Batstone, David. 2007. *Not for Sale*. New York: HarperOne.

Bechard, Raymond. 2005. *Unspeakable: The Hidden Truth behind the World's Fastest Growing Crime*. New York: Compel Publishing.

Bernstein, Elizabeth. 2007. *Temporarily Yours: Intimacy, Authenticity, and the Commerce of Sex*. Chicago: University of Chicago Press.

Bishop, Ryan, and Lillian Robinson. 1998. *Night Market: Sexual Cultures and the Thai Economic Miracle*. New York: Routledge.

Blakey, G. Robert. 1994. "RICO: The Federal Experience (Criminal and Civil) and an Analysis of Attacks against the Statute." Pp. 451–490 in *Handbook of Organized Crime in the United States*, edited by Robert Kelly, Ko-lin Chin, and Rufus Schatzberg. Westport, Conn.: Greenwood Press.

Boonchalaksi, Wathinee, and Philip Guest. 1998. "Prostitution in Thailand." Pp. 130–169 in *The Sex Sector: The Economic and Social Bases of Prostitution in Southeast Asia*, edited by Lin Lean Lim. Geneva: International Labour Office.

Brazil, David. 2004. *No Money No Honey! A Candid Look at Sex-for-Sale in Singapore*. Singapore: Angsana Books.

Brennan, Denise. 2002. "Selling Sex for Visas: Sex Tourism as a Stepping-Stone to International Migration." Pp. 154–168 in *Global Woman: Nannies, Maids, and Sex Workers in the New Economy*, edited by Barbara Ehrenreich and Arlie Russell Hochschild. New York: Metropolitan Books.

———. 2004. *What's Love Got to Do with It? Transnational Desires and Sex Tourism in the Dominican Republic*. Durham: Duke University Press.

———. 2010. "Sex Tourism and Sex Workers' Aspirations." Pp. 307–323 in *Sex for Sale: Prostitution, Pornography, and the Sex Industry*, 2nd ed., edited by Ronald Weitzer. New York: Routledge.

Brown, Louise. 2000. *Sex Slaves: The Trafficking of Women in Asia*. London: Virago Press.

Busza, Joanna, Sarah Castle, and Aisse Diarra. 2004. "Trafficking and Health." *British Medical Journal* 328: 1369–1371.

Caldwell, Gillian, Steve Galster, Jyothi Kanics, and Nadia Steinzor. 1999. "Capitalizing on Transition Economies: The Role of the Russian Mafiya in Trafficking Women for Forced Prostitution." Pp. 42–73 in *Illegal Immigration and Commercial Sex: The New Slave Trade*, edited by Phil Williams. London: Frank Cass Publishers.

Chang, Leslie. 2009. *Factory Girls: From Village to City in a Changing China*. New York: Spiegel & Grau.

Chen, Hsiang-shui. 1992. *Chinatown No More: Taiwan Immigrants in Contemporary New York*. Ithaca: Cornell University Press.

Chepesiuk, Ron. 2003. *The Bullet or the Bribe: Taking Down Colombia's Cali Drug Cartel*. Westport, Conn.: Praeger.

Chin, Ko-lin. 1990. *Chinese Subculture and Criminality: Non-Traditional Crime Groups in America*. Westport, Conn.: Greenwood Pres.

———. 1996. *Chinatown Gangs*. New York: Oxford University Press.

———. 1999. *Smuggled Chinese: Clandestine Immigration to the United States*. Philadelphia: Temple University Press.

———. 2003. *Heijin: Organized Crime, Business, and Politics in Taiwan*. Armonk, N.Y.: M. E. Sharpe.

Chin, Ko-lin, and Roy Godson. 2006. "Organized Crime and the Political-Criminal Nexus in China." *Trends in Organized Crime* 9: 5–44.

Choo, Kyungseok, Joon Oh Jang, and Kyungshick Choi. 2010. "Methodological and Ethical Challenges to Conducting Human Trafficking Studies: A Case Study of Korean Trafficking and Smuggling for Sexual Exploitation to the United States." *Women & Criminal Justice* 20: 167–185.

Chu, Yiu Kong. 2000. *Triads as Business*. London: Routledge.

———. 2005. "Triad Involvement in the Sex Service Industry in Hong Kong and Its Impacts on Southeast Asia." Paper presented at "The Shadow Areas of the Chinese Diaspora in Southeast Asia: Factors of Regional Integration or Threats to Stability" Symposium. Bangkok, Thailand, January 6–7.

Clarke, Ronald, and Derek Cornish. 2001. "Rational Choice." Pp. 23–42 in *Explaining Crime and Criminals. Essays in Contemporary Criminological Theory*, edited by Raymond Paternoster and Ronet Bachman. Los Angeles: Roxbury Publishing.

Cohen, Sharon. 1986. "Fighting a Shadowy Foreign Trade in Sex." *Bergen Record*, September 26, p. A1.

Constable, Nicole. 2002. "Filipina Workers in Hong Kong Homes: Household Rules and Relations." Pp. 115–141 in *Global Woman: Nannies, Maids, and Sex Workers in the New Economy*, edited by Barbara Ehrenreich and Arlie Russell Hochschild. New York: Metropolitan Books.

Cook, Elisebeth. 2008. Letter to the Editor, Re "The Justice Department, Blind to Slavery," *New York Times*, July 22.

Crawford, Mary. 2010. *Sex Trafficking in South Asia: Telling Maya's Story*. London and New York: Routledge.

Cwikel, Julie, and Elizabeth Hoban. 2005. "Contentious Issues in Research on Trafficked Women Working in the Sex Industry: Study Design, Ethics, and Methodology." *Journal of Sex Research* 42: 306–316.

David, Fiona. 2008. *Trafficking of Women for Sexual Purposes*. Research and Public Policy Series No. 95. Canberra: Australian Institute of Criminology.

DeStefano, Anthony. 2007. *The War on Human Trafficking: U.S. Policy Assessed*. New Brunswick: Rutgers University Press.

Dewey, Susan. 2008. *Hollow Bodies: Institutional Responses to Sex Trafficking in Armenia, Bosnia, and India*. Sterling, Va.: Kumarian Press.

Dimitrova, Dessi, ed., 2007. *Marshaling Every Resource: State and Local Responses to Human Trafficking*. Princeton: Woodrow Wilson School of Public and International Affairs, Princeton University.

Di Nicola, Andrea. 2007. "Researching into Human Trafficking: Issues and Problems." Pp. 49–72 in *Human Trafficking*, edited by Maggy Lee. Cullompton, Devon, U.K.: Willan Publishing.

Di Nicola, Andrea, Andrea Cauduro, Marco Lombardi, and Paolo Ruspini, eds. 2009. *Prostitution and Human Trafficking: Focus on Clients*. New York: Springer.

Doezema, Jo. 2010. *Sex Slaves and Discourse Masters: The Construction of Trafficking*. London: Zed Books.

Edelman, Murray. 1964. *The Symbolic Use of Politics*. Urbana: University of Illinois Press.

Emerton, Robyn. 2001. *Trafficking of Women into Hong Kong for the Purpose of Prostitution: Preliminary Research Findings*. Occasional Paper No. 3. Hong Kong: University of Hong Kong.

Emka, Moammar. 2002. *Jakarta Undercover*. Singapore: Monsoon Books.

Enright, Michael, Edith Scott, and Ka-mun Chang. 2005. *Regional Powerhouse: The Greater Pearl River Delta and the Rise of China*. New York: Wiley.

Farley, Mellisa, ed. 2003. *Prostitution, Trafficking, and Traumatic Stress*. Binghamton, N.Y.: Haworth Maltreatment & Trauma Press.

Farr, Kathryn. 2005. *Sex Trafficking: The Global Market in Women and Children*. New York: Worth Publishers.

Ferrell, Jeff, and Mark Hamm. 1998. *Ethnography at the Edge: Crime, Deviance, and Field Research*. Boston: Northeastern University Press.

Finckenauer, James. 2001. "Russian Transnational Organized Crime and Human Trafficking." Pp. 166–186 in *Global Human Smuggling*, edited by David Kyle and Rey Koslowski. Baltimore: John Hopkins University Press.

———. 2007. *Mafia and Organized Crime*. Oxford, U.K.: Oneworld Publications.

Finckenauer, James, and Ko-lin Chin. 2006. "Asian Transnational Organized Crime and Its Impact on the United States." *Trends in Organized Crime* 10: 18–107.

Finckenauer, James, and Elin Waring. 1998. *Russian Mafia in America*. Boston: Northeastern University Press.

Frederick, John. 2005. "The Myth of Nepal-to-India Sex Trafficking: Its Creation, Maintenance, and Its Influence on Anti-Trafficking Interventions." Pp. 127–148 in *Trafficking and Prostitution Reconsidered: New Perspectives on Migration, Sex Work, and Human Rights*, edited by Kamala Kempadoo. Boulder, Colo.: Paradigm Publishers.

Gambetta, Diego. 1993. *The Sicilian Mafia: The Business of Private Protection*. Cambridge: Harvard University Press.

Gilmartin, Christina. 1990. "Violence against Women in Contemporary China." Pp. 203–226 in *Violence in China: Essays in Culture and Counterculture*, edited by Jonathan Lipman and Stevan Harrell. Albany: SUNY Press.

Gittings, John. 2005. *The Changing Face of China: From Mao to Market*. New York: Oxford University Press.

Global Alliance Against Trafficking in Women (GAATW). 2007. *Collateral Damage: The Impact of Anti-Trafficking Measures on Human Rights around the World*. Bangkok: Global Alliance against Traffic in Women.

Gozdziak, Elzbieta, and Micah Bump. 2008. *Data and Research on Human Trafficking: Bibliography of Research-Based Literature*. Institute for the Study of International Migration, Walsh School of Foreign Service, Georgetown University. A Final Report Submitted to the National Institute of Justice, U.S. Department of Justice.

Gozdziak, Elzbieta, and Elizabeth Collett. 2005. "Research on Human Trafficking in North America: A Review of Literature." Pp. 99–128 in *Data and Research on Human Trafficking: A Global Survey*, edited by Frank Lack and Elzbieta Gozdziak. Geneva: International Organization for Migration.

Haugen, Gary, and Gregg Hunter. 2005. *Terrify No More*. Nashville, Tenn.: W Publishing Group.

Hilgartner, Stephen, and Charles Bosk. 1988. "The Rise and Fall of Social Problems: A Public Arena Model." *American Journal of Sociology* 94: 53–78.

Hill, Peter. 2003. *The Japanese Mafia: Yakuza, Law, and the State*. New York: Oxford University Press.

Hoigard, Cecile, and Liv Finstad. 1986. *Backstreets: Prostitution, Money, and Love*. University Park, Pa.: Pennsylvania University Press.

Hsu, Francis. 1967. *Under the Ancestor's Shadow: Kinship, Personality and Social Mobility in China*. Stanford: Stanford University Press.

Hughes, Donna. 2000. "The 'Natasha' Trade: The Transnational Shadow Market of Trafficking in Women." *Journal of International Affairs* 53: 625–651.

———. 2008. "Wilberforce Can Free Again." National Review Online.

Human Rights Watch. 1995. *Rape for Profit: Trafficking of Nepali Girls and Women to India's Brothels*. New York: Human Rights Watch.

———. 2000. *Owed Justice: Thai Women Trafficked into Debt Bondage in Japan*. New York: Human Rights Watch.

Hyde, Sandra Teresa. 2007. *Eating Spring Rice: The Cultural Politics of AIDS in Southwest China.* Berkeley: University of California Press.

Ignatius, Sarah. 1993. *An Assessment of the Asylum Process of the Immigration and Naturalization Service.* Cambridge: Harvard Law School.

International Organization for Migration (IOM). 2002. *Counter-Trafficking Unit: Return and Reintegration Project Situation Report.* Pristina, Kosovo.

———. 2003. *IOM Bosnia and Herzegovina Counter Trafficking Program.* Sarajevo, Bosnia and Herzegovina.

Jacobs, James. 1994. *Busting the Mob: United States vs. Cosa Nostra.* New York: NYU Press.

———. 1999. *Gotham Unbound: How New York City Was Liberated from the Grip of Organized Crime.* New York: NYU Press.

———. 2006. *Mobsters, Unions, and Feds: The Mafia and the American Labor Movement.* New York: NYU Press.

Jahic, Galma. 2009. "Analysis of Economic and Social Factors Associated with Trafficking in Women: Thinking Globally, Research Locally." Ph.D. dissertation, School of Criminal Justice, Rutgers University–Newark.

Jahic, Galma, and James Finckenauer. 2005. "Representations and Misrepresentations of Human Trafficking." *Trends in Organized Crime* 8: 24–40.

Jeffrey, Leslie Ann. 2002. *Sex and Borders: Gender, National Identity, and Prostitution Policy in Thailand.* Chiang Mai: Silkworm Books.

Jeffreys, Elaine. 2004. *China, Sex and Prostitution.* London: RoutledgeCurzon.

Jones, Gavin, Endang Sulistyaningsih, and Terence Hull. 1998. "Prostitution in Indonesia." Pp. 29–66 in *The Sex Sector: The Economic and Social Bases of Prostitution in Southeast Asia,* edited by Lin Lean Lim. Geneva: International Labour Office.

Jordan, Jan. 1997. "User Pays: Why Men Buy Sex." *Australian and New Zealand Journal of Criminology* 30: 55–71.

Kaplan, David, and Alec Dubro. 2003. *Yakuza: Japan's Criminal Underworld.* Berkeley: University of California Press.

Kara, Siddharth. 2009. *Sex Trafficking: Inside the Business of Modern Slavery.* New York: Columbia University Press.

Keefe, Patrick Radden. 2009. *The Snakehead: An Epic Tale of the Chinatown Underworld and the American Dream.* New York: Doubleday.

Kelly, Liz. 2005. "You Can Find Anything You Want: A Critical Reflection on Research on Trafficking in Persons within and into Europe." Pp. 235–266 in *Data and Research on Human Trafficking: A Global Survey,* edited by Frank Laczko and Elzbieta Gozdziak. Geneva: International Organization for Migration.

Kelly, Robert, Ko-lin Chin, and Rufus Schatzberg, eds. 1994. *Handbook of Organized Crime in the United States.* Westport, Conn.: Greenwood Press.

Kempadoo, Kamala. 2004. *Sexing the Caribbean: Gender, Race, and Sexual Labor.* New York: Routledge.

———. 2005. "From Moral Panic to Global Justice: Changing Perspectives on Trafficking." Pp. vii–xxxiv in *Trafficking and Prostitution Reconsidered: New Perspectives on Migration, Sex Work, and Human Rights,* edited by Kamala Kempadoo, with Jyoti Sanghera and Bandana Pattanaik. Boulder, Colo.: Paradigm Publishers.

Kempadoo, Kamala, and Jo Doezema, eds. 1998. *Global Sex Workers: Rights, Resistance, and Redefinition.* New York: Routledge.

Kenney, Dennis, and James Finckenauer. 1995. *Organized Crime in America*. Belmont, Calif.: Wadsworth Publishing.

King, Gilbert. 2004. *Woman, Child for Sale: The New Slave Trade in the 21st Century*. New York: Chamberlain Bros.

Koken, Juline, David Bimbi, and Jeffrey Parsons. 2010. "Male and Female Escorts: A Comparative Analysis." Pp. 205–232 in *Sex for Sale: Prostitution, Pornography, and the Sex Industry*, 2nd ed., edited by Ronald Weitzer. New York: Routledge.

Konisberg, Eric. 2008. "Couple's Downfall Is Culminating in Sentencing in Long Island Slavery Case." *New York Times*, June 23, p. B1.

Kurtz, Steven, Hilary Surratt, James Inciardi, and Marion Kiley. 2006. "Violent Victimization of Street Sex Workers." Pp. 148-158 in *In Their Own Words: Women Offenders' Views on Crime and Victimization*, edited by Leanne Alarid and Paul Cromwell. Los Angeles: Roxbury Publishing Co.

Kwong, Peter. 1997. *Forbidden Workers: Illegal Chinese Immigrants and American Labor*. New York: New Press.

Kyle, David, and John Dale. 2001. "Smuggling the State Back In: Agents of Human Smuggling Reconsidered." Pp. 29–57 in *Global Human Smuggling*, edited by David Kyle and Rey Koslowski. Baltimore: John Hopkins University Press.

Kyle, David, and Rey Koslowski, eds. 2001. *Global Human Smuggling*. Baltimore: John Hopkins University Press.

Laidler, Karen Joe, Carole J. Petersen, and Robyn Emerton. 2007. "Bureaucratic Justice: The Incarceration of Mainland Chinese Women Working in Hong Kong's Sex Industry." *International Journal of Offender Therapy and Comparative Criminology* 51: 68–83.

Lee, Maggy. 2007. "Introduction: Understanding Human Trafficking." Pp. 1–25 in *Human Trafficking*, edited by Maggy Lee. Devon, U.K.: Willan Publishing.

Light, Ivan. 1974. "From Vice District to Tourist Attraction: The Moral Career of American Chinatowns, 1880–1940." *Pacific Historical Review* 43: 367–94.

Lim, Gerrie. 2004. *Invisible Trade: High-Class Sex for Sale in Singapore*. Singapore: Monsoon Books.

Lim, Lin Lean, ed. 1998. *The Sex Sector: The Economic and Social Bases of Prostitution in Southeast Asia*. Geneva: International Labour Office.

Lindquist, Johan, and Nicola Piper. 2007. "From HIV Prevention to Counter-Trafficking: Discursive Shifts and Institutional Continuities in South-East Asia." Pp. 138–158 in *Human Trafficking*, edited by Maggy Lee. Devon, U.K.: Willan Publishing.

Lintner, Bertil. 2002. *Blood Brothers: The Criminal Underworld of Asia*. New York: Palgrave.

Liu, Min. 2010. "Prostitution, Migration, and Human Trafficking." Ph.D. dissertation, School of Criminal Justice, Rutgers University–Newark.

Lo, Sonny Shiu-hing. 2009. *The Politics of Cross-Border Crime in Greater China*. Armonk, N.Y.: M. E. Sharpe.

Looi, Sylvia, Paul Choo, and A. Raman. 2007. "Caning for 'China Doll.'" *The Star*, July 24, p. N33.

Lowman, John, and Chris Atchison. 2006. "Men Who Buy Sex: A Survey in the Greater Vancouver Regional District." *Canadian Review of Sociology* 43 (3): 281–296.

Malarek, Victor. 2003. *The Natashas: Inside the New Global Sex Trade*. New York: Arcade Publishing.

Mam, Somaly. 2007. *The Road of Lost Innocence*. New York: Spiegel & Grau.

Markon, Jerry. 2007. "Anti-Human Trafficking Bill Would Send FBI Agents on Trail of Pimps." *Washington Post*, November 29, p. A5.

Martilla, Anne Maria. 2003. "Consuming Sex: Finnish Male Clients and Russian and Baltic Prostitution." Paper presented at Gender and Power in the New Europe, the 5th European Feminist Research Conference, August 20–24, Lund University, Sweden.

Martin, Mildred Crow. 1977. *Chinatown's Angry Angel: The Story of Donaldina Cameron*. Palo Alto, Calif.: Pacific Books.

Massey, Douglas, Joaquin Arango, Graeme Hugo, Ali Kouaouci, Adela Pellegrion, and J. Edward Taylor. 1993. "Theories of International Migration: A Review and Appraisal." *Population and Development Review* 19: 431–66.

Massonnet, Phillippe. 2000. *The New China: Money, Sex, and Power*. Boston: Tuttle Publishing.

Merry, Sally Engle. 2009. *Gender Violence: A Cultural Perspective*. West Sussex, U.K.: Wiley-Blackwell.

Miller, Jody. 2001. "Reconciling Feminism and Rational Choice Theory: Women's Agency in Street Crime." Pp. 219–240 in *Rational Choice and Criminal Behavior*, edited by Alex Piquero and Stephen Tibbetts. New York: Garland Publishing.

Miller, John. 2008. "The Justice Department, Blind to Slavery." Op-ed, *New York Times*, July 11, A17.

Miller, J. Mitchell, and Richard Tewksbury. 2001. *Extreme Methods: Innovative Approaches to Social Science Research*. Boston: Allyn and Bacon.

Miriam, Kathy. 2005. "Stopping the Traffic in Women: Power, Agency and Abolition in Feminist Debates over Sex-Trafficking." *Journal of Social Philosophy* 36: 1–17.

Mix, Prapairat Ratanaloan. 2002. "Four Cases from Hamburg." Pp. 86–99 in *Transnational Prostitution: Changing Global Patterns*, edited by Susanne Thorbek and Bandana Pattanaik. London: Zed Books.

Monto, Martin. 2010. "Prostitutes' Customers: Motives and Misconceptions." Pp. 233–254 in *Sex for Sale: Prostitution, Pornography, and the Sex Industry*, 2nd ed., edited by Ronald Weitzer. New York: Routledge.

Morawska, Eva. 2007. "Trafficking into and from Eastern Europe." Pp. 92–115 in *Human Trafficking*, edited by Maggy Lee. Devon, UK: Willan Publishing.

Murray, Allison. 1998. "Debt-Bondage and Trafficking: Don't Believe the Hype." Pp. 51–64 in *Global Sex Workers: Rights, Resistance, and Redefinition*, edited by Kamala Kempadoo and Jo Doezema. London: Routledge.

New Straits Times (Malaysia). 2006. "'Ambassadors of Love' from Past to Help Prostitutes." December 24, p. 8.

O'Connell Davidson, Julia. 2005. *Children in the Global Sex Trade*. Cambridge, U.K.: Polity Press.

Outshoorn, Joyce. 2004. "Introduction: Prostitution, Women's Movements and Democratic Politics." Pp. 1–20 in *The Politics of Prostitution: Women's Movements, Democratic States and the Globalisation of Sex Commerce*, edited by Joyce Outshoorn. London: Cambridge University Press.

Parrenas, Rhacel. 2011. *Illicit Flirtations: Labor, Migration, and Sex Trafficking in Tokyo*. Stanford: Stanford University Press.

Pearson, Elaine. 2002. *Human Traffic Human Rights: Redefining Victim Protection*. London: Anti-Slavery International.

Phongpaichit, Pasuk, and Sungsidh Piriyarangsan. 1994. *Corruption and Democracy in Thailand*. Chiang Mai: Silkworm Books.

Phongpaichit, Pasuk, Sungsidh Piriyarangsan, and Nualnoi Treerat. 1998. *Guns, Girls, Gambling, Ganja: Thailand's Illegal Economy and Public Policy*. Bangkok: Silkworm Books.

Piper, Nicola. 2005. "A Problem by a Different Name? A Review of Research on Trafficking in South-East Asia and Oceania." Pp. 203–233 in *Data and Research on Human Trafficking: A Global Survey*, edited by Frank Laczko and Elzbieta Gozdziak. Geneva: International Organization for Migration.

Plumridge, Elizabeth, S. Jane Chetwynd, Anna Reed, and Sandra Gifford. 1997. "Discourses on Emotionality in Commercial Sex: The Missing Client Voice." *Feminism & Psychology* 7: 165–181.

Porter, Judith, and Louis Bonilla. 2010. "The Ecology of Street Prostitution." Pp. 163–185 in *Sex for Sale: Prostitution, Pornography, and the Sex Industry*, 2nd ed., edited by Ronald Weitzer. New York: Routledge.

Ren, Xin. 1993. "China." Pp. 87–107 in *Prostitution: An International Handbook on Trend, Problems, and Policies*, edited by Nanette Davis. Westport, Conn.: Greenwood Press.

Richard, Amy O'Neill. 2000. *International Trafficking in Women to the United States: A Contemporary Manifestation of Slavery and Organized Crime*. Washington, D.C.: Center for the Study of Intelligence.

Rigger, Shelley. 1999. *Politics in Taiwan: Voting for Democracy*. London: Routledge.

Sage, Jesse, and Liora Kasten. 2006. "Behind the Stories: Modern Day Slavery in Context." Pp. 1–10 in *Enslaved: True Stories of Modern Day Slavery*, edited by Jesse Sage and Liora Kasten. New York: Palgrave MacMillan.

Sanders, Teela. 2008. *Paying for Pleasure: Men Who Buy Sex*. Devon, U.K.: Willan Publishing.

Sanghera, Jyoti. 2005. "Unpacking the Trafficking Discourse." Pp. 3–24 in *Trafficking and Prostitution Reconsidered: New Perspectives on Migration, Sex Work, and Human Rights*, edited by Kamala Kempadoo, with Jyoti Sanghera and Bandana Pattanaik. Boulder, Colo.: Paradigm Publishers.

Scarpa, Silvia. 2008. *Trafficking in Human Beings: Modern Slavery*. New York: Oxford University Press.

Schifter-Sikora, Jacobo. 2007. *Mongers in Heaven: Sexual Tourism in Costa Rica and in the United States*. Lanham, Md.: University Press of America.

Schloenhardt, Andreas. 2001. "Trafficking in Migrants: Illegal Migration and Organized Crime in Australia and the Asia Pacific Region." *International Journal of the Sociology of Law* 29: 331–378.

Seabrook, Jeremy. 2001. *Travels in the Skin Trade: Tourism and the Sex Industry*. London: Pluto Press.

Segrave, Marie, Sanja Milivojevic, and Sharaon Pickering. 2009. *Sex Trafficking: International Context and Response*. Portland, Oreg.: Willan Publishing.

Shannon, Sarah. 1999. "Prostitution and the Mafia: The Involvement of Organized Crime in the Global Sex Trade." Pp. 119–144 in *Illegal Immigration and Commercial Sex: The New Slave Trade*, edited by Phil Williams. London: Frank Cass Publishers.

Shelley, Louise. 2007. "Human Trafficking as a Form of Transnational Crime." Pp. 116–137 in *Human Trafficking*, edited by Maggy Lee. Devon, UK: Willan Publishing.

———. 2010. *Human Trafficking: A Global Perspective*. New York: Cambridge University Press.

Shu, Xiaoling, and Yanjie Bian. 2002. "Intercity Variation in Gender Inequalities in China: Analysis of a 1995 National Survey." Pp. 269–309 in *The Future of Market Transition*, Volume 19, edited by Kevin Leicht. Oxford, U.K.: Elsevier Science, Ltd.

Simon, Herbert. 1982. *Models of Bounded Rationality*, Vols. 1 and 2. Cambridge: MIT Press.

Skeldon, Ronald. 2000. "Trafficking: A Perspective from Asia." Pp. 7–30 in *Perspectives on Trafficking of Migrants*, edited by Reginald Appleyard and John Salt. Geneva: International Organization for Migration.

Skinner, E. Benjamin. 2008. *A Crime So Monstrous: Face-to-Face with Modern-Day Slavery*. New York: Free Press.

Skrobanek, Siriporn, Nattaya Boonpakdi, and Chutima Janthakeero. 1997. *The Traffic in Women: Human Realities of the International Sex Trade*. London: Zed Books.

Smith, Paul, ed. 1997. *Human Smuggling*. Washington, D.C.: Center for Strategic and International Studies.

Sobieszczyk, Teresa. 2002. "Risky Business: Debt Bondage International Labour Migration from Northern Thailand." Paper presented at the IUSSP Regional Population Conference on "Southeast Asia's Population in a Changing Asian Context," Bangkok, Thailand, June 10–12.

Soderlund, Gretchen. 2005. "Running from the Rescuers: New U.S. Crusades against Sex Trafficking and the Rhetoric of Abolition." *NWSA Journal* 17: 64–87.

Stetson, Dorothy McBride. 2004. "The Invisible Issue: Prostitution and Trafficking of Women and Girls in the United States." Pp. 245–264 in *The Politics of Prostitution: Women's Movements, Democratic States and the Globalisation of Sex Commerce*, edited by Joyce Outshoorn. London: Cambridge University Press.

Stolz, Barbara Ann. 2007. "Interpreting the U.S. Human Trafficking Debate through the Lens of Symbolic Politics." *Law & Policy* 29: 311–338.

———. 2010. "Identifying Human Trafficking Victims." *Criminology & Public Policy* 9: 267–274.

Sulainmanova, Saltanat. 2006. "Trafficking in Women from the Former Soviet Union for the Purposes of Sexual Exploitation." Pp. 61–76 in *Trafficking and the Global Sex Industry*, edited by Karen Beeks and Delila Amir. Lanham, Md.: Lexington Books.

Sykes, Gresham, and David Matza. 1957. "Techniques of Neutralization: A Theory of Delinquency." *American Sociological Review* 22: 664–670.

Thorbeck, Susanne. 2002. "Prostitution in a Global Context: Changing Patterns." Pp. 1–9 in *Transnational Prostitution: Changing Global Patterns*, edited by Susanne Thorbek and Bandana Pattanaik. London: Zed Books.

Tommaso, Maria, Isilda Shima, Steinar Strom, and Francesca Bettio. 2009. "As Bad as It Gets: Well-Being Deprivation of Sexually Exploited Trafficked Women." *European Journal of Political Economy* 25: 143–162.

Tyldum, Guri, and Anette Brunovskis. 2005. "Describing the Unobserved: Methodological Challenges in Empirical Studies on Human Trafficking." Pp. 17–34 in *Data and Research on Human Trafficking: A Global Survey*, edited by Frank Laczko and Elzbieta Gozdziak. Geneva: International Organization for Migration.

United Nations. 2000. *Protocol to Prevent, Suppress and Punish Trafficking in Persons, Especially Women and Children, Supplementing the United Nations Convention against Transnational Organized Crime*. Vienna: United Nations.

United Nations Inter-Agency Project on Human Trafficking (UNIAP). 2008. *Guide to Ethics and Human Rights in Counter-Trafficking*. Bangkok: Regional Project Management Office.

United Nations Office on Drug and Crime (UNODC). 2006. *Trafficking in Persons: Global Patterns.* Vienna: United Nations.

———. 2010. *Smuggling of Migrants: A Global Review and Annotated Bibliography of Recent Publications.* Vienna: United Nations.

U.S. Department of Justice. 2008. "Chinese Woman Sentenced for Role in Saipan Sex Trafficking Ring." Press release. February 26.

U.S. Department of State. 2007. *Trafficking in Persons Report.* Washington, D.C.: Office to Monitor and Combat Trafficking in Persons.

———. 2008. *Trafficking in Persons Report.* Washington, D.C.: Office to Monitor and Combat Trafficking in Persons.

———. 2009. *Trafficking in Persons Report.* Washington, D.C.: Office to Monitor and Combat Trafficking in Persons.

———. 2010. *Trafficking in Persons Report.* Washington, D.C.: Office to Monitor and Combat Trafficking in Persons.

U.S. Government Accountability Office (GAO). 2006. *Human Trafficking: Better Data, Strategy, and Reporting Needed to Enhance U.S. Antitrafficking Efforts Abroad.* Washington, D.C.: U.S. Government Accountability Office.

U.S. Senate. [1877] 1978. *Report of the Joint Special Committee to Investigate Chinese Immigration.* Reprint. New York: Arno Press.

van Kemenade, Willem. 1997. *China, Hong Kong, Taiwan, Inc.* New York: Alfred A. Knopf.

Varese, Federico. 2001. *The Russian Mafia: Private Protection in a New Market Economy.* New York: Oxford University Press.

Vocks, Judith, and Jan Nijboer. 2000. "The Promised Land: A Study of Trafficking in Women from Central and Eastern Europe to Netherlands." *European Journal of Criminal Policy and Research* 8: 379–388.

Warren, James Francis. 2003. *Ah Ku and Karayuki-San: Prostitution in Singapore 1870–1940.* Singapore: Singapore University Press.

Weitzer, Ronald. 2007. "The Social Construction of Sex Trafficking: Ideology and Institutionalization of a Moral Crusade." *Politics & Society* 35: 447–475.

———. 2009. "Sociology of Sex Work." *Annual Review of Sociology* 35: 213–234.

———. 2010a. "The Mythology of Prostitution: Advocacy Research and Public Policy." *Sexuality Research and Social Policy* 7: 15–29.

———. 2010b. "Sex Work: Paradigms and Policies." Pp. 1–43 in *Sex for Sale: Prostitution, Pornography, and the Sex Industry,* 2nd ed., edited by Ronald Weitzer. New York: Routledge.

Whitehead, Kate, and Nury Vittachi. 1997. *After Susie: Sex in South China.* Hong Kong: Chameleon Books.

Widgren, Jonas. 1994. *Multilateral Co-Operation to Combat Trafficking in Migrants and the Role of International Organizations.* Vienna: ICMPD.

William Wilberforce Trafficking Victims Protection Reauthorization Act of 2008 [United States of America] Public Law 110-457, 23 December 2008.

Williams, Phil, ed. 1999. *Illegal Immigration and Commercial Sex: The New Slave Trade.* London: Frank Cass.

Wilson, Carol Green. 1974. *Chinatown Quest.* San Francisco: California Historical Society.

Winick, Charles, and Paul Kinsie. 1971. *The Lively Commerce: Prostitution in the United States.* Chicago: Quadrangle Books.

World Health Organization (WHO). 2003. *WHO Ethical and Safety Recommendations for Interviewing Trafficked Women.* Geneva: World Health Organization.

Yang, Yeehsan. 2006. *Whispers and Moans: Interviews with Men and Women of Hong Kong's Sex Industry*. Hong Kong: Blacksmith Books.

Zarembka, Jy. 2002. "America's Dirty Work: Migrant Maids and Modern-Day Slavery." Pp. 142–153 in *Global Woman: Nannies, Maids, and Sex Workers in the New Economy*, edited by Barbara Ehrenreich and Arlie Russell Hochschild. New York: Metropolitan Books.

Zhang, Sheldon. 2007. *Smuggling and Trafficking in Human Beings: All Roads Lead to America*. Westport, Conn.: Praeger.

———. 2008. *Chinese Human Smuggling Organizations*. Stanford: Stanford University Press.

———. 2009. "Beyond the 'Natasha' Story—A Review and Critique of Current Research on Sex Trafficking." *Global Crime* 10: 178–195.

Zhang, Sheldon, and Ko-lin Chin. 2002. "Enter the Dragon: Inside Chinese Human Smuggling Organizations." *Criminology* 40: 737–768.

Zheng, Tiantian. 2008. "Anti-Trafficking Campaign and Karaoke Bar Hostesses in China." *Wagadu: A Journal of Transnational Women's and Gender Studies* 5: 73–92.

———. 2009. *Red Lights: The Lives of Sex Workers in Postsocialist China*. Minneapolis: University of Minnesota Press.

Zhou, Jinghao. 2006. "Chinese Prostitution: Consequences and Solutions in the Post-Mao Era." *China: An International Journal* 4: 238–262.

Zhou, Min. 1992. *Chinatown*. Philadelphia: Temple University Press.

IN CHINESE

Chang, Tseng-liang. 2002. "A Study on the Problem of 'Fake Marriage' across the Taiwan Strait, Focusing on Fake Marriage for the Purpose of Prostitution." *Central Police University Journal of Police Science* 33: 203–236.

Chen, Guyuan. 1971. *History of Marriage in China*. Taipei: Commercial Press.

Liang, Jiefen, and Lu Xing. 2010. *Casino Development and Its Impact on China's Macau SAR*. Hong Kong: City University of Hong Kong Press.

Wang, Chi-kun, Chin Ko-lin, and Lin Li-sen. 1997. *Preventing the Illegal Entry of Mainland Chinese*. Taipei: Executive Yuan Mainland Affairs Council.

Wang, Huan, Pang Lien-hui, Lu Yen-san, Lo Xiao-lan, Li Fung-er, Jen Jin wen, and Chu Xio-ji. 2002. *The Sex Trade in Hong Kong*. Hong Kong: Purple Ivy.

World Journal. 2008. "The Story of an Old Prostitute." March 7.

Yang, Wen-yu. 1985. "Chinese Commercial Sex in New York City." *Rainbow Biweekly*, August 2, p. 5.

Zhao, Fengjie. 1973. *Women and Law in Chinese Society*. Taipei: Shihuo Publisher.

Ko-lin Chin is Professor II (Distinguished) at the School of Criminal Justice at Rutgers University–Newark and author of many books, including *Hei-jin: Organized Crime, Business, and Politics in Taiwan,* and *Golden Triangle: Inside Southeast Asia's Drug Trade.*

James O. Finckenauer was Professor II (Distinguished) at the School of Criminal Justice at Rutgers University–Newark, where he had been since 1974, and author or coauthor of many books, including *Asian Transnational Organized Crime.* Professor Finckenauer was formerly Director of the International Center at the National Institute of Justice, and past President of the International Association for the Study of Organized Crime and of the Academy of Criminal Justice Sciences.